Pride, Not Prejudice

PRIDE, NOT PREJUDICE

*National Identity as a Pacifying Force
in East Asia*

Eunbin Chung

University of Michigan Press
Ann Arbor

Copyright © 2022 by Eunbin Chung
Some rights reserved

This work is licensed under a Creative Commons Attribution-NonCommercial-NoDerivatives 4.0 International License. *Note to users:* A Creative Commons license is only valid when it is applied by the person or entity that holds rights to the licensed work. Works may contain components (e.g., photographs, illustrations, or quotations) to which the rightsholder in the work cannot apply the license. It is ultimately your responsibility to independently evaluate the copyright status of any work or component part of a work you use, in light of your intended use. To view a copy of this license, visit http://creativecommons.org/licenses/by-nc-nd/4.0/

For questions or permissions, please contact um.press.perms@umich.edu

Published in the United States of America by the
University of Michigan Press
Manufactured in the United States of America
Printed on acid-free paper
First published February 2022

A CIP catalog record for this book is available from the British Library.

Library of Congress Cataloging-in-Publication data has been applied for.

DOI: https://doi.org/10.3998/mpub.12010257

ISBN 978-0-472-13294-2 (hardcover : alk. paper)
ISBN 978-0-472-03905-0 (paper : alk. paper)
ISBN 978-0-472-90293-4 (OA)

*Dedicated to
My Parents,
Joo-Taek Chung and Jin-Sook Lee*

Contents

List of Figures — ix
List of Tables — xiii
Acknowledgments — xvii
Chapter 1. Are Strong National Identities Harmful for Peace? — 1
Chapter 2. Why Can't We Move Beyond the Past? Distrust, Guilt Avoidance, and Negative Images — 18
Chapter 3. Theories of Identity Affirmation: Trust, Guilt, and Images — 39
Chapter 4. National Identity and Trust: Experiments in China, Japan, and South Korea — 83
Chapter 5. National Identity and Guilt Recognition: Experiments in Japan — 113
Chapter 6. National Identity and the Ally Image: Surveys in South Korea — 156
Chapter 7. Application to Policy 1: Security Cooperation — 171
Chapter 8. Application to Policy 2: Reparation Endorsement — 196
Chapter 9. Conclusion — 219
Appendix A: Survey Materials — 239
Appendix B: Supplementary Empirical Materials — 249
Notes — 257
References — 263
Index — 299

Digital materials related to this title can be found on the Fulcrum platform via the following citable URL: https://doi.org/10.3998/mpub.12010257

Figures

Figure 1. South Koreans' trust of other countries — 27
Figure 2. South Koreans' assessment of threats from surrounding countries and categories of those threats — 36
Figure 3. Assessment and prospect of South Korea's relationship with surrounding countries — 37
Figure 4. The proposed effects of NIA on postconflict reconciliation — 53
Figure 5. The proposed effects of NIA on trust — 65
Figure 6. Effects of NIA in the long run — 67
Figure 7. NIA can move inflictor and receiver sides closer together on reparatory attitudes — 71
Figure 8. Experiment structure — 85
Figure 9. Distribution of latent trust variable ("Moralistic Trust") — 96
Figure 10. People affirmed of their national identity report more moralistic trust (as measured by trust questions) regarding their opponent country, compared to individuals who are not affirmed — 97
Figure 11. Distribution of tokens ("Strategic Trust") — 103
Figure 12. People affirmed of their national identity report more strategic trust (as measured by tokens given in the trust game) regarding their foreign opponent, compared to individuals who are not affirmed — 103
Figure 13. Model of NIA and guilt recognition — 117
Figure 14. Experiment structure — 120
Figure 15. Prosocial attitudes mediate NIA and declared personal guilt in game — 124

Figure 16. Across affirmation conditions, the most people in the NIA condition exhibited prosocial attitudes — 126

Figure 17. Prosocial attitudes mediate NIA and reported in-group guilt in game — 127

Figure 18. Prosocial players reported more personal declared guilt than proself players (overall sample) — 132

Figure 19. Prosocial players reported more in-group declared guilt than proself players (overall sample) — 133

Figure 20. People who admitted more guilt for their personal action sent back more in the following dictator game — 136

Figure 21. People who admitted more guilt for an in-group member's action sent back more in the following dictator game — 137

Figure 22. Prosocial attitudes mediate NIA and revealed (personal and in-group) guilt in game — 139

Figure 23. Prosocial players reported more personal revealed guilt — 139

Figure 24. Prosocial players reported more in-group revealed guilt — 140

Figure 25. Prosocial attitudes mediate NIA and declared in-group guilt in game — 147

Figure 26. Prosocial attitudes and historical guilt, by opponent nationality — 148

Figure 27. Japanese' reported affect levels toward South Korea and China — 152

Figure 28. The NIA condition had the largest number of people exhibiting prosocial attitudes when paired with a Chinese counterpart — 153

Figure 29. Country favorability by South Koreans (Scale: 0–10. Least favorable = 0; Most favorable = 10) — 158

Figure 30. How South Koreans assess their country's relationship with the United States, China, and Japan — 159

Figure 31. South Koreans' opinions on support for and necessity of GSOMIA (%) — 173

Figure 32. South Koreans' opinions on security cooperation with Japan (%) — 174

Figure 33. South Koreans' perceived necessity for GSOMIA over time — 175

Figure 34. South Koreans' responses to survey question "How do you view the relations between South Korea and Japan?" (%, 2013) — 176

Figure 35. Percentage of respondents (by age groups and
ideology) who replied their perceived intensity of the
division between liberals and conservatives was "strong"
(6–10, on a scale from 0 to 10. 0 was presented as Not Strong;
5: Normal; and 10: Very strong) 180
Figure 36. South Korean public support for GSOMIA by ideology 182
Figure 37. Strategic trust is positively correlated with support for
GSOMIA (South Korean sample) 188
Figure 38. Strategic trust is positively correlated with support for
GSOMIA (South Korean sample with Japanese counterpart) 189
Figure 39. Support for GSOMIA by political ideology 190
Figure 40. Support for GSOMIA by political ideology and linked fate 191
Figure 41. Progressives who believed in linked fate came to support
GSOMIA more affirmed of their national identity 192
Figure 42. Trust in the other country's people as well as trust
in their tendencies to act in fair, prosocial ways mediate Japanese
NIA and general perceived need for compensation. Results from
overall sample and South Korean conditions, with overall sample
in bold 212
Figure 43. Trust in the other country's people as well as trust in
their tendencies to act in prosocial ways mediate Japanese NIA
and personal willingness to partake in compensation. Results
from overall sample and South Korean conditions, with
overall sample in bold 213
Figure 44. Trust in the Chinese and South Korean governments
mediate NIA and Japanese motivation for personal reparative
action. Findings from Chinese condition are in bold 214
Figure 45. NIA boosted various types of moralistic trust,
which enhanced Japanese openness to several
reparation measures 215
Figure 46. Trust in South Korean people, their tendencies to act
prosaically, and the South Korean government mediate NIA
and Japanese perceived general need for compensation toward
South Korea 216
Figure 47. South Koreans prefer forging a new cooperative
relationship with China over maintaining alliance with the
United States at the risk of damaging relations with China 229
Figure 48. Plot of data clusters found by mixture model 252

Tables

Table 1. Hypothesized effect of NIA on image change	78
Table 2. Two-by-two experimental design (South Korean example)	84
Table 3. Moralistic trust by NIA and subject nationality	98
Table 4. Moralistic trust with NIA and opponent nationality interaction	99
Table 5. Test of moralistic trust including NIA and "commonness" variables	100
Table 6. Moralistic trust by affirmation and affect	102
Table 7. Strategic trust by NIA and subject nationality	105
Table 8. Strategic trust by NIA and opponent nationality	106
Table 9. Test of strategic trust with NIA and opponent nationality interaction	107
Table 10. Selection model on strategic trust with commonality variables	108
Table 11. Selection model on strategic trust with commonality variables and controls	109
Table 12. Experimental conditions	120
Table 13. Number and percentage of respondents in each condition	123
Table 14. NIA as predictor of prosocial attitudes (simple model)	128
Table 15. NIA as predictor of prosocial attitudes (long model)	128
Table 16. Number of people who reported no guilt, some guilt, or a lot of guilt following personal action in the game	130
Table 17. People who exhibited prosocial attitudes reported more personal declared guilt in overall sample, and in samples matched with Chinese and South Korean counterparts each	131

Table 18. Number of people who reported no guilt, some guilt, or a lot of guilt following in-group member's action in the game — 131
Table 19. Prosocial players reported more in-group declared guilt in overall sample, and in samples matched with Chinese and South Korean counterparts each — 133
Table 20. Prosociality did not depend on opponent nationality — 134
Table 21. Linear regression: declared guilt (survey questions) and revealed guilt (amount given back in dictator game) following personal action — 136
Table 22. Linear regression: declared guilt (survey questions) and revealed guilt (amount given back in dictator game) following in-group member's action — 137
Table 23. Prosociality was positively associated with personal and in-group revealed guilt — 140
Table 24. Declared guilt due to in-group member's action vs. my action in the game: overall sample — 142
Table 25. Declared guilt due to in-group member's action vs. my action in the game: sample with South Korean opponents only — 143
Table 26. Declared guilt due to in-group member's action vs. my action in the game: sample with Chinese opponents only — 143
Table 27. Revealed personal and in-group guilt, simple model — 144
Table 28. Revealed personal and in-group guilt with controls — 145
Table 29. Historical guilt factor analysis — 147
Table 30. Prosocial people report more historical guilt in overall sample as well as South Korean/Chinese counterpart conditions — 149
Table 31. People who felt guilty for a fellow in-group member's action in the game also tended to report more historical guilt — 150
Table 32. Predictors of prosocial attitudes among Japanese with Chinese counterparts, simple model — 154
Table 33. Predictors of prosocial attitudes among Japanese with Chinese counterparts, with controls — 154
Table 34. Summary statistics: South Koreans' images of United States, Japan, China, and Russia, 2007–2012 — 163
Table 35. South Koreans' images of four neighbor counties with national pride as main predictor — 165
Table 36. South Koreans' images of four neighbor counties with economic satisfaction and democracy as main predictors — 168

Table 37. Cross tab analyses with South Korea-Japan security cooperation (%)	175
Table 38. Strategic trust in experimental game as predictor of support for GSOMIA (South Korean sample)	186
Table 39. Strategic trust in experimental game as predictor of support for GSOMIA (South Korean sample paired with Japanese counterpart)	188
Table 40. Results of t-test and descriptive statistics for GSOMIA support by political ideology	190
Table 41. NIA and linked fate on South Korean progressives' support for GSOMIA	192
Table 42. NIA and linked fate on South Korean progressives' support for GSOMIA, controlling for gender	193
Table 43. Factor score weights (all countries—default model)	250
Table 44. Factor score weights—South Korea	251
Table 45. Factor score weights—Japan	251
Table 46. Summary statistics for groups 1 and 2 identified in mixture model	253
Table 47. Summary statistics for strategic and moralistic trust, by nationality, opponent, and affirmation conditions	254
Table 48. Number of subjects by condition, excluding the people who gave 100 token	255

Acknowledgments

This book would not have been possible without a great deal of support, encouragement, and patience from an embarrassingly long list of people, whom I attempt to list here. I may very well and completely by accident be omitting others who also deserve thanks, in which case I sincerely apologize.

Like many first academic books, this one is based on a doctoral dissertation. At the time I was a doctoral student I had the good fortune of working with an incredibly supportive advisor, Richard Herrmann, who encouraged me with his belief in the value of the project and my ability as a scholar. On several occasions, a meeting with him was all it took to revive my motivation and focus to proceed forward again, even after moments of losing direction. Besides awakening my interest in political psychology, he led me to see the "big picture" and political significance of my ideas that reach farther beyond what I had initially envisioned. Bear Braumoeller provided reliable and constructively critical feedback, especially for methods sections. William Minozzi introduced me to behavioral decision-making and gave practical advice for a beginning academic. Equally important to my dissertation committee was Amanda Robinson, who was extremely generous with her time and advice, and an exemplar of an amazing mentor and role-model. Earlier drafts of many chapters benefited from Jennifer Mitzen's feedback, particularly on the conceptualization of the history problem and a richer literature review on post-conflict justice and reparatory policy. Thomas Nelson guided me step-by-step to think through the psychological mechanism of my theory, and the project is all the better thanks to his intellectual generosity.

I had the great honor of winning a number of awards for the dissertation this book is based on, which resulted in flattering and memorable award ceremonies where the chairs of the award committees made some very kind remarks about my dissertation. I wish to acknowledge the immeasurably encouraging input from the 2016 chairs of the following award committees: Zoe Oxley, for the American Political Science Association (APSA) Best Dissertation in Political Psychology; Jonathan Ladd, for the APSA Best Dissertation in Experimental Research; and Jonathan Renshon, for the International Society of Political Psychology Best Dissertation (Honorable Mention), all of whom provided the generous words and confidence that motivated me to turn the dissertation into a book and helped to improve the quality of the project.

Across many chapters, this book shares results from experiments conducted in other countries. I am grateful to a large number of people for their assistance in fielding my experiments overseas: Aiji Tanaka and members at the GLOPE II office including Motoki Watabe, Kumiko Yanagisawa, and Yoko Hiraide at Waseda University in Tokyo, Japan, and Taehyun Kim at Chung-Ang University in Seoul, South Korea. Special thanks go to Minru Li for help in improving the experiment's instrumentation and conducting field research in China.

The project was generously supported in part by research grants, awards, and fellowships from the Korea Foundation, the Japan Foundation, the Academy of Korean Studies, Waseda University, Department of Political Science, College of Social and Behavioral Science, and the Asia Center at the University of Utah, and the Mershon Center for Security Studies, Decision Sciences Initiative, and Department of Political Science at the Ohio State University. I am also grateful for the Global Gateway Research Abroad Grant from the Ohio State Council of Graduate Students and the Coca-Cola Critical Difference for Women Research Grant for providing additional financial support.

For insightful suggestions and queries on drafts of various chapters, I am indebted to Manfred Elfstrom, Joshua Kertzer, Tongfi Kim, Anna Pechenkina, Katy Powers, Alex Thompson, and Alex Wendt. In particular, chapter 6 could not have existed without Byungwon Woo's generous help with the data and analysis. A huge thank you goes to Byungwon for his thoughtfulness, patience, and rigor. Austin Carson deserves special thanks, for being extraordinarily generous with his time and his wonderful insights on several chapters as well as the subtitle of this book. Xiaoyu Pu also offered remarkably helpful suggestions on many versions of my chapters, as well as supportive words and advice on the process of book publishing. Colleagues from graduate school, including Bentley Allan, C. Travis Bunner, Zoltan Buzas, Dustin Carnahan, Nyron Crawford, Raphael Cunha, Marina Duque, Erin Graham, Matthew Hitt, Benjamin Jones, Jason Keiber, Emily Lamb, Emily Lynch, Meri Ellen Lynott, Sebastien Mainville, Eleonora Mattiacci, Vittorio Mérola, Hye Bin Rim, Dan Schley, Jiwon Suh, Joshua Su-Ya Wu, and Wei-Ting Yen provided me an invaluable service by reading and providing feedback on very early (and often very rough) drafts.

Previous versions of this project benefited from probing questions and useful suggestions during presentations at the University of Utah, Ohio State University, Yale-NUS College, Princeton University Conference on Experiments in International Relations, NYU-CESS Experimental Political Science Conference, East-West Center at the University of Hawaii, Ewha Women's University, and too many APSA, ISA, MPSA, and ISPP conference meetings to count. For encouragement, compliments, and constructive criticism, among these audiences I especially thank R. William Ayres, Joslyn Barnhart, Michael Findley, Donald Green, Peter Gries, Eran Halperin, Sam Handlin, David Hendry, Tobias Hofmann, Brendan Howe, Susan Hyde, Dong-Hun Kim, Jiyoung Ko, Rose McDermott, Helen Milner, Daniel Nielson, Ngoc Phan, Daniel Posner, Brian Rathbun, Daniel Rothbart, Dustin Tingley, and Seanon Wong.

I have several colleagues and friends to thank, without whom this book could not have been completed. As soon as I arrived at the University of Utah, I realized I was in an incredibly supportive and collegial environment. Tabitha Benney, James Curry, John and Leslie Francis, Claudio Holzner, Baodong Liu, Steven Lobell, Ella Myers, J. Steven Ott, Peri Schwartz-Shea, Lina Svedin, and M Hakan Yavuz generously shared their insights and experiences as recent authors of incredible books. I especially wish to thank Mark Button and Brent Steele for research support and course releases that helped me finish this book. Matthew Burbank saved me at critical moments with his help and kindness as the absolute best department mentor one could ask for. I also wish to extend a special thank you to Janet Theiss and Kim Korinek, who both provided generous research support and mentorship as directors of the Asia Center.

I had the fortune of working with many of our wonderful graduate students, who read and copyedited several chapters of the book: Samuel Baty, Devon Cantwell, Benjamin Krick, Anne Peterson, and Charles Turner. Thanks are also due to Daniel Adkins and Pascal Deboeck at the University of Utah Consortium for Families and Health Research for their statistical assistance. Colleagues from other departments at the University of Utah, Lien Fan Shen, Jaehee Yi, Gaben Sanchez, Sarah Sinwell, and

Jane Hatter also provided warm advice, mental support, and friendship at a much-needed time.

Just before COVID-19 struck the world, I started working with Elizabeth Demers at the University of Michigan Press (UMP) for this book, who continued with her unwavering guidance throughout the challenging times of the pandemic. I thank Elizabeth and the team at UMP for their efforts in helping this work come to its final steps of fruition as a published book. For thoughtful feedback and comments, I am grateful to Letitia Moffitt, whose copyediting work was nothing short of fantastic, and who suggested the brilliant idea that became the title of this book.

I have several friends and family to thank, without whom this book could not have been completed. For friendship of incalculable value, I thank Seowon Lee, Jungmin Lee, Sara Kim, Morana Song, Yi Chu Su, Youn Ki, Diana Cortes-Selva, Jianing Song, Marwa El-Turky, Da Kim, Hyeyoung Kang, Yoonjin Chae, Sara Haq, Joan Cheng, Tian-Yeh Lim, Ryan and Bertie Stoker, Remy the dog, Hanzoom, and Army. My deepest thanks go to my grandparents, Youna Chung, Heejoo Kim, furry friends Santa, Prince, Mocha, Pablo, Gus-Gus, and friends from Ewha DIS—Jihye Sophie Chung, Esther Haerim Heo, Bobae Kim, Mina Kwon, Minyoung Lee, Ri Yoo—and Baekseok High School.

Most importantly, a final and very special thank you goes to my parents: Joo-Taek Chung and Jin-Sook Lee. Their unwavering support and belief in what I can become and accomplish are what keep me going. My father, a distinguished scholar and educator himself (not to mention the smartest man I know), was the first inspiration that enlightened me to the world of academia and steered me toward this path. My mother's love was the steady rock that helped me through the vicissitudes of book-writing oceans away from family. Though this journey took me to many faraway places, I always felt them believing in and cheering for me. This book is dedicated to my beloved parents. Without their dear love, understanding, and encouragement, I am nothing.

October 2021
Eunbin Chung

ONE

Are Strong National Identities Harmful for Peace?

A history of conflict and distrust can inflame disputes between neighboring countries. Conflict between states may evoke resentment, but some regions have found it especially difficult to overcome painful history. In Northeast Asia, negative remnants of history continue to shape the current political fault lines (Cho and Park 2011). Historical animosity filters down into all aspects of relations, keeping states from agreeing to put the past in the past and move forward (Cha 2003). In media and government circles, this phenomenon—where remnants of aggression and injury serve to inhibit present-day cooperation—is commonly referred to as the "history problem" (Berger 2008).[1]

In numerous unresolved historical disputes between China, Japan, and South Korea concerning wartime atrocities, national pride has been blamed as a cause. In April 2005, when anti-Japanese mass movements broke out in more than thirty Chinese cities following then-Japanese Prime Minister Junichiro Koizumi's visits to the controversial Yasukuni Shrine,[2] pundits emphasized the elements of national pride that still plague the countries' relations well into the twenty-first century (Chan and Bridges 2006). When Japanese and South Korean civil society clashed over a statue commemorating wartime sex slaves, or "comfort women," commentators highlighted the "deep [. . .] national identity and pride" rooted in the issues that make resolution challenging (Everard 2014; Fisher 2013; Hamilton 2014; Kimura 2019; Kindig 2019).

Throughout the twentieth century, strong pride in and love of one's nation have been noted as major contributory factors in war. From this perspective, distinctive attachment and allegiance to different nations divide people and generate conflict between countries, prompting ego-enhancing social comparisons and discriminatory behavior toward other nations (Dunn 1999; Herrmann, Isernia, and Segatti 2009; Nussbaum et al. 1996; Spinner-Halev and Theiss-Morse 2003). In Asia, specialists have written that "the power and persistence of national identity is one of the most important obstacles to the forging of a productive partnership" between Northeast Asian states (Glosserman and Snyder 2015).

Noting clashes of strong nationalism around the world, particularly in areas like Northeast Asia, numerous researchers argue that more peaceful relations are likely only if countries submerge or paper over existing national identities by promoting universalism, through cultural convergence or the embracing of overarching commonalities such as "Asian-ness" (Gaertner and Dovidio 2014; Kupchan 2010). This could also be achieved through the formation of a tighter community like the European Union (Haas 1958; Rosamond 2000), emphasis on cosmopolitan humanity (Held 2003), or through the homogenizing effects of globalization (Ohmae 1995). According to these scholars, the persistence of individual national identities in each country leads to a continuation of conflict. Yet some have questioned whether strong national identities are always impediments to peace, as they have coexisted with international cooperation. How do we make sense of this?

This book argues that nations can in fact build trust and reconcile with each other when each affirms[3] its own national identity.[4] To "affirm" a national identity means to bolster a positive image of one's country (Čehajić-Clancy et al. 2011). Researchers have identified that national identity is an attachment to one's country with no necessary implication for how one feels toward other countries (Huddy 2013; Mummendey et al. 2001; Sniderman et al. 2004). In other words, national identity can generate a sense of liking for conationals but does not necessarily confer a hatred of outsiders (Huddy and Del Ponte 2020). Therefore, national identity is not always manifested in prejudice toward other nations and does not always translate into xenophobia (Hopkins 2001). I focus on national identity as the psychological foundation of belonging to a nation upon which national pride, attachment, and nationalistic attitudes form (Smith 1993; Tajfel 1978; Wimmer 2017).[5] I distinguish and highlight a positive element of national identity from its frequently linked darker components: one that emphasizes attachment to one's nation, without an attitude of arrogant superiority over other nations. Affirmation is thus a seemingly counterintuitive approach that stresses that through a reflection on group values, people actually come to act in less defensive ways toward other groups. This book argues that affirmation of strong national identities can have pacifying effects in world politics and serve as a more feasible and effective way to build peaceful relations.

Sharpened national identity can have positive aggregate effects in times when widespread national pride is framed as inward-looking. For example, political, economic, or cultural pride and confidence of one's country may spring from awareness of how far one's country has come in comparison to its past, rather than perceived superiority over another country. Throughout the book I give examples of historical cases such as the Sino-Japanese "honeymoon" phase of the 1970s and early 1980s, which coincided with a period of revitalized national identity in both countries (He 2009; Sasaki 2001). With the help of policy, media, and rhetoric in framing the heightened national self-confidence toward a willingness to reach out to its neighbor and overcome the past, the China-Japan dyad—which has been portrayed as the most war-prone in the world (The Economist 2012, 2013, 2015)—exhibited a series of reconciliatory gestures and reciprocation, creating a period experts describe as "representing the peak of the bilateral relationship not just in the postwar era, but in all of history" (Reilly 2012; see also Ijiri 1996; Soeya 1995). On the other hand, strengthening national identity based on xenophobia and supremacy over a coexistent other can invite prejudicial effects and downsides of national pride.[6]

I investigate three main impediments to international reconciliation[7] and ways to overcome them. If each national population reaffirms positive aspects of its own distinctive identity, countries with a history of conflict can move closer to overcoming distrust, reluctance to admit guilt, and negative perceptions of one another. My results point to the promise of turning a strong national identity *upon itself*—or, in other words, activating salience in the public's positive meanings of national belonging to switch off rather than fuel the negative aspects of nationalism such as xenophobia or chauvinism.

1.1 "Embrace Commonality, Downplay Differences"

Numerous studies have suggested that for antagonistic groups to reconcile, they must promote a sense of commonality through a shared identity that sets aside existing subidentities and downplays differences (Allport 1954;

Gaertner and Dovidio 2014; Nussbaum 1994; Putnam 2007; Riek et al. 2010), as the distinction between groups itself promotes bias (Brewer 1999; Jackson and Smith 1999; Simon, Kulla, and Zobel 1995; Stets and Burke 2000; Tajfel and Turner 1979; Tajfel 1981; Turner et al. 1987). However, this is much easier theorized than done.

What's wrong with the prevailing prescription? A review of news headlines from around the world suggests that the prospect of achieving reconciliation through an erosion of existing identities is doubtful. Even with forces of globalization, regional integration (e.g., the European Union, the Association of Southeast Asian Nations), and the proliferation of transnational organizations, we have not seen a decline in national identities. Predictions of withering nationalism or an obsolete nation-state (Ohmae 1995) have yet to be borne out, and nationalist interstate tensions loom ominously large in many parts of the world. Furthermore, even within states, conflicts based on ethnic, linguistic, or religious identities remain undiminished today, as witnessed in areas of intrastate uprising such as Iraq, China, and Russia.

Strategies that involve a weakening of existing identities are also costly in terms of difficulty, time, and risk. National identities are usually deeply ingrained and socialized into their members' mindsets. These identities influence feelings, cognition, and behavior in everyday life. People do not, and in many cases cannot, simply abandon or switch identities associated with family or heritage overnight.

Moreover, integrating countries into a larger group carries the risk of backfiring. Most people crave some sense of belonging (Brewer 2003). Since national identities are deeply ingrained in people's minds, any seemingly forced attempt to weaken or alter these identities may be perceived as a threat to ontological security and thus meet fierce resistance (Mitzen 2006; Steele 2008). Consequently, reconciliation may be much harder to achieve when the process requires doing away with identities that are deeply socialized into people's minds from a very young age. For these reasons, attempts to achieve trust, cooperation, or reconciliation between countries by weakening national identities appear highly questionable.

It seems that we have not yet found an adequate means of coexisting peacefully in all our global diversity. A key step may lie in challenging two existing notions. First, while distinctive national identities may appear to be the cause for international conflict, peace does not require cultural homogeneity or assimilation around some united commonality—the clichéd "melting pot." Instead, recognition of subgroups in their diverse authenticity, and a world where such groups can be respected by and coexist with their different identities, is a better and more realistic route to peace.

Second, strong national identities and pride can have positive effects for peace. This approach reflects the liberal nationalist thesis that emphasizes the virtues of independent nations and nationalisms. According to liberal nationalists, respect for independent nations and national belonging secures a sense of dignity in people that provides a basis for international peace and cooperation (Glover 1997; Kymlicka 1998; Mazzini 2009; Miller 1995; Tamir 1995; Taylor 1998; Walzer 2008). As will be seen, compromising or converging existing national identities are not necessary for reconciliation between past adversaries.

1.2 How Can National Identity Affirmation Promote International Reconciliation?

Rather than try to weaken categories of identification, I suggest an alternative approach to boosting trust, guilt recognition, and positive perception between countries: through strengthening of existing national identities. Building on psychological theories of identity affirmation, I apply them to the national identity level as a way to promote peace between countries. By reflecting on values that are important to one's country, people of a given country are able to be less defensive in their dealings with another country (Sherman et al. 2007; Steele 1988). This tendency to be less defensive is consistent with the idea that clarity and security in the sense of who you are, or what it means to be part of a group, increases tolerance toward others, even a past adversary. I investigate how identity affirmation works at a group level, in particular with regard to national identities.

How can affirming one's national identity promote reconciliation? Psychologists have made an important distinction between out-group hate and in-group love (Brewer 1999). Attachment to a nation can be similarly separated into two components: an outward-looking component of chauvinism (the nastier variant of nationalism), which entails comparison and superiority; and a purely inward-looking component, which involves affirmation and reclarification of what it means to be part of a group (Spinner-Halev and Theiss-Morse 2003). This inward-looking component applied to countries denotes a reinforcement of one's national identity, and it can have positive effects for public sentiment across countries. Indeed, recent studies find national attachment increases trust, while chauvinism has the opposite effect (Gustavsson and Stendahl 2020). In other words, attachment to one's own country does not automatically mean hostility toward other countries (Herrmann, Isernia, and Segatti 2009). Affirmation of national identity does not have to involve comparison with an "other"—it can promote the effect of elevating the self without necessarily putting down the other. In this sense, affirmation provides a route to peaceful coexistence of groups and should be promoted in a way that is distinct from chauvinism and xenophobic self-esteem.

1.3 Three Obstacles to Peace and Security: Distrust, Guilt Avoidance, and Negative Images

In separate chapters, I empirically examine trust, guilt recognition, and perception in international reconciliation. I use these three variables as central to reconciliation for three reasons. First, relations between numerous countries have been fraught with distrust. Chronic distrust between people in countries with lasting memories of conflict prevents institutional cooperation and heightens the publics' perception of threats to security. In order for states suffering from a negative past to overcome historical grievances, an increase in interstate trust is essential. In my study of trust, I focus on trust among the general public, assuming that small changes in the public psyche can alter overall public opinion and eventually affect political change between states on a larger level. As we will discover, two different types of trust—strategic and moralistic—are required for institutional cooperation and alleviation of security dilemmas, respectively.

A second issue that recurs in postconflict areas and seriously impedes reconciliation is guilt recognition. This often becomes an important matter for the comparatively weaker state or group of people who believe they were victimized in a conflict. To them, acknowledgment of guilt by the more dominant power becomes an issue of achieving justice and restoration.

Conflict resolution specialists stress that denials of past aggression or atrocities elevate fear and tension between past adversaries, but this is not always a simple matter (Berger 2003; Lebow 2004). When it comes to guilt for historical deeds, there is a temporal gap between today's younger generation and their ancestors who were directly involved in past conflict. For example, among Japanese today there is a divide between those who argue the current Japanese government and people must admit guilt for the country's past actions, and those who think it is unfair to demand reparation from a younger generation of Japanese who have no memory of war. Should those who personally have no responsibility for atrocities of the past need to pay for something they never did? To address this problem, I examine when people will or will not admit guilt about an in-group member's behavior, even when they themselves never participated in the act.

Experts note numerous areas around the world where the issue of guilt recognition and reparation for the past are at the core of whether groups with a history of conflict can successfully mend relations or not. These cases include Israeli-Palestinian relations, Bosnian Serbs' involvement in the Srebrenica genocide and other incidents against non-Serbs (Čehajić-Clancy et al. 2011), Canadian treatment of Aboriginal people (Gunn and Wilson 2011), and racial politics within the United States (Harvey and Oswald 2006). For decades, Chinese and South Koreans have denounced Japanese remembrance as unapologetic, citing statements made by Japanese leaders and omissions from Japanese history textbooks (Kim 2008; Tselichtchev 2018). In Northeast Asia, the inability of states to come to terms with their past has become a powerful symbol for a host of problems that define the area's international relations. At the time of writing, seventy-four years have passed since the end of World War II and Japan's hold on the Korean peninsula as well as parts of China, but the countries have yet to come to grips with their painful history.

Finally, besides distrust and guilt avoidance, overall negative perceptions of other countries have toxic consequences for international relations as well. People might perceive another country as a potentially cooperative ally or a competitive enemy. Perceptions that this country has ill motives and goals that are incompatible with one's own can threaten international security and even initiate war (Kray et al. 2010; Lebow 1984). When citizens base such judgments solely on what happened in the past, this can have particularly chilling prospects for already-strained relations in the present.

Perceptions of other countries and their implications for international relations have a lot to do with the concept of *images* (Herrmann and Fischerkeller 1995). Image theory—which specifies the conditions under which an ally or enemy image of a country is expected to appear—will aid our examination of the relationship between the public's psychology of perception and how it can boost positivity in images in world politics.

1.4 Policy Implications

This project focuses on how to shift entrenched public opinion that otherwise impedes foreign policy developments. Specifically, chronic distrust and negative images of other countries among the public in China, Japan, and South Korea often inhibit cooperative foreign policy that would be beneficial to those nations. In a region where nationalist sentiment is of great importance to the public, it is unlikely that any state leader who decides to drastically shift to cooperative foreign policy with neighbor states by setting aside nationalism will be popular. This is especially true for leaders who must win elections in democracies. In Japan and South Korea, where leaders are selected through democratic elections, low popularity means low public support through votes.

National identity affirmation (NIA) can help detach the public from historical bitterness and dominant negative images, and move toward cool-headed reasoning of self-interest in cooperation. Affirming national identities could be a more viable and appealing approach for national leaders who wish to obtain the benefit of international cooperation with a past adversary but are hesitant to take actions objectionable to their own citizens. Nationalisms remain vigorous in China, Japan, and South Korea, so leaders must take them into account as they build new international ties. Consequently, when elites find economic, strategic, or geopolitical reasons to build new forms of cooperation among nations with histories of conflict, mutual affirmation of national identities offers a better route forward than attempting to downplay long-standing group identities.

"Cold politics, warm economics" is a phrase that a Chinese official used to characterize international relations in Northeast Asia.[8] China, Japan, and South Korea already trade heavily, and it would make a lot of sense for them to work more closely together because they have much to gain from cooperation. They are arguably three of the most economically successful countries of the past half-century. All three countries came out of World War II and/or post-World War II conflicts deeply impoverished and politically broken, but they have since become the two largest economies (China and Japan) and fourth-largest economy (South Korea) in Asia. With shared concerns about North Korea, the countries stand to gain significantly from working together. However, the three countries have had very limited success at cooperating with one another (Reynolds and Lee 2019).

In this sense, the workings of NIA theory can present a useful guide for elites and policymakers. Even when leaders perceive possible win-win benefits from cooperation, mutual suspicion and fear in the public may prevent leaders from pursuing cooperative policy and amplify the excessive tension between the countries. In cases where there is clear interest in cooperating but the public is openly hostile toward and thus unwilling to support cooperation with another nation-state, NIA can offer a way for these publics to dispassionately realize the benefit of cooperation. As we will see in chapters 7 and 8, NIA can move those who are most extremely opposed to a policy into a more moderate middle-zone, through a lowered defensiveness about their in-group.

1.4.1 Implications for the United States and the World

Antipathy between these three prosperous economies has broader implications for the world, and is especially troubling for the United States. First, heightened security fears between the countries threaten to embroil the United States and other states in their disputes. Territorial disputes over Diaoyu/Senkaku between China and Japan and the Takeshima/Dokdo islands between Japan and South Korea raise the dreaded prospect that the United States and Russia, among others, may face entrapment issues over the need to support allies should tensions escalate to militarized conflict (Glosserman and Snyder 2015). Regarding controversy in disputed waters between Japan and South Korea, Mintaro Oba, a former U.S. diplomat who worked on Korean Peninsula issues, remarked, "That this is the area where we've seen so much tension lately is undoubtedly very worrying to Washington" (Reynolds and Lee 2019).

Second, obstacles that impede cooperation between the triangular alliance of the United States, Japan, and South Korea are a cause for concern (Choe and Gladstone 2018). At a time of difficult transitions and diplomacy on the Korean Peninsula and unease in U.S.-China relations, repeated antagonism between Japan and South Korea is worrisome to American officials (Sneider, in Choe and Gladstone 2018). Both countries are U.S. allies, and the unremitting quarrels between Japan and South Korea can impede the protection and advancement of America's strategic and geopolitical interests (Glosserman and Snyder 2015). For example, hostile relations between the states can undermine U.S. efforts to disarm North Korea. Tension between Japan and South Korea could negatively affect America's potential collaboration with these states in the event of a North Korean crisis. In August 2017, a North Korean ballistic missile flew over northern Japan, and Tokyo, already uncomfortable with South Korean President Moon Jae-in's attempts at detente with North Korea, emphasized a hard line on sanctions enforcement on North Korea. Reports that followed indicated Japan would skip joint naval exercises with the United States and South Korea that were planned for April 2019 (Reynolds and Lee 2019).

1.5 Contributions

Political elites and experts have yet to reach a consensus on best practices for existing national identities when it comes to reconciliation between antagonistic countries. Theoretical predictions that globalization would accompany an erosion of national identities have not been confirmed (Calhoun 2007; Guibernau 2001; Kaldor 2004; Kymlicka 2003). In the European Union, one of the most closely integrated regional entities in the world, historical trends demonstrate that regional identities form alongside extant national identities, adding to rather than replacing them (Hoffmann 1966).

Under these conditions, this study presents possibilities for a more plausible approach of what to do with existing boundaries of identity. The findings in this study shed light on potential robustness of the mechanism of NIA and its connection to intergroup reconciliation.[9] Making a case for how stronger identification to subgroups can actually improve relations between larger groups, in a broad sense my study offers timely implications for debates on multiculturalism, as well as interethnic and interracial conflict in domestic politics. If making salient existing subgroup identities via affirmation paves ways for a more peaceful coexistence within a supragroup, there is reason to be hopeful that multicultural communities where a number of different cultures coexist while defending each of their cultural traditions and practices can be free of conflict.

In the context of Northeast Asian states, affirmation effects could potentially suggest a more feasible way of overcoming historical animosity than its alternatives, for example China and South Korea pressuring Japan for a public apology. State leaders are sensitive to issues of losing or saving face relative to other governments and how that is displayed to their domestic audiences. For this reason, Japanese atonement via political pressure from other states rather than inward-looking NIA within the Japanese public is neither likely nor desirable (Lind 2008a; see also Barkan 2011; Gibney et al. 2008; O'Neill 1999; Torpey 2004). Unfortunately (yet also perhaps unsurprisingly), recurring pursuits by Chinese and South Koreans for a "sufficient" public apology from Japan have been unrewarding for decades.

NIA could propose appealing policy advice for state leaders who wish to obtain the benefit of international cooperation with a past adversary but who are hesitant to do so due to public objections. With the current nationalistic vigor in South Korea, China, and Japan, it is unrealistic to expect a rapid diminishing of nationalisms in Northeast Asia. State leaders will thus need to engage nationalism for public support. As previously noted, this will be especially important in democratic states, where leaders must appear as politically attractive enough to win votes into office. Thus when elites find economic, strategic, or geopolitical reasons to cooperate, NIA could present a path to pursue this while still advocating popular nationalism.

In sum, when leaders hope to ease relations with other states but encounter challenges due to pervasive enemy images in public opinion, NIA may help move the people toward a moderate direction. If this process works congruently with the proposed mechanism of NIA, it would be through heightened ability of the masses to process the benefits of international cooperation. Conversely, however, leaders may have vested interests in actively perpetuating distrust and hatred between countries. In these cases there will be limits to the affirmation effects.

1.5.1 Broader Impacts

The implications of what NIA can do for peaceful relations reach far beyond Northeast Asia. Around the world, there is no shortage of examples of countries whose relations with their neighbors suffer from a failure to reconcile. Besides Japan's relations with its neighbors, relations between India and Pakistan and between Palestine and Israel vividly illustrate this phenomenon. In these countries the past is still very much present, as suspicions about each other's intentions and negative perceptions rooted in history often lead to disruptions in diplomacy.

Chronic distrust and hostile images of each other destabilizes institutional cooperation and regional security. In August 2014, for example, all three "hot-bed" areas experienced upheavals that demonstrate the lasting effects of historical animosity. On August 15, 2014, a day that marked the sixty-ninth anniversary of Japanese defeat in World War II as well as independence of Manchuria and Korea from Japanese colonialist rule, Japan's Prime Minister Abe Shinzo sent an offering to the controversial Yasukuni Shrine (Martin and Connect 2014; Varandani 2014). This move enraged both China and South Korea, weakening ties already strained by territorial disputes and differences over wartime history (Fifield 2014). Likewise, on August 18, 2014, with just a week remaining before foreign secretary-level talks, Indian Foreign Secretary Sujatha Singh called off planned meetings with her Pakistani counterpart, Aizaz Ahmad Chaudhry, expressing resentment over Pakistan's engagement with Kashmiri separatist leaders (BBC 2014). Similarly, in the midst of a ceasefire between Israel and Palestine in the deadly conflict of August 2014, opinion gaps between the two sides remained wide as Israeli and Palestinian negotiators hardened their positions in Egypt-mediated Gaza truce talks (Fitch, Mitnick, and Najib 2014). Just days before the expiration of the ceasefire, both sides staked out unyielding positions, coming no closer to a solution. These are all cases wherein memories of a tumultuous past disrupted interstate interactions and intensified geopolitical security fears.

Researchers note that the potential benefits of ending tensions and building more cooperative measures between these states could be immense. From the Chinese perspective for example, critics contend that China should increase ties with Japan and South Korea to counter the United States in an intensifying competition of hegemony. Even government researchers in Beijing note that China has become economically dependent on trade relations with the United States, and that China should leverage relationships with Tokyo and Seoul to drive regional economic development instead (Lee 2019). In addition, to many observers the tension between Japan and South Korea is especially puzzling. Both countries are liberal democracies and longtime U.S. allies that have extensive trading relationships with each other. With numerous shared interests, including apprehension about North Korea and the growth of China's power, the two countries have much to gain from closer ties. In a similar vein, Pakistan and India likewise have a great deal in common with each other politically, culturally, economically, and strategically; their economies are closely bound and their citizens have common social and family ties going back generations (Hajari 2015). And with the unprecedented death and injury tolls between Palestine and Israel (for example, 561 children were killed, 3,000 wounded, and 1,000 permanently disabled just during a fifty-day conflict in 2014), the benefits from peace are urgent and obvious (Patten 2015).

Many observers blame the history problem. The common claim is that unresolved historical issues stand in the way of reconciliation. Regarding South Korea and Japan, for example, commentary in *The New York Times* (2012) stated that "old animosities are still making it difficult for [the countries] to establish a reliably productive relationship."

But sometimes a shared security threat, or the view that a country is an indispensable strategic partner, may prompt leaders to seek cooperation. At such times, leaders can have a difficult time convincing the public that a drastic change in their foreign policy from hostility to cooperation is beneficial, given the tendency for negative images to persevere. Leaders of past inflictor states may struggle to convey to their public that acknowledging past violence and showing empathy for the other country's suffering is an effective way of showing they are a reliable international partner and/or politically expedient ally. Given the political costs of pursuing unpopular policies, leaders typically find it easier to embrace popular nationalism than abandon it. For example, the General Security of Military Information Agreement (GSOMIA)—a military cooperation agreement—revealed the difficulties encountered in collaborative efforts between Japan and South Korea's due to public reluctance, regardless of the eagerness initiated by leaders.

I offer NIA as a way toward trust and reconciliation between countries without having to demolish national identities, which are highly salient and important in all of the areas mentioned in this book and their "history problem." NIA does not require promotion of an overarching group, a supranational entity like the European Union, or a common historical identity—though many previous accounts promote these methods as effective tools to accomplish reconciliation. In the results of my experimental, survey, and case studies, I find that an opposite strategy of empowering national identities can have the effect of increasing trust and support for cooperation with past adversaries, and leading inflictors to acknowledge greater need to atone for their past.

1.6 Method

This book provides an in-depth analysis of the psychological underpinnings of international reconciliation in the populace of Northeast Asia, using a multidisciplinary framework that combines three research methods and five subfields popular in social science. The research methods are experiments, fieldwork, and large-N survey analyses; the connected fields are international security, social psychology, conflict resolution, behavioral economics, and history. Drawing from these various fields and methods, I illustrate how NIA can increase trust, guilt, and positive perception of other countries, despite the countries being burdened with traumatic memories of conflict.

Original experiments and observational data support these findings. First, through a series of field experiments conducted in China, Japan, and South Korea, I provide evidence that NIA increases the level of trust people from these countries feel toward another country traditionally perceived as a rival or enemy. These countries were chosen as research sites because their relations are strongly marked by past conflict, and because the legacy of such conflict continues to impede and undermine present-day diplomacy. I examine two measures of trust: (1) strategic trust, as a crucial element in institutional cooperation, and (2) moralistic trust, the lack of which can lead to a security dilemma. Trust on both measures was greater for individuals who had a firm sense of their national identity.

These positive initial findings suggest that NIA could be effective in the real world. To investigate the matter further, this book also looks at attitudinal measures on real, unresolved issues of reconciliation between the countries. With these measures, we can see the effect of NIA on both sides of past aggression—the side of past "inflictors" and of the "receivers." Specifically, I study the effect of NIA on (a) South Koreans' willingness to cooperate with Japan on a contested military agreement involving intelligence sharing, and (b) Japanese willingness to endorse acts of reparation to Chinese and South Koreans for losses during World War II. In the examination of guilt, I analyze a sample of 1,597 Japanese to find the affirmation of national identity increases guilt recognition and willingness to compensate for personal and other Japanese persons' transgressions.

I also consider observational data on perceptions 7,200 South Koreans held over a period of six years regarding countries South Korea had the most turbulent interactions with throughout history.[10] The results indicate that individuals with an affirmed sense of national identity held more positive perceptions of these countries, seeing them as allies with reasonable intentions and as a potential partner to cooperate with.

1.7 Plan of the Book

This book is organized into nine chapters. Chapter 2 introduces the state of Northeast Asian international relations and delves deeper into the problems of unresolved history addressed throughout the book. In particular, I examine the problem in regions that suffer from traumatic memories of history—in other words, the "history problem." This chapter provides a detailed definition of the history problem and how its perpetuation limits reconciliation between states. Next, I explore examples of how distrust, negative imagery, and reluctance to admit guilt inhibit practical steps toward accord and heighten security-threat perceptions between states, using the examples of Sino-Japanese and Japanese-South Korean relations. Focusing on the current state of countries that suffer from a lack of trust and guilt recognition, as well as preponderance of negative imagery, chapter 2 is devoted to outlining the problem before proposing a solution.

Chapter 3 provides a presentation of this book's central theory, which argues that affirming national identities can increase trust, guilt recognition, and positive imagery between countries with a history problem. First, I examine the independent variables, or predictors, of the study—ways to increase trust, guilt, and positive images between states struggling from negative memories of history. I review numerous studies, borrowing from political science, social psychology, and literature on conflict resolution, that advocate a "commonality" of downplaying existing subidentities as a way of overcoming the past. This leads us to the theory of group-affirmation, from where we can focus on how NIA can promote reconciliation between states by emphasizing national identities. This provides potential for a better understanding of how NIA works, by exploring how affirmation of one's national identity decreases defensiveness toward other countries.

Having examined the independent variables in the first section of chapter 3, in the second section I present the dependent variables, or outcomes, of interest—trust, guilt, and images. I discuss my theory on the two types of aforementioned trust and argue that affirming national identities can help increase trust between countries with a history problem. I then propose the theory that NIA can encourage guilt recognition and willingness to cooperate between states with unresolved issues of reparation. Through reduced defensiveness, NIA can lead a country that has historically adopted a relatively powerful position—a past "inflictor" position—to acknowledge guilt, while those who believe they were "receivers" of harm simultaneously come to objectively recognize the potential benefit of cooperating with the former inflictor country. NIA is offered as a more feasible remedy than existing prescriptions for increasing guilt recognition from past inflictors and willingness to cooperate from past receivers. Finally, the chapter incorporates insight from image theory and summarizes the importance of perceptions and images in international relations, as well as suggestions of how NIA can increase positive images between countries with a turbulent past.

Chapters 4 through 6 provide experimental, observational, and cross-national evidence to show how affirmation of national identity can decrease defensiveness and thus promote reconciliation between adversarial countries. Chapter 4 explores the relationship between NIA and trust, which is first examined on the individual level by integrating techniques developed in social psychology and behavioral economics in novel field experiments in China, Japan, and South Korea. The experiment manipulates NIA and examines whether this makes a difference in levels of trust as reported by subjects. Levels of trust were measured in two ways: first, strategic trust was measured through a trust game that examines the number of tokens individuals send to an opponent whom they believe is from another country; and second, moralistic trust was measured through survey questions that asked subjects how much they trusted another country. The experiments found that individuals who were affirmed of their national identity reported higher levels of trust across both trust measures, as compared to individuals in the control condition. Other predictor variables from the survey represented alternative remedies proposed in the extant literature, such as the creation of an overarching identity, a pursuit of regional integration with the European Union as a model, or a constructivist vision of common historical interpretation. These variables were not significantly correlated with trust.

Chapter 5 reports results from another novel field experiment on NIA and guilt conducted in Japan. I examine whether NIA, by circumventing the defensiveness often elicited by transgressions of one's country, frees people to acknowledge guilt. For Japan, the most challenging issue in dealing with its past colonies is not public opposition to cooperation but political and public fatigue with regard to China and South Korea's constant demands for acknowledgment of past guilt. Admitting past guilt of one's group can hurt its members' self-image as a moral body that treats other groups fairly, so many past inflictor countries exhibit defensive reactions with regard to past actions. This can be through denial of violence, justification of actions as self-defense, or even glorification of wartime history.

Existing research shows, however, that when aggressors of history develop a proud and positive group identity, they have been found to accept more guilt and shame about their group's past wrongdoing (Čehajić-Clancy et al. 2011; Gunn and Wilson 2011). Studies on dominant majority groups in society have also found that when secure in their group identity, such groups come to admit the oppression practiced and prejudice held against minority groups (Adams, Tormala, and O'Brien 2006). Drawing a connection with these studies, I analyze original data collected from a sample of 1,597 Japanese. Results reveal that people come to admit higher levels of guilt for either their own or in-group members' actions after they were affirmed of their national identity. In addition, to address the policy challenge of the mismatch between deceased perpetrators and contemporary Japanese in reparation policy, I highlight the mechanism that connects NIA and guilt recognition, which is prosociality.

Chapter 6 builds on the experiments conducted on the three countries for a more comprehensive examination of NIA. Data from representative surveys conducted on 7,200 South Korean adults from 2007 to 2012 supports the correlation between survey responses that approximate measures of NIA and images of other countries. Consistent with the experimental findings in earlier chapters, results indicate that people who felt prouder of their national identities reported more positive perceptions of other countries as candidates for cooperation—the ally image (Herrmann and Fischerkeller 1995). Strikingly, this effect of NIA was consistent throughout the six-year duration of the data and across different age groups.

How would NIA influence actual policy? Chapters 7 and 8 take us a little deeper into actual unresolved policies surrounding countries with the history problem. By focusing on specific policies at hand that are intertwined with diplomatic friction and security threats, I examine how NIA can be effective in bringing the countries closer to cooperation and reconciliation. Using my experimental data, each of these chapters focuses respectively on how NIA could have an effect on the past inflictors' and receivers' side of history. Starting with the receivers, chapter 7 focuses on the specific case of South Korean public opinion toward GSOMIA. While this agreement was cancelled in 2012 due to public opposition, opinion polls suggest that when systematically processing through the benefits of the treaty, most South Koreans acknowledge the necessity of it. As it turns out, NIA can serve to, in effect, nudge those most opposed to a policy into a more moderate middle-zone.

Chapter 8 then shifts focus to Japan's perspective. Public opinion polls reveal Japanese distrust in the sincerity of continued pressure for compensation from South Korea and China. Much of the Japanese public believes the two countries exaggerate and continue with such demands for political reasons, by strategically playing the history card. I find from my experiments that Japanese with a strong sense of national identity are more open to endorsing compensation with affected countries, due to increased trust of the people and governments of the countries making reparation claims.

Finally, chapter 9 discusses historical cases that provide an examination of qualitative evidence of NIA as well as lessons we can take away from them. I provide examples where leaders applied NIA frames in speeches and policy to encourage the public toward international cooperation with a past enemy. The utility of NIA in areas beyond Asia is also discussed, citing examples from American foreign policy. The chapter concludes the book by examining the larger policy implications of this study, presenting the ramifications of the findings for scholars and policymakers more generally.

TWO

Why Can't We Move Beyond the Past?

Distrust, Guilt Avoidance, and Negative Images

This chapter starts by describing the "problem" in the "history problem." I provide an overview of the current state of international relations in Asia. In particular, I look at examples of how distrust, disagreement on the extent of guilt recognition necessary, and negative images resulting from turbulent history continue to haunt relations between China, Japan, and South Korea today. As the book focuses on NIA within public opinion, this chapter also offers a broader account of why public opinion is important in world politics.

The next section describes the scope of this book, which areas in which the history problem stumps reconciliation. In these areas, unforgettable traumas breed distrust and negative perception, as well as disagreement over who is guilty and responsible to what extent in historical interpretation. All of this hampers peace and cooperation. Specifically, the distrust and negative images that remain tangible for generations in the public make it difficult for elites to revise policies toward past adversaries.

2.1 The Puzzle

The puzzle regarding the emergence of the history problem as a prominent source of tension is that it goes against conventional wisdom across all prominent international relations theories. First, according to realists, on a systemic level China would have incentive to partner more closely with

Japan and South Korea to offset the impact of competition with the United States (Lee 2019). Academics comment that "China needs to better leverage Japan, to relieve or even resolve the conflict with the U.S." (Zhang, cited in Lee 2019). An alliance would be beneficial to all three states as they face new military and security environments in the world order.

Even within the three countries, on a regional scale, the rise of China should prompt at least the two countries of Japan and South Korea to ally in a balancing act of power distributions. International relations scholars' work examining rapprochement posits that complementary economies and geopolitical interests are strong facilitating conditions for rapprochement (Rock 1989). Japan and South Korea share common security concerns and wider geopolitical interests against potential threats a rapidly growing China imposes. This creates a significant opportunity for alliance in bilateral defense and technical cooperation (Yoon 2019). In addition, Japan and South Korea need a security partner to check and cope with possibilities of revisionist policies from North Korea or Russia.[1] However, even as Japanese and South Koreans become more aware of what China's growing economic and political influence, hardline policy from Russia, and North Korean provocations mean for Japanese and South Korean security policies, tension between the two countries has not subsided (Glosserman and Snyder 2015). Unlike realist predictions, distrust and negative perception originating from history seven decades ago outweigh the urgency of upcoming security threats of China, Russia, and North Korea.

Second, areas bedeviled by the history problem challenge the liberal notion that increasing interaction and communication should dilute political grievances (He 2006). Liberals emphasize that interdependence in trade relations (Gartzke and Li 2003; Keohane and Nye 1977) and similar political systems reduce likelihood for conflict (Oneal and Russett 1999[2]). Other liberals have also stressed the importance of international exchange in "soft power" arenas (Nye 2004).

However, these prospects appear to be limited in areas where the history problem persists. In economic terms, intraregional trade and investment are strong. China and Japan already trade heavily: China has emerged as Japan's greatest trading partner and Japan as second biggest to China, after the United States (Simoes and Hidalgo 2011; World Bank 2017).[3] In fact, bilateral trade volume between China and Japan increased about six times from 1980 to 1999, and this was certainly not a period of amiable relations (MITI, Bureau of Statistics; Japan Statistical Yearbook, Trade Statistics of China, Japanese Ministry of Justice Annual Report of Immigration, in He 2006). In addition, Japan and South Korea are both liberal democracies and each other's third-largest trading partner, a good portion of the goods being cultural products (Reynolds and Lee 2019). Japanese and South Korean pop culture—a typically cited source of soft power—is avidly consumed in China (Berger 2008). But developments in the region have shown that trade relations or cultural exchange have not been binding, and meaningful and trustful cooperation is still elusive. Even cultural products that are exchanged reflect or have been used to promote anti-other sentiments (Chung 2015a).

Overall, liberal prospects of interdependence and soft power have not been realized in Northeast Asia (Hoffman 1966). Furthermore, when politically sensitive issues arose, previous cooperation was put in peril, strengthening the claim that such approaches are enclosed with limitations within regions with the history problem (Lee 2008).

Finally, in response to the history problem, constructivists in international relations theory emphasize the importance of a common historical interpretation. Oftentimes with reference to reconciliation in Rwanda, experts have suggested the creation of an official narrative of memory (Longman and Rutagengwa 2004; Rutayisire, Kabano, and Rubagiza 2004). Especially in Northeast Asia, where history textbooks are at the center of controversy, attempts to construct a common historical narrative have been made in Northeast Asia as well (Akio 2017; Lawson and Tannaka 2011). On several occasions since the 1990s, UNESCO initiated official textbook talks between Japan, South Korea, and China. However, on an official level dialogue failed, with these talks repeatedly breaking down and being suspended again.

To summarize, despite many shared geopolitical and economic interests, the three states never developed genuine strategic cooperation over the past decades. As a matter of fact, notwithstanding commercial ties, since the 2000s China and Japan have evinced a trend toward thinly veiled or open rivalry (He 2013).

2.1.1 The History Problem

Where does the history problem come from? The history problem can start and spread from both leaders with chauvinistic interests and the public, even though the threats and losses from a long-term failure to reconcile hurts everyone. Leaders may portray or "scapegoat" another country in an enemy or imperialistic image for votes or to promote national unity. Sometimes leaders reinforce stereotypes of another country as untrustworthy and threatening in order to mobilize their public for war. Other leaders emphasize their adversaries' past violence in order to justify, deny, or simply forget their own (Halperin et al. 2010). In such ways, political authorities seek to create official historical narratives that give themselves legitimacy and the power to serve their own interests (Berger 2008). Noting the examples of the failure of Palestinian-Israeli negotiations in 2000–2001 and the ongoing outbreak of the Palestinian-Israeli wars, Kaufman (2009) contends that political elites construct competing narratives of group identity that reinforce stereotypes of the other. This creates group fears that would justify hostility, thereby making peace between groups harder to reach.[4] These narratives enable hardline leaders on both sides to block compromise and escalate conflict. Governing elites use their control to shape historical "myths" (He 2006) about historical reality in terms of their interests (Kim and Schwartz 2010). For example, Wirth (2009), Peattie (2007), and Pilling (2009) note that since the 1980s, Chinese leaders have strategically used the "history card" against Japan, exploiting its "victim status" in order to advance their own interests and divert public attention away from internal disunity.

However, when negative history continues to bring about distrust and negative images in people's minds, leaders suffer as much as they benefit from the history problem. These same leaders fall prey to those very images (Herrmann and Fischerkeller 1995), as leaders themselves suffer from setbacks due to the way in which history is solidified in the public's minds. When leaders are socialized into a "sticky" image, one that breeds certainty that the other country is up to no good, the image will heighten the elites' threat perception, concern for their own gain, and willingness to risk conflict. In sum, the losses, harm, and risk caused by the history problem are too excessive compared to any short-term self-interest or support sought by chauvinistic leaders or entrepreneurs.

Sometimes the history problem is perpetuated by the public, and leaders are constrained by these public expressions of outrage and injustice (Vogel 2003). For example, the public can prolong the history problem through demonstrations, petitions, and boycotts targeting another country for what they believe to be inappropriate historical treatment (Pei 2010). Against these movements, the Chinese government struggled with various means to stop the spread of violent, autonomous anti-Japanese mass protests in 2005. Beijing tried to limit the activities of anti-Japanese activists and used more policemen to prevent and disband demonstrations. On university campuses, seminars were held to educate students to be practical in their attitudes toward Japan (Chan and Bridges 2006). However, there are Chinese youths and nongovernmental actors who are patriotic and hold strong resentment against Japan, although they have never experienced war firsthand (Pei 2010). In such ways, public opinion centering on history can constrain government policies and press leaders to choose hostile actions over conciliatory ones (Kelman 1997).

2.1.2 Images Are Sticky—But Can Change

As formidable as the perceived obstacles caused by the history problem might seem, it is important to remember that perceived images of countries are never completely static (Herrmann 2013; Berger 2008). Image theorists predict that imagery can change dramatically and quickly, once a benefit from cooperating with the other is perceived. Herrmann (2013) notes that when groups conceive of their goal in terms of compatibility and interdependence, those previously dehumanized or seen as radical extremists can become human or moderate overnight. Even very intense enemy images can be forgotten quickly, as seen in the American public's views of Russia, Japan, or China with the 1979 U.S.-PRC Joint Communique following Beijing's willingness to cooperate with the United States.

Readiness to cooperate causes a dramatic reversal of a country viewed in a colony image as well, as seen in the shift in American perceptions of Ethiopia and Somalia in the 1980s or the transformation of American pictures of the good Afghan mujahideen into the bad Afghan Taliban in the 1990s. In Iraq, the Sunni resistance was initially seen as radical extremists tied to al-Qaeda, but in a remarkably short time was reimagined as the Sons of Iraq—moderate and responsible leaders of the Sunni Awakening (White 1991). What brought this change was willingness to cooperate with the occupation forces (Herrmann 2013).

In sum, one of the main weaknesses in the existing literature on the history problem lies in its view of historical animosity as a constant—without noting any conditions and contexts under which the distrust and negative images can be changed for the better (Cho and Park 2011). While the history problem may be persistent, it can be alleviated. Taking into consideration the nonstatic nature of image construction and the damaging features of the history problem, it is possible and indeed necessary that we ask in what ways we can lessen its harmful effects. Before getting into ways of how, the section below describes the importance of public opinion, as this book suggests identity affirmation in the public as a way toward this. Either an affirmed public could push an elite for rapprochement or elites might find NIA an attractive way to help move the public in a more cooperative direction. The remaining parts of the chapter introduce the state of international relations in Northeast Asia, in particular why boosting trust, guilt recognition, and positive images are critical to overcoming negative history.

2.2 Why Does Public Opinion Matter?

This book focuses on identity affirmation in the public. Does public opinion matter in international politics? International relations theorists have various views on the role of mass publics in world politics. Although realists see citizens as primarily constrained by the international system and the state, they accept that the public's actions may be reflected in national interest. Liberals believe mass publics matter because they help formulate the state's interests. According to liberals, the public may affect international relations through mass actions that pressure state decision makers. Constructivists contend that the public can become agents of potential change through discourse and the formation of collective identities. In more recent postmodernist and feminist scholarship, the role of private citizens and their stories have found salience.

Various experts have noted the importance and influence of public opinion on politics and foreign policy. Some emphasize the role of public opinion in affecting voting behavior (Aldrich, Sullivan, and Borgida 1989), while others underscore its impact on public policy (Chanley 1999; Page and Shapiro 1992; Jacobs and Shapiro 2000). The public can also have a profound impact on international politics through collective action. Autonomous acts of thousands of people fleeing East Germany led to the construction of the Berlin Wall in 1961, while the spontaneous exodus of thousands of East Germans through Hungary and Austria led to the tearing down of the wall twenty-eight years later in 1989 (Major 2010). Sometimes the public provides direct input on foreign policy decision-making. Citizens have voted in public referendums on issues with foreign policy significance such as the Maastricht Treaty, EU Constitution, and Treaty of Lisbon in the EU. In 2016, British people voted to leave the EU, and in 2002 Swiss people voted in a referendum to join the United Nations.

Numerous other examples illustrate the power of the public in politics, especially amplified today with mass communication. In October 2000, aided by new technology of the time—cellular phones—Serbians were able to mobilize citizens from all over the country against Yugoslavian leader Slobodan Milosevic's rule (Pavlović 2016). A group of young private citizens in late 2010 organized a Facebook and YouTube campaign, calling on more than 130,000 followers for the ouster of the government of President Hosni Mubarak of Egypt (Vargas 2012). Frequent mass movements against each other in China, Japan, and South Korea, added with the tech savviness of the countries' citizens, have opened a vast array of opportunities for the publics to influence international politics.

Evidence from the United States suggests that elites do care about the preferences of the public, as the popularity of presidents affects their ability to work (Brody 1991). In other words, leaders may lose popularity if they pursue policy against the general mood of the masses. Given the contemporary policy relevance of influencing public opinion through national identities, NIA can provide valuable insights for leaders who feel constrained in initiating new cooperative measures with a past enemy country.

Recently, public opinion and international relations scholars have been giving more attention to the significance of *trust* and *images* in the public. Research finds that trust the public holds of other countries influences mass beliefs on international relations, adding a new layer to our understanding of how citizens affect foreign policy (Brewer et al. 2004). In addition, recent accounts have shown that citizens base such opinions on internalized images of specific foreign nations (Herrmann, Tetlock, and Visser 1999; Hurwtiz and Peffley 1987; Peffley and Hurwitz 1992; Wittkopf 1990). That is, citizens base their opinions about world affairs in part on the perceived image of how trustworthy they believe other countries to be. In demonstrating the role of international trust—defined as generalized beliefs about whether one's country can trust another country—in shaping public opinion, scholars have found that international trust shapes whether Americans perceive the image of specific foreign nations as unfriendly or threatening, whether they endorse internationalism or isolationism, and whether they favor certain foreign interventions overseas (Brewer et al. 2004).

Public opinion, sentiment, and movements among the citizenry are particularly important in areas where violent nationalist movements in the populace are rampant. Northeast Asia is an example of such an area today. Scholars caution that with regional-level security threats between China and Japan, along with systemic-level competition between the United State and China that could shift the international order, the feasibility of healthier international relations in Northeast Asia depends most on the development of a genuinely resilient and robust civil society (Park 2017; He 2013). Critics also note that although elite-level meetings between the states can help ease tensions, a meaningful and durable rapprochement remains a dim prospect in Asia until the public in each country espouses more positive views of each other country (Hardy-Chartrand 2014).

Public views influence foreign policy, international relations, and the prospects for future conflict in Asia (Glosserman and Snyder 2015). In liberal democracies like South Korea and Japan, public opinion directly influences the parameters of foreign policymaking by shaping or enlarging cooperation with countries perceived as allies. Even in China, public opinion is currently seen as playing a larger role than that in a traditional Marxist society. Recent studies demonstrate that Chinese politics increasingly relies on public opinion, and Chinese leaders show actual responsiveness to public demands (Chen, Pan, and Xu 2016; Jiang 2018; Landry, Lü, and Duan 2018). For example, despite the authoritarian elements of China's system, officials in the Communist Party of China (especially at lower levels) are being evaluated based on performance, in attempts to boost the legitimacy of the party.

However, despite its importance, systematic analysis of public opinion in Asia is surprisingly thin. There has been little effort to analyze Northeast Asian public opinion in an interactive way that paints a fuller picture of how publics view relations with their neighbors. Many scholarly analyses of foreign policy in Asian countries tend to emphasize systemic and structural factors and a model for understanding decision-making that privileges elites over individuals. However, it is apparent that the interaction between public opinion and political leadership increasingly influences national preferences in foreign policy and gives insight into international relations in Asia. This requires a deeper exploration of the root causes underlying changes in public opinion.

The survey experiments in this book probe the individual-level effects of NIA on trust, guilt, and perception. How can we connect psychological findings based on the individual level to international politics? We can find answers in the large body of literature that exists on public opinion and foreign policy. Research in this tradition finds that individual dispositions compose public opinion and ultimately impact policy (Page and Bouton 2008). Previous findings identify individual-level internationalist or isolationist tendencies as well as cooperative or militant policy preferences in the citizens. Kertzer (2016) studies psychological individual-level variations in persistence and resolve regarding the use of force, to study public opinion toward military interventions. These studies attribute such dispositions to ideological, partisan, and sociodemographic differences (Hurwitz and Peffley 1987, 1990). None of these studies, however, focuses on national identity and its impact on international trust and reconciliation.

In sum, the effects of NIA proposed throughout this book can certainly apply to both leaders and the public. However, this book tests its theories on the general public as a way to suggest how psychological change in public opinion may affect public sentiment, thereby nudging foreign policy and international relations over time.

2.3 Trust in Asia

Considering that leaders sometimes intentionally exacerbate negative memories of history (for example, to promote domestic unity through a common, external enemy), one might ask what the actual "problem" of negative memories is. Do the potential losses outweigh the political benefits of keeping the mistrust alive? This section provides examples within the Northeast Asian context of how the history problem has aggravated distrust in international relations, thereby severely undermining institutional cooperation and increasing security fears.

For the purposes of this investigation, I define trust as the belief that others will cooperate when one cooperates, and distrust as the lack of this belief (Kydd 2007; Rathbun 2009). In Northeast Asia, historical issues have become powerful symbols for a host of problems that stump efforts at rebuilding trust. The overall consensus of the existing work on the region is unmistakable: the troubled past has been, and continues to be, a defining feature of how countries judge and interpret each other's intentions. Historical animosity drives mistrust, which in turn drives the behavior affecting these nations' relations (Cha 2003).

Results from a public opinion poll conducted by Genron NPO and *China Daily* in 2014 reveal that the majority of the Japanese (66.0 percent) and Chinese (76.1 percent) respondents reported that they view each other as untrustworthy. In particular, Japan's past participation in expansionism and colonialism in Asia during World War II left behind a legacy of mutual suspicion, which foils opportunities for institutional cooperation between Japan and its neighbors. In his speech on the country's Liberation Day in 2001, former South Korean president Kim Dae Jung exclaimed: "How can we make good friends with people who try to forget and ignore the many pains they inflicted on us? How can we deal with them in the future with any degree of trust?" (Kirk 2001). Figure 1 highlights the low trust Koreans have of their Northeast Asian members. Compared to the United States and European Union, South Koreans regard the Chinese—and Japanese to a larger extent—to be untrustworthy.

Debates regarding Japan's recent efforts to amend its constitution, which

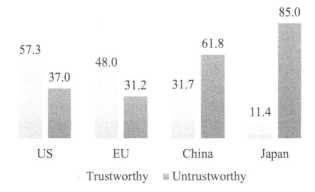

Figure 1. South Koreans' trust of other countries. July 2013 (%).
Modified and recreated from The Asan Institute for Policy Studies.

would allow it to have an army rather than its current self-defense forces, illustrate how distrust amplifies Chinese and South Koreans' security fears of Japan. Japan claims these endeavors are aimed at becoming a "normal country"—just like any other country that can practice its "normally considered" rights of having a national military force. This move, however, has greatly alarmed China and South Korea, as both feel an urgent need to guard against any "resurgent Japanese militarism" and thus contain Japanese power (Cha 2003). Chinese and South Koreans have even expressed unease over Tokyo's dispatch of peacekeepers abroad (Lind 2009a).

2.4 Guilt: How World War II-Era Reparations Are Still Roiling Asia[5]

Chinese and Korean demands for more explicit apologies and extensive compensation from Tokyo have not succeeded in reducing long-standing tensions in Northeast Asia (Harris and Harding 2018a, 2018b). In addition, ongoing problems such as arguments over territory, history textbooks, war memorials, fishing rights, and oil deposits all become intertwined with the issue of historical guilt. In each of these areas, Chinese and Koreans point to Japan's inadequate atonement for its wartime conduct as the root cause (Pilling 2012).

From the Japanese perspective however, apologies have already been made (New York Times 2015). The 1995 Murayama Statement, in which then Japanese Prime Minister Tomiichi Murayama spoke of his "feelings of deep remorse" and his "heartfelt apology for Japan's colonial rule and aggression (which) caused tremendous damage and suffering to the people of many countries, particularly to those of Asian nations," is just one example (Ministry of Foreign Affairs of Japan 1995). In 2001, Prime Minister Junichiro Koizumi personally wrote a letter to surviving comfort women that Japan is "painfully aware of its moral responsibilities" and "as Prime Minister of Japan, I thus extend anew my most sincere apologies and remorse to all the women who underwent immeasurable and painful experiences and suffered incurable physical and psychological wounds as comfort women." He also added, "We must not evade the weight of the past, nor should we evade our responsibilities for the future" (Ministry of Foreign Affairs of Japan 2001).

But how likely is it that present-day Japanese will feel responsible for seventy-four-year-old events? There is growing concern that the younger generation, with no memory of war or colonization, is further against compensating for something they were never personally involved in (Yasuaki 2002). Many Japanese express a sense of fatigue regarding the constant accusations from China and South Korea, especially now that most of those who committed wartime atrocities are deceased (Dudden 2014). Chinese and Koreans problematize textbooks approved for use in Japanese schools that seem to soften Japanese guilt in such events, but these demands from China and South Korea are seen as arduous by the youth of Japan, causing a reluctance in the youth to deal with the issues at all (Evans 2015). In this regard, younger Japanese may feel it is unfair that they are still asked to pay for action their great-grandfathers committed and, as such, further lose interest in soothing Japan's relations with its neighbors (Yasuaki 2002).

On the other hand, the belief that current Japanese should admit guilt and pay compensation for their county's past is very much alive in China and South Korea. Bitterness over Imperial Japan's occupation of Asian neighbors is still robust, and from Chinese and Korean perspectives, the public and leaders of Japan today do not sufficiently feel the "weight of the past" as they should (Evans 2015). In 2018, for example, the Korean Supreme Court ordered Nippon Steel & Sumitomo Metal, a leading Japanese steelmaking company, to compensate Korean men forced to work as slave laborers during World War II (Choe and Gladstone 2015). The ruling stirred age-old resentments, inflaming Japan-South Korea relations once again, and the Japanese government was quick to criticize the decision. From the view of Japanese, postwar agreements such as the 1965 Treaty on

Basic Relations between Japan and South Korea already settled claims for damages caused by Imperial Japan's colonial conquests (Kim 2019).

However, any past Japanese attempts at penitence have been insufficient in the Chinese and Koreans' eyes (Choe and Gladstone 2018). Why? Observers note that Japanese leaders and the public tend to "eviscerate" past apologies, either by reversing prior admissions of the past or carefully choosing words that are just a little too subtle, raising doubt in the sincerity of such attempts (Evans 2015). For example, notwithstanding Japanese Chief Cabinet Secretary Yohei Kono's 1993 statement that acknowledged the Imperial Japanese Army was involved in the establishment of comfort women stations (Ministry of Foreign Affairs of Japan 1993; Tatsumi 2018), in 2012 a conservative Japanese civil society group paid for an advertisement denying comfort women were sex slaves in a daily newspaper in New Jersey. The advertisement emphasizes that many of the women were not sex slaves but worked under a system of licensed prostitution and earned incomes exceeding what was paid to field officers and even generals (Evans 2015). According to some progressive sources, the publication took place six months after Palisades Park in New Jersey turned down Japanese officials' offer of one hundred cherry blossom trees in exchange for removing a small plaque memorializing comfort women.[6]

Some of the people behind the advertisement also referred to the Nanjing Massacre as the "Nanking Hoax," denying the incident ever took place. The massacre is another major issue of tension regarding the historical guilt between China and Japan. Disagreement over the scale of civilian killings by Japanese forces has caused heated debate between the countries. Chinese sources contend that up to 300,000 civilians, many of them women and children, were sacrificed when Nanjing city was occupied by Imperial Japanese forces in 1937 (Evans 2015). In 2014, Chinese President Xi Jinping presided over China's first state commemoration of the massacre (Evans 2015). Commentators have noted that for descendants of Asians who suffered in wars started by Imperial Japan, the period "was their holocaust" (Choe and Gladstone 2018).

Finally, Chinese and Koreans also take issue with the wording of apologies issued by Japanese leaders. When Japanese Prime Minster Shinzo Abe expressed "deep remorse over the past war," skeptics from China and South Korea argued that the word remorse does not imply apology, casting doubt on the sincerity of statement (Evans 2015).

I suggest that NIA offers an easier way for Chinese, Japanese, and South Korean political leaders to pursue cooperative foreign policy toward each other where there is perceived benefit, rather than succumbing to popular domestic sentiment. Regarding guilt admission, ultimately China and South Korea will have to decide exactly which actions it will accept from Japan as expressions of remorse that will enable the countries to move their relations forward. On the other side, Japan will need the courage to meet those requirements sufficiently (Glosserman and Snyder 2015). I argue that NIA can help with both of these. If NIA enlarges the win-set for both sides, by boosting, even if just slightly, current Japanese willingness to admit past guilt, and by lowering Chinese and Korean thresholds of what will be accepted as "sufficient remorse" and increasing willingness to cooperate with Japan, the countries can enjoy more flexibility and leniency in international interaction and negotiations.

2.5 Images in Asia

The images between Japan and its immediate neighbors to the west are profoundly negative. In public opinion polls in 2013 and 2014, when asked about the impressions the Japanese and South Korean publics held of each other, the majority of both sides reported predominantly negative images. In both years, more than 70 percent of South Korean respondents stated they held unfavorable perceptions of Japanese. This image is largely mutual—the percentage of Japanese respondents who answered that they had an unfavorable image of South Koreans reached 54.4 percent in 2014 (Genron NPO and East Asia Institute 2014).

Meanwhile, according to a 2014 BBC World Service Poll, Japanese people held the most negative perception of China in the world, while Chinese people held the most negative perception of Japan in the world. Of the Japanese respondents, 73 percent negatively viewed China's influence, while only 3 percent expressed positive views. Unfortunately, this sentiment is echoed in China as well: 90 percent of Chinese people viewed Japanese influence negatively, while only 5 percent of Chinese people had a positive view of Japanese influence (BBC World Service Poll 2014).

Images that people of one country hold of other countries matter in international conflict or cooperation for at least three reasons. First, negative images of an adversary's motivations have been found to stimulate mass public decisions for military action (Herrmann, Tetlock, and Visser 1999). Second, when negative images persist, they can construct habitual behavior that repeats itself. These routines can lead to spirals of conflict (Jervis 1976). Third, images determine learning behavior. People draw different lessons from historical outcomes based on the images they hold of others (Tetlock and Lebow 2001). Failure to rethink and adjust preexisting beliefs to new information becomes a key reason for intelligence failures in international conflict (Jervis 2010).

Present negative images as well as future images can be analyzed and predicted using theoretical terminology. Insights from image theory help to describe how the three Northeast Asian states perceive of each other.[7] Image theorists define five types of images resulting from perceived international relations: *ally*, *enemy*, *imperialist*, *colony*, and *barbarian* (Herrmann and Fischerkeller 1995). The theory specifies the conditions under which each image is expected to appear, as well as behavioral orientations in foreign policy we can expect from them (Alexander, Brewer, and Livingston 2005).

During the period of war and colonization, it can be argued that China and Korea held an imperialist image of Japan, while Japan perceived an opportunity to dominate and exploit Korea and China, thus viewing the countries in a colony image. Recently, however, with the rapid rise in Chinese power, China can be perceived as a major upcoming threat to Japan. If Japan sees China as being superior in power but inferior in relative cultural status (due to not being a democratic state, for example) and having incompatible goals with Japan, this would result in a barbarian image.

People with positive or negative images of their neighbor states will have different constructions of reality, and therefore different beliefs in the need for certain policies. An enemy image both generates and justifies a motivation for conflict. Therefore to avoid tension in Asia, strategies that can alleviate such motivations are necessary. As we will see, NIA can increase the positivity in images between states.

Japanese Images of China and Korea

Considering Japanese expansion into China between 1894 and 1945 and the power and status differences between Japan and China during that period, it can be inferred that the Japanese held a colony image of China. Japan perceived opportunity for exploitation from the country's relatively inferior power and status. Incidents such as the Sino-Japanese War, Japan's colonization of Manchuria, and the Nanjing Massacre corroborate this. Gruenfeld et al. (2008) find that when there is a large asymmetry in power, the more powerful are likely to engage in objectification. Indeed, men who served in the Japanese military at the time have testified to being trained and brainwashed to perceive Chinese as "less than human" (Castano and Giner-Sorolla 2006).

Considering that China was stronger in power for many centuries, even up to just before the Japanese modernization, we can imagine that the socialization and education of Japanese people to dehumanize or infrahumanize the Chinese (that is, to make them appear as "lower" forms of humanity) could have justified an image of the country as one between enemy and colony. This combination of images comes with behavioral consequences of attack and exploitation (Herrmann and Fischerkeller 1995).

For many decades before the First and Second World Wars, China reigned as the superpower of Northeast Asian civilization (Gernet 1996). However, in the late nineteenth century, both China and Korea were late in importing Western military technologies compared to Japan. Japan opened its borders to Western civilization and influence much earlier, modernizing quickly with the Meiji Restoration (Gordon 2003). With rapid acceptance of Western civilization during this time, many Japanese came to consider China as culturally backwards (by Western perspectives and by standards of industrialization). This was while China was rapidly deteriorating in relative power as well. The idea of "escaping Asia" or Datsu-A Ron[8] reflects this Japanese view of its neighbors.

Datsu-A Ron is a national political theory of Japan that was organized and promoted by Meiji political thinker Yukichi Fukuzawa, which has been quoted as an example of Japanese militarism in the Meiji period (Korhonen 2013). Datsu-A Ron reveals a Japanese aspiration to accommodate the "wind of Westernization" and "taste the fruit of civilization." Kwok (2009) interprets the aims of Datsu-A Ron as the following: "to display to the West and Japan itself that Japan was different and better than other 'weak links' (in Fukuzawa's and Western terms) in Asia. Then, with this aim successfully achieved, Japan would be able to proclaim its right to *assist* (*enjo* in Japanese) the vitalization of a newer and stronger Asia."

The goal of Datsu-A Ron is to emulate the advanced Western powers rather than China and Korea, two countries that are described as "not different from the case of the righteous man living in a neighborhood of a town known for foolishness, lawlessness, atrocity, and heartlessness. His action is so rare that it is always buried under the ugliness of his neighbors' activities." Further, Datsu-A Ron emphasizes that "We do not have time to wait for the enlightenment of our neighbors [. . .]. It is better for us to leave the ranks of Asian nations and cast our lot with civilized nations of the West." This view of China and Korea reflects a colony image, one where the target countries are seen as culturally backwards and unenlightened. With Western imperialist powers as role model, Japan joined the bandwagon of colonizing weaker states and utilizing them as a platform for further advancement of military might (Kwok 2009).

Even after the popularity of Datsu-A Ron or the "escaping Asia" discourse declined, a perception of Chinese cultural backwardness remained in Japan. Cho and Park (2011) note that even until the late 1980s, there existed in Japan the "ideal of reentering Asia [. . .] [as a] cultural bridge between a backward, authoritarian China and the West's human rights agenda."

Japan's image of Korea was likely also a colony image in the past, where Japan perceived opportunity for exploitation from Korea's inferior power and status. The late 1800s was a period when Western imperial powers expanded their reach into Northeast Asia. In 1875, just four years after the first U.S. expedition to Korea (also known as the Korean Expedition[9]), Japanese warship *Un'yō* landed in the vicinity of an island in Korea. The military clash that followed led to the signing of the Japan-Korea Treaty of 1876, which opened the Korean Peninsula to Japanese and foreign trade.

The colony image is both a cause and consequence of a group perceiving the other as nonthreatening (thus low in power and status) but offering an opportunity to expand. If Japan viewed China and Korea in the late nineteenth century and earlier half of the twentieth century in this image, it would create or justify a motivation to exploit or dominate these countries for self-interest.

China's Rise

In the past, China may have been seen in a colony image to Japan, while Japan was viewed as imperialist from China's perspective. However, with China's rapid growth in power, there is a possibility the image of China from Japan's perspective could shift from a colony to an enemy or barbarian image. This has grave implications for regional security.

There are several indicators that while Japan held a colony image of China, China held an imperialist image of Japan. When Japan opened its ports to trade following pressure from the Western world,[10] Shimazu Nariakira, who was a Japanese feudal lord (*daimyō*) of the Edo period, concluded that "if we take the initiative, we can dominate; if we do not, we will be dominated." Witnessing this, Chinese general Hongzhang Li declared Japan a principal security threat (Kissinger 2011).

More recently in the twenty-first century, however, we saw a reversal in overall economic power of the two states. China took Japan's place as the second-largest economy in the world in the final months of 2010 (Barboza 2010). Furthermore, China has been anxious to expand militarily and signal that growth to the world (Ross 2009; Suzuki 2008). According to image theory, with China's massive power expansion, an enemy or barbarian image can ensue from Japan's perspective. Chapter 3 provides more theoretical detail of this and then continues to propose that NIA can help prevent past Japanese perceptions of China in a colony image from transforming into an enemy or barbarian image and can move them into an ally image instead.

Chinese and Koreans' Images of Japan

South Korea holds a long-standing negative image of Japan. In modern Asian history, particularly from the late nineteenth to early twentieth century and during World War II, Japan grew exponentially in military capabilities, winning wars against and colonizing Korea and parts of China (Jansen 2002). During this period when the perceived threat from Japan was extreme and China and Korea were relatively weaker in power, the psychological perception China and Korea held of Japan can be classified as an imperialist image.

After the end of World War II, however, Japan's military power was limited by the no-war clause, or Article 9 in Japan's peace constitution (Ienaga 1993). Due to this restriction, the power of China and South Korea each rose relative to Japan. This implies a shift in how Chinese and South Koreans perceive their countries' relative power in comparison with Japan. Specifically, the countries' images of Japan moved from the imperialist image closer to the enemy image. Images identified in image theory are ideal types and can be thought of as extremes on a continuum or spectrum of images (Herrmann and Fischerkeller 1995). The image one country's public holds of another can be anywhere in between the ideal types, or it can be a combination of two or more images.

In particular, the enemy image is defined as cases of conflict in which the adversaries are roughly comparable in power/capability and have somewhat comparable status, and in which leaders perceive great threat from the other state. Even with restrictions to expansion of Japanese military might written in the country's constitution, many Chinese and South Koreans still perceive of Japan as having sinister intentions. Statements from conservative Japanese leaders, right-wing interest groups, and civil society that deny Japanese guilt or glorify Japan's wartime past are frequently taken in China and South Korea as signals that aggressive Japanese motives have never changed (Ye 2013).

What are the consequences of a possible shift to an enemy image? An enemy image justifies a scenario of war, due to a perception of the other's motivation as being unchangeably "evil and unlimited" (Herrmann and Fischerkeller 1996). When asked about the prospects of a full-scale military conflict in Northeast Asia, interdependence theorists in international relations would have a difficult time rationalizing the possibility of war between China and Japan, considering the scale of economic interdependence between them (Keohane and Nye 1977; Copeland 1996; Oneal and Russet 1997). Similarly, neofunctionalists of integration theory argue that state cooperation in functional or economic areas will automatically activate a "spill-over" to political cooperation (Haas 1958; Rosamond 2000).

However, public opinion polls point to the contrary. The negative images in Asia threaten regional security. Results from a recent public opinion poll that may appear surprising to neofunctionalists show how Chinese and Japanese perceive of the future of relations between the two countries. About 30 percent of Japanese and *more than half* of Chinese respondents mentioned that they think there will be future military conflict with the other country (Genron NPO and China Daily 2014), and 80 percent of Japanese fear military clash around the Diaoyu/Senkaku Islands (Johnson 2016).

South Koreans' Images of Surrounding Countries

South Koreans responded in a public opinion poll (figure 2) that they feel more threatened by their neighbor states geographically closest to them in East Asia than they do by the United States. In response to two-step questions that asked, "Do you believe that [the U.S./China/Japan] will pose a threat to South Korea?" and "If you agree with the above, in which category would these countries pose the greatest threat?," more than 50 percent of the South Korean respondents answered that China and Japan will pose a threat to South Korea. Of those who reported that they perceived potential threats from the countries, the largest proportion of respondents thought that a security threat would come from Japan. This is astonishing considering Japan, a country without military power, was still perceived as such a strong security threat to South Koreans. This points to the power of sticky images and also the severe degree of perceived untrustworthiness South Koreans still hold of Japan.

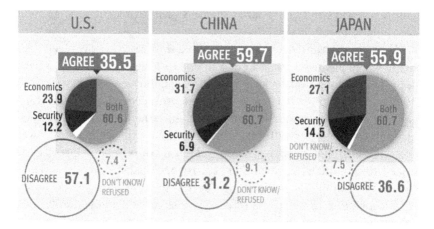

Figure 2. South Koreans' assessment of threats from surrounding countries and categories of those threats. The Asan Poll 2013.

In addition, when asked whether South Koreans think relations between their country and other influential countries—the United States, China, and Japan—have improved or worsened, as well as whether those relations will improve in the future, South Korean respondents gave disproportionately negative answers about relations with Japan. These reports are illustrated in figure 3. More than 80 percent of the survey participants stated that South Korea's relations with Japan had worsened, and more than 60 percent expected them to further worsen in the future.

In sum, while South Koreans felt a considerable degree of threat from both China and Japan, they perceived of Japan in a far more negative light and held very little hope for improvement of relations in the future. Only about 22 percent of the respondents predicted that relations with Japan would improve, which is in stark contrast to the 75 percent optimistic view for prospects with the United States, and 66 percent hopeful for better relations with China.

2.6 Conclusion

This chapter laid out an introduction to the problem motivating this book's study. As discussed, the book's specific scope of study are areas—China, Japan, and South Korea—that continue to suffer from the history problem. We learned what the history problem is and why it is perpetuated in certain areas that suffer from its effects. The chapter also outlined our

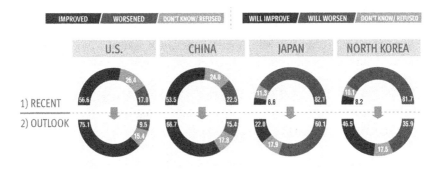

Figure 3. Assessment and prospect of South Korea's relationship with surrounding countries. The Asan Poll 2013 (%).

region of interest, as a case wherein history continues to poison international relations today, and asks what can help us escape this predicament. I surveyed how each of the variables of distrust, guilt, and images have been prominent in the three Asian states' failure to reconcile. This chapter focused on the unstable state of international relations today, emphasizing the dependent variables of the study.

Many people celebrate the advent of an "Asian century." However, in this region, promise of the future appears subject to limits imposed by the history problem. Paradoxically, in Northeast Asia the conventional wisdom on injury reparation that time can heal wounds, or at least let us forget pain, has not been substantiated (He 2006). The enduring historical distrust and negativity that dominate relations between the countries are puzzling, even to experts who know of their unpleasant past. In particular, with new security threats impending in the shifting frameworks of the world and regional orders today, why are the countries unable to get out of age-old perpetuating cycles of distrust and animosity? Why do the countries, all of which have enjoyed extraordinary success in the postwar era, repeatedly dwell on distant and ugly history instead, producing self-defeating outcomes and abandoning opportunities for strategic cooperation (Glosserman and Snyder 2015)?

Building on the painful issues of history in Northeast Asia explained in this chapter, this book argues that a psychological shift that nudges public perception from hostility and competition to reconciliation and cooperation is crucial in Asia. Especially today, at least three shifting dynamics unraveling in Asia make it critical for Northeast Asian states to view each other in an ally image, or a partner for cooperation. These are: first, North

Korean nuclear provocations; second, rivalry between Japan and a rapidly rising China that destabilizes regional security; and third, America and China's hedging strategies against each other on a systemic level. At these complex, intricate, and delicate crossroads, distrust and negative imagery within publics sustains tension and bitterness between neighbors, thereby threatening regional security. Cooperation between countries with a difficult history problem presents a huge challenge, but the benefits of cooperation outweigh the costs of competition.

The next chapter provides a discussion of predictor variables. We begin with a review of the different kinds of remedies put forward in previous research as ways to overcome history of conflict. In particular, numerous existing studies argue for "commonality" across parties, most often in the form of an overarching, superordinate identity that erases existing subidentities. From there we move to a remedy of national identity affirmation in an international context, which takes an alternative approach. NIA provides a way of bringing states closer to reconciliation by putting existing national identities front and center, rather than downplaying them.

THREE

Theories of Identity Affirmation
Trust, Guilt, and Images

In this chapter I describe my theories that NIA can enhance trust, guilt recognition, and positive images between countries. The chapter consists of five main sections. Having examined the state of distrust, disagreement over the degree of necessary guilt recognition, and negative images in Asia in the previous chapter, we start by focusing on the *predictors* that can improve this unfortunate state of affairs (section 3.1). Here I provide an interdisciplinary review of previous research that advocates a "commonness" that downplays existing subidentities as a solution, along with some unsuccessful historical cases of attempts at reconciliation based on Asian commonality. Through a discussion of these previous accounts, we will see why NIA is a more viable way of overcoming the past.

This leads to an introduction of theories of identity affirmation. To better understand how NIA works, I describe the theory and explain the leap from self to group-affirmation (3.2). I then illustrate the mechanisms through which affirmation of one's national identity can lead to its *outcomes* of trust, guilt recognition, and positive images vis-à-vis another country. We start with trust (3.3), introducing its importance in producing desirable outcomes proposed by various international relations theories: 1) the achievement of mutual gain through institutional cooperation, and 2) alleviation of the security dilemma. Two types of trust are required in each of these outcomes: strategic trust and moralistic trust, respectively. Regions that suffer from a traumatic "history problem" are deficient in these two types of trust. This section ends with a diagram of my proposed theory and hypothesis on how to increase trust, which are tested in chapter 4.

The fourth section moves to a discussion of guilt and includes a review of the existing literature on guilt in postconflict justice and reconciliation (3.4). One of the primary reasons state dyads with a tumultuous history find it difficult to get along is because of disparate views on how to deal with reparation and repentance. The book proposes NIA as an alternative for states to narrow these disagreements. Namely, through reduced motivation to defensively protect the in-group, identity affirmation can decrease past inflictors' proself attitudes and increase prosocial tendencies. This concern for others, in turn, increases guilt recognition for personal and in-group members' deeds that harmed an out-group's well-being. While NIA boosts a willingness to provide compensation on the past inflictor state's side in this way, NIA can also increase the past receiver state's willingness to cooperate with the past inflictor. Here I present another diagram of the hypothesized effects of NIA for the inflictors and receivers. The reparative issues introduced here are empirically analyzed using experimental data in chapters 5 and 8.

The fifth section of this chapter discusses the theory behind the last of the three dependent variables: perception (3.5). Image theory in international relations describes how perception between countries form stereotypes that both initiate and justify particular behavior. This is the theoretical background for chapter 6, which finds that South Koreans who are affirmed of their national identity also hold positive perceptions regarding other countries Korea had the most eventful and dynamic relations with throughout history. The chapter presents the book's hypotheses, before beginning our empirical analyses in chapter 4. Historical examples are embedded throughout the chapter.

3.1 Road to Reconciliation

A lasting question in the literature as well as in policy debates on international conflict has regarded whether countries with a history of war and/or colonization are able to approach cooperation and reconciliation without having to weaken their national identities. As noticeable from the many problematic situations presented in the previous chapter, nationalism seems to be particularly intractable in Asia. Various researchers have prescribed weakening national identities as a path to peace. From this perspective, national identities are regarded a source of the harmful aspects of nationalism. These scholars equate chauvinistic phenomena to natural by-products of the boundaries of belonging that divide people into different categories. Since the dividing line of identity creates an "us" and an "other," this generates in-group and out-group differentiation. These identifications are considered what we need to abandon in order to reach sustainable peace.

Along these lines, much of previous research in political science and social psychology has proposed, as a way to peaceful relations, a promotion of universalism that downplays extant identities (Kinder and Kam 2009; Mansfield and Mutz 2009; Rousseau and Garcia-Retamero 2007; Sniderman, Hagendoorn, and Prior 2004). This could be based on a sense of "we-ness" in a common in-group (e.g., that would promote "Asian-ness") (Gaertner et al. 1993; Kupchan 2010); a neofunctionalist spillover (Haas 1958; Rosamond 2000); the homogenizing effects of globalization (Ohmae 1995); a common interpretation of history (He 2013; Lind 2008); integration that submerges previous group categories through individual contact (Allport 1954); an overarching identity founded on cosmopolitan values (Held 2003); strategies of assimilation (Barry 2002; Waldron 2002); or supranational regionalism (Neyer 2012; Schlenker 2013).

To the contrary, others emphasize the value of strong national identities, contending that confidence in national identification affirms a sense of worth and belonging, which inspires cooperative over selfish attitudes toward others (Ariely 2012; Collingwood, Lajevardi, and Oskooii 2018; Johnston et al. 2010; Nussbaum 2008; Soroka et al. 2017; Theiss-Morse 2009). Positive effects of national identification have been identified as increased political and intergroup trust (Berg and Hjerm 2010; Foddy et al. 2009; Platow et al. 2012; Robinson 2014), interethnic cooperation (Charnysh, Lucas, and Singh 2015; Miguel 2004), interpartisan affinity (Levendusky 2018), and support for minority-favoring policies (Transue 2007). Liberal nationalists argue that distinct nations and national identities ensure a sense of dignity conducive to international peace and cooperation (Glover 1997; Gustavsson and Miller 2019; Kymlicka 1995; Miller and Ali 2014; Mounk 2018; Tamir 1995; Walzer 2008). From this perspective, an overarching identity of "we-ness" that stresses unity, commonality, or cultural convergence is not necessary for cooperation with others.

I offer NIA as a way of reducing conflict and opening gateways for cooperation by *strengthening*, not weakening, existing national identities. Salient national identities can enhance international reconciliation through trust, guilt recognition, and positive perception. While this idea may at first seem unlikely, it is consistent with the intuition that people who have a secure and confident sense of identity are better able to deal with others in a calm, collected, and objective manner.

3.1.1 Whither National Identities? Remedies of Commonness

National identity affirmation is an easier and more realistic route to peace between states for three reasons. First, few of the prescriptions from previous studies mentioned have proved to be effective in Northeast Asia. Integration theorists claim that cooperation in technical, functional areas can automatically spill over into a larger, overarching peace (Haas 1958; Rosamond 2000). However, a political spillover has not happened in Asia. In fact, there is no guarantee that functional cooperation automatically brings political peace—if that were the case, East Asia, with its long-standing and large degree of interdependence, would have integrated into an Asian community long ago. To the contrary, interdependence can actually lead to uncertainty and conflict, especially when dependent entities feel vulnerable due to little trust or negative perception of the other's intentions (Waltz 1979; Barbieri 1996, 2002). Even in Europe, where integration theory originated, recent studies find that EU integration has pushed citizens to value their national identities more than a common European identity. The number of people who have primarily a European identity has grown smaller, while more citizens identify only with their nation and look to their national governments to protect them (Polyakova and Fligstein 2016).

Psychologists have argued that increased individual contact between members in groups that don't get along can break down stereotypes (Allport 1954). In Asia, individual contact is already dense, as millions of Chinese, Japanese, and South Koreans visit each other's countries for business trips, school, or tourism (Berger 2008)—yet these have not led to a dismantling of prior categorizations of identity, creation of an overarching ingroup, or, most importantly, an improvement in perceptions of each other that breaks down barriers.

The second reason has to do with the robustness of the nation. We live in an *age of nationalisms*. Even with accelerating and intensifying forces of globalization, closer regional integration in multinational entities like the EU or ASEAN, the proliferation of multinational corporations, transnational interest groups, and international organizations such as the UN, we have not seen a decline in the nation (Chung 2015b; Chung and Woo 2015). Hyperglobalists predicted from as early as the 1960s that the nation-state would become obsolete, but the validity of this claim is doubtful (Ohmae 1995). Ironically, nationalisms are strongest in East Asia, which is also one of the most globalized areas of the world (Chung 2015a). Therefore the idea of diminishing nation identities as a starting point for international peace is questionable.

Third, people *want* some sense of belonging (Brewer 2003). Because of this, integrating into a larger group while removing existing identities is costly in terms of time and feasibility—and it could backfire. National identities are often deeply ingrained and socialized. People do not simply join or abandon group identities when the identities have some association with culture, heritage, or common bloodline. Even within states, identification on the lines of ethnic, linguistic, or religious differences remain undiminished today, as witnessed in areas such as Iraq, China, and Russia. Any attempt at integration that feels forced, unnatural, or at a faster pace than people are ready for can create backlash, triggering a threat to ontological security (Mitzen 2006; ; Steele 2008). Therefore it is unlikely that a process that requires doing away with national identities can lead to positive outcomes of cooperation or integration with another country.

For these reasons, national identities are usually sticky and difficult to alter. There have been rare exceptions where a rapid change of national identities was witnessed. These, however, were in unusual circumstances where large structural transformations or external shocks in the preexisting social system occurred. For example, Reséndez (2005) explains how the unique combination of the Mexican-American War, various national projects in North America, and the "crucible of anticolonial movements, civil wars, intertribal alliances, utopian schemes, and harebrained land ventures" generated a period of exceptionally fluid identities in Texas and New Mexico. According to Reséndez (2005), these major transformations led Spanish-speaking frontier inhabitants, nomadic and sedentary Native American communities, and Anglo Americans to adopt new national or ethnic identification as Mexican, American, or Texan. While it is possible for national identities to change, they are most likely to do so in the context of major changes in social structure and state forms (Todd, Bottos, and Rougier 2013).

Large structural transformations are uncommon, however, and generally changes in national identity take a long time. For example, Barucco (2007) selects a period as long as the past century and a half to describe evolving patterns of Indian national identity. Bechhofer and McCrone (2009) describe national identities as something to which "we belong whether we like it or not, and most of us like [. . .]. Hardly any of us question it."

3.1.2 Unsuccessful Attempts at Asian Commonality

There have been unsuccessful historical cases in Northeast Asia where promotion of commonality was attempted. In each of these, when political clashes arose, people were quick to prioritize nationalistic ideas, and efforts to bring the countries together under some umbrella of commonality proved unrealistic. First, in the early 2000s, witnessing the heyday of integration in Europe in the 1990s, elites raised the possibility of discussions for regional integration in a supranational entity like the EU—in other words, a "Northeast Asian Community" (Bowles 2002; Chopparapu 2005; Hund 2003; Jones and Plummer 2004; Ravenhill 2001; Soesastro 2006; Yahuda 2006). Scholars argued that the potentially achievable benefits from this new community would widely range from security and economic gains to larger influence on an international level (Corning 2011; Dent and Huang 2002; Harvie, Kimura, and Lee 2005). However, when these ideas met public sentiment, they quickly lost momentum. With publics that did not seem to like each other enough to be part of a tighter community, proposals of regional integration lacked palpable and practical substance (Yoon 2008).

Second, congruent with ideas put forward by constructivists in international relations scholarship, there have also been collective efforts to achieve a common version of historical interpretation the countries could agree on. Between 2006 and 2009 the governments of China and Japan sponsored a Joint History Research Committee for this purpose (Goh 2011; Kitaoka 2010). However, these efforts were ultimately disrupted by the political sensitivity of dissemination of information between the countries, and the final results of the joint research were not issued in full form due to political interference.

Finally, countless endeavors that actualize the vision of contact theorists were attempted but without success in reducing historical grievances. Japan's Genron NPO, in partnership with *China Daily*, launched the Tokyo-Beijing Forum in 2005, providing a large annual platform for dialogue between politicians, business leaders, academics, and journalists. In 2006, members from two major universities in the two countries—the University of Tokyo and Peking University—gathered and voluntarily started a forum. Since its creation, this student association has held an annual exchange program of collaborative research and discussion. Following the recommendation of the New Japan-China Friendship Committee of the 21st Century, Prime Minister Abe invited approximately 4,000 Chinese youths to Japan every year through the Japan-East Asia

Student and Youth Exchange Network program. Despite these efforts, bilateral public opinions again plunged when politics resurfaced. Repetitively, the publics' sentiment of one another would freeze as a result of political squabbles, such as the deadlocks in the Senkaku/Diaoyu Islands in 2010 and 2012 and subsequent media coverage (Akio 2017). Historical evidence does not corroborate previous ideas of universalism as a remedy for international conflict.

3.2 National Identity Affirmation

3.2.1 Self-Affirmation

Individuals strive to protect a positive image of the self. When their image of self-worth is threatened, people respond in ways to restore it (Sherman and Cohen 2006). One way is through defensive biases that directly reduce the threat (Fein and Spencer 1997; Riek, Mania, and Gaertner 2006). Although self-integrity can be restored via this route, the rejection of threatening information can narrow the chances of learning.

The theory of self-affirmation (Steele 1988) suggests that by feeling positive about themselves in one domain, people can replenish their self-worth and accept incoming information with regards to another domain in an objective way, even if that information was something they would have otherwise acted toward in defensive ways. This is possible because the overall perception individuals have of themselves is maintained through various sources of the self. For example, an individual can have a concept of the self that consists of being a mother, Christian, vegetarian, and a polite and hardworking individual, all at the same time. People strive to keep a global sense of self-integrity as a combination of their worthiness in all of these domains, rather than necessarily maximizing their self-worth in every single domain (Sherman and Cohen 2006).

The multiplicity of the domains allows for flexibility in how people react to new information. People can respond to threats by affirming the self-worth using alternative resources that are unrelated to the threat at hand, as they realize that their self-worth does not rely on the immediate situation (Spencer, Fein, and Lomore 2001).

One often-cited case of the workings of self-affirmation concerns smokers (Gibbons, Eggleston, and Benthin 1997). When heavy smokers were shown a video that explains the negative effects of smoking to health, the majority of the smokers rejected the video as being unscientific or unreliable. Objective acceptance of the information would cause a threat to the positive self-image as a wise person who makes healthy and sensible decisions, thus prompting defensive responses (Nisbett and Ross 1980). However, when these smokers performed a simple self-affirmation task prior to watching the video, which normally asks people to think and write about an alternative source of self-worth (Crocker, Niiya, and Mischkowski 2008), they were able to accept information in the video in an unbiased way. In other words, affirming an alternative value opened the door to logical updating.

With rising popularity of identity affirmation in psychology, the dependent variables researchers study have grown diverse as well, as they pioneer different effects of affirmation. The first is trust. Affirmation has been found to increase trust across partisan lines in the context of negotiation (Cohen, Aronson, and Steele 2000). For example, affirmation cultivates trust across racial lines, and with lasting effects (Cohen and Garcia 2005). A study of seventh-grade minority students found that throughout a school year, self-affirmed minority students sustained a high level of trust in their teachers and school administrators and perceived fairness in their grades and treatment. By contrast, the nonaffirmed minority students typically displayed a decline in trust in their teachers and school administrators, judging their grades and treatment as less fair and more biased at the end of the year than they had at the beginning (Aronson, Fried, and Good 2002). In other words, self-affirmation made a significant difference throughout the year, which indicates it is not merely a priming effect.

Studies on self-affirmation have also scrutinized its effects on the dominant class. Adams, Tormala, and O'Brien (2006) discover that self-affirmation helps majority groups in society realize the oppression practiced and prejudice they held against minority groups. That is, self-affirmation leads those "inflicting" harm on others to acknowledge guilt and shame for their wrongdoings. Normally the idea that one may have been unfairly privileged or benefited from the oppression of other groups damages the self-integrity of one's egalitarianism. Building on this logic, Adams, Tormala, and O'Brien (2006) found that when European Americans were affirmed, they perceived significantly more racism against minorities in the United States. Affirmed European-American participants also agreed, to a far greater extent than their nonaffirmed peers, that European-Americans in general tend to understate the impact of racism in daily life. Thus the otherwise threatening idea that one's group may have been inflicting harm on another group was more acceptable among those who were buffered by self-affirmation. The "inflictors" came to acknowledge their guilt in an evenhanded way rather than defensively protecting their group's image.

Finally, research has extended to studying dependent variables with implications for political elites. Sivanathan et al. (2008) establish that self-affirmation can reduce the possibility of an irrational increase in an individual's level of commitment to an idea or action. For example, political leaders might feel a need to continually defend a certain policy even if it is proving counterproductive. This kind of process leads to an extremitization of politics. In an international context, this could be the reason for snowballing incidents of nationalism or antagonistic sentiment against another country. Sivanathan et al. (2008) thus conclude that self-affirmation can be used to de-escalate commitment in political leaders.

To summarize, the theory of self-affirmation offers one way people respond to threats to self-worth by building on the fact that the self is composed of several domains. By restoring some self-integrity through another source that makes an individual feel better about her/himself, (s)he is able to accept incoming information in a less defensive way, even if the information undermines prior beliefs.

3.2.2 Group-Affirmation

Recent studies in psychology have found that self-affirmation on a group level is also possible, working through the same proposed mechanism and having similar effects as self-affirmation (Sherman and Kim 2005). Existing research finds that affirming values central to a group can reduce group-serving judgments, just as affirming values central to the self can reduce self-serving judgments (Sherman and Cohen 2006). Scholars suggest there is a direct link between representations of one's self and one's group, implying that these are overlapping constructs (Smith and Henry 1996). People are therefore motivated to maintain not only their own integrity but also that of their group (Harvey and Oswald 2000; Cohen and Garcia 2005; Norton et al. 2003).

Much research in self-affirmation effects on a group level looks at how affirming *self*-identities on an individual level can reduce biases and defensiveness that stem from *group* identities (Sherman and Kim 2005). Self-affirmed individuals are reminded of other sources that uphold self-worthiness other than their group membership, thereby enabling objective judgment and releasing them from the need to make group-serving judgments. In this way, self-affirmation allows people to evaluate their groups independently of how they evaluate themselves (Sherman and Cohen 2006). These studies view social identity as just another source of the *self*-concept.

In contrast, I propose that affirmation of a social identity on a group level is possible, as there are aspects of social identity that are shared collectively by group members. Across fields, scholars have found that there are aspects of national identity that are commonly shared across its members, and common emotions felt on a group level is possible. Sociologists argue that national identity entails a set of common understandings and aspirations, sentiments and ideas, that bind the population (Smith 1993), allowing similarities to be assessed in a national identity on a general level (Hjerm 1998). Psychologists also find that a "group emotion" is real, as intergroup emotions are experienced by individuals when they identify with a social group (Mackie, Devos, and Smith 2000; Smith, Seger, and Mackie 2007). Since individuals can feel on a group (country) level, affirming a group (country) collectively on a value they share and uphold together is also plausible.

People could therefore restore integrity as country members by affirming alternative values that are important to their country, preparing a buffer against threatening information. Doing this, people are reminded that the integrity and importance of their national identity do not hinge on opposition against another country, and they can react in a more evenhanded manner toward other countries while retaining a sense of national attachment. Although perceived threat in group relations has been found to lead to prejudice, highlighting an alternative positive value of one's group identity can shift the focus away from perceived threat from the out-group as the primary motivator in dealing with them (Stephan and Stephan 2000).

Many South Koreans dislike having closer relations with Japan, as the idea runs contrary to popular perception and awareness that Koreans suffered from Japan's actions in the past, were treated unfairly without compensation, and should thus hate Japan. Therefore this feature of social identity involves a sense of deprivation and victimization; "hating Japan" functions as a uniting force. A researcher once attested that "in South Korea, labeling an opponent a 'Japanese collaborator' continues to be an effective way to win a political debate," and "working toward a compromise [with Japan] runs the risk of denunciation for failing to uphold national pride" (Reynolds and Lee 2019). Consequently, trusting and/or working in close cooperation with Japan poses a threat to that identity domain, and to protect themselves many South Koreans oppose closer relations. Information that depicts possible benefits from closer relations are met with defensive reactions that question or reject the information, leading to difficulty in learning from it.

But social identity, like self-identity, has several aspects. For instance, while many South Koreans would agree that a sentiment against Japan is commonly shared in the majority of its people, the social identity of "being South Korean" entails many elements such as Confucian family values, a high enthusiasm for education, or pride in achievements of rapid economic and political development. People could restore integrity as a country member by affirming values that are important to their national belongingness, which could happen via policy, media, education, leaders' rhetoric, or some significant national or international event that affirms national identity. I provide a historical case in Asia as an example, this time focusing on Japanese NIA in Sino-Japanese relations.

The Sino-Japanese Honeymoon Period

The 1970s and early 1980s are referred to as a rare "honeymoon" period in Sino-Japanese relations (He 2009). Analysts remark that during this time China and Japan were "more friends than foes" (Kraus, Radchenko, and Kanda 2014). This period can be seen as a case where elites used NIA as a strategy to garner public support for trust-building, changing the image of a longtime enemy toward an ally image. Public affirmation of national identity appeared as an effective policy-framing device. How were elites able to achieve the cordial atmosphere, especially in democratic states like Japan where leaders are sensitive to public support?

In the shifting world order of the 1970s, with profound transformation of U.S.-China-USSR trilateral relations leading to the détente and the Chinese-American Joint Communiqué, Japanese and Chinese leaders realized the benefits and necessity of amicable bilateral relations. Kakuei Tanaka, prime minister of Japan in 1972, pursued a policy of rapprochement with China, and in a reciprocating manner China's Deng Xiaoping traveled to Japan in 1978, soon after the signing of the Treaty of Peace and Friendship between the two countries. In 1984, Japanese Prime Minister Nakasone Yasuhiro visited China for a summit with Deng—a meeting that many experts describe as "representing the peak of the bilateral relationship not just in the postwar era, but in all of history" (Ijiri 1996; Reilly 2012; Soeya 1995).

The honeymoon period suggests that public support for thawing relations between even the "world's most nationalist" countries with the history problem is possible (Tang and Darr 2012). While the temporal proximity, fresh memory and wounds of wartime events would have likely posed even harsher public resistance compared to today, political leaders at the time were able to utilize NIA tactics to help convince their public. Experts point out that this period coincided with a period of revitalized Japanese national identity (Sasaki 2001). Japan was experiencing accelerated economic growth, which may have led to a greater national self-confidence. In mid-1973, Japan's admission into the world's "Group of Five" (later G7) epitomized a national identity and pride based on economic success (Lai 2013). This identity peaked soon after, as Japan gained economic superpower status (McCormack 2000), and the Japanese "developmental state" model grew popular as a model to emulate in developing states (Hook et al. 2003; Vogel 1979, 1986). This confident national identity also facilitated the development of cultural discourses wherein Japan's economic success was associated with pride in Japanese cultural uniqueness and its social system (Crawcour 1980).

NIA is not the same as economic and cultural strength, however; what matters more is public perception. Satisfaction in one's elevated status and affluent conditions encourages a mentality that can now afford to reach out to a previous adversary to mend relations and realize mutual benefit, which would have been more difficult in conditions where self-perception is low and mental resources for confidence are scarce. NIA makes use of this mentality. The basis of the newfound confidence and pride in Japanese national identity was inward-looking and did not entail comparison with or superiority over a contemporary out-group. Japanese were leaving the postwar shambles behind and shifting their national identity to incorporate new economic and political prowess. Alternative positive foundations of national identity were brought into light, replacing the wartime identity of militaristic might and hard power. The "other" to feel a sense of superiority over, if any, was the in-group's own past. In such a manner, national greatness was affirmed in ways free from zero-sum competition with neighbor states, opposite to what had been the case during wartime. Japanese elites used this newfound pride toward a willingness to reach out, resulting in the reduction of public animosity (Sasaki 2001).

In theory, most people would expect hardline policies to easily gain more popularity in the public at a time of heightened national pride. However, since the type of national identity that was emphasized and made salient featured inward-looking pride, the period of national greatness did not necessarily stir out-group hostility. Lai (2008) notes that national confidence and pride at the time "reaffirmed the essence of Japanese identity." Thus it can be inferred that the public felt little need to act defensively or use their rising strength to put adversary countries in lower positions, although it would have been an advantageous time to do so. Policy, media, education, and leaders' rhetoric played roles in directing widespread national pride into positive and beneficial affirmation effects toward others. Japanese Prime Minister Nakasone issued a friendly statement that close Sino-Japanese relations were "the basis for peace in the Asian region, and [. . .] a powerful pillar for world peace," portraying China in a clear ally image (Kraus, Radchenko, and Kanda 2014). As an indication of NIA's effects on guilt recognition, Japanese history textbooks from the 1970s markedly increased coverage of the wartime suffering of Asian peoples (He 2013). When domestic conservatives advocated stronger political and military roles commensurate with Japan's economic strength, antirevisionist forces in the public, media, and Diet stymied such agendas (Saeki 2001).

3.2.3 Expected Psychological Mechanism

In this section I examine the psychological micromechanisms of how NIA could increase trust, guilt recognition, and positive perception in both the "inflictors" and "receivers" of past atrocities and colonization. Mainly, the defensiveness that NIA releases concerns dissatisfaction and rage of having been treated unequally but without proportionate compensation afterwards in the receivers, and motivation to deny past shame and guilt in the inflictors.

Expanding the theory of self-affirmation from an individual to intergroup level opens up a subjective space of emotions between the groups. First, "receivers" feel victimized from being unfairly treated by the "inflictors" and not sufficiently compensated for their sufferings. This creates a facet of social identity reflecting a unified anti-inflictor sentiment, and "receivers" find it undesirable to work in close cooperation with "inflictors." When a branch of identity is threatened, individuals feel their self-worth is also threatened and react in defensive ways to protect it. Affirming the self using an unrelated resource allows for restoration of self-worth beforehand so that individuals do not feel as threatened. Doing so also mends the sense of deprivation. Similarly, affirming values distances group members from the immediate need to react defensively, allowing them to focus on more objective considerations of working closely with the other group. "Receivers" are thus more content because their internal sense of their group worth has been replenished beforehand, and with this increased assurance they believe their state is resilient to any immediate threatening information.

For example, since there are other facets that make up the social identity of "being Korean," affirming another group value rather than anti-Japanism can fill in the hollow space that is the sense of deprivation. In this way victim-states can correct for defensiveness, as well as objectively accept and learn from information indicating that trust and cooperation are beneficial.

NIA thus offers a way of elevating a sense of self without putting down the other. Those who feel they have been treated unfairly become more moderate in their need to express extreme forms of irrational hatred—including situations that harm the self, such as exaggerated feelings of the other as a security threat (aggravated security dilemma) or forgoing possible benefit from cooperation (undermined gain).

A similar mechanism goes for "inflictors" in history. On this side, acknowledging past actions creates moral dissonance; thus, when met with evidence of past deeds or when dealing with "receivers," the "inflictors" act to protect their self-worth. However, when one's feeling of group integrity is restored by affirmation, this "switches off" the need for defensiveness, allowing inflictors to face the past in an unbiased way.

By this mechanism, affirmation reduces reluctance to accept guilt or shame of the past on the inflictor's side. This in turn lessens motivations to glorify or deny the past (Sullivan et al. 2012). Research has shown that those who have imposed harm on others in the past come to recognize it in a more objective manner when they are self-affirmed (Adams, Tormala, and O'Brien 2006). The proposed effects of affirmation for both sides are summarized in figure 4.

To conclude, on the receiver's side, victims find it hard to trust past offenders if they feel they have not yet received proportionate compensation for past sufferings. This creates a sense of deprivation and unfairness of being on unequal status. Pressuring the inflictors for apology and compensation reflects the wish to correct this inequality. For the offenders, acknowledging some injustice by their group is difficult because it harms their moral well-being as a group, and they will tend to deny the past or exhibit group defensive behavior regarding their (or their ancestors') past deeds (Gunn and Wilson 2011).

If a sense of injury of the victim and a motivation of denial of the offender are the mindsets underlying enduring hostility, then we need to focus on what can work to resolve these feelings and motivations. I theorize that NIA can be a correction to such responses, working as a "first move" to gaining initial trust and positive perception. This initial step could de-demonize the offenders in the victims' eyes and allow the offend-

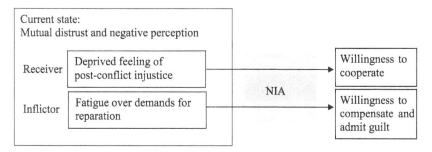

Figure 4. The proposed effects of NIA on postconflict reconciliation. Source: Eunbin Chung

ers to realize the damage of their past actions. After this first move that breeds positive out-group sentiment, interactions that follow would look more like a game that has an added social aspect to it—where both players make moves based on reciprocated compensation or judicious calculations of future gain.

3.3 How Distrust Undermines Gain and Intensifies Security Threats

3.3.1 Problem of Distrust 1: Undermined Mutual Gain

Publics who suffer from the history problem are often unable to realize the benefit from cooperation. Painful historical memories breed subjective enmity, which in turn causes countries to forgo opportunities that are objectively in their interests—or to undertake actions that are clearly self-detrimental (Cha 2003). This has negative consequences for regional institution building (Cho and Park 2011).

There is an increasing need for cooperation through institutions in Northeast Asia, as regional and global challenges become more significant. These include issues related to security, the economy, the environment, and other areas that states cannot manage alone (Harvie, Kimura, and Lee 2005; Yamamoto 2008). But any type of institution-building requires some initial trust (Rathbun 2011), and enduring suspicion from the past has been a key impediment. Kim and Schwartz (2010) assert that debates over historical events in Asia complicate "every negotiation table" and continue to shape or provoke political crises.

The rational gain from institutions has been widely noted across institutionalists, ranging from reduced transaction costs, enhanced compliance and transparency, and guarantee of credible promises (Koremenos, Lipson, and Snidal 2001). If Northeast Asian states are able to build a level of trust sufficient to create and jointly operate institutions, these institutions could benefit member states in many ways. First, by maintaining an ongoing dialogue, states would achieve a way of conveying state intentions and thus increase the transparency of their activities. In this way institutions in Asia could enhance mutual reassurance and build confidence. Second, institutions would provide fundamental principles and codes of conduct for conducting dialogue and cooperation in the region. This is a useful step for effective collective action in emerging issues that require multilateral attention (Lee 2008).

Yamamoto (2008) notes that Northeast Asia is the least institutionalized region in most topic areas. The area lacks an institutional framework for intergovernmental cooperation with no regional power playing a leading and responsible role in the cooperative process (Lee 2008). While loose regional economic ties in the form of intraregional trade and investment linkages are relatively common, these have been developed in the absence of a formal cooperative scheme (Nicolas 2014). Moreover, institution-based regional cooperation in the areas of security and the environment has been far less advanced.

Given the issues Northeast Asia faces, more institutions are needed to solve problems and maintain stability, and demand for institutionalization in this region has increased tremendously (Yamamoto 2008). There have been new, transnational threats to security such as bird flu and other health epidemics, pollution and yellow sandstorms from China, international terrorism, the proliferation of weapons of mass destruction, and trafficking in humans and drugs, as well as problems posed by environmental degradation and disasters. Nations increasingly understand that such threats can no longer be tackled by any one country (Timmerman 2008). The Asian Financial Crisis of 1997 provided an opportunity for state leaders to pay considerable attention to regional cooperation from the perspective of "institutionalized collaboration," not only in the economic sphere but also in the political and social arenas (Berger 2008). However, mistrust in the public arena from persisting deep-seated nationalist rivalries has been a principal obstacle. Fear that they may again become military rivals makes it difficult for these countries to talk to one another and to agree on the creation of binding international institutions.

Disagreements over historical issues have frequently disrupted mutual gains in diplomacy (Berger 2008). Unable to trust Japan, both South Korea and China have continuously issued numerous criticisms of Japan's failure to atone for its past. For this reason, dialogue often regresses to polem-

Theories of Identity Affirmation 55

ics and resolution becomes more difficult (Cha 2003). A case in point is South Korea's recall of its ambassador from Tokyo and halt to the process of opening South Korean markets to Japanese cultural products in 2001, when the revisionary content of Japanese history textbooks became an issue.[1] The government in Seoul at the time had been initially willing to chart a new course of diplomatic relations with Japan, holding a joint communiqué in 1998 to lift earlier bans on Japanese cultural products and to address more than forty issues ranging from security and the economy to the environment (Lee 2005; Rozman 2008). Due to unease in South Korean public opinion, however, all efforts stopped (Cho and Park 2011). Crises over textbooks and shrine visits have caused Japan's neighbors to recall ambassadors from Tokyo and cancel summits, even when the countries were negotiating about critical issues such as North Korea's nuclear program. For every failure in diplomacy or trade negotiations, distrust in the populace has been raised as a main cause (Cha 2003).[2]

The history problem has had substantial impact on Japan's efforts in institution building as well. Many Chinese and South Korean people are adamantly against the idea of Japan becoming a permanent member on the United Nations Security Council (Lind 2009). Kim Sam Hoon, the South Korean ambassador to the UN in 2005, argued that due to the distrust Japan's neighbor states hold, Japan could not assume the role of a world leader (Lind 2009). In addition, when the Democratic Party of Japan took power in 2009, it proclaimed a grand vision to improve relations with China. In a world moving from U.S. unipolarity to multipolarity, in the words of then prime minister Yukio Hatoyama, Japan would rediscover Asia as its "basic sphere of being" (Pilling 2012). In three years the government found the vision lying in shreds, replacing its ambassadors in Beijing and Seoul following public outrage from territorial disputes with China and South Korea.

In sum, historical animosity gives rise to an atmosphere of distrust in the public, and this harms the possibility of rational negotiations (Cha 2003). As a prime example, the public in Northeast Asian states suffer from a lack of trust that undermines mutual gain. Historical memories lie at the core of these problems, casting a shadow over every interaction that disrupts the building of, and cooperation through, institutions.

3.3.2 Problem of Distrust 2: Aggravation of the Security Dilemma

Uncertainty in intentions adds another layer of distrust, constituting a security dilemma. With the animosity created by memories of the past, relations between states easily deteriorate. The increased suspicion raises possibility for more aggressive policy and excessive hostility, which could lead to, in worst cases, a spiral of military competition (Jervis 1978). Had states been able to trust each other, they could have avoided this type of security dilemma, waste of energy and resources, and excessive tension.

Increasingly today, with China rapidly growing in power, Japanese leaders displaying nationalistic attitudes, and unpredictable action from North Korea, distrust could light a fire on the explosive tension. The riskiest situation could come from a security dilemma between a rising China and rearming Japan. Coupled with the insecurity distrust provides, this volatile situation could quickly lead to disaster.

Media reports note that "a nationalistic storm is building throughout the region," and "conflict [. . .] between China and Japan now looks possible" (Bandow 2013). Several experts note a growing assertiveness in Chinese foreign policy (Swaine 2010; Twining 2012). Goldstein (2013) contends that the threat of Chinese military action is real. Johnston (2013) argues that the mainstream description of Chinese foreign policy underrates the degree of China's military assertiveness, and Beijing's active movements to legitimize their arguments in contentious naval areas have contributed to escalated tension. In the spring 2014 Global Attitudes Survey, survey respondents from at least twelve countries expressed concern that territorial disputes with China and China's neighboring states could lead to a military conflict (Pew Research Center 2014).

On a systematic level, with a rapidly growing China as a challenger to the current world order, the instability of the shifting balance of power could create conflict (Gilpin 1981; Organski 1958). On a regional level, this type of conflict could occur if Chinese vow to make a comeback from what they remember to be "100 years of humiliation" under imperial Japanese influence, or if Japan aims to deter or defeat Chinese efforts to gain primacy in East Asia. As expected, Japanese are especially sensitive to Chinese actions that suggest China may be assuming a more hegemonic approach to the region.

The Global Attitudes Survey revealed that both Japan and South Korea are highly concerned that territorial disputes with China could lead to a military conflict. If mistrust fuels traditional scenarios of self-help and conflict (Bernstein and Munro 1998; Betts 1993; Bracken 1999; Buzan and Segal 1995; Friedberg 1993; Klare 1993; Roy 1994), the emboldening effects of Chinese economic prosperity could provoke a regional arms race (Cha 2003).

On a state level, experts highlight the decline of communism as a source of legitimacy for the Chinese government and predict a turn to other sources for domestic support—most possibly a nationalistic story (Hughes 2013; Pei 2010). The Chinese Communist Party may seek alternative bases for legitimacy as it strives to maintain its one-party rule in the face of pluralist pressures (Hughes 2013). In this case, the most likely "Other" China nationally posits itself against in Asia will be Japan. Some go as far as to say "nationalism/patriotism has now virtually replaced Marxism as the official ideology justifying the legitimacy of the party-state system, making history and collective memory even more important than ever [. . .]."[3] The Chinese government could mobilize anti-Japanese nationalist behavior to generate national unity. Pilling (2009) argues that Chinese leaders have strategically used the "history card" against Japan as an easy target to exploit, diverting public attention away from internal disunity.

A public opinion poll found that about 30 percent of Japanese and more than half of the Chinese respondents think there will be military confrontation with the other in the future. According to political scientist Etel Solingen (2007), Northeast Asian states have prioritized economic development and trade, which helped them escape an arms race. However, in the case that Chinese leadership turns around and takes a "statist-nationalist stand" (Solingen 2007)—which "feeds on nationalistic emotion against other states and prioritizes military buildup"—we could witness an arms race in an East Asian security dilemma, just as Solingen explains as the situation in the Middle East.

Another reason moralistic trust is urgently needed in East Asia now is because, as several experts argue, Japanese leaders have recently been more actively actualizing a desire to remilitarize (Denyer 2018; Heydarian 2018; Rajagopalan 2018; Rich 2017a, 2017b). Coupled with chronic distrust, such a move is bound to come with tension and unease. China and South Korea want to contain Japanese power and guard against a rearming Japan.

In Japan early warning signals are already noticeable, as Japanese leaders have been taking a stronger nationalistic stance. Suzuki (2015a) warns that Japan has been constructing a national identity with the Chinese "Other" as a focal point, depicting China as an overbearing state that unfairly browbeats Japan into making diplomatic concessions. Coincidentally, as the leadership in China faces a crisis of legitimacy, a similar sense of bankruptcy of competence in the governing elites is rising in Japan, making it all the more tempting to turn to nationalism to compensate (Hughes 2013). In addition, frustrated with restrictions on expanding military might, Japan has been repositioning itself as a "normal country" in the world (Suzuki 2008), reflecting dissatisfaction with defense policies that are considered "abnormal" for their country's size and power (Soeya,

Welch, and Tadokoro 2011). Tokyo's defense spending is on average only 1 percent of Japan's GDP, a number that has not changed since 2002 (The World Bank 2013). One of Prime Minister Shinzo Abe's top policy priorities since his reelection in December 2012 has been to "reclaim Japanese sovereignty" by amending the current pacifist constitution, which "fails to provide a necessary condition for an independent nation" (Kawasaki and Nahory 2013).

Such intentions seem noticeable in Japan's actions toward territorial disputes. One of the most dangerous and serious situations in terms of militarized conflict has been its disagreement with Beijing over the five Diaoyu/Senkaku Islands (Branigan 2012; Hughes 2013). Competition over the islands has sparked naval clashes, aerial chases, activist flotillas, and domestic protests. Abe declared that "there is no room for diplomatic negotiations over [the islands]," and that the solution necessitated, "if I may say at the risk of being misunderstood—*physical force*" (Bandow 2013). The issue was then further politicized by Tokyo's purchase of three of the islets in 2012.

Despite Japanese claims that the country just wants to reclaim the right to defend itself with its military, fundamental distrust leads many Chinese and South Koreans to fear a rebirth of Japan's past militarism—and to distrust it as a true partner (Lind 2012). The Chinese and South Korean public continuously criticize Japanese failure to atone for its past as the main obstacle to reconciliation, but nationalistic forces in Japan are tired of being blamed for the past. They believe China and South Korea are using the "history card" to secure further compensation from Japan (Reilly 2011).

Some recent prime ministers of Japan have made tributes to Yasukuni Shrine. Chinese and South Korean citizens have criticized this as paying homage to Japan's wartime aggressions, as some of the war dead enshrined there include those that could be considered war criminals from Chinese or South Korean perspectives (Park 2013). Abe appeared at first to respect such political sensitivities, avoiding visits to the shrine. This provoked a nationalist Japanese citizen to cut off and send his pinkie finger in protest to Abe's political party, the Liberal Democratic Party (Japan Times 2007). In addition, in the Koreatown of Shin-Okubo in Tokyo, rightist Japanese groups held anti-Korean protests against South Korean claims that Japan must apologize for its past (Hayashi 2013). These movements in the citizenry make it further difficult for state leaders to abandon nationalist policy. Such public sentiment has not just inflamed emotional tension but also worsened economic relations by drastically reducing the exchange of cultural goods (Torres 2013).

Finally, trust between Northeast Asian states is critical in addressing serious security flashpoints, such as the Korean Peninsula and the Taiwan Strait, and several territorial disputes between countries within the region (Gries 2005). While there has been no actual military conflict in the region after China and Korea gained independence (despite tensions over North Korea and Taiwan), beneath the surface nationalist rivalries simmer on.

3.3.3 The Importance of Trust in International Relations Theory

Across theoretical perspectives, social scientists have long noted the inability to trust others' motives as a central cause of states' failure to cooperate, as well as the tendency to resort to conflict (Copeland 2000; Jervis 1976; Keohane 1984; Kydd 2007; Larson 1997; Mearsheimer 1994; Waltz 1979; Wendt 1999). Low levels of trust add to chronic uncertainty in international relations, causing mainly two problems: 1) the hindrance of gain (Beugelsdijk, de Groot, and van Schaik 2004; Knack and Keefer 1997; Whiteley 2000; Zak and Knack 2001), and 2) the aggravation of security dilemmas (Glaser 1997; Herz 1950; Jervis 1978).

Distrust is itself corrosive, creating attitudes and behaviors that contribute to greater distrust (Lieberthal and Jisi 2012). States that are unable to overcome their mutual distrust will be locked in a security dilemma, where conflict can result (Kydd 2007). However, many scholars note the possibility of changes that can have macro-level effects on international relations over time. According to Wendt (1999), trust is the mechanism in the redefinition of self and other from adversary to partner to friend (Rathbun 2009). Once trust is generated, through a transformative process of interaction, trust can create a reinforcing spiral of cooperation (Wendt 1999).

One example constructivists use to epitomize how trust can over time create a deep change that affects the development of states is the idea of security communities (Alder and Barnett 1998). A security community is a region in which war has become unlikely or unthinkable (Deutsch 1957). Areas such as the European Union, as well as the American-Canadian and American-Mexican dyads have been noted as examples of security communities (Tusicisny 2007). The development of a widespread understanding that military means are out of the question is a high ideal of a peaceful world from a constructivist point of view, since actors will act in accordance with how they believe the world to be (Wendt 1999). I use the term security communities as a highly desirable outcome in international relations from a constructivist perspective that lies at the opposite extreme of a security dilemma.

Therefore, two main ways to overcome mistrust, put forward by liberal and constructivist theorists in international relations, are 1) institutions, and 2) a shared understanding that conflict is unthinkable, exemplified by the notion of a security community. The realization of these ideas has been particularly difficult in regions where negative memories of the past persist, as a certain level of trust is necessary to construct an institution or security community in the first place. Once institutions and security communities come to exist, each of them can have a mutually constitutive relationship with trust, and through repeated confidence-building interaction, even more trust could be generated.

Neoliberal institutionalists would hope that institutionalized cooperation can create mutually beneficial relationships through ties of trust that mute historical enmities (Cha 2003). In areas where the nightmares of the past persist, however, inability to trust each other limits the creation of institutions to begin with. Former Japanese Prime Minister Koizumi's 2001 visit to Yasukuni brought a halt in high-level meetings between Japan and China for as long as five years (Berger 2003). In these areas the idea of institutionalists draws a vicious cycle, where the prescription is to create institutions to overcome mistrust but mistrust becomes a hurdle to building and running institutions.

Rathbun (2011) maintains that trust does not follow the creation and operation of institutions but is rather a cause of these institutions. This argument fits areas suffering from history particularly well, as in these places lack of trust may prevent institutionalizing efforts that could provide win-win benefits. Even in a few functional areas where early institution building has been possible, political tension has repeatedly caused disruptions in their operation, disallowing eventual cultivation of the trust neoliberals expected would follow institutions.

A security community also becomes unlikely where states constantly suffer from perceived untrustworthiness and are more prone to assign hostile motives to each other's actions, which exacerbates uncertainty and fear in the international system. Receiver countries will tend to link current moves of the inflictor state to aggressive ambitions. Historical narratives populated in receiver states create a sense of victimization that fuels grievances and perpetuates severe distrust of the inflictor (He 2009). Meanwhile, past inflictor states might find the receiver country's distrust unjustified and view its unfriendly reactions as a disguise for that country's own hostile intentions.

In sum, Asia's history of expansionism and colonialism during World War II left behind a legacy of mutual suspicion that periodically roils relations between Japan and its neighbors. Distrust is shared in the publics and amplifies unnecessary tension. Japan is barely a serious security threat to either of its neighbors, considering that Japan does not officially have a national military force or incentive to militarily invade the countries anytime soon. Still, mistrust resulting from past experiences leads more than 90 percent of Chinese respondents in a contemporary survey to have a negative opinion of Japan and between 40 and 60 percent of South Koreans to typically identify Japan as South Korea's next security threat (Lind 2009). Associating Japan with militarism and colonial abuse, Chinese and South Koreans are constantly wary of the possibility of a militarily resurgent Japan.

3.3.4 Strategic Trust and Moralistic Trust

Strategic Trust

The lack of trust in international relations causes two main problems, which countries with vivid memories of conflict and colonialization are particularly prone to: 1) the hindrance of mutual gain from cooperation (Keohane 1984), and 2) the aggravation of security dilemmas (Rathbun 2007). The types of trust that are lacking in each of the two cases are related but different types. The kind of trust required in realizing mutual gain is strategic trust, while chronic suspicion that causes a constant security fear corresponds to a lack in moralistic trust.

Strategic trust is a calculative belief that other actors will exhibit cooperative behavior (Uslaner 2002) because they have a rational interest in building or maintaining a long-term, mutually beneficial relationship (Rathbun 2009). Keohane (1984) is referring to strategic trust when he notes that cooperation is based on a strategic calculation where each party changes his or her behavior contingent on changes in the other's behavior, improving the rewards of both parties.

Incentives for states to demonstrate trustworthy behavior in institutions, at large, are based on strategic trust. States engage in diplomacy because it provides incentives to both sides. Based on the information that actors will abide by a set of institutional rules because doing so is in their interest, actors trust each other to honor their commitments. As actors' images (Herrmann and Fischerkeller 1995) and reputations become involved, as more linkages are created, and as shadows of the future are lengthened, the level of strategic trust further increases (Rathbun 2007). Gradually, actors' interests come to encapsulate one another (Axelrod 1984; Keohane 1984; Oye 1985).

In a trust game[4] or prisoners' dilemma situation, players would mutually benefit through cooperation but are under the risk of ending up with the sucker payoff (Camerer 2003). In game theoretic terms, by tracking backwards from the final rewards parties would gain from cooperation, one could infer that the other party would cooperate as well. The belief that the other will take those steps for self-interested gain—even if it is unconnected to a moral intention or goodness in the other's character—is strategic trust. For example, you could strategically trust someone as reliable enough to engage in business interactions with, even if you assess that person to be unethical in character.

Findings in behavioral games show us that the Nash equilibrium alone does not explain recurrent experimental results and that psychological notions like trust are a necessary supplement (Camerer and Fehr 2004). Without trust, a mechanism of complete rationality would expect that the proposer in a trust game would not offer anything.[5] Strategic trust, however, would lead players to *break with* the trust game's Nash equilibrium. The trust that the receiver in the game will reciprocate cooperation, since that is more beneficial for the receiver than defecting, is strategic trust, and with this trust proposers will come to invest in the situation.

In iterated games, or at least when players are uncertain of how many rounds they will play, we may expect strategic cooperation as a more obvious choice. However, even when there are expectations for repeated interactions or long-term exchange—thus self-interested reason for players to exchange tokens—profound distrust can remove the expectation for the other's cooperation. This has frequently been the case in settings of institutional cooperation in international relations. Various cases in Northeast Asia, including bilateral and trilateral institutional agreements between China, Japan, and South Korea, were proposed but had a difficult time becoming realized.

Moralistic Trust

Moralistic trust is a subjective belief of the other's ethical character.[6] This is a "social conception of trust" in which people believe that the other will behave in trustworthy ways because that is her/his disposition, and not because of the situation (Booth and Wheeler 2007; Larson 1997; Tyler and Degoey 2004; Yamagishi and Yamagishi 1994).

What lies at the core of a security dilemma is a lack of moralistic trust. Due to uncertainty in the moral nature of the other, actors struggle from a constant security fear even when it is unwarranted. Especially in international relations where a tumultuous history exists, countries might readily assign evil intentions to another, exacerbating the security dilemma and heightening perceptions of threat.

The confident attribution of benign motives to other states springs from moralistic trust. Moralistic trust is deeper than strategic trust in that it does not rely on specific reciprocity and therefore provides a more durable foundation for cooperation, allowing actors to draw broader conclusions of others without the need to collect information in every new situation (Rathbun 2007).

Security communities epitomize moralistic trust. They are not intentionally formed but develop through a process of repeated interactions that engender social learning. Adler and Barnett (1998) define the trust needed here as "a social phenomenon [. . .] dependent on the assessment that another actor will behave in ways that are consistent with normative expectations." In other words, the trust involved in creating a security community is a moralistic judgment of the integrity of the other.

While strategic and moralistic trust are different, they are not mutually exclusive. Strategic trust can eventually breed moralistic trust (although moralistic trust is not only borne through strategic trust). Strategic trust is based on more immediate reciprocity than moralistic trust. Yet even security communities begin with shallower interactions in institutions. Governments do not explicitly seek to create a security community but attempt to coordinate their relations in order to enjoy the benefits of institutions, as mentioned by neoliberal institutionalists (Koremenos, Lipson, and Snidal 2001). Through time and repeated interaction in institutions, actors engage in a social learning process that enhances trust. This process occurs at both the masses and elite level (Adler and Barnett 1998). The trust eventually expands into a normative realm, where expectation of behavior evolves into "logic of appropriateness" (March and Olsen 2004), which is possible due to an expectation that other actors will act in certain ways because it is "appropriate" to do so, not out of self-interest (i.e., logic of consequences).

Similarly, international relations scholars specializing in rapprochement have noted the instrumental role of "first gestures" made through institutions that potentially have catalytic effects in the long run. Proponents of a reconciling strategy called Graduated and Reciprocated Initiative in Tension-Reduction (GRIT) argue that instrumental behaviors that rationally reveal mutually benign intentions can transform dyadic relationships from enmity to amity through reciprocal acts of accommodation (Osgood 1962). Starting with that grand gesture that becomes the first nudge of accommodation, both sides in the dyad progress through a dynamic of adjusting national images until they become compatible (Boulding 1978). Eventually, instrumental behaviors of pursuing mutual gain through strategic trust will lead to an adjustment of divergent geopolitical interests, building toward a security community based on moralistic trust. In this way, positive incentives can induce short-term desirable behavior and extend to stable long-term peace (Nincic 2011).

I employ the concept of security communities as an example of a desirable outcome in international relations, but there is a difference between previous observations of a security community and my proposed way of progressing toward one. Existing research advocates the creation of the security community through a common identity (Adler and Barnett 1998). In contrast, this book proposes that making existing identities salient can increase trust—both strategic and moralistic—and thus pave the way to reconciliation.

Figure 5 encapsulates the overall structure of this book's theoretical expectations on trust. In this study we look at the psychological microfoundations that can initiate trust, which can eventually lead to desirable outcomes in international relations. In this sense, we are examining what can initiate the change in the first step of the diagram, which can eventually lead to the second step.

Tests of NIA's effect on trust, the first dependent variable, are described in chapter 4. In the chapter, trust is measured in two ways: by direct, verbal indications of trust measured by responses to survey questions, and by a trust game. The former expression of trust is a measure of moralistic trust and the latter is a way to measure strategic trust. I hypothesize that individuals affirmed of their national identity report higher levels of both measures of trust. In contrast to the effects of NIA, I also suggest that emphasizing a sense of overarching commonness across Asia is not associated with trust between Chinese, Japanese, and South Koreans.

Hypothesis 1 = Individuals affirmed of their national identity trust the other country more than individuals that are not affirmed.

3.3.5 Long-Term Effects of the Two Measures of Trust

I hypothesize that NIA boosts two types of trust: moralistic and strategic. How are these related, and what does this mean for international politics in terms of policy implications, public opinion, and reconciliation?

Theoretically, strategic trust could be the initial catalyst that triggers a string of interaction that is mutually beneficial for both parties in bilateral

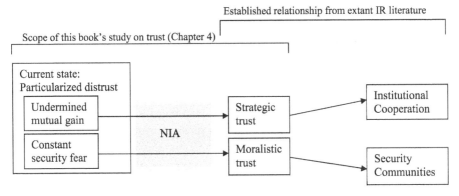

Figure 5. The proposed effects of NIA on trust. Source: Eunbin Chung

relations. Since strategic trust is based more on a cold calculation of self-interest, it could be easier to initiate than moralistic trust, which entails a normative appraisal of the character of the other. Once a certain level of strategic trust is established, it could be that iterated games of reciprocated cooperation smoothly follow (Boulding 1978; Osgood 1962). Naef and Schupp (2009) find that past trusting behavior is a good predictor of behavior in economics-style trust games. If this is true, then we have reason to be hopeful that once NIA assists in the establishment of the first, minimum necessary level of strategic trust, this could lead to a number of interactions that are productive for both sides.

The repetition of interactions involving strategic trust could, over time, develop into moralistic trust. Many existing studies have examined the relationship between trust experimentally measured in trust games and trust assessed through direct survey questions and found that the two are correlated (Fehr et al. 2003; Gächter, Herrmann, and Thöni 2004; Naef and Scupp 2009). Glaeser et al. (2000) and Gächter et al. (2004) also find that their experimental measures of trust are clearly correlated with survey questions on past trusting behavior and a question on trust in strangers.

I hypothesize that NIA is correlated with moralistic trust, measured through direct survey questions that entail no reward or loss for the survey respondent. Therefore while strategic trust can eventually lead to an increase in moralistic trust, moralistic trust can be boosted directly from NIA.

What would all of this look like if the hypothesized effects were to unfold between states over time? The stream of positive events NIA could generate can be summarized in figure 6. NIA can open the doors to the first initiation of strategic or moralistic trust. Since strategic trust is the basis for institution building, as was described in previous chapters, once the required amount of strategic trust is built, this could lead to institutions that states can more effectively cooperate through, in a more formal and technical environment. Once the infrastructure for institutions is up and running, repeated games that are mutually beneficial like the trust game could more easily and frequently take place. Institution states then come to enter more binding commitments, which allows for confidence building and a mitigation of uncertainty. Through these institutions, states that had previously been suffering from practices that undermine gain due to negative memories of history could increasingly become able to realize mutual gain from cooperation.

Strategic trust could also directly increase iterations of reciprocated cooperation that do not necessarily need to be through institutions. As these interactions are repeated, they could themselves contribute to the building of new institutions. As previously discussed, repeated positive interaction could over time build moralistic trust—the basis needed for security communities.

In sum, NIA can provide the first step in alleviating the two main problems regions with the history problem struggle from: "undermined gain," which inhibits the realization of mutual gain through institutions, and a "constant security fear," which makes the formation of a security community difficult. Once strategic and moralistic trust are initiated, this could gradually lead to a responsive and reflexive flow of reciprocal interaction (Osgood 1962).

3.4 The Challenge to Guilt Recognition

The second dependent variable I focus on after trust is guilt admission in postconflict reconciliation. I describe the two possible extremes for reparation policy in the aftermath of international conflict, and how Japan and its neighbor states have been unsuccessful in reconciliation because their desired policy points are on different locations between the extremes. I propose that NIA can offer a more viable way of bringing the inflictors' and receivers' approaches closer together via tendencies for prosocial attitudes.

3.4.1 NIA as a Catalyst for Reconciliation: The Inflictor's Side

There are two opposite extremes of how inflictor states can go about reparatory policy. On the inflictor's side there is complete denial, forgetting,

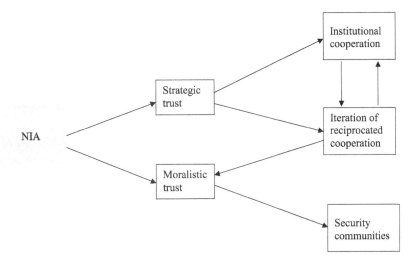

Figure 6. Effects of NIA in the long run. Source: Eunbin Chung

or even glorification of the past. For decades, Chinese and Koreans have criticized Japan's approach for being closer to this end. Japan has expressed contrition at times, such as the Kono Statement in 1993 and the Murayama Statement in 1995 (New York Times 2015). However, Japan's dominant action on several occasions since World War II has been one of denial. For example, current Prime Minister Abe has denied that "comfort women" were forced into brothels by Japan's Imperial soldiers, implying that they were willing prostitutes. Abe also selected cabinet members who have denied past wartime actions (Hayashi 2008).

For "inflictors," acknowledging that their group undertook inhumane deeds to others hurts the in-group's integrity as a fair and moral entity (Crocker and Luhtanen 1990; Tajfel and Turner 1979). These countries might be relatively less averse toward cooperating with receivers than vice-versa, but frustration of constant demands by receivers for repentance can cause disinclination for cooperation (Branscombe and Miron 2004; Peetz, Gunn, and Wilson 2010; Rotella and Richeson 2013; Sahdra and Ross 2007). For example, with regards to GSOMIA—the military cooperation agreement between Japan and South Korea that fell apart in 2012 due to fierce opposition from the latter country (Harlan 2012)—there was less reluctance in the Japanese public about signing a security agreement with South Korea per se, but news about the South Korean opposition added to fatigue in the Japanese public about Korean discontent and demands for reparation (Friedhoff and Kang 2013).

NIA may reduce such defensive reactions. Group-affirmation has been found to diminish inflictors' tendencies to deny guilt (Adams, Tormala, and O'Brien 2006; Čehajić-Clancy et al. 2011). When individuals reflect upon the core values of their group, they become more confident about their priorities and qualities. As a result, they are more receptive to unfavorable information; they do not act as defensively and become open to acknowledging guilt.

The larger perspective offered by the effects of affirmation allows people to exhibit more prosocial attitudes. With a calm and objective mindset, people can afford the mental space to have more concern for others. In this way, individuals in past inflictor countries become better able to embrace information about their country's history, and thus experience guilt. To override this guilt, they become receptive to reparation. Gunn and Wilson (2011) found that group-affirmed Canadians expressed more collective guilt and shame about their past action against Aboriginal children. Chapter 5 takes a close look at the relationship between NIA and guilt recognition on the Japanese side.

3.4.2 The Receiver's Side

On the receiver country's side, aversion against the inflictor is oftentimes prevalent in society to the extent that it is considered a part of the in-group identity. The strong negative image of the other creates an unwillingness for the receiver to work in closer cooperation with the inflictor, even if it means forgoing potential benefit. By decreasing defensiveness and allowing individuals to view the larger picture, NIA is expected to enable the public of receiver states to realize the benefit of cooperation.

Receiver states also find themselves in between the two opposite extremes of reparatory policy. Surprisingly, several scholarly accounts find that directly demanding explicit reparation is not always the most beneficial approach for the receiver country either. Experts who study post-conflict justice and reconciliation are divided by the critical question of whether to penalize those responsible for past human rights abuses or not (Sarkin 2001). First, those who advocate official trial of past inflictors contend that "ignoring history leads to collective amnesia, which is not only unhealthy for the body politic, but is essentially an illusion—an unresolved past that will inevitably return to haunt the citizens" (Čehajić and Brown 2010; Čehajić-Clancy et al. 2011; Cohen 2013; Gilbert 2001; Lederach 1997; Minow 1998; Sarkin 1999; Tutu 1999). From this perspective, past receivers' needs to heal cannot be disregarded.

Those who oppose trials point out that bringing past inflictors to justice will be at the expense of other ideals. They maintain that the goals of reconciliation—bringing groups together and building unity for peaceful coexistence, reconstructing the institutions necessary for stable political and economic systems—are in conflict with directly confronting the past (Orentlicher 1991). In particular, when institutional structures looking over both groups are still fragile, they will not have the capability to survive any destabilizing effects of politically charged trials, making the prosecutions ineffective (Mutua 1997). Experts with this view often argue that rather than some explicit form of prosecution, granting amnesty to former inflictors does more to consolidate a new, peaceful order.[7]

In Northeast Asia, granting complete amnesty to the inflictors is bound to stir harsh resistance from Chinese and South Koreans, and thus may not be a reasonable policy (Lazare 2004). For decades since the end of World War II, the unmistakably dominant (yet unsuccessful) approach by the Chinese and South Korean masses has been to pursue the policy advocated on the other extreme: pressuring Tokyo for sufficient atonement and reparation (Christensen 1999; Friedberg 1993; Kydd 1997; Lebow 2004; Onishi 2007). However, the feasibility and utility of such policy are doubtful.

An often-quoted example in comparison to the Japanese case is Germany's postwar approach to guilt and reconciliation. Experts agree that Germany and Japan are of central importance in Europe's and Asia's regional orders, respectively (Berger 2012; Katzenstein 2003, 2005). But those who emphasize the importance of sufficient remorse and reparation claim that European states were able to successfully reconcile because of Germany's clearly expressed remorse for World War II crimes (Dujarric 2013; He 2011; Kristof 1998). Specifically, Bonn's willingness to accept responsibility for the actions during the Nazi era, and the absence of denials among mainstream West Germans, reassured Germany's neighbor countries to the extent that a security community has developed in Western Europe (Lind 2008). Evidence from this viewpoint suggests that official contrition for past violence facilitates international reconciliation. It is this same logic through which Chinese and South Korean masses pressure Japan (He 2006; Scanlon 2005).

Scholars who take a different stance on reconciliation contend that pressuring Tokyo as the best way to initiate peace in Asia is debatable, for three reasons. First, an official policy of penitence is not necessary for reconciliation. A closer look at European history reveals that past enemies in the region were able to successfully mend relations *without* coming to terms with the past. For example, in the early years after the war, West

German education, commemoration, and public discourse ignored Nazi Germany's atrocities and instead mourned only German wartime sufferings (Hein and Selden 2000; Lind 2008). However, West German-French relations drastically changed during this time. By the early 1960s, *before* Bonn started expressing atonement, French already viewed the West Germans as a security partner (Lind 2008).

Second, it is not plausible to expect a public apology from Tokyo in the foreseeable future. For decades, Chinese and South Korean elites have unsuccessfully attempted to push Japan into official repentance and reparation. Governments have incentives to save face to their domestic audience, and an official apology entails costs to reputation (O'Neill 1999). In addition, considering the divergence between Japan and its neighbors' positions so far—with Tokyo arguing that expressions of remorse have already been offered, and Beijing's and Seoul's stance being that any expressions to date have been far from sufficient—it is difficult to imagine a policy of explicit contrition where all sides will agree and be satisfied enough to move on.

Finally, such a policy can backfire, further harming relations. Evidence from Europe and elsewhere suggests that governmental apologies tend to prompt conservatives to promote a competing narrative that glorifies, justifies, or denies the country's past.[8] These narratives in turn alarm the receiver countries, spawning distrust and negative images once again. The paradox of public apologies is they can make reconciliation further unlikely (Lind 2008).

A strategy that nudges inflictors and receivers closer toward each other between the extremes of reparation policy will be one that can widen inflictors' willingness to acknowledge a little more guilt than before, while at the same time open receivers' minds to cooperating. Directly pressuring an inflictor for a public apology will likely trigger that country to protectively guard its self-esteem, leading to more bitterness. For this reason, a policy of official contrition is not a panacea to rebuilding relations and might not even be in the receiver country's best interest. Figure 7 summarizes how NIA can theoretically allow both sides to meet in the middle.

Denials or glorification of past violence are indeed toxic for peaceful relations. But rather than seeking ways to receive an apology, NIA focuses on how psychological change within a group can improve relations with another group. Instead of pushing Tokyo for reparation as a first step, it is a more viable and effective strategy to find alternative routes that can break from the cognitive inertia that prevents reconciliation (Biletzki 2013). Prior beliefs often have greater weight and influence the acceptance of the

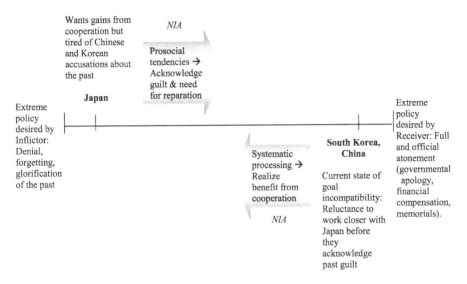

Figure 7. NIA can move inflictor and receiver sides closer together on reparatory attitudes. Source: Eunbin Chung.

information. Therefore information that is inconsistent with preexisting beliefs is likely to be disregarded as unreliable or unimportant. Because cognitive inertia can inhibit humans from learning in a prudent manner, animosity between countries with a history of conflict can be perpetuated even when facing information that promises potential benefits of cooperation. Affirmation shifts psychological focus to provide the mental space for coolheaded updating.

Chapters 7 and 8 focus on specific policy issues in the dynamic of inflictors and receivers in a postconflict situation and discuss the implications of NIA on reconciliation within these dynamics. I propose through empirical findings that NIA can bring states closer to reconciliation, as affirmation of national identities reduces group members' defensiveness.

Chapter 5 examines how NIA impacts guilt. I test the proposed mechanism of this relationship: whether NIA increases guilt recognition through an increased concern for others, which can be referred to as prosociality. I thus hypothesize that NIA works through an enhanced tendency for prosocial attitudes.

> Hypothesis 2 = Individuals affirmed of their national identity report higher levels of guilt toward other country members through inducement of prosociality.

How can NIA impact an in-group's image or perception of an out-group? In the next section, I discuss the importance of images in international relations and how affirmation can help move perceptions of other countries toward a positive, ally image. I then view the theory of NIA in more detail through a review of existing research and the proposed mechanisms of how it works.

3.5 Perception of Others in a Negative Image

Perceptions and images matter in international relations. Images can be defined as a subject's cognitive construction or mental representation of another actor in the political world (Herrmann and Fischerkeller 1995). Such images reflect the stereotypes people hold about people from other countries, and at the same time serve to justify certain attitudes and behavior toward another country (Alexander, Brewer, and Livingston 2005). Based on images, people evaluate whether the other country is a candidate for cooperation (ally) or competition (enemy).

Stereotypes cause people to act based on positive or negative images of the other, which may differ from consequences of systematic processing of information. I argue that NIA can induce more positive images, therefore removing these motivated stereotypes. The findings presented in chapter 6 confirm this by empirically examining the effect of NIA on positive images of other countries from the South Korean perspective.

Theoretically, identity affirmation works through two mechanisms to improve individuals' perceptions of out-groups in a more positive way. These are through a realization of the perceived opportunity of cooperating with the out-group (as opposed to a perceived threat from the out-group) and through an elevation of the in-group's status. First, affirmation enhances evenhanded processing, thus helping people realize the benefits of cooperating with the other country. This implies a shift from perception of the other country as a target for competition to one of cooperation. The increased positivity in the image of another country entails a perception that the two countries' goals are compatible (as is the case in institutional cooperation between countries) and not necessarily zero-sum (as would be in cases of a security threat). Second, NIA elevates perceived in-group status. As mentioned, identity affirmation offers a way to elevate a sense of self, or one's status, without necessarily putting down the other. NIA can thus help move imperialist images (in which observers would view the out-group as being superior in status) into an ally image (in which observers perceive their status to be equal with the out-group) by increasing perceptions of goal compatibility as well as perceived in-group status.

The following section provides a brief overview of why perceptions of other countries matter in international relations, and then discusses this in the context of Northeast Asia.

3.5.1 Why Do Perceptions Matter?

Increasingly from the 1950s, scholars have noted that international relations cannot be explained by material factors alone, and how actors psychologically perceive of others' images affects the outbreak of war and the conclusion of peace in various ways.[9] Indeed, the stakes are high when it comes to the images people hold in the international realm. First, images influence public decisions to go to war. Morgenthau (1973) emphasized that subjective judgments shape decisions regarding the use of force, and consequently incorrect perception of the other country's motivation is perilous, often leading to war. Jervis (1976) argued that how people perceive of their adversary's intentions can result in spiral or deterrence models of conflict. Herrmann, Tetlock, and Visser (1999) find empirical support that the image of an adversary influences mass public decisions for military action. The pictures people have of other countries become central building blocks in their identification of the threats and opportunities their country faces (Herrmann 2013).

Second, images construct routine behavior in world politics. Constructivists have long asserted the importance of habit in international relations (Hopf 2010). When images are hardened into habit, they become assumptions that are taken for granted. Habit produces basic parameters of what is seen as being in or contrary to a country's interest (Herrmann 2013). When negative images become habit, they can create and reproduce undesirable and dangerous patterns of state interaction such as enduring rivalries.

Finally, images influence learning behavior. People draw different lessons from historical outcomes based on the images they hold (Tetlock and Lebow 2001). In cases of intractable conflict or enduring rivalries, failure to rethink and adjust preexisting beliefs to incoming information is a major cause of intelligence failure (Jervis 2010).

In sum, the idea of images heightened the significance of perception in international relations (Jervis, 1976; Jervis and Snyder, 1991). During the Cold War the enemy image received a great deal of attention in scholarship, reflecting the significance of studying images in critical situations for international security and peace (Brofenbrenner 1961; Cottam 1977; Holsti 1967; Shimko 1991; Silverstein 1989; Stuart and Starr 1981; White 1965, 1968).

3.5.2 Image Theory

Image theorists define five types of images resulting from perceived international relations: ally, enemy, imperialist, colony, and barbarian (Herrmann and Fischerkeller 1995). The theory specifies the conditions under which each image is likely to appear, as well as behavioral orientations in foreign policy we can expect from them.

Images can be predicted based on three factors between the countries: goal compatibility, relative power, and relative status. The three dimensions are critical to stereotype formation between groups (Alexander, Brewer, and Herrmann 1999). Each dimension represents an assessment of the perceived relationship between one's country and another (in other words, is the other country higher or lower or equal in power and status relative to my country) (Alexander, Brewer, and Livingston 2005).

The first dimension, goal compatibility, refers to the perceived threat or opportunity one country believes another actor represents. This reflects what one views to be the intention of the other. The other country can either be seen as having motivations that threaten the realization of one's own country goals or be a candidate for mutual gain through cooperation. Neoliberal institutionalists in the field of international relations underline the significance of perception of the opportunity for mutual gain (Keohane 1984; Koremenos, Lipson, and Snidal 2001).

Second, relative status reflects how a country perceives of or values the other country or its culture. One source of international violence is the inclination of one country to see itself as more culturally advanced and the other as backward (Horowitz 1985).[10]

The final dimension of power differences refers to disparities in military, political, and economic resources (Alexander, Brewer, and Livingston 2005). Although realists often dismiss the importance of psychological perception in international relations, perceived relative power provides and constrains the options decision makers can seriously consider pursuing (Herrmann 2013). Power can be correlated with status of groups, although not necessarily. For example, it is possible for people of a country to perceive another country as lower in cultural status but with stronger military capabilities.

When countries' goals are seen as compatible, members of a country view the other country in a positive, ally image.

This image creates nonthreatening assessments and behavioral inclination to cooperate with the other country. Countries in the ally image are positively perceived, having cooperative and trustworthy attributes. Since image also serves the function of justifying cooperative treatment of the other country, an ally image, once it is established, can facilitate further cooperative behavior.

Other images are negative and stem from relations where the countries' goals are viewed as incompatible.

The *enemy* image is the flip side of the ally image, also arising when the perceived status and power of one's country are equal to the other's. However, the country in an enemy image is perceived as having threatening motivations. The relationship is characterized by intense competition, and the other country is considered a candidate for attack or containment. The enemy image depicts another country as having untrustworthy, hostile, manipulative, and opportunistic characteristics.

The remaining three images arise in situations characterized by unequal power and status. When the in-group perceives itself as superior and sophisticated in cultural status compared to the out-group but weaker than the out-group in power, the out-group is seen in a threatening *barbarian* image. This image describes the out-group as strong but culturally inferior, violent, ruthless, irrational, and destructive (Alexander, Brewer, and Livingston 2005).

When one group thinks it has higher status and power than another group, it perceives an opportunity to eliminate the goal incompatibility between groups by ways of exploitation or paternalism. Because exploitation is morally incorrect, the tension between this behavioral preference and the moral constraint against it is balanced by developing a representation of the other country as lazy, lacking discipline, naïve, incompetent, and vulnerable. This *colony* image justifies exploiting out-groups to help or protect them. Social and political psychologists have explained how such justifications occur as attempts to achieve psychological balance (Elster 1998; Festinger 1957; Heider 1946; Kuran 1998; Thies 2009). A colony image motivates observers to deny any guilt or need for reparation regarding past invasion and colonization, because the image provides a justification that the target country in some way deserved such "enlightenment."

A complement to the colony image is the *imperialist* image, generated when the in-group perceives itself as weaker in power and lower in status than a threatening out-group. Rather than directly attacking the out-group to deal with the goal incompatibility (not a viable option given the out-group's strength), the in-group responds with indirect resistance, sabotage, and acts of revolt or rebellion. Here the out-group is seen as arrogant, paternalistic, controlling, and exploitative, and the in-group may further believe that some of their members have sold out and allowed themselves to be used by the imperialists.

3.5.3 National Identity Affirmation and Images

In this section, I propose my theory of how NIA can influence the three determinants for images, as well as the implications for Northeast Asian states. I argue that NIA helps shift negative images toward a positive ally image. In particular, NIA provides 1) increased recognition of goal compatibility or mutual benefit from cooperation, and 2) an elevation of in-group status that does not necessitate putting down the relative status of the out-group. In other words, for groups that perceive their status to be lower than the out-group, NIA can help enhance perceptions of comparable cultural status.

First, among the three elements of images, NIA can increase awareness of goal compatibility, with the main sentiment toward the other moving from perceived threat to perceived opportunity in mutual gain from cooperation. How? Group-affirmation releases defensiveness in one's reaction toward an out-group and allows for objective processing of information (Sherman et al. 2007). In casual terms, affirmation takes people out of their angry little selves, or little holes they live in, and lets them realize the larger picture. The initial step toward investment necessary in cooperation is difficult, because one does not want to be left with the sucker's payoff. However, with the minimum necessary trust to take that first step, further solidified by iterated interaction, recurring rounds of cooperation that benefit both sides are possible (Axelrod and Hamilton 1981; Berg, Dickhaut, and McCabe 1995; Duffy, Xie, and Lee 2013; Grieco 1988). Therefore identity affirmation can bring about a transition from perceived threat of the other to the realization of perceived opportunity of cooperation. The resulting effect is a nudge toward perception of the other in a positive, *ally* image.

Second, relative status reflects how the other country (or culture of the country) is regarded or valued in the international context. Importantly, perceived group status is affected by a collective sense of self-esteem rooted in group membership (Alexander, Brewer, and Livingston 2005). It is this connection between how one views the status of one's own group relative to an out-group where group-affirmation comes in. In chapter 6, I study whether NIA among South Koreans affects their perception of three neighboring states—China, Japan, and Russia—and the United States, which together have the heaviest influence on South Korean politics and history. As will be seen, affirmed South Koreans, who have a heightened sense of self-esteem in their national identity, are more likely to view the neighboring powers in a positive image. Specifically, affirmed South Koreans responded that they perceive the other countries as candidates for cooperation rather than as competition or with hostility—an ally image. Through NIA, any perceived gaps between the perceived status of South Korea and the other four powers would narrow.

The third criterion determining images is power inequality. Power differences generally refer to military capabilities in the context of international relations. The reality of material differences may seem relatively difficult to challenge just with psychological change—a point frequently made by realists to underscore the limits of psychological approaches in international relations (Walt 1987; Waltz 1979). However, the perception of relative power is in fact central to realist theory (Kray et al. 2010; Lebow 1984; Morgenthau 1973). Power cannot be examined as a merely objective factor, and perceptions of security rest on estimates of relative power and assumptions about the motives of other countries (Herrmann 2013). In addition, political psychologists have noted that perceptions of material capabilities do not necessarily go proportionately hand in hand with measures of hard power. On the contrary, how people perceive of the other's material capabilities is very much a function of psychological perception (Heider 1946). For example, Fitzsimons and Shah (2008) find that once an out-group is evaluated as instrumentally valuable for the in-group, the out-group is observed in a more positive light.

Also recall that these images should be regarded as extreme points on a continuum of images, and any image in-between those or a combination of two or more is possible. Although power inequalities are more explicit between South Korea and great powers like the United States, China, and Russia (Japan's case is less clear due to its lack of a military force, but can be considered protected under a U.S.-provided security umbrella), NIA can still have the effect of pushing South Koreans' perception of neighboring states *further toward* the ally image.

TABLE 1. Hypothesized effect of NIA on image change

Perception	Goal Compatibility	Outgroup Image	Judgment of Out-group the Image Reveals	Foreign Policy Orientation
Positive	Mutual Gain	Ally	Equal Power Equal Status	Institutional Cooperation
Negative	Threat	Enemy	Equal Power Equal Status	Containment, Attack
		Imperialist	Superior Power Equal Status	Resistance, Rebellion
		Barbarian	Superior Power Inferior Status	Defensive Protection
	Opportunity to Exploit	Colony	Inferior Power Inferior Status	Intervention, Exploitation, or Paternalism

Table 1 summarizes image theory predictions of out-group images and their behavioral orientations, which in international relations would appear in a form of foreign policy. The empirical tests in chapter 6 study the proposed effect of NIA on perceptions as shown by the arrow in table 1, examining whether individuals affirmed of their national identity hold more positive perceptions of other countries, and view the other countries as candidates for cooperation (i.e., in an ally image) rather than competition, caution, or hostility. Based on these findings, we can expand our theoretical expectations to predict behavioral orientations.

Incorporating insight from image theory, we can expect the perceptions individuals hold of other countries to accompany and engender public support for associated policy. For example, the negative images can initiate a security dilemma or spiral model situation, where countries build military strength for self-protection purposes but find themselves in an increasingly threatening situation (Glaser 1997; Jervis 1976, 1978). Countries that hold enemy, imperialist, or barbarian images of another country will seek security by responding to the other state's military buildup with similar measures, ironically only increasing tension, straining political relations and fueling conflict, even when no side desired it. A colony image may also cause military conflict, motivating the country holding the image to take advantage of or exploit the other country through invasion or colonization. On the other hand, the realization of mutual gain between countries can transfer the images these countries hold of each other to the first row in table 1, leading to an ally image.

How Can NIA Change Images in Asia?

Chapter 6 uses observational data from South Korea to examine the relationship between NIA and perception of other countries. Although I have only tested this in South Korea, based on the findings and by expanding my theory behind it, we can assume affirmation can have positive effects on perceptions from other countries as well. In Northeast Asia, NIA may help relocate the imperialist image Chinese and South Koreans held of Japan in the past closer toward an ally image, and Japanese perception of South Korea and China from a colony image to an ally image. Moreover, with the rapid rise in China's power, there is a possibility China is perceived as a major upcoming threat to Japan. The psychological effect of NIA can attenuate this threat by helping Japan realize the opportunity of cooperating with China, moving China into an ally image.

Japanese Images of China and South Korea

Goal incompatibility can pose a threat through a number of images. China's power is on a rapid rise, and if the Japanese come to believe that China is equivalent in power and status as Japan and thus a candidate for competition, then threat appraisals may result and an enemy image will arise. If the Japanese think China has grown to match the power of Japan but is still lacking in areas of cultural sophistication such as a democratic system, treatment of human rights, intellectual property, or environmental issues, Japan can come to see China in a barbarian image. Thus if the Japanese perceive China to be incompatible in goals but high in power, either of the negative images can be generated, leading Japan toward competition or self-defense.

What inhibits the recognition that cooperation can be beneficial for both sides is psychological defensiveness that disables objective reasoning and systematic processing. Affirmation can thus help prevent past Japanese perceptions of China in a colony image from transforming into an enemy or barbarian image, and instead into an ally image.

NIA can also encourage a shift in Japan's image of South Korea from a past colony to a present ally. This shift engenders stronger motivation for cooperation. It can be inferred that the Japanese viewed Korea in a colony image in the past, perceiving opportunity from Korea's inferior power and status. Although South Korea's economic development since the end of World War II has weakened the image the Japanese held of Korea during the period of colonization, some phenomena witnessed today might be rooted in remnants of it.

Chinese and South Korean Images of Japan

Let's now examine what NIA can do for the three determinants of images of Japan from the Chinese and South Korean perspectives, or the past "receiver" states. First, as asserted, NIA can move adversarial actors into the realm of *goal compatibility*, where countries perceive opportunity for mutual benefit as a product of cooperation. Second, with regard to *relative status*, NIA raises one's in-group status by making one feel good about one's self as a group member without putting down the out-group (Sherman and Cohen 2006). Finally, since the military capabilities of Japan have undeniably waned in comparison to each of the other two countries since the end of World War II, it can be assumed that Chinese and South Korean perceptions of *relative power* have shifted with this dynamic. Therefore, even if China and South Korea previously held an imperialist image of Japan, with the combination of the three dimensions NIA can move this image closer into one of an ally.

Chapter 6 empirically examines whether people who are affirmed of their national identity held more positive perceptions of other countries. Specifically, I analyze South Korean perception toward Japan, China, Russia, and the United States—four important states that share dynamic and turbulent histories with Korea. I find that people who held robust national identities also perceived of other countries as potential allies to cooperate with.

> Hypothesis 3 = Individuals affirmed of their national identity exhibit more positive images of other countries.

In addition to my main hypotheses, I conduct additional tests of NIA in actual policy areas of contention between Asian states. This chapter described the reasons it is difficult for past inflictors and receivers of conflict to reconcile. Chapters 7 and 8 extend that discussion to apply NIA's effects on real policy issues that have important symbolic value in reconciliation between China, Japan, and South Korea. Chapter 7 first focuses on the receivers' side. The publics in receiver states find it difficult to accept cooperation with inflictor countries due to deprivation of what they judge to be adequate compensation, even when cooperation would benefit them. Focusing on the case of a military agreement (GSOMIA) between

South Korea and Japan, I hypothesize that South Koreans affirmed of their national identity are more open to the idea of signing the agreement with Japan, and this occurs through a boost in strategic trust.

> Hypothesis 4 = NIA nudges South Koreans most extremely against GSOMIA into a more moderate middle zone, leading them to become more supportive of it.[11]

Chapter 8 then moves to the "inflictor" side. Building on the findings of chapter 5, chapter 8 empirically examines Japanese citizens' willingness to personally initiate or participate in reparatory efforts. Inflictors typically find it less difficult to sign cooperative agreements with the past receivers; the main challenge instead is the demand for adequate reparation from receivers. I hypothesize that by releasing group members from a need to react defensively, NIA can lessen inflictors' tendencies to deny past guilt. In particular, Japanese fatigue regarding the issue of reparation concerns doubt about the sincerity of Chinese and South Korean claims for "adequate" compensation, to the extent that Japanese public opinion polls reveal a belief in a dispositional "anti-Japanese DNA" in Chinese and South Koreans that facilitates political use of the "history card" (Friedhoff and Kang 2013). This distrust in the ethical character of the other leads to tendencies to disregard Chinese and South Korean demands, often reproducing sour relations. I hypothesize that NIA boosts Japanese trust of the moralistic character of other parties, which leads to openness in endorsing compensation toward China and South Korea.

> Hypothesis 5 = Japanese affirmed of their national identity are more willing to endorse reparatory policy.[12]

3.6 Conclusion

We began this chapter with a discussion of NIA's prospects for reconciliation. I described why trust is important generally in international relations, and the two main problems distrust causes, which is the hindrance of mutual gain and aggravation of the security dilemma. The type of trust necessary in realizing gains from cooperation is strategic trust, while the trust needed to overcome the security dilemma is moralistic trust. The consequences especially hit hard for states with the history problem.

While I disagree that pressuring Japan into a government-level apology is the most feasible strategy, it should be noted that I am not arguing that actions of the past should be forgotten. Rather, NIA suggests a more feasible way to approach a reconciliatory outcome that can satisfy both inflictor and receiver with less resistance and friction. With this application of psychology, we can strike a balance between the extremes of the debate on postconflict justice. Rather than employing legally forceful and institutional measures to judge offenders and make them pay, NIA paves a way for offenders to realize within themselves any collective guilt and need for reparatory measures.

Identity affirmation has been known to take individuals out of their defensive selves and enable them to see the "bigger picture," leading to a dispassionate learning process. This allows group members to overcome defensive reactions that would otherwise aim to protect the in-group's image. In this light, NIA can increase inflictors' openness to acknowledging past guilt and therefore endorsing compensation, and can increase receivers' willingness to cooperate with the inflictor for mutual benefit.

Therefore what we need to promote is neither extremes of a blanket strategy of totally forgetting nor aggressive demands of atonement. NIA is an easier way of resolving the psychological and policy distances between how inflictors and receivers view the past. NIA is not just more efficient than using political resources to pressure Japan to apologize but also more effective in moving the psychological underpinnings of the inflictor and receiver toward agreement.

In the next five chapters, these theories of NIA are tested in different settings. In chapter 4 I examine NIA in several field experiments in China, Japan, and South Korea and find that NIA is correlated with increased levels of both moralistic trust and strategic trust in a country-to-country setting. Chapter 5 experimentally examines guilt recognition in the Japanese public. Building on my experimental findings, chapter 6 provides a boost of external validity through analysis of survey data that explicitly asks about the positive or negative perceptions people hold of other countries. This allows for a focused analysis into the power of NIA in changing the images people have in an international context. Chapters 7 and 8 show results of additional analysis from the experiments in which we find that NIA can affect real, unresolved policy issues between the countries.

FOUR

National Identity and Trust

Experiments in China, Japan, and South Korea

To test the theory that national identity affirmation increases trust between people in different countries, I conducted cross-national experiments. This chapter begins with a description of how moralistic and strategic trust can be interrelated and meaningful in international relations. I then explain my experimental design and results. The experiments manipulated national identity affirmation and measured levels of trust using techniques developed in behavioral economics and social psychology. Across my three countries of interest, individuals who were affirmed of their national identities reported more trust of people in the two other countries, a finding which held in both attitudinal and behavioral measures of trust. On the other hand, ideas that emphasize an overarching homogeneity or commonality across the countries were not associated with trust.

4.1 Method

I tested the following hypothesis on national identity affirmation and trust in the context of Northeast Asian states, in a lab-in-the-field experiment with a total of 1,118 undergraduate and graduate students recruited from three universities in South Korea, Japan, and China.

> Hypothesis 1 = Individuals affirmed of their national identity trust the other country more than individuals that are not affirmed.

To describe my experimental design, I begin by explaining how the experiment was conducted in South Korea as one example for the sake of simplicity. The same experiment was conducted in Japan, and a slightly shorter version of the same experiment was completed in China, with just the country and opponent country names changed as needed.

Over the course of two weeks at a university in Seoul, 484 students came to a computer lab to participate in a paid survey. The survey was advertised on a board of announcements listed on the homepage of the university website as an opportunity for students to complete a computer-based survey and receive a small cash reward for participation.[1] Although advertised as a plain survey on students' opinion on foreign affairs, the survey was in fact a survey-based experiment designed to test the effects of NIA on trust.

Roughly a quarter of the sample was randomly assigned to each of four conditions illustrated in table 2. Participants were not paired with people from their own country, so they were randomly assigned to either one of the "two other countries" conditions.

4.1.1 Research Design and Materials

The structure of the experiment is summarized in figure 8.

Participants were randomized to either first receive the affirmation treatment (control) or a set of three questions reflecting previous prescriptions for overcoming historical animosity that promote a sense of overarching commonness between countries. These measured 1) how much subjects retained an overall "Asian" attachment, as opposed to the attachment that subjects felt only to their country, 2) the extent to which subjects championed the idea that Asia would become an integrated community like the European Union in the future, and 3) how much subjects agreed to the constructivist idea of a common interpretation of history. These three questions were included in order to examine their correlations with trust. All three questions were measured on a modified Likert scale.

TABLE 2. Two-by-two experimental design (South Korean example)

	Opponent Country: Japan	Opponent Country: China
National Identity Affirmed	N = 90	N = 86
Nonaffirmed (Control)	N = 91	N[1] = 217

[1] In all three countries, I aimed for approximately 100 subjects per condition; however, in some conditions like this one, the number of participants responding to the survey advertisement was higher than others.

Figure 8. Experiment structure. Source: Eunbin Chung

The first question involved the idea that attachment to a superordinate identity that includes both current in-group and out-group—that is, a redefinition of the in-group as a larger entity that contains both of "us"—is a way to achieve overarching peace (Gaertner and Dovidio 2014). This is the common stream of thought behind studies suggesting the promotion of universalism that submerges existing identities: proponents of a supranational type of regionalism (Schuman 1950), homogenizing strategies of assimilation (Barry 2002; Waldron 2002), regional integration via a functionalist spillover (Haas 1958; Rosamond 2000), or merging into a larger in-group that dismantles subcategories through individual contact (Allport 1954). In order to assess this, subjects were asked to report how strongly they identified with Asia as a whole, or how important it was to the subjects that they were "Asian."

Witnessing the relatively successful "overcoming of history" in Europe, some scholars suggest the European Union as a forward-looking model for Asia (Chopparapu 2005; Dent and Huang 2002; Hund 2003; Ravenhill 2001; Soesastro 2006; Yahuda 2006). In accordance with this thought, and in order to offer a narrower focus from the first question that assessed a sense of regional attachment, the second question provided a short paragraph describing that some scholars believe Northeast Asia could integrate into a tighter community like the EU in the future, and asked subjects how much they agreed with that view.

The last question attempted to assess the constructivist assertion that an intersubjective understanding of history is a more successful way of reconciliation (Kupchan 2010; Wendt 1999). Borrowing sentences from previous research (He 2008; Lind 2008), I provided a short paragraph depicting a common interpretation of history, one that both inflictor and receiver countries of aggression could reach agreement on: that the traumatic past of East Asian states was a tragedy of the time in history, due to the imperialistic and militaristic world order at the time, rather than the doing of one country alone. Participants were asked to indicate their level of agreement toward this understanding of history, to see if the subjects who shared this interpretation in inflictor and receiver states reported higher levels of trust of each other.

Participants in the affirmed condition performed the NIA treatment, which followed common practice in psychological affirmation studies. The affirmation treatment is a straightforward, nonpolitical task. Self-affirmation on an individual level in social psychological experiments is typically done by asking subjects to either write about an important value to the self such as family or religion or to rank values in order of importance. The manipulation in my experiment looked similar but was done on a group level, by affirming social identities. Since the group I was interested in affirming was the subjects' countries, the treatment asked subjects to choose from a list of nineteen values the one they deemed most important for their country and people from their country, and then write a short essay on why they think so. The list of qualities aimed to affirm their self-worth as a group and was chosen carefully so that none were specifically related to out-group sentiment or competition with another country. The order in which the response options were presented was randomized.

Participants in the control group performed the nonaffirmation task, in which questions were identical in format but completely irrelevant to group values. Subjects chose out of a list of nineteen exotic-sounding jelly beans one that soundest tastiest and were to write a short essay on why they chose that flavor (Critcher, Dunning, and Armor 2010).

Then began measurements of trust, the dependent variable. As a measure of particularized moralistic trust, subjects were asked a series of questions that directly asked how much they trusted the government and people of their opponent country, which depended on the condition they were randomly assigned to. These questions were borrowed and adapted from the questions on trust in the World Values Survey.[2]

Questions measuring moralistic trust were removed from my survey in China; thus only data from South Korea and Japan are used in my analysis of moralistic trust. Items that were regarded as politically sensitive were deleted as a condition for permission of carrying out the survey, leading to a shorter survey conducted in China. Consequently, questions directly asking about levels of trust regarding the other country's government or people, as well as questions measuring affect levels of other countries, were omitted.

Box 1

Circle which one among the following values you think is most important to Koreans generally.

self-discipline	family	democracy
loyalty	creativity	originality
appearance / fashion	honesty	concern for others
patience	religion / spirituality	working hard
self-respect	friendships	personal liberty
health/fitness	achieving your dream	
social skills	courtesy/ manners	

In the box provided below, write 1–2 paragraphs about why you think this value tends to be important to Koreans.

In the box provided below, write 1–2 paragraphs about what you think Koreans have done to demonstrate this value.

For this reason, I had other explanatory factors in the Japanese and South Korean surveys that I couldn't measure in China. Since I could not measure all the covariates I wanted to measure in China, I was unable to include data from China in my model on moralistic trust. I provide a list of the trust questions below.

I will briefly discuss why I chose these five questions to assess subjects' moralistic trust of another country. Q1 and Q3 directly ask how much subjects trust the other country's government or people. I have both of

---

Box 2

Q1. How much trust do you have in the [Korean / Japanese / Chinese] (opponent country, given depending on condition subject was in) government?

No trust at all / Little trust / Quite a bit of trust / A lot of trust

Q2. Do you feel the [Korean / Japanese / Chinese] government would try to take advantage of [your country's] government if they got a chance, or do you feel it would be fair?

Take advantage / Try to be fair

Q2-a. How strongly do you feel about this?

Very strongly / Strongly / Weakly / Very weakly

Q3. How much trust do you have in [Korean / Japanese / Chinese] people?

No trust at all / Little trust / Quite a bit of trust / A lot of trust

Q4. Do you feel the [Korean / Japanese / Chinese] people would try to take advantage of [your country's] people if they got a chance, or do you feel it would be fair?

Take advantage / Try to be fair

Q4-a. How strongly do you feel about this?

Very strongly / Strongly / Weakly / Very weakly

Q5. Would you say that most of the time [Korean / Japanese / Chinese] people try to be helpful, or that they are mostly just looking out for themselves?

Try to be helpful / Just looking out for themselves

Q5-a. How strongly do you feel about this?

Very strongly / Strongly / Weakly / Very weakly

these components of trust—toward people and toward the government—because "trust of another country" can mean either one or both. When asked a question such as "*How much do you trust China?*," the respondent could be confused as to whether they are being asked about Chinese people in general or asked for a perspective on Chinese government and policy.

Aside from those questions that directly ask subjects' level of trust vis-à-vis a country's people or government, supplementary questions such as Q2, Q4, and Q5 were added for a broader and more accurate assessment of trust toward another country. These three questions were chosen as other ways to ask the level of trust subjects have in other countries.

As in the case for questions 2, 4, and 5, when possible, questions were divided into two steps. In the first step, subjects were asked to choose one out of a dichotomous response option. Then the following question asked subjects to report how strongly they felt about their previous assessment, on a modified 4-point Likert scale ranging from "very strongly" to "very weakly." Sniderman, Hagendoorn, and Prior (2004) note that disaggregating a survey question into these two steps, in particular when asking politically sensitive survey questions, has been known to be a more effective measure in terms of processing time accuracy in assessment of subject attitudes. Consequently, the survey questions were designed in these two steps when possible.

Finally, subjects played a simulated trust game, which is often used in experimental economics to measure trust between players (Berg, Dickhaut, and McCabe 1995).[3] Subjects were told they would be connected in real time via the Internet with another participant from their opponent country, where they would exchange numeric responses (representing numbers of tokens).[4] In the game there is a proposer and a responder, where the proposer is given one hundred tokens. The proposer must decide how much, if any, of the one hundred tokens to send to the responder with the proviso that every token sent is tripled before it reaches the responder. So if the proposer sends ten tokens, the responder receives thirty, and if the proposer sends fifty tokens, then the responder receives 150, and so forth. Once the responder receives the tokens, then the responder must decide how much, if any, of the amount received to send back to the proposer.

The amounts sent from proposer to responder are commonly taken as measures of trust—indications that the proposer expects the responder to reciprocate. Economic theory predicts that if both players are rational and selfish and that this is common knowledge, the Nash Equilibrium of the trust game is that neither player will transfer a single token to the other (Naef and Schupp 2009). A self-interested rational proposer will keep the entire amount of tokens for themselves, and if the responder does receive any tokens they will not send any back. If the proposer trusts the responder enough to believe the responder will return some tokens, however, the proposer will send tokens to the responder, as the proposer realizes that paying more to the responder gives them a higher chance of receiving back a larger amount of money. In this way, the trust game measures how much trust the proposer holds with regard to the responder. Likewise, amounts sent back reflect trustworthiness—the extent to which money sent elicits an obligation to reciprocate on the part of the responder (Leland, Houser, and Shachat 2005). I am interested in the levels of trust subjects exhibit toward their foreign opponents, and thus focus on the first move by the proposer.[5]

My analysis focuses on the first number of tokens participants offer as proposers to their receivers in the game for two reasons. First, I employ the trust game to measure the amount of trust participants have of their counterpart, when the only information given is the nationality of the counterpart. This setting allows for an investigation of each subject's perceived trustworthiness in their counterpart solely based on abstract images subjects hold of the people from the other country, and any stereotypes that originate from those images. In order to avoid undesirable cues or influence from any other information besides the counterpart's nationality, such as gender, age, or external features, there is no communication[6] other than the exchange of numbers. Second, any interaction beyond the very first move from the proposer is unlikely to avoid influence from unwanted cues, because the moment playing history starts accumulating, the behavior of the counterpart becomes a lesson for the participant's next move. Therefore, in order to remove this type of updating, the best data to focus on is the very first amount participants-as-proposers offer to their foreign opponents.

It is most likely that any behavior players exhibited in the second round was highly influenced by the amount they received back in the last step of the first round of the game. Due to logistical constraints, however, I was unable to make the game truly interactive when conducting the experiments in the three countries. Therefore, while subjects were told they were being paired with a foreign opponent in real time, the responses they actually received at the end of the first trust game were actually programmed beforehand into the survey to return half of what the receiver in the game was given. Since this amount was not random, and all players would have found their opponents to play in completely "fair" ways by dividing the enlarged pie equally in half, this could very well prompt a different action in the second round of the game than what players would have otherwise displayed.

Participants were told they would play multiple rounds of the game. This is because iterated games most closely simulate the interactions in an international setting where institutional cooperation occurs. According to scholars who advocate the possibility of cooperation through institutions, repeated interaction elongates the shadow of the future, leading actors to invest in trusting behavior for an increase in self and overall benefit (Axelrod 1984; Keohane 1984; Oye 1985). The repetition itself by nature becomes an institutional rule that actors abide by, because defecting when future interaction is likely harms one's reputation and will most likely lead to a decrease in the next round's gains.

Likewise, when participants have expectations of iterated games, the type of trust the proposer reveals via their first move in the trust game is strategic trust. This is because the proposer endows a certain amount in their opponent in the interest of maximizing their own gain.[7] When participants are told that they will play multiple rounds with the same player, consideration for reputation and long-term exchange comes into play. Since participants believed that they would be playing iterated rounds with a foreign player in a different country in real time, it can be expected that participants would take into account the possibility of reputation building over multiple rounds. Because this "shadow of the future" exists in iterated games, the tokens proposers offer in the first step of the game represents strategic trust. In actuality, all subjects played just one round of the game as proposer, and then one more round of the game as responder.

If the proposer has absolutely no trust of their counterpart, then they would send zero tokens from the very beginning. This is congruent with the unique subgame perfect equilibrium for a one-shot trust game. In the case that the proposer has sufficient level of trust, however, they will engage in a joint endeavor with the responder to enlarge the size of the pie so that returns increase for both players.

While experimental games are stylized and offer participants interaction in abstract form, they involve real stakes, risks, and opportunities, mostly in the form of gaining or losing money. In a game where subjects are paid directly according to how much they earn, there is little incentive for individuals to pay their counterparts unless there is the expectation, or trust, that doing so will in turn benefit the self. This is the strategic element of trust, where people trust each other enough to, for example, do business together—they are trusted to uphold their agreements, which will then produce mutual benefits.

In strategic trust, there must be a potential gain to provide incentive to trust the opponent. Unlike the trust game, survey questions asking subjects directly to self-report their level of trust toward another country are measures of subjective moral assessments—verbal indications that do not entail any potential reward for the subject. Trust in the trust game, however, represents strategic trust that reveals attitudes in the process of economic exchange that subjects can gain from. It is a trust that allows for the maximization of rewards when players trust each other enough to mutually "use" each other for strategic means. The reason proposers invest some, if any, in the responder in the first place is because they are aware this will amplify the gains (by three times) the two players can divide later, and they sufficiently trust the responder will give some of this enlarged return back. Existing research has found strong statistical correlation between the expectations proposers have as to how much the responder will return and the amount the proposer actually sends (for a review, see Naef and Schupp 2009).

As a measure of strategic trust, the trust game is a useful way to predict the trust necessary in readiness to cooperate, because interaction in the game is analogous to situations states find themselves in when cooperating with each other in international relations. States must first invest some costs into the process with some vulnerability, as there is a time lag before the fruits of cooperation are available to all participants. Trust between states is what will allow them to invest with these costs in the first place, with faith that there will be an increasing return. This corresponds to the first move of the proposer. When looking at the responder's side, their decision to give back a certain amount to the proposer is much like situations where cooperating states are finally dividing the pie. The pie is now bigger due to cooperation, just as symbolized with the multiplication of the tokens by three. Division of the amplified pie at that point allows for mutual benefits. On the other hand, a failure to endow the minimum necessary level of trust results in an inability for both sides to enjoy a larger pie. Just like states that are unable to actualize the growth of the pie through collaboration due to lack of trust, players who do not exchange tokens will be unable to realize the larger gain that was possible for them. In other words, distrust stymies potentially rewarding collaboration (Rathbun 2009).

As with institutional cooperation between states, there lurks in the game the possibility of receiving a "sucker" payoff (Grieco 1988; Mearsheimer 1994; Stein 1982). The responder may defect at the end of the game by not returning anything to the proposer. However, this kind of cheating in collaboration would only be beneficial for a responder in a one-shot game, or in the final round of a series of games when participants are aware of the number of rounds they are playing. When players expect to play multiple rounds, without knowledge of how many, players are less likely to easily defect, as interaction entails some shadow of the future. Considering that bilateral relations is never a one-shot game but a series of repeated games, defecting would not be a strategic choice.

Because there were other trust questions in-between the manipulation and the trust game, in order to make sure the effects of the manipulation were not watered down I built a "reinforcement" of affirmation into the game. While subjects were waiting for their opponent to decide how many tokens to give back (which was built into the survey and forced participants to wait), they were again shown the (non)affirmation questions and their written answers. This time, the screen stated that subjects had the chance to review and/or edit their answers should they wish. By refreshing (non) affirmation in participants' minds, we could check the effect of affirmation on trust with added confidence.

At the end of the game, in order to reimburse subjects based on how much they trusted their opponents, each subject was paid the amount that they earned in the first round of the trust game. Thus the size of the award was proportionate to what subjects would have earned considering they were paired with the same type of opponent. At this stage participants were debriefed and then left the room.

Due to logistical constraints, participants in Japan and China were asked to complete the survey at home, or wherever they had access to the Internet and could complete the survey without distraction. After having completed the survey, students came to a specified classroom during a given time slot to receive their payment from the researcher. All participants were assigned a random number so that they could accurately receive the payment corresponding to how they played the game.

Payment was roughly equivalent across countries. Taking into consideration the foreign currency exchange rates vis-à-vis each other as well as different currency values with regard to living costs in each country at the time, payments were made to be similar across countries. The exact amount of the initial award for participation and additional reward from the trust game needed to be adjusted following discussion and agreement with staff and faculty members at the universities.[8] In South Korea, subjects received 5,000 Won for participation, with the chance to gain up to 5,000 Won more from the game. In China, participants were paid 20 Yuan for participation, with an opportunity to earn up to 10 Yuan more depending on how they played the game. Finally, Japanese participants received up to 1,000 Yen, of which 500 Yen was given for participation.

4.2 Results

I open the results section with a presentation of demographics of the sample I gathered. First, the gender distribution was roughly half, with the proportion of males being slightly higher at 54 percent of the sample. Having recruited participants from university students, the analyses of age and education levels of my sample are fairly predictable. The ages of the subjects ranged from seventeen to sixty-one, excluding missing values; 97 percent of the sample, or 1,090 participants, reported that they were between seventeen and thirty-five years old.

Participants were also asked to self-report how politically liberal or conservative they were on a 4-point Likert scale. In the overall sample, a little more than half of the sample self-reported as liberal. While this is not a terribly lopsided distribution considering that most college populations would be expected to be predominantly liberal, it should be noted that what it exactly means to be politically liberal or conservative varies by country. For example, China is a socialist republic under the one-party leadership of the Communist Party of China. With vastly different political systems, the definitions and connotations of being liberal or conservative might be too divergent and distinct in nature to group together across different countries. If the whole spectrum of political orientations is skewed to the left in China, for example, the possible range of political ideologies that Chinese people are aware of or perceive as desirable might be on completely different scales than that in Japan or South Korea. For these reasons, the political orientation variable is not included in my analyses of trust. My overall sample seemed fairly even in its ideological divide, with 56.31 percent self-reporting as politically liberal and 43.68 percent as politically conservative. However, when just the Chinese sample was examined in isolation, it was found that the majority of the sample (over 82 percent) self-reported to be politically liberal in China.

I now turn my analyses to trust. For each of my trust measures, the results are discussed in three phases. First, I briefly describe the process of how I examine my dependent variables of interest, preparing them for analysis. I then present the results of my analyses of NIA's effect on trust on the overall sample as well as variations across different dyads. Finally, I test whether the "commonness" variables being compared with NIA have an effect on boosting trust.

In a nutshell, I find that in both cases of moralistic and strategic trust, individuals affirmed of their national identity reported higher levels of trust in other countries, thus confirming my hypotheses. The effect of

NIA on each of the trust measures somewhat varied in quantity across the dyads but did not have conflicting effects across any of them. Discussion of the theoretical implications of these findings is embedded throughout this section.

4.2.1 NIA and Moralistic Trust

Unlike physical attributes such as height, weight, and volume, trust is a broad and abstract term that is difficult to measure directly in a survey (Byrne 2013). Accordingly, it is common practice for social scientists in survey research to combine a larger number of items aimed at measuring trust, rather than using just one survey question. This adds a degree of reliability and accuracy in measuring unobservable variables such as trust. Such measures are called *latent variables* in social science research (Bollen 2002; Borsboom, Mellenbergh, and Van Heerden 2003; Edwards and Bagozzi 2000; Sobel 1994).

As such, from my set of questions that measure moralistic trust, I have five trust variables, which I combine to create an overall trust index. This allows for a more reliable measure of subjective trust than using participants' answers to just a single survey item as a dependent variable. However, in order to see if the combined items are indeed sufficiently homogenous in nature and thereby all measuring the same variable of trust, I used a confirmatory factor analysis to combine them.

Treating "overall moralistic trust" as a latent factor, factor analysis helps determine the contribution of each of the five trust variables toward measuring that latent factor. I then scale this new variable so that it ranges from 0 to 1. This process is described in detail in the appendix.

Figure 9 shows the distribution of this newly created latent trust variable. For convenience of comparison in analysis, I scaled the trust variable to range from 0 to 1. The mean of this variable is .342, with a standard deviation of .189. Since no Chinese subjects are included in the model, the N drops to 826, which is the number of valid data points from Japanese and South Korean subjects combined. Figure 9 shows that the distribution of the trust variable seems close to normal.

Figure 10 illustrates the distribution of the trust variable data by affirmation and nationality of subject and opponent. This is based on all of the data I collected with the trust questions, and it compares the responses by the nationality of the subject who was surveyed and the countries they were asked about. At a glance, it is noticeable that across all conditions the subjects who were affirmed of their national identity reported stronger

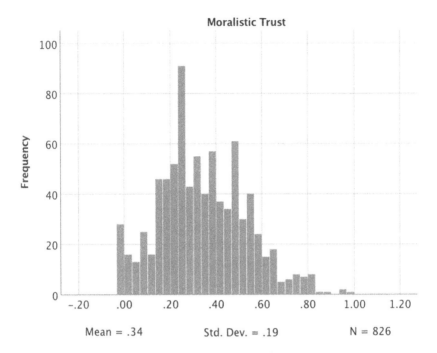

Figure 9. Distribution of latent trust variable ("Moralistic Trust")

levels of trust in the trust questions compared to nonaffirmed subjects who were asked about the same country. A large table that compares the exact numeric values of means and standard deviations of the trust variables across all eight conditions (two nationalities Japan and South Korea X two possible opponent countries X affirmation and nonaffirmation conditions) is included in the appendix.

Does national identity affirmation boost moralistic trust?

The hypotheses I am testing in this study of trust are twofold. The first argument is that affirmation of each person's own national identity increases trust between people from different countries. The second argument is that existing theoretical claims that advocate a sense of similarity across nations, in contrast to the first argument, are not associated with higher trust. These theories that claim an inclusive commonness can be summarized as the following: 1) an all-encompassing "Asian" identity, 2) an idea that the EU is a forward-looking model for Asia and Asia should

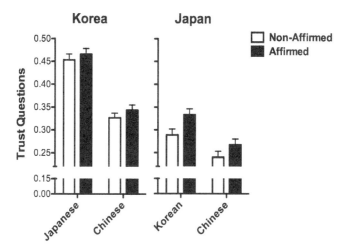

Figure 10. People affirmed of their national identity report more moralistic trust (as measured by trust questions) regarding their opponent country, compared to individuals who are not affirmed.

thus integrate into a regional community like the EU, and 3) the claim that a common interpretation of history across states is necessary for trust between them.

In order to test my first hypothesis, I first present simple models to focus on the effect of affirmation on trust, controlling just for subject nationalities. I start my analysis with a simple test that examines whether affirmed individuals reported more moralistic trust toward the other country, and whether there was a difference between trust as reported by South Korean and Japanese respondents in the survey questions.

Table 3 shows that affirmation did have a boosting effect on trust: individuals affirmed of their national identities reported significantly higher levels of trust toward the countries they were paired with, compared to nonaffirmed individuals. Controlling for the nationalities of respondents, affirmed individuals reported on average .028 point or approximately 3 percent higher levels of moralistic trust compared to nonaffirmed individuals. This .028 point margin was based on the 0–1 scaled latent variable that I created combining participants' answers to questions on how much they subjectively trust the other country.

TABLE 3. Moralistic trust by NIA and subject nationality

Moralistic Trust	Coef (SE)
NIA	.028*
	(.013)
Subject Nationality (Japan)	–.105**
	(.013)
Constant	.270
N	826
R^2	.076

Note: Linear regression, robust standard errors in parentheses. ** Indicates statistical significance at the 1 percent level, * significant at the 5 percent level, † significant at the 10 percent level.

Also, when affirmation effects are not taken into consideration, South Korean subjects reported more trust toward the countries they were paired with overall compared to Japanese subjects, which is also observable in figure 10.

The next step is to see whether the effect of affirmation differed depending on nationality of the subjects. To do this I employed another test that included an interaction term of subject nationality and affirmation. If NIA had the effect of boosting trust only for South Korean participants, for example, an interaction term of subject nationality and affirmation would be statistically significant. This would indicate that NIA did not have an effect on Japanese participants. However, when I introduced an interaction term of nationality and affirmation in the model, it was not significant: [F (1, 822) = 0.00, p = .994]. Therefore there was no significant difference in the effect of affirmation on trust depending on the nationality of participants.

The interaction did not become significant when opponent's nationalities were controlled for either. The results of this test are summarized in table 4.

In addition, the effect of affirmation did not depend on the nationalities of the subject and opponent country. A three-way interaction of affirmation, the subjects' nationality, and the nationality of the paired opponent was also not significant: [F (3, 819) = 1.877, p = .132], which implies that the effect of affirmation did not diverge specifically based on the nationality of subjects or their counterparts.

Across all country dyads affirmed individuals reported more trust toward the other country, as was predicted in my theory and hypotheses and as is directionally observable from figure 10. Although the boosting

TABLE 4. Moralistic trust with NIA and opponent nationality interaction

Moralistic Trust		Coef (SE)
NIA		.031†[1]
		(.019)
NIA X Nationality	(NIA X South Korea)	–.020
		(.025)
Subject Nationality	(South Korea)	.095**
		(.021)
Opponent	(South Korean)	.060**
		(.018)
	(Japanese)	.123**
		(.017)
Constant		.430
N		826
R²		.142

Note: Linear regression, robust standard errors in parentheses. ** Indicates statistical significance at the 1 percent level, * significant at the 5 percent level, † significant at the 10 percent level. The p-value for the NIA variable in this test is .06.

effect of NIA on trust occurred across dyads, a closer examination by country reveals that more specifically the comparative quantities of reported trust did vary by country. First, regardless of the specific opponent country, South Korean participants reported significantly more trust in the countries whose trust levels they were asked about, compared to Japanese participants.

Second, when South Korean or Japanese participants were asked about how much they trust China, they reported less trust compared to when their trust was measured toward each other. In a larger context outside of the game, we can be reminded that both Japan and South Korea are key allies of the United States, which is in increasing competition with China and both economic powers in Asia. Therefore China's rapid growth, which seemingly challenges American hegemony and regional economic powers, could pose threats to other countries, making it harder for them to trust China. It is noteworthy, however, that NIA effects still occurred in these difficult dyads, boosting South Koreans' and Japanese' trust in their moral assessments of China.

Model of Moralistic Trust with Commonness Variables

In order to study the relationship between existing theories of overarching commonness (Asian identity, EU model, and common interpretation of history) and trust, I measured how much subjects held such perceptions in my survey. I include those variables in my next model. Table 5 presents the results. I estimated a linear regression that includes the "commonness" variables, controlling for where the countries subjects were from and which countries subjects' levels of trust was asked about in the survey.

Consistent with my hypotheses, and contrary to many existing prescriptions for increasing trust between people from rival states, none of the commonness variables were associated with moralistic trust. How closely subjects identified with Asia overall, how much they agreed that Asia could be integrated into a regional community like the EU, or how much they

TABLE 5. Test of moralistic trust including NIA and "commonness" variables

Moralistic Trust		Coef (SE)
NIA		.021*
		(.010)
Attachment to Asia	(not much attachment)	−.022
		(.046)
	(some attachment)	−.002
		(.041)
	(strong attachment)	−.000
		(.041)
EU	(somewhat disagree)	.016
		(.015)
	(somewhat agree)	.016
		(.016)
	(totally agree)	.016
		(.024)
Common understanding of history	(somewhat disagree)	.000
		(.028)
	(somewhat agree)	−.000
		(.027)
	(totally agree)	.018
		(.030)
Subject Nationality	(Japan)	−.061**
		(.014)
Opponent	(Japanese)	.066**
		(.020)
	(Chinese)	−.036*
		(.015)
Affect		.004**
		(000)
Constant		.391**
		(.069)
N		776
R^2		.441

Note: Linear regression, robust standard errors in parentheses. ** Indicates statistical significance at the 1 percent level, * significant at the 5 percent level, † significant at the 10 percent level.

supported the idea of a common interpretation of history were not correlated with trust. Remarkably, in a model that included all of these commonness variables and NIA, only NIA had a positive effect on enhancing moralistic trust.

I controlled for how much subjects reported that they liked the other country (i.e., affect). Affect toward the other country had a significant and positive effect on how much subjects said they trusted the country. Having affect variables as explanatory variables in my model, one thing worth checking was whether there was any correlation between those who already liked the other country and those who were affirmed of their national identity. Although people were randomly assigned to the NIA or nonaffirmation conditions in order to avoid such possibilities, I estimated a t-test with affect and affirmation to double-check that those who were affirmed in my study didn't just happen to already like the other country more. Results of the 2-tailed t-test indicated that affirmed and nonaffirmed groups did not have significantly different answers to the affect questions, $t(776) = .25$, $p = .79$, adding confidence to my decision of including both affirmation and affect variables in the model.

Affirmation and Affect

Could it be that those who reported more moralistic trust simply liked the other country more? Even when controlling for affect, or how much participants reported they liked the other country, affirmation still had a positive and significant effect on moralistic trust.

To measure affect, all participants were asked to indicate how much they liked or disliked ten countries. The list included both China and Japan, and the order of countries was randomized. Inclusion of other countries and order randomization were done to disguise the fact that I was getting at their affect toward the two countries and to avoid social desirability bias. I tried to pick evenly across regions and knowledge subjects may have of the countries, so that the overall affect levels of the participant toward the countries were not skewed to overly negative or positive. Subjects self-reported their level of affect on a slide-bar ranging from extremely negative to extremely positive.

As shown in table 6, affect had a significant effect on moralistic trust. It is less surprising and can be expected that those with a higher affect score of the other country (i.e., they like the other country more) report that they trust the other country more as well, compared to those who express a dislike of the country. Therefore it is noteworthy here that something as

TABLE 6. Moralistic trust by affirmation and affect

Moralistic Trust		Coef (SE)
NIA		.022*
		(.010)
Subject Nationality	(Japan)	−.081**
		(.017)
Opponent	(Japanese)	.066**
		(.020)
	(Chinese)	−.036*
		(.015)
Affect		.004**
		(.002)
N		776
R^2		.434

Note: Linear regression, robust standard errors in parentheses. ** Indicates statistical significance at the 1 percent level, * significant at the 5 percent level, † significant at the 10 percent level.

counterintuitive as national identity affirmation can have similar effects. When one thinks of the policy implications of these findings, affect toward other countries is certainly an other-regarding emotion and one that would not be easily nudged by a change in policy. After decades of conflictual interaction and colonization, it is unlikely that people will easily change their feelings about another country and quickly change their emotion of enmity to one of amity. However, affirmation of one's identity is inward-looking. It does not entail how one views the other. Therefore affirmation presents more viable policy implications for increasing trust between countries with a rough history.

4.2.2 NIA and Strategic Trust

Since I was able to have subjects play the trust game in all three countries including China, the number of participants I could examine for the tokens model grew from the 826 subjects I had in the "moralistic trust" model to 1,046.[9] The descriptive statistics and distribution of the second dependent variable, the number of tokens given by the proposer in the trust game, are shown in figure 11.

Figure 12 graphs how strategic trust differs by nationality of subjects and opponents, as predicted by the model. It can be observed that across all twelve conditions, participants who were affirmed of their national identity paid more tokens to their counterparts in the trust game, compared to participants who were not affirmed of their national identities.

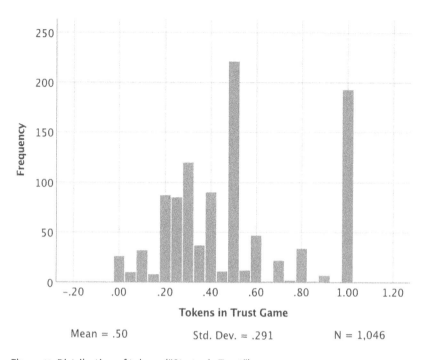

Figure 11. Distribution of tokens ("Strategic Trust")

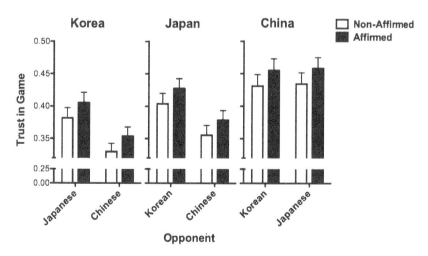

Figure 12. People affirmed of their national identity report more strategic trust (as measured by tokens given in the trust game) regarding their foreign opponent, compared to individuals who are not affirmed

Noticing the peak in the 100 tokens proposers gave to the responders in the game, as shown in the histogram of figure 11, I estimated a mixture model in R, using package flexmix (Leisch 2004), to take a closer look at what was going on. A mixture model is a regression model that allows my response variable (strategic trust, represented by tokens) to be the mixture of two normal distributions with different means and standard deviations (Leisch 2004). The mixture model gives each observation a probability of belonging to each of the two clusters. The two distributions are mixed together with a certain probability. In order to do this, flexmix assigns observations to group 1 or 2 based on the variables provided and estimates parameters separately. This process is laid out in more detail in the appendix.

In my data, the model identified people who said they gave 0–99 and 100 tokens as two distinct groups with a 100 percent probability. In other words, based on all variables in the data, the two groups are very different. Since there is no variation in the dependent variable in the group that gave 100 tokens, however, I chose to figure out what makes these groups distinct in a different manner.

To do this, I estimated a two-step Heckman selection model. The Heckman method is used to model which observations select themselves into a given subset (Gronau 1974; Heckman 1976, 1979; Lewis 1974). The first stage of the method finds the determinants of selection into a subgroup of the sample, and the second stage models variation within that group.

The first stage of the two-step methodology uses a probit model to obtain consistent estimates of the parameters of the selection equation. In my case, this step models which people select themselves into the 0–99 tokens group. Results from the probit model are reported in the columns on the far right in tables 10 and 11. The positive rho (ρ) in the two tables implies that the probit and OLS error terms are highly correlated.

In the second step of the method, the equation is estimated using OLS for the uncensored observations only. This second stage in my analysis is thus only of the people who gave their opponents less than 100 (0–99) tokens. The results from this OLS regression are reported in the second columns from the right in tables 10 and 11.

Which people tended to select themselves into the 0–99 tokens group? In my survey, all subjects were asked about their experience of living overseas. This was captured by the question, "Have you ever lived out of your home country? Check this box only if you have lived overseas for at least three years." I find that responses to this question—whether people had the experience of living abroad for a moderately long period of time—affect selection into the subgroup (Sartori 2003). Specifically, people who did not have the experience of living abroad for more than three years tend to select themselves into the 0–99 tokens group. This could be because the experience of living in other countries affected the subjects' concept or idea of national identity, which in turn may have brought about different mechanisms or effects of NIA. The experience of living overseas may have also led people to become more open-minded in a way that makes them more trusting of foreigners. These are all promising avenues for further investigation and specification in future research.

Does national identity affirmation boost strategic trust?

Since the mixture model identified those who gave 100 tokens as a separate minority group, and the first-stage analysis of the Heckman selection model found through a probit selection that those who gave the maximum number of tokens to their counterparts as having spent a significant portion of their lives overseas, I took a closer look at the other majority of the data that gave under 100 tokens. Tables 10 and 11 include the analyses of both of the groups in one figure. For convenience in reading and comparing the results, I again scaled the dependent variable to range from 0 to 1. Before that, I show the results of my various examinations of the majority group.

First, as I did with moralistic trust, I start by checking whether affirmed individuals gave more tokens to their opponents in the game compared to nonaffirmed individuals, simply controlling for subject nationality. The results of this test are summarized in table 7.

Just as for moralistic trust, NIA had a positive effect of boosting strategic trust, when controlling for subject nationality. In other words, affirmed

TABLE 7. Strategic trust by NIA and subject nationality

Strategic Trust		Coef (SE)
NIA		.027*
		(.013)
Subject Nationality	(Japan)	.028†
		(.015)
	(China)	.083**
		(.016)
Constant		.431
N		857
R^2		.036

Note: Linear regression, robust standard errors in parentheses. ** Indicates statistical significance at the 1 percent level, * significant at the 5 percent level, † significant at the 10 percent level.

subjects gave more tokens to their opponents compared to nonaffirmed subjects. On average, affirmed participants gave about three more tokens, out of 100 possible tokens, to their opponents when comparing to participants who were not affirmed, controlling for subjects' nationalities. When not taking into account affirmation effects, Chinese subjects gave the most tokens, and South Koreans gave the least tokens to their opponents overall. Compared to South Korean subjects, Japanese players on average gave about three more tokens to their counterparts, while Chinese subjects gave an average of eight more tokens.

As shown in table 8, affirmation had a similar effect when controlling for the nationality of opponents as well. Although Chinese gave the most tokens to their counterparts, they were least trusted as opponents in the game, controlling for affirmation effects.

Witnessing the low trust South Korean and Japanese subjects expressed particularly with regard to China across both measures of trust, I considered a test that examined whether the effect of affirmation differed depending on the nationality of the opponent player. Table 9 shows the results from a test that includes an interaction between affirmation and the opponent country. In this model, the interaction variable for neither of the opponent nationalities was significant. This indicates that the effect of NIA on boosting strategic trust did not differ depending on the nationality of the opponent subjects were paired with. In addition, a three-way interaction of nationality, opponent, and affirmation was tested to see if the effect of affirmation was particular to certain dyads. The three-way interaction was not significant (p = .636), implying that the affirmation effects were not unique to nationalities of subjects and opponents.

TABLE 8. Strategic trust by NIA and opponent nationality

Strategic Trust		Coef (SE)
NIA		.025*
		(.013)
Opponent	(Japanese)	–.010
	(Chinese)	(.017)
		–.074**
		(.015)
Constant		.414
N		857
R^2		.040

Note: Linear regression, robust standard errors in parentheses. ** Indicates statistical significance at the 1 percent level, * significant at the 5 percent level, † significant at the 10 percent level.

TABLE 9. Test of strategic trust with NIA and opponent nationality interaction

Strategic Trust		Coef (SE)
NIA		.045†
		(.024)
Subject Nationality	(Japan)	.027
		(.017)
	(China)	.055**
		(.019)
Opponent	(Japanese)	.017
		(.026)
	(Chinese)	−.031
		(.025)
NIA X Opponent	(NIA X Japanese)	−.024
		(.034)
	(NIA X Chinese)	−.032
		(.031)
Constant		.366
N		857
R^2		.050

Note: Linear regression, robust standard errors in parentheses. ** Indicates statistical significance at the 1 percent level, * significant at the 5 percent level, † significant at the 10 percent level.

Model of Strategic Trust with Commonness Variables

Affirmed individuals reported higher levels of strategic trust. That is, affirmed subjects gave more tokens to their opponents compared to non-affirmed subjects. I estimated a two-step Heckman selection model on the whole sample of 1,046 respondents, using the number of tokens as a dependent variable representing strategic trust. The second step of the selection model is an OLS regression. The results are presented in table 10. As I did with moralistic trust, in this model I include the commonness variables to see if they had a positive effect on strategic trust. Again, none of commonness variables boosted trust. Table 11 then estimates the model again while controlling for nationalities of the subjects and opponents in the game. The findings in table 11 reinforce my findings once again that NIA encourages strategic trust across people from rival countries, confirming my hypotheses.

The section following table 11 provides a more detailed discussion of the results on both measures of trust.

I estimated the same selection model again, this time controlling for nationality of subjects and opponents. Again, the model censored the

TABLE 10. Selection model on strategic trust with commonality variables

Strategic Trust		OLS Coef (SE)	Probit, Selection Equation Coef (SE)
NIA		.036*	.083
		(.014)	(.087)
Attachment to Asia	(not much attachment)	−.027	.025
		(.030)	(.174)
	(some attachment)	.005	.136
		(.030)	(.178)
	(strong attachment)	.022	.467*
		(.036)	(.213)
EU	(somewhat disagree)	.050*	.285*
		(.023)	(.131)
	(somewhat agree)	.034	.202
		(.024)	(.137)
	(totally agree)	.022	−.086
		(.037)	(.204)
Common understanding of history	(somewhat disagree)	.042	.200
		(.066)	(.400)
	(somewhat agree)	.101	.002
		(.062)	(.368)
	(totally agree)	.119†	−.135
		(.062)	(.370)
Lived Abroad			−.287**
			(.096)
Constant		.207**	.932*
		(.066)	(.376)
Rho			.890**
			(.032)
Sigma			.222**
			(.007)
Lambda			.199**
			(.012)
Log pseudo likelihood			−244
No. of obs			1046
Censored obs			189
Uncensored obs			857

Note: Selection model, standard errors in parentheses. ** Indicates statistical significance at the 1 percent level, * significant at the 5 percent level, † significant at the 10 percent level.

minority group and conducted an OLS regression on the uncensored observations. Again, when controlling for the countries that participants were from and the countries their strategic trust was measured about, NIA had a positive and significant effect in increasing trust. In this model as well, none of the commonality variables had such an effect.

The subjects who gave the most tokens to their opponents, regardless

TABLE 11. Selection model on strategic trust with commonality variables and controls

Strategic Trust		OLS Coef (SE)	Probit, Selection Equation Coef (SE)
NIA		.027†[1]	.057
		(.014)	(.087)
Attachment to Asia	(not much attachment)	–.027	.052
		(.029)	(.173)
	(some attachment)	.005	.136
		(.030)	(.178)
	(strong attachment)	.004	.442*
		(.036)	(.219)
EU	(somewhat disagree)	.043†	.272*
		(.023)	(.131)
	(somewhat agree)	.029	.190
		(.024)	(.137)
	(totally agree)	.030	–.043
		(.037)	(.204)
Common understanding of history	(somewhat disagree)	.042	.234
		(.066)	(.396)
	(somewhat agree)	.101	.033
		(.062)	(.361)
	(totally agree)	.112†	–.114
		(.062)	(.362)
Subject Nationality	(Japan)	.045*	.036
		(.019)	(.123)
	(China)	.075**	.290*
		(.022)	(.140)
Opponent	(Japanese)	.009	.062
		(.022)	(.136)
	(Chinese)	–.019	.254*
		(.020)	(.123)
Lived Abroad			–.168†
			(.100)
Constant		.159**	.544
		(.069)	(.385)
Rho			.904**
			(.031)
Sigma			.220**
			(.007)
Lambda			.199**
			(.012)
Log pseudo likelihood			–224
No. of obs			1046
Censored obs			189
Uncensored obs			857

Note: Selection model, standard errors in parentheses. ** Indicates statistical significance at the 1 percent level, * significant at the 5 percent level, † significant at the 10 percent level.

[1] The p-value for the NIA variable is .05.

of the nationality of their opponents, came in the order of Chinese, Japanese, South Korean. The nationality of opponents (not taking into regard the nationality of the subjects) was not significant in the model, but by comparison, Japanese opponents were most trusted, then South Koreans, then Chinese. Chinese were therefore the most trusting nation, but at the same time the least trusted by other nationalities. South Koreans were the group that gave the least tokens to their opponents, thus least trusting, and came in second place after the Japanese when it came to how trusted they were. Japanese subjects came second in terms of how trusting they were, but were most trusted by other nationalities. This is an interesting point considering that in modern history of the three countries, Japan was the inflictor country, whereas Korea and a part of China (Manchuria) were colonies of Japan. There could be a number of reasons as to why these results came about in my study. First, as was inferred from the tests on moralistic data, it could be that a rapidly rising China today poses the most salient threat to neighbor states in the region. The commonly mentioned ambiguity of China's intentions (Goldstein 2013; Ikenberry 2008; Ross 2009; Suzuki 2008) mixed signals on the revisionist or status-quo nature of China's rise, and the sense of threat and insecurity provided by such perceptions of uncertainty may have reduced China to a less trustworthy actor.

Alternatively, due to the fact that measurement of strategic trust was based on a setting of monetary exchange, it is possible that how subjects perceived the general infrastructure of the other country, and the image they had of how credible and committed the people of the other country might be in investment and business, had an effect. Also, while distrust of Japan in the South Korean and Chinese publics is undoubtedly low (as illustrated in the earlier chapters), the behavior of my sample of undergraduate students could reflect a generational difference. Younger people who have more access to and enjoy the consumption of Japanese culture might feel more open to and comfortable in trusting Japanese opponents in situations of monetary exchange.

Besides statistical significance, the substantive size of the effect of affirmation is roughly 2 percent of the range of the dependent variable for moralistic trust, and 3 percent for strategic trust. At first glance, this might seem like a slim quantity. However, it is key to note here that NIA was found to have a significant and positive effect for both measures of trust, significantly departing from the equilibrium, especially in a setting where participants were asked about countries they shared a turbulent history of conflict and colonialism with.

I measure the first move of trust with the *expectation* that a player and her/his opponent will engage in repeated interactions in the future, where there will come repeated opportunities for cooperation and thus mutual gain. The mutual gain is amplified as a result of the player and her/his opponent's trust in working together. Since the first move is the hardest to initiate, any trust value larger than 0, which departs from the "rational" equilibrium, becomes all the more meaningful and interesting, especially in this setting where one is matched with a past adversary rampant with distrust in relations with one's country.

In addition, since the economic equilibrium of 0 trust and 0 trustworthiness is not based in cases of interaction between adversarial actors, the mere push beyond 0 to a positive number associated with affirmation is certainly worth highlighting. That is, the motivation for the proposer to send no tokens in the first place is not based on negative images of the responder but on the motivation to ensure that one doesn't end up with the sucker payoff. So the finding that proposers and receivers from countries suffering from severe distrust and an ugly history of war and colonization were able to invest more of their own resources in each other in a trust game is striking. It is possible that reciprocated games, or investment and return in larger quantities, may follow after this first nudge toward cooperation. These findings have implications for policies of cooperation and reconciliation between Northeast Asian states and elsewhere. The implications of my experimental findings for policy, public opinion, and reconciliation are discussed in more detail in the concluding chapter of this book.

4.3 Conclusion

The conventional wisdom on group identity and conflict is that the existing group identities are negative for trust. Because of this, even a slight positive finding refutes those existing notions of identity and group conflict. Therefore, for purposes of this study, it is worth focusing on the direction of affirmation effects rather than exact magnitude (of precisely how many more tokens affirmation can encourage participants to exchange, for example). The fact that NIA can boost trust between past adversaries into a positive direction implies that with additional insight in future research and policy measures, an amplification of the magnitude is also possible. In particular, in the trust game, since participants are in a difficult situation where they are paired with an unknown opponent who is a member of a past adversary country, any finding that departs from the subgame perfect equilibrium of zero becomes an interesting and unexpected finding.

How generalizable and applicable are my results to real world international politics? Some caveats to the possible policy connections of my experiment are equivalent to key points in general debates on the validity of experimental political science. One common critique hints at the artificiality of lab environments.[10] Aronson et al. (1990) nonetheless explain that lab experiments are not necessarily limited in generalizability compared to field experiments. In fact, labs offer scholars tighter control over the treatment and experiment overall, making them a preferred option for those focusing on the internal validity and performance of their models. Aronson et al. (1990) also note that "bringing the research out of the laboratory does not necessarily make it more generalizable or 'true'; it simply makes it different. [. . .] The generalizability of any research finding is limited."

Experts on lab experiments have responded in such ways against criticisms about the validity and reliability of the method. Besides these points, my experiments hold the additional strength that they were lab experiments conducted in the field. As the key variable of interest in my experiment, NIA, was performed through an experimental manipulation that evoked national identity, it was particularly crucial that the subjects in my sample held deeply engrained national identities into which they were sufficiently socialized. So fielding the experiment was essential. This could also give us hints as to why those who had prolonged experience of living overseas had tendencies of selecting themselves into a particular subgroup in the sample. It can be expected that the experience of living in another country for longer periods of time had some particular effect on the subjects' strength of national identity or broadened its concept. For those subjects, national identity and affirmation of it could have meant different things than to those who had only been socialized into their national identities growing up in their home countries.

Nonetheless, while utilizing a sample with deeply engrained national identities socialized from their home countries may hold greater implications for the applicability of this study to the real countries, extensions of the experiment can deliver further promise into the external validity of NIA theory. For this reason, in chapter 5 I utilize tests conducted on a sample that is representative by age and gender. Chapter 6 further escapes the artificiality of lab experiments with surveys conducted on a larger sample. Then I perform additional analyses based on the initial experimental findings. In chapters 7 and 8, I discuss results from my analyses of real, unresolved policy issues between the countries. Chapter 9 further strengthens the feasibility of NIA in actual politics and foreign policy through a discussion of historical cases.

FIVE

National Identity and Guilt Recognition
Experiments in Japan

"We must not let our children, grandchildren, and even further generations to come, who have nothing to do with the war, be predestined to apologize."

—Japanese Prime Minister Shinzo Abe, in his message commemorating the seventieth anniversary of the end of World War II, August 14, 2015

Experts highlight strong national identities in the public as obstacles to reconciliation between countries. In this chapter, I turn this conventional perception around to propose a way to increase guilt recognition through a reinforcement of national identities. In field experiments conducted with a sample of 1,597 Japanese citizens, I find that people come to admit higher levels of guilt for either their own or in-group members' actions after they are reminded of the worthiness of their national identity. This effect is inward looking in that it does not entail specific comparison with an outgroup. In addition, I examine the mechanism that connects identity affirmation and acknowledgment of guilt in the game, to find that this occurs through an increased awareness and concern for others, or "prosocial" tendencies.

Just as with our examination of trust in the previous chapter, the assumption of my analysis on guilt in this chapter significantly departs from rationalist expectations of behavior predicted by traditional economists. The equilibrium of human behavior according to rational choice theory would be to report no guilt at all, across any strategic conditions. If humans are hardwired to be intrinsically self-interested by nature, then it would make little sense to acknowledge guilt for maximally acquiring what is available on the table for them to take.

The rational choice model of decision-making has been astoundingly resilient due to its quantifiability and permeation in modern policy as well as economic and political processes, although often at a cost of lacking relationship to reality. Recently, however, research across multiple disciplines has advanced with regard to important determinants of decision-making in addition to the rational choice framework. Behavioral theories have attempted to deepen understanding of the links between other cognitive processes that affect decision-making, producing political behavior that diverges from the predicted rationalist equilibria. In fact, various studies find that many individuals care not only about gain for themselves in a "proself" way of behavior typically assumed in a game-theoretic model but also show that people have concern for fairness and reciprocity to others (i.e., "prosocial" behavior) (Kertzer and Rathbun 2015).

However, many of these studies remain disconnected and underspecify how and under which conditions psychological variables like values and identity relate to prosociality to affect moral perceptions of guilt, justice, or reciprocity. In addition, research on the motives identified to underlie reciprocal or fair behavior has been mixed. In the field of international relations, for example, there is a body of literature on reciprocity and mixed-motive cooperation; however, it largely assumes egoistic motivations rather than prosocial ones (Axelrod 1984; Keohane 1984).

The study in this chapter attempts a contribution in filling this research gap, by integrating interdisciplinary insights to develop a model of guilt in international relations that has larger explanatory power than rational choice. I aim to investigate the dynamic interaction and interdependence between different levels of identity—national, regional, and self—and willingness to contribute one's own resources to make up for a situation where one's actions have negatively affected the well-being of an out-group member. In the last stage of the study I investigate whether such prosocial concerns are extended to the actual historical context of Asian countries, strengthening the policy relevance and external validity of my experiments.

Guilt in Conflict Resolution

Guilt is an emotion people feel when the self is perceived as being responsible for violating a moral standard (Baumeister, Stillwell, and Heatherton

1994). Beyond the individual level, people are able to experience guilt on behalf of their group (Smith 2014). Guilt at the level of a group identity, which is also referred to as group-based or collective guilt, can be experienced when people feel a sense of in-group membership in the group they perceive as having committed wrongs against another group (Branscombe and Miron 2004).

However, reluctance to admit group-based guilt is commonly found in postconflict areas where parties have not successfully reconciled (Roccas, Klar, and Liviatan 2006). On the side of those accused as inflictors, admitting in-group wrongdoing can present challenges to a positive image of the group or be damaging to group self-esteem (Branscombe and Wann 1994; Paez and Liu 2011; Strelan 2007). In particular, regarding actions that occurred decades ago, current generations in the inflictor group may resist taking responsibility simply by association with the group (Wohl, Branscombe, and Klar 2006).

How and when, then, do people admit guilt in international interactions, namely for past deeds committed by an in-group? To investigate this question I conducted a survey-based experiment, measuring guilt in both a simulated game, where Japanese participants were told they were matched with a South Korean or Chinese participant, and through questions directly asking about whether Japan should or should not feel guilty about their past interactions with Korea or China.

I argue that affirming individuals of their national identity can increase reports of guilt. The affirmation of identity replenishes people's sense of the worthiness of their national identity, creating a boosting effect that elevates one's own group without putting down the other (Sherman et al. 2007). This elevation effect releases people from defensive response, allowing them to more readily admit guilt for past deeds (Steele 1988). I find that NIA increases guilt levels in both game settings and also in direct reference to Japan's history with China and Korea. NIA increases concern for others, allowing for prosocial attitudes. I discover that this is the mechanism through which NIA works to increase guilt—the other-regarding attitude of prosociality, which leads to an openness to admit guilt.

5.1 Prosociality and Guilt Recognition

Why might prosociality matter in guilt recognition? In conflictual dyads where there is a power asymmetry, recognition of guilt in the public of the stronger state requires some concern for fairness. Kertzer and Rathbun (2015) point out that when in positions of strength relative to a counterpart, prosocials are more dedicated to fairness and equality. Because a common response to demands from an out-group for penitence is to defensively protect the in-group, a psychological trigger to release people from this defensive reaction can activate prosocial tendencies, leading to increased penitence.

Previous research has examined various ways in which prosocial attitudes matter in international relations. For example, the existence of prosocial people in negotiations and foreign policy increases likeliness for bargaining parties to reach fair agreements (Kertzer and Rathbun 2015). The positive effect of the prosocials shines most, in particular, when they are in positions of strength. Since prosocials are more committed to equality and motivated by concern for others than proselfs, they do not exploit their greater bargaining leverage. The result is a greater preference for fair agreements, regardless of power differences. Therefore the presence of prosocials in a dyad makes bargaining failure less likely. This has implications for policy decisions like the extent of reparation between states, where countries would strive to find a comfortable midpoint for both sides to settle on.

I suggest that prosociality induced by NIA can boost guilt recognition in both game settings and when Japanese subjects are asked directly about their guilt levels in a historical context. I summarize my model here (see fig. 13).

I include two ways of measuring guilt in this study. My first measure is a behaviorally revealed guilt in an abstract game setting, and the second measure is a declared guilt, measured with survey questions about guilt. Some of the latter questions expand beyond guilt in a game setting, asking about Japanese participants' guilt regarding the actual historical context of Northeast Asian countries.

There is good theoretical reason to include measures of declared and revealed guilt. People have a subjective perception of whether they should pay responsibility toward past action or not, but this might not coincide with their revealed preferences. In answering a series of questions on guilt, participants are essentially summing up their subjective evaluation of how guilty they should feel toward another country. This subjective measure may or may not hold in actual encounters when members from the countries strategically interact with one another, especially when there are stakes of gain or loss at hand. Therefore it is helpful to have a subjective measure and a behavioral measure. While survey answers provide primary evidence of guilt, they do not capture behaviors. In my experimental games, subjects exchange money (represented by virtual points) through the Internet.

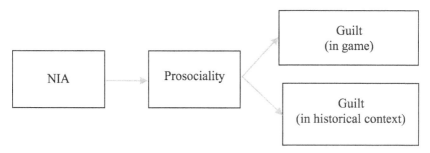

Figure 13. Model of NIA and guilt recognition. Source: Eunbin Chung

In the following section, I lay out the theoretical foundations of my model, which leads to a reminder of my hypotheses. After describing my methods, I discuss my findings and the implications of this study.

5.1.1 Theory and Hypotheses

The Psychological Mechanism of NIA and Guilt

While extant research has found that group-affirmation increases guilt (Gunn and Wilson 2008), the actual mechanisms through which group-affirmation works have been understudied. In experimental game settings, I examine the mechanism between identity affirmation and acknowledgment of guilt. I hypothesize that group-affirmation leads individuals to choose prosocial ways of behavior toward out-group members in the game. Prosocial attitudes have been found in existing studies to be associated with a concern for fairness (Kertzer and Rathbun 2015). If this is true, then it can be assumed that people who behave in prosocial ways come to realize more guilt for their past acts that may have harmed others. This leads to the following hypothesis:

> Hypothesis 2 = Individuals affirmed of their national identity report higher levels of guilt toward other country members through inducement of prosociality.
>
> H2a = NIA increases prosociality.
>
> H2b = People with prosocial tendencies report more guilt when their actions harm an out-group member.

When do individuals perceive personal guilt from an in-group member's behavior?

Another issue of contention from the Japanese perspective concerns the "guilt by association" fallacy. This point of view emphasizes the fact that more than seventy years have passed since Korea was a colony of Japan. In other words, the generation has changed in Japan so that the main elites in government and the socially, politically, and economically active Japanese in the public are those without memory of war or colonialism. Many of these people express fatigue and perception of unfairness when accused of their ancestors' deeds. The inability of Northeast Asian states to resolve issues of postconflict justice shortly after independence of Japan's colonies has led to these new problems.

Earlier studies have found that group members are capable of feeling guilt as a consequence of the behavior of other in-group members (Baumeister and Hastings 1997; Feagin and Hernan 2000; Landman 1993; Steele 2006). In particular, when one's group has a negative history, group members have been known to acknowledge collective guilt (Doosje et al. 1998). Theorists of social identity (Tajfel 1978; Tajfel and Turner 1979) and self-categorization (Turner et al. 1987) in social psychology have found that individuals derive their self-image from their social group. Individual guilt occurs when there is a discrepancy between how one thinks one should have behaved and how one actually behaved (Devine et al. 1991), but since individuals derive their self-concept from their group membership, a personal sense of guilt that derives from the group membership is also possible.

Scholars have found that the self-image of Japan as a peaceful nation (due to Article 9, the nonwar clause in the nation's peace constitution) has created a sense of ontological security among Japanese who feel threatened when their more violent history is brought up (Gustafsson 2014; Hagström and Gustafsson 2015; Zarakol 2010). In such circumstances, the recognition of responsibility for past generations' actions may be especially challenging.

This question of whether the current generation of Japanese needs to apologize and pay for a past in-group member's behavior can be connected to ideas of linked fate to the nation (Dawson 1994). Academics have noted the concept of linked fate as an attitude that equates one's destiny to the trajectory of their country, where one believes their identity is inextricably intertwined with and wholly dependent on their nation (McClain et al. 2009; Tate 1994). The literature on linked fate originated from the idea that due to one's ethnic identity, individuals in minority communities consider the destiny of the community and one's well-being to go hand in hand. While linked fate can refer to various categories of identity (the best-known studies have focused on racial politics in a domestic setting), here I focus on beliefs of linked fate on a national level.

Recognizing guilt for an in-group's harmful actions in which the self personally played no role depends on whether one perceives of a categorical association between the self and the in-group that committed those actions (Branscombe, Doosje, and McGarty 2002). Therefore linked fate will have a strong effect on the experience of group-based guilt.

I assume that Japanese who have a stronger belief of linked fate to their country will report more guilt about Japan's past actions and a greater need to compensate for those actions. This is because they believe in a sense of continuity of the nation. Conceptions of linked fate thus connect unresolved issues left by ancestors and the responsibility of the current generation to continue to work on those issues. I hypothesize that people with a stronger belief in linked fate to the nation report higher levels of guilt regarding behavior of somebody else from their country.

> Hypothesis 2 = Individuals who believe in linked fate report higher levels of guilt for another in-group member's behavior.
>
> H2a = Individuals who report guilt for an in-group member's deed in the game also report more guilt regarding Japan's history.

5.2 Method

In summer 2017 in Tokyo, I conducted a survey experiment with a sample of 1,597 Japanese respondents, representative by age and gender. Participants were collected by staff at a survey research firm, who distributed the survey in the form of an Internet link to Japanese people. The survey had eight conditions, to which participants were randomly assigned.

This study has more conditions compared to my previous tests on trust in chapter 4. First of all, rather than merely measuring the attachment subjects already hold toward Asia, this time I manipulate the "commonness" variable of an overarching Asian identity. Having a separate treatment condition that affirms an Asian identity of participants allows for a stronger test that directly compares the effects of national identity affirmation and affirmation of a supranational "Asian" identity.

Second, recent findings in studies on guilt are mixed in the social psychological literature, with some finding that group identity affirmation increases group guilt recognition (Gunn and Wilson 2011), but other studies finding only that self-affirmation is helpful for admitting group guilt (Čehajić-Clancy et al. 2011). Due to these mixed findings in the effect of group-affirmation on group-based guilt recognition, it is fair to say the relationship between the two in existing studies is unclear. In order to reexamine the difference between effects of self and group-affirmation, I include the condition of self-affirmation separately in this model. Table 12 shows my eight experimental conditions.

TABLE 12. Experimental conditions

Manipulation	Japanese National Identity Affirmation	Asian Identity Affirmation	Self-Identity Affirmation	Nonaffirmation (Control Group)
Other country 1: China	Group 1	Group 2	Group 3	Group 4
Other country 2: South Korea	Group 5	Group 6	Group 7	Group 8

Figure 14 shows the survey flow. After answering questions on simple demographics, participants completed either an affirmation treatment or control task, depending on the group they were in. With the exception of the nonaffirmation (control group) condition, individuals performed a task that affirmed either their Japanese national identity, and overarching Asian identity, or their individual self-identity. The list of values provided was equal across conditions, but the order in which each participant received the values was randomized.

Then all participants started the simulated game, where they were asked to suppose they were playing with a South Korean or Chinese oppo-

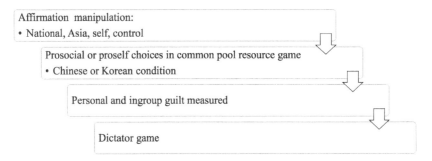

Figure 14. Experiment structure. Source: Eunbin Chung

nent, connected with them in real time through the Internet. In this game, subjects chose a way to distribute a common pool of resources (described as "points" in the game) between themselves and their foreign opponent. Participants were to choose one of three response options across five questions. An example is given below.

Box 3

Q.   Here's an example of how this task works:

	A	B	C
You get	500	500	550
Your Chinese/Korean counterpart gets	100	500	300

In this example, if you chose A you would receive 500 and the other would receive 100 from the common pool of resources. If you chose B, you would receive 500 and the other 500; and if you chose C, you would receive 550 points and the other 300. So, you see that your choice influences both the amount of resources you receive and the amount of resources the other receives from the common pool.

Before you begin making choices, please keep in mind that there are no right or wrong answers—choose the option that you, for whatever reason, prefer most. Also, remember that the points have value; the more of them you accumulate, the better for you. Likewise, from the "other's" point of view, the more points s/he accumulates, the better for her/him. Your answers here won't affect any other part of the survey.

(Van Lange 1997, Rathbun and Kertzer 2015)

This game was intended to measure the social preferences of each participant. For each choice situation, one of these response options represents a prosocial choice, an individualistic choice, and a competitive choice. In the questions shown, each of these choices are represented by the respective response options of B, C, and A; across all of the questions, the order of the response options was randomized. Both individualistic and competitive orientations are forms of proself orientations, but individualistic orientations maximize what political scientists would call "absolute gains" and competitive orientations maximize "relative gains": subjects with a competitive social value orientation would rather receive a smaller payoff if it meant their opponent received even less. This is a method that borrows the Triple-Dominance Measure created by Van Lange et al. (1997) and adapted by Kertzer and Rathbun (2015).[1]

After answering five of these questions, participants were told that their personal action in the game caused harm to their foreign opponent's well-being by overdrawing from a common pool of resources. They reported how guilty they felt about this at this point. Then participants played a dictator game where they could offer anywhere from 0 to 500 points to send back to their opponent. This amount represents the compensation will of the participant, even if it takes away from her/his own resources.

Then I measured guilt in another scenario. This time the survey indicated that another Japanese participant, a survey respondent who had also been playing this game, had overdrawn from the resource pool, harming the opponent's group. The perceived guilt participants personally felt for this was measured. Then participants played a dictator game where this time they could offer anywhere from 0 to 500 tokens to send back to their opponent's group.

Finally, participants were told the survey was proceeding to a second study. Across all conditions subjects were measured of their beliefs in linked fate. Then everyone answered a number of questions about the extent of guilt they felt toward China or South Korea, in the actual historical context between the countries.

Participants were debriefed at the end of the survey. Unlike the trust study in chapter 4, I could not pay all participants what they earned in the game due to logistical considerations. After consultation with staff that distributed my survey and collected the data, the survey was finalized to randomly pick a number of participants and grant to them an award for their participation. The amount of this award was proportionate to the number of virtual points subjects earned in the game. Therefore due to logistical constraints not all participants were guaranteed payment, but because participants played the game with a probability in mind of being paid according to how they played the game, the revealed guilt in this study can be assumed as a reasonable behavioral expression of guilt.

5.3 Results

5.3.1 Summary Statistics

I first discuss the demographics of the sample. Only adult participants between the ages of twenty and seventy were collected. The sample was designed to be nationally representative by age group, and reflected the aging tendencies of the Japanese population, with a distribution that appeared to be negatively skewed farther to the left than a normal distribution, with more than 65 percent of the sample being over the age of forty. In terms of the gender distribution of the sample, a little under half identified as male, and a slightly higher percentage of participants identified as female.[2] 50.32 percent of the sample responded that they had a university education. 64.11 percent of the sample self-reported their political orientation as somewhat conservative, which may be a reflection of the age distribution of the Japanese. Only 27 percent of the sample self-identified as politically liberal.

Table 13 shows the number and percentage of the respondents that were randomly assigned into each condition. Roughly an eighth of the sample was assigned into one of the eight conditions.

Having examined the basic demographics and various distributions in the data, we now move on to the results of the tests on our main hypotheses on NIA, prosociality, and various types of guilt. These are discussed in the following section.

5.3.2 Guilt in the Game

National identity affirmation leads to prosocial attitudes, which in turn increases guilt recognition.

The first finding in the overall sample is that NIA and reported guilt are mediated by prosocial attitudes. Depending on respondents' answers to multiple choice questions on how they would distribute resources between themselves and a foreign opponent, I categorized each respondent as either a prosocial or proself player. Examining the mechanism between NIA and

TABLE 13. Number and percentage of respondents in each condition

Manipulation	Japanese National Identity Affirmation	Asian Identity Affirmation	Self-Identity Affirmation	Nonaffirmation (Control Group)	Total
Other country 1: China	213 (13.5%)	195 (12.3%)	170 (10.8%)	199 (12.6%)	777 (49.2%)
Other country 2: South Korea	226 (14.3%)	190 (12.0%)	200 (12.7%)	186 (11.8%)	802 (50.8%)
Total	439 (27.8%)	385 (24.3%)	370 (23.5%)	385 (24.4%)	1,579 (100%)

acknowledgment of guilt, I find that NIA leads individuals to choose prosocial ways of behavior in the game, which in turn leads to guilt recognition. This holds for all our measures of guilt—declared and revealed guilt both in the personal and group-based setting (i.e., following personal action and another in-group member's action), as well as historical guilt based on the actual past of the countries' international relations.

Japanese individuals who were affirmed of their national identity were more likely to exhibit prosocial attitudes compared to those who were not affirmed of their national identity. Prosociality has been found in existing studies to be associated with a concern for fairness. If this is true, then it is intuitive that people who behave in prosocial ways come to realize more guilt for their past acts that may have harmed others. The following describes findings across declared and revealed guilt in the game, both in the settings of personal and in-group guilt, and historical guilt.

Personal Declared Guilt

What is the mechanism through which NIA affects international guilt recognition? Mediation analyses revealed that NIA worked through prosocial tendencies to increase declared guilt following personal action in the game. Figure 15 displays these results.

Multiple regression analyses were conducted to assess each component of the proposed mediation model. First, it was found that NIA was posi-

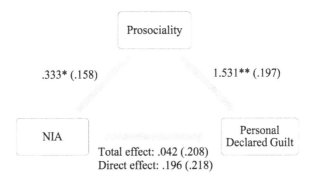

Figure 15. Prosocial attitudes mediate NIA and declared personal guilt in game.
Mediation with indirect effect. Numbers represent unstandardized beta coefficients, with standard errors in parentheses. **Indicates statistical significance at the 1 percent level, *significant at the 5 percent level, †significant at the 10 percent level. Source: Eunbin Chung

tively associated with prosociality (B = .333, exp(B) = 1.395, p < .05),[3] indicating that Japanese who were affirmed of their national identity exhibited more prosociality in dealing with a Chinese or South Korean counterpart in the game. It was also found that prosociality was positively related to perceived guilt Japanese participants declared in the game, after they were told they had withdrawn too many resources from the common pot, thus harming their counterpart (B = 1.531, exp(B) = 4.623, p < .01). It should be noted that the numbers on this second path are not simply the effect of prosociality on personal declared guilt. Rather it represents the effect of prosociality on personal declared guilt while controlling for NIA.

Because both of the first two paths were significant, mediation analyses were tested. This was a mediation with an indirect effect, where the total effect was not significant. Results of the mediation analysis confirmed the mediating role of prosociality in the relation between NIA and personal guilt reported in the game (B = .196, exp(B) = .822, p = .369). This is the direct effect, or the effect of NIA on personal declared guilt controlling for prosociality, which was statistically nonsignificant.

In other words, subjects who were affirmed of their national identity tended to take prosocial action in the game, and although these subjects were more generous to their counterparts in the game compared to those who exhibited proself behavior, these actually reported more guilt regarding the possibility that they could have harmed another group.

This could be because subjects who act in prosocial ways had more concern for others. As affirmation theory maintains, NIA can remove the need for people to act defensively toward people from other countries. This tendency to act evenhandedly toward out-group members could have led to prosocial rather than proself decisions in the game, which was further connected to perceived guilt when it was revealed that one's actions negative affected the well-being of others. In this sense, in can be inferred that prosocial tendencies are a mechanism through which NIA increases concern for people in other countries.

NIA Increases Concern for Others

People in the NIA conditions were most likely to exhibit prosocial attitudes. Since prosociality had a direct impact on increasing guilt in our model, I took a closer look at the relationship between affirmation and prosociality in the raw data.

Figure 16 shows the distribution of people who had prosocial versus proself tendencies by affirmation condition and opponent country. When

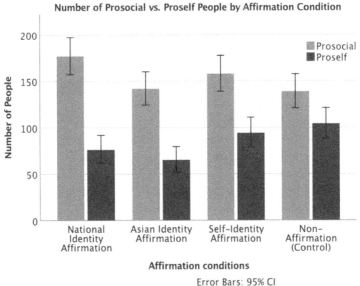

Figure 16. Across affirmation conditions, the most people in the NIA condition exhibited prosocial attitudes. Source: Eunbin Chung.

comparing across all the different affirmation conditions, the most people in the NIA condition exhibited prosocial attitudes. That is, across different levels of identity (national, Asian, or self-identity) affirmation, the most people who displayed prosocial attitudes in the game had been affirmed of their national identity.

In-group Declared Guilt

How about group-based guilt? It was found across all participants that prosociality was positively related to perceived guilt Japanese participants reported in the game after they were told it was not themselves but another in-group member (i.e., a fellow Japanese participant concurrently playing the game) who had withdrawn too many resources from the common pot, thus harming the Chinese or South Korean counterpart group (B = .888, exp(B) = 2.429, p < .01). It can thus be interpreted that NIA increased a concern for fairness to others (or in other words, prosocial tendencies), which boosted acknowledge guilt regarding an in-group member's action as well (B = .005, exp(B).995, p = .979). In other words, prosocial tendencies

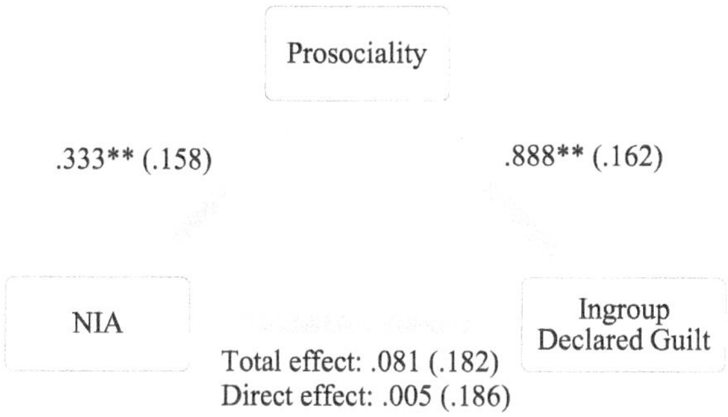

Figure 17

```
                  Prosociality

    .333** (.158)              .888** (.162)


    NIA                          Ingroup
                              Declared Guilt
          Total effect: .081 (.182)
          Direct effect: .005 (.186)
```

Figure 17. Prosocial attitudes mediate NIA and reported in-group guilt in game. Source: Eunbin Chung

mediated NIA and group-based declared guilt. These results are illustrated in figure 17.

Besides NIA, other types of affirmation and opponent nationality did not make a difference in prosociality.

In the mediation analyses so far, it can be observed that NIA increases prosocial attitudes, which then boosts subjective and behavioral guilt. All of these mediation analyses were conducted on the overall sample of Japanese, that is, where participants who were paired with Chinese and South Korean counterparts were combined.

The next step is to examine whether these effects differed by opponent country, as well as whether other modes of affirmation had an effect. Unlike the tests on trust in chapter 4, in these guilt experiments in Japan I had included other modes of affirmation besides NIA, all in separate conditions. This allows for a rigorous examination of whether affirmation on other identity levels have similar or opposite effects (or any effect at all) in direct comparison to NIA.

Since in our mediation analyses NIA boosted guilt recognition across several measures of guilt *through* prosociality, I conducted tests with prosociality as the dependent variable and opponent country and different types of affirmation as predictors. In order to study whether the effect NIA differed depending on the opponent country, I created an interaction variable of the different levels of affirmation and opponent country. Table 14 summarizes these results.

It can be seen above that across the different conditions of affirmation, only NIA had a significant and positive correlation with prosociality. In addition, the interaction variable of NIA and opponent country was not

128 Pride, Not Prejudice

TABLE 14. NIA as predictor of prosocial attitudes (simple model)

Prosocial Attitudes	B	SE	Wald	Exp(B)
Affirmation				
National Identity Affirmation (NIA)	.693	.273	6.422	1.999*
Asia-Affirmation (AA)	.183	.277	.439	1.201
Self-Affirmation (SA)	.341	.269	1.613	1.407
Opponent (South Korean)	–.149	.259	.329	.862
Affirmation X Opponent				
NIA X South Korean Opponent	–.263	.379	.481	.769
AA X South Korean Opponent	.625	.398	2.468	1.869
SA X South Korean Opponent	–.195	.369	.278	.823
Constant	.365	.184	3.924	1.440*
χ^2	17.591	p = .014		
Nagelkerke R^2	.025			

Note: Logistic regression, ** indicates statistical significance at the 1 percent level, * significant at the 5 percent level, † significant at the 10 percent level.

significant, indicating that the effect of NIA on prosociality did not vary by the opponent country that was paired with Japanese participants.

In order to control for demographic variables, I also estimated a longer model that included measurements of participants' gender, education, age, and political ideology. See table 15 for these results.

Again, even when controlling for basic demographics, only NIA had a significant and positive effect on prosociality, across all different types of affirmation. Also, the opponent country Japanese were paired with did

TABLE 15. NIA as predictor of prosocial attitudes (long model)

Prosocial Attitudes	B	SE	Wald	Exp(B)
Affirmation				
National Identity Affirmation (NIA)	1.011	.324	9.759	2.747**
Asia-Affirmation (AA)	.297	.310	.914	1.347
Self-Affirmation (SA)	.398	.306	1.688	1.488
Opponent (South Korean)	.130	.300	.186	1.138
Affirmation X Opponent				
NIA X South Korean Opponent	–.832	.445	3.493	.435
AA X Korean Opponent	.480	.455	1.116	1.617
SA X South Korean Opponent	–.668	.427	2.441	.513
Gender (Male)	–.510	.161	10.059	.601**
Education	–.047	.089	.287	.954
Age	.018	.006	9.542	1.018**
Political Ideology (Liberal)	.248	.178	1.944	1.281
Constant	.086	.441	.038	1.090
χ^2	36.409	p = .000		
Nagelkerke R^2	.065			

Note: Logistic regression, ** indicates statistical significance at the 1 percent level, * significant at the 5 percent level, † significant at the 10 percent level.

not make a difference in the effect of NIA on prosociality, meaning that Japanese did not respond significantly differently to Chinese counterparts compared to South Korean counterparts.

When controlling for simple demographics, the positive effect of NIA on prosociality appeared to actually be even stronger. Compared to participants who were not affirmed at all, which was the baseline, Japanese who were affirmed of their national identity were almost three times more likely to divide resources between themselves and a Chinese or South Korean opponent in a prosocial way. Here the group of participants who were in the control condition were not affirmed at all of any level of identity, and instead completed a different task with a similar structure to the affirmation task but completely irrelevant in substance. Borrowing from the nonaffirmation task used by Critcher, Dunning, and Armor (2010), the participants not to be affirmed were asked to choose from a list of exotically named jellybeans that they imagined to be tastiest and write a short essay to explain their choice.

The study was conducted on a sample representative by gender and age group, with the participants' ages ranging from twenty to sixty-nine, with a median age of forty-seven. In our model, age was also significant, as older participants were slightly more likely to be generous to their counterparts. At first glance, this might seem counterintuitive, as the older generation of Japanese have more salient memories of past war and colonialism in Asia. However, this finding actually supports the context and assumption of tests on in-group guilt that follow later in this chapter. The younger generation of Japanese people have often expressed a sense of fatigue over Chinese and South Koreans' repeated demands for reparation, particularly with regard to the fact that they are held guilty "by association" for action their ancestors committed several decades ago. If this fatigue existed in the younger Japanese in my sample, it could be that the nationality of people they were told they were paired with in the game acted as a cue that invoked some frustration or discontent that prompted participants against playing the game in prosocial ways. In addition, the older generation who were more directly involved in past atrocities might be more remorseful as they feel a closer personal connection or responsibility to the turbulent past.

As can be predicted based on existing research on prosocial and proself tendencies, participants' gender made a significant difference, as females tended to exhibit more prosocial attitudes (Crick and Grotpeter 1995). However, unlike previous studies that find political liberals act in more prosocial ways (Kertzer and Rathbun 2015), I did not find here a significant relation between political ideology and prosociality.

Declared Guilt and Prosocial Attitudes

This section provides an in-depth analysis of both measures of declared guilt—personal and group-based. Specifically, I focus on the relationship between prosociality and the guilt measures, both in the overall sample as well as in each subgroup paired with either a Chinese or South Korean opponent in the game. I find various results that challenge game theoretic predictions of the rational choice model, and discuss their implications.

We start by observing the distribution of personal declared guilt, summarized in table 16. When told they had personally taken too many points in the game, roughly 80 percent of the sample reported some or a lot of personal guilt for this, while about 20 percent reported that they personally felt no guilt at all. Noticing this, one might question whether those who reported no guilt at all did so because they were aware they actually only played the game in prosocial ways. In this scenario, a completely fair distribution of points in the game would not necessarily cause any personal guilt. However, the cross-tabulation table below (table 17) demonstrates that people who played the game in prosocial ways actually reported more guilt, while those who maximized self-interested gain reported less guilt. This held across the overall sample, and in each of the sample subgroups where participants were matched with Chinese and South Korean counterparts.

Furthermore, Mann-Whitney tests indicated that prosociality in the game was in fact very strongly and positively associated with more personal declared guilt (U = 66056.5, p = .000) *and* in-group declared guilt (U = 78107.5, p = .000). In other words, it was the prosocial players, or people who were fair and gave more points to their counterparts in the game compared to proself-type people, who actually admitted more guilt. This held for both personal and in-group declared guilt, as well as in the overall sample and in each of the groups matched with South Korean and Chinese opponents. Table 17 categorizes the results on personal declared guilt. Figure 18 plots the number of prosocial and proself players by how much personal guilt they declared.

TABLE 16. Number of people who reported no guilt, some guilt, or a lot of guilt following personal action in the game

	Self-Report of Perceived Personal Guilt	N
Personal Declared Guilt in Game	No Guilt	138
	Some Guilt	615
	A Lot of Guilt	189

TABLE 17. People who exhibited prosocial attitudes reported more personal declared guilt in overall sample, and in samples matched with Chinese and South Korean counterparts each

		\multicolumn{6}{c}{Social Preference (SP) (Prosocial, Proself)}
		\multicolumn{2}{c}{Overall Sample}	\multicolumn{2}{c}{Chinese Counterpart}	\multicolumn{2}{c}{South Korean Counterpart}
Personal Declared Guilt (PDG)		Prosocial	Proself	Prosocial	Proself	Prosocial	Proself
No Guilt	% within PDG	34.1	65.9	37.3	62.7	31.0	69.0
	% within SP	7.7	27.5	8.1	27.1	7.3	27.8
Some Guilt	% within PDG	64.1	35.9	65.9	34.1	62.2	37.8
	% within SP	64.5	66.8	66.3	68.4	62.6	65.3
A Lot of Guilt	% within PDG	89.9	10.1	91.9	8.1	88.3	11.7
	% within SP	27.8	5.7	25.6	4.5	30.1	6.8
Total	% within PDG	64.9	35.1	66.6	33.4	63.2	36.8
	% within SP	100.0	100.0	100.0	100.0	100.0	100.0
Mann-Whitney Test	U	\multicolumn{2}{c}{66056.5}	\multicolumn{2}{c}{15926.5}	\multicolumn{2}{c}{17014.5}
	p-value	\multicolumn{2}{c}{.000}	\multicolumn{2}{c}{.000}	\multicolumn{2}{c}{.000}

Similar findings hold between prosocial players and in-group declared guilt. Table 18 shows the distribution of people who reported no or some in-group guilt.

Interestingly, a comparison between tables 16 and 18 reveals that a larger proportion of the sample reported in-group declared guilt compared to personal declared guilt; 80 percent of the sample reported some or a lot of guilt for personally taking too many points, while 86 percent of the sample declared some or a lot of guilt when they were told another group member overdrew from the pot.

TABLE 18. Number of people who reported no guilt, some guilt, or a lot of guilt following in-group member's action in the game

	Self-Report of Perceived In-group Guilt	N
In-group Declared Guilt in Game	No Guilt	204
	Some Guilt	594
	A Lot of Guilt	133

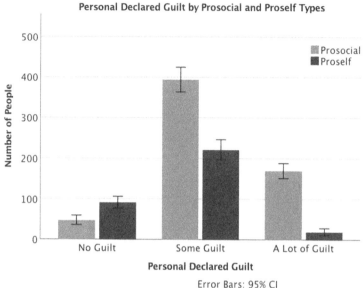

Figure 18. Prosocial players reported more personal declared guilt than proself players (overall sample). Source: Eunbin Chung.

As with personal declared guilt, people who played the game in prosocial ways actually reported more in-group guilt, while those who maximized self-interested gain reported less guilt even when they were told an in-group member's selfish action in the game had hurt the out-group. Cross-tabulation and Mann-Whitney test results in table 19 demonstrate that this finding held across the overall sample, and in each of the sample subgroups where participants were matched with Chinese and South Korean counterparts. Figure 19 plots the number of prosocial and proself players by how much in-group guilt they declared.

Tables 17 and 19 organize the number of prosocial and proself players according to the level of declared personal and in-group guilt they reported. Two things can be noted here. First, confirming the results of our statistical tests, people who acted in prosocial ways declared more guilt than proself players. Additionally, across both personal and in-group guilt measures, more proself than prosocial players declared that they felt absolutely no guilt at all for personal or in-group member's overdrawing from the common pool.

TABLE 19. Prosocial players reported more in-group declared guilt in overall sample, and in samples matched with Chinese and South Korean counterparts each

		Social Preference (SP) (Prosocial, Proself)					
		Overall Sample		Chinese Counterpart		South Korean Counterpart	
In-group Declared Guilt (IDG)		Prosocial	Proself	Prosocial	Proself	Prosocial	Proself
No Guilt	% within IDG	48.5	51.5	46.7	53.3	50.0	50.0
	% within SP	16.4	32.2	14.0	32.0	18.8	32.4
Some Guilt	% within IDG	67.3	32.7	70.4	29.6	64.1	35.9
	% within SP	66.1	59.5	70.4	59.5	61.7	59.5
A Lot of Guilt	% within IDG	79.7	20.3	78.7	21.3	80.6	19.4
	% within SP	17.5	8.3	15.6	8.5	19.5	8.1
Total	% within IDG	65.0	35.0	66.7	33.3	63.3	36.7
	% within SP	100.0	100.0	100.0	100.0	100.0	100.0
Mann-Whitney Test	U	78107.5		18473.5		20578.0	
	p-value	.000		.000		.000	

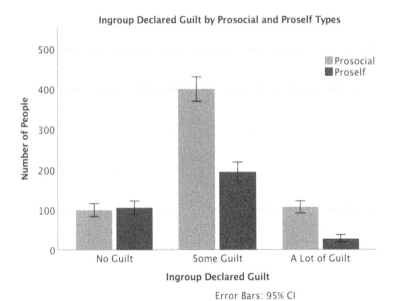

Figure 19. Prosocial players reported more in-group declared guilt than proself players (overall sample). Source: Eunbin Chung.

This might seem counterintuitive, since the proself players are those who played the game in selfish ways. However, we can be reminded here that such behavior is actually what is expected from a rational choice perspective. Traditional economic and game theory would expect all humans, in fact, to belong to this condition where people maximize their gains and report zero guilt for doing so.

In this sense, four findings here notably contradict predictions of the dominant rational choice model from a social science perspective. The first is that the number of prosocial players exceeded the number of proself players. This was true in the overall sample, as well as in each of the groups paired with a South Korean or Chinese opponent. A chi-square test found no significant difference between opponent country and prosociality ($\chi 2(1, N = 931) = 38.37, p = .311$). In other words, Japanese' prosociality did not differ depending on the country their opponents were from. The exact numbers in each condition can be found in the contingency table (table 20). Second, more than 80 percent of people across all conditions of declared guilt settings reported some level of guilt above zero. Third, interestingly, people who behaved in fair ways to their opponents were actually the ones who reported more guilt than proself players. Fourth, more than 85 percent of people reported guilt for something they themselves never even did. These people admitted guilt just by the fact that they shared the same national identity with someone else who was said to have committed an act that harmed an out-group. The participants did not even personally know this person at all; in fact, they were given no information other than the fact that the person was Japanese.

These various findings lead us to question the rational choice model's validity and connection to reality. It can be supposed for example that the purely self-interested and perfectly calculative prototype of human cogni-

TABLE 20. Prosociality did not depend on opponent nationality

Opponent Country (OC)		Social Preference (SP) (Prosocial, Proself)		
		Prosocial	Proself	Total
South Korean	% within OC	63.0	37.0	100.0
	% within SP	49.7	53.1	50.9
Chinese	% within OC	66.1	33.9	100.0
	% within SP	50.3	46.9	49.1
Total	% within OC	64.5		35.5
	% within SP		100.0	100.0
Chi-square Test	$\chi 2$			1.025
	df			1
	p-value			.311

tion and behavior assumed by rationalist models refer to a certain type of smaller subgroup within the population. In fact, judging from the proportion of prosocial versus proself performances in my study, rational choice might be the exception of human behavior rather than the norm, or a particular mode of action that rarely surfaces.

In the next section, I prepare my analyses for revealed guilt. I start by first examining revealed guilt in both personal and in-group settings before using them as dependent variables.

Declared Guilt and Revealed Guilt Go Hand in Hand

Having examined declared (personal and in-group) guilt, we now prepare to move on to our study of revealed guilt. Before doing so, however, this section helps us with the transition. I explain my findings here that declared guilt, measured by survey questions on the level of guilt subjects subjectively felt, was directly connected to behaviorally revealed guilt, represented by the amount subjects were willing to pay from their own pot of money (points) to the other in the dictator game. Therefore it can be inferred that the amount sent back in the dictator games is an accurate behavioral proxy of and directly related to perceived guilt. In other words, the subjective measure of declared guilt and behavioral measure of revealed guilt went together hand in hand.

In the game, those who reported more guilt for their own behavior also sent back larger amounts of points in the following dictator game. Likewise, the reported guilt for an in-group member's behavior was a strong predictor for the amount sent back to make up for the harm caused by a fellow in-group member. Recall that this amount of money was coming from what participants were told to perceive as a personal pot. It is noteworthy that players who felt very guilty for an in-group member's deed were willing to pay out of their individual pot of money to make up for this. Table 21 and figure 20 summarize this finding.

After playing the game in the survey, participants were told they overdrew from the common pool of resources shared by themselves and their opponent, thus harming the opponent. At this point, survey questions measured how much guilt the subjects felt for this. Table 16 presents the distribution of participants' responses to the survey questions.

Results of a linear regression of personal revealed guilt on personal declared guilt find that revealed guilt increased hand in hand with declared guilt. That is, the stronger dose of guilt subjects reported in survey responses, the more likely they were to offer larger amounts out of their

TABLE 21. Linear regression: declared guilt (survey questions) and revealed guilt (amount given back in dictator game) following personal action

Personal Revealed Guilt	Coef (SE)
No Guilt (Baseline)	0
Some Guilt	.016**
	(.001)
A Lot of Guilt	.023**
	(.002)
Constant	.015**
	(.001)
N	942
R^2	.182

Note: Linear regression, robust standard errors in parentheses. ** Indicates statistical significance at the 1 percent level, * significant at the 5 percent level, † significant at the 10 percent level.

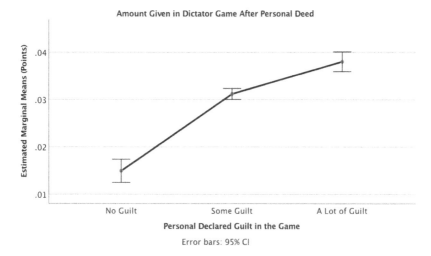

Figure 20. People who admitted more guilt for their personal action sent back more in the following dictator game. Source: Eunbin Chung.

virtual points to their opponent player to make up for the opponent's loss in the game. Table 21 presents the results of the regression analysis, and figure 20 graphs personal revealed guilt by personal declared guilt, based on the findings in table 21. In both figures the dependent variable, or personal revealed guilt, was rescaled to range from 0 to 1 for ease of comparison. Before rescaling the variable, its possible range was from 0 to 500 points.

I found very similar results analyzing in-group declared and revealed guilt as well. The two measures were very strongly and positively correlated.

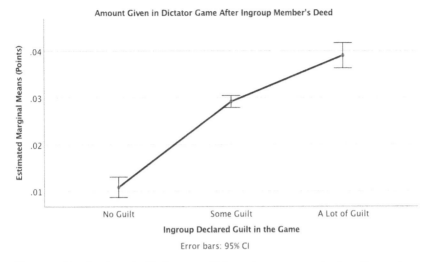

Figure 21. People who admitted more guilt for an in-group member's action sent back more in the following dictator game. Source: Eunbin Chung

Just like in the case with personal guilt, in-group revealed guilt appeared to be a reasonable proxy for in-group declared guilt as well. It can be seen from table 22 that the amount participants gave back to their opponents following an in-group member's overdraw grew proportionally to how much guilt they reported for the group member's action. This finding is graphed in figure 21.

The amounts sent back in the dictator games were accurate representations of perceived guilt, both in the personal guilt condition and group-based guilt condition. The amount participants paid back in the dictator

TABLE 22. Linear regression: declared guilt (survey questions) and revealed guilt (amount given back in dictator game) following in-group member's action

In-group Revealed Guilt	Coef (SE)
No Guilt (Baseline)	0
Some Guilt	.018**
	(.001)
A Lot of Guilt	.028**
	(.002)
Constant	.011**
	(.001)
N	931
R^2	.241

Note: Linear regression, robust standard errors in parentheses. ** Indicates statistical significance at the 1 percent level, * significant at the 5 percent level, † significant at the 10 percent level.

game increased proportionally to reported personal guilt. Likewise, the amount paid back in the dictator game after an in-group member's harm was proportional to the reported guilt for an in-group member's action. Therefore my behavioral measure of guilt and willingness to compensate appear to be a reasonable measure of guilt, especially considering that subjects were told that the compensation was to be made directly from their own personal resources in the game.

Revealed Guilt

Just as with declared guilt, prosociality mediated NIA and revealed guilt. That is, NIA induced prosocial tendencies, which were positively associated with revealed guilt. The mediation analyses still held when the dependent variable of interest from the previous mediation was changed to the amount of virtual tokens participants offered in the dictator game following a personal overdraw from the common pot of resources (B = .386, CI = .074 to .739), as well as the amount participants offered in the dictator game after they were told another Japanese player had overdrawn (B = .339, CI = .096 to .658). Each of these amounts in the dictator games can be seen as a behavioral proxy for perceived personal guilt and in-group guilt, respectively. In other words, the power of NIA extended beyond just personal guilt participants declared they felt after their own deed, into reported guilt regarding another in-group member's acts, *and* a willingness to take action for these feelings of guilt. Although this was a simulated game, these findings indicate that participants were willing to behaviorally draw out of their own resources to pay back more to a counterpart following both personal and an in-group member's deeds.

Ideally, the game would have been truly interactive, had the logistics of the environment of the experiment allowed that to be possible. But if the simulated nature of the game had rendered the game ineffective, then we would not likely see these striking and consistent effects of NIA across the various measures of guilt. Figure 22 combines the mediation analyses across the two measures of revealed guilt (personal and group-based) to summarize them into one figure.

Figures 23 and 24 present the mean amount of personal and in-group revealed guilt prosocial and proself players reported, across the samples paired each with South Korean and Chinese counterparts. The revealed guilt on the y-axis is represented by the number of points participants sent back to their counterparts in the dictator game. It is noticeable that across

National Identity and Guilt Recognition 139

```
                              .009** (.001)    ┌─────────────┐
                                               │  Personal   │
                                               │Revealed Guilt│
                                               └─────────────┘
           .333* (.158)
┌─────┐                  ┌─────────────┐
│ NIA │                  │ Prosociality│
└─────┘                  └─────────────┘
                                               ┌─────────────┐
                                               │   Ingroup   │
                              .008** (.001)    │Revealed Guilt│
                                               └─────────────┘
```

Figure 22. Prosocial attitudes mediate NIA and revealed (personal and in-group) guilt in game. Source: Eunbin Chung.

the conditions, those who played the distribution game with greater concern for others also returned more back in the later dictator game when they were told the opponent or out-group had been hurt in the game.

Table 23 displays results of several linear regression tests. People who exhibited prosocial attitudes in the distribution game reported more personal and in-group revealed guilt for a personal or in-group member's act, respectively, that harmed the opponent or opponent's group.

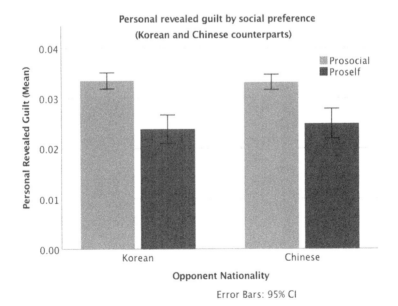

Figure 23. Prosocial players reported more personal revealed guilt. Source: Eunbin Chung.

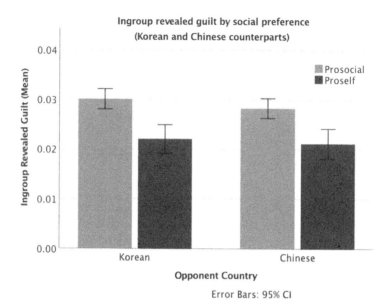

Figure 24. Prosocial players reported more in-group revealed guilt. Source: Eunbin Chung.

TABLE 23. Prosociality was positively associated with personal and in-group revealed guilt

	Personal Revealed Guilt			In-group Revealed Guilt		
	Overall Sample	South Korean Counterpart	Chinese Counterpart	Overall Sample	South Korean Counterpart	Chinese Counterpart
Variables	Coef (SE)			Coef (SE)		
Prosocial	.009**	.024**	.008**	.008**	.008**	.007**
	(.001)	(.001)	(.001)	(.001)	(.002)	(.002)
Constant	.024**	.024**	.025**	.022**	.022**	.021**
	(.001)	(.001)	(.001)	(.001)	(.001)	(.001)
N	942	478	464	931	471	460
R^2	.071	.079	.062	.039	.044	.035

Note: Linear regression, ** indicates statistical significance at the 1 percent level, * significant at the 5 percent level, † significant at the 10 percent level.

From the various positive outcomes of prosociality we have observed, it should be noted that NIA was a strong initiator of prosociality. Synthesizing our findings on guilt so far, it can be summarized that NIA boosted prosocial tendencies, which led to increased guilt. Prosociality is thus a mechanism through which NIA works to influence guilt. In my experiments, prosocial subjects in the game reported more guilt and paid their counterpart more—even after they had treated their counterpart more fairly than proself players. The self-reports of guilt, or declared guilt, were responses to survey questions asking whether participants felt guilt either for a personal deed (as a measure of personal guilt) or an in-group member's deed (as a measure of group-based guilt). The paid amount to counterparts represented revealed (personal or in-group) guilt.

Interestingly, prosocial players played the game in more fair ways to the other and still reported more guilt when told they did harm to the other. Furthermore, prosocial players were willing to pay more back to make up for that harm—even though those prosocial players in fact would have caused the least harm. On the other hand, proself players played the game to maximize self-interest, reported less guilt for doing that, and were willing to pay less back for any harm their selfish actions may have caused the other.

In the results so far, there were not huge differences between how personal and in-group guilt operate. Despite their conceptual distinctions, it was found that NIA and prosocial tendencies work together in similar ways to affect both personal and in-group guilt. In the next section, I focus on the differences between the two types of guilt.

A prime issue that recurs in policy circles in Japan as well as discussions in international discourse with Chinese and South Koreans is whether present-day Japanese need to pay for their country's past. Some younger generation Japanese refer to this as a "guilt by association" fallacy, pressuring current Japanese to repair actions committed by their great grandfathers many years ago. However, group-based guilt that claims validity over several generations is not unheard of in other areas of the world. German remembrance of its international relations history, for example, reinforces salience of past atrocities and urges present and future generations to be aware of the continuing responsibility to keep alive today's difficultly gained peace based on harsh lessons from the past (Lind 2008).

In-group and Personal Guilt

Subjects who acted in prosocial ways declared higher guilt due to a personal deed as well as an in-group member's deed. Prosociality in the game was also a strong predictor of the payback amount in the dictator game for personal guilt, and following guilt caused by an in-group member's act. This implies that declared and revealed guilt were connected, and the two can be reliable indicators of each other—the guiltier subjects feel, the more they are willing to pay their opponent or opponent's group from their own pot of money. If declared and revealed guilt go hand in hand in so many ways, what are some differences between the two? I find that linked fate was significantly associated with all measures of in-group guilt but had no relevance to personal guilt across any conditions.

Included in my survey were questions aimed at gauging participants' beliefs in the concept of linked fate. Linked fate was measured by combining the responses to the following questions: "How strongly do you feel what happens to Japan in general is related to your own fate?" and "When someone speaks badly about Japan, how strongly do you feel they are speaking badly about you?"

Consistent with my hypotheses, those who held stronger beliefs in linked fate also declared more guilt for something an in-group member did, even when the respondent herself had no personal responsibility. Japanese people who reported that what happened to their nation was directly significant for their individual destiny, i.e., held a strong belief in linked fate, acknowledged guilt for other Japanese people's deeds that may have harmed the well-being of other groups. These findings on in-group and personal declared guilt are reported in table 24.

Notably, these effects held across both samples with South Korean and Chinese counterparts, indicating the robustness of these findings. When focusing on individual declared guilt for a personal deed, linked fate did

TABLE 24. Declared guilt due to in-group member's action vs. my action in the game: overall sample

Variables	In-group Declared Guilt			Personal Declared Guilt		
	B	SE	Exp(B)	B	SE	Exp(B)
Prosocial	.955	.193	2.599**	1.530	.239	4.619**
Linked Fate	.257	.099	1.293*	.157	.117	1.170
Gender (Male)	−.767	.202	.464**	−.993	.258	.370**
Education	−.037	.108	.964	−.093	.135	.911
Age	.002	.007	1.002	−.003	.008	.997
Political Ideology (Liberal)	−.219	.207	.803	.033	.257	1.034
Constant	1.359	.487	3.894	2.117	.604	8.307
χ^2	61.640	p = .000		73.146	p = .000	
Nagelkerke R^2	.126			.174		

Note: Logistic regression, ** indicates statistical significance at the 1 percent level, * significant at the 5 percent level, † significant at the 10 percent level.

TABLE 25. Declared guilt due to in-group member's action vs. my action in the game: sample with South Korean opponents only

	In-group Declared Guilt			Personal Declared Guilt		
Variables	B	SE	Exp(B)	B	SE	Exp(B)
Prosocial	.739	.263	2.095 **	1.468	.343	4.341 **
Linked Fate	.120	.058	1.128*	.188	.158	1.207
Gender (Male)	−.716	.270	.489**	−1.386	.382	.250**
Education	−.132	.150	.876	−.189	.202	.828
Age	.009	.009	1.009	.011	.012	1.011
Political Ideology (Liberal)	.015	.287	1.015	.489	.391	1.631
Constant	.216	.827	1.242	2.192	.897	8.951
χ^2	24.582	p = .000		47.248	p = .000	
Nagelkerke R^2	.098			.220		

Note: Logistic regression, ** indicates statistical significance at the 1 percent level, * significant at the 5 percent level, † significant at the 10 percent level.

not matter, unlike when declared guilt for a fellow in-group member's deed was measured. Table 25 shows that these findings still hold when just focusing on participants matched with a South Korean counterpart: Japanese who acted in prosocial ways in the game and who believed in the idea of linked fate declared more guilt for a deed committed by a fellow in-group member. However, linked fate did not matter in the recognition of personal guilt.

Results for just the sample paired with a Chinese counterpart are summarized in table 26.

TABLE 26. Declared guilt due to in-group member's action vs. my action in the game: sample with Chinese opponents only

	In-group Declared Guilt			Personal Declared Guilt		
Variables	B	SE	Exp(B)	B	SE	Exp(B)
Prosocial	1.220	.294	3.387**	1.603	.340	4.970 **
Linked Fate	.351	.161	1.421*	.110	.175	1.117
Gender (Male)	−.947	.319	.388**	−.649	.360	.523†
Education	.094	.161	1.099	−.008	.189	.992
Age	.009	.009	1.009	−.015	.012	.985
Political Ideology (Liberal)	−.483	.306	.617	−.300	.350	.741
Constant	1.430	.735	4.179	2.067	.855	7.903
χ^2	45.442	p = .000		34.869	p = .000	
Nagelkerke R^2	.191			.168		

Note: Logistic regression, ** indicates statistical significance at the 1 percent level, * significant at the 5 percent level, † significant at the 10 percent level.

These findings on linked fate also applied to revealed guilt, represented by the number of virtual tokens Japanese participants sent back in the dictator game. Beliefs in linked fate had no effect on personal guilt but was strongly associated with group-based revealed guilt. That is, when respondents were asked to draw from their own virtual pot of resources to make up for another Japanese action that harmed the out-group, those who believed their fate was closely connected to their nation expressed more group-based guilt and also gave more resources to make up for this.

Table 27 summarizes these findings. The difference between personal and in-group revealed guilt is strikingly similar to that in the analysis of personal and in-group declared guilt. Again, linked fate had no significant effect across any of the samples—the overall sample or the group of Japanese paired with a Chinese or South Korean counterpart each. The distribution of both in-group and personal revealed guilt appeared close to normal, allowing for multiple linear regression analyses. In the actual game, respondents had the option of returning 0 to 500 virtual tokens back to their opponents in the dictator game. For convenience of comparison, in this analysis the dependent variables as well as the combined variable of linked fate were scaled to range from 0 to 1.

In the overall sample as well as in each of the samples where participants were paired with a Chinese and South Korean counterpart, linked fate was a significant predictor of in-group revealed guilt. That is, the more participants believed their destiny was critically connected to the nation of the whole (i.e., believed in the idea of continuity in the nation), the more

TABLE 27. Revealed personal and in-group guilt, simple model

	In-group Revealed Guilt			Personal Revealed Guilt		
	Overall sample	South Korean counterpart	Chinese counterpart	Overall sample	South Korean counterpart	Chinese counterpart
Variables	Coef (SE)			Coef (SE)		
Prosocial	.008**	.008**	.007**	.009**	.010**	.009**
	(.001)	(.002)	(.002)	(.001)	(.002)	(.002)
Linked Fate	.009**	.007†	.012**	.002	.000	.004
	(.003)	(.004)	(.004)	(.002)	(.003)	(.003)
Constant	.018**	.019**	.016**	.023**	.023**	.023**
	(.002)	(.002)	(.002)	(.001)	(.002)	(.002)
N	923	467	456	923	467	456
R^2	.051	.050	.055	.077	.087	.068

Note: Linear regression, ** indicates statistical significance at the 1 percent level, * significant at the 5 percent level, † significant at the 10 percent level.

TABLE 28. Revealed personal and in-group guilt with controls

	In-group Revealed Guilt			Personal Revealed Guilt		
	Overall sample	South Korean counterpart	Chinese counterpart	Overall sample	South Korean counterpart	Chinese counterpart
Variables	Coef (SE)			Coef (SE)		
Prosocial	.007**	.007**	.007**	.008**	.008**	.008**
	(.001)	(.002)	(.002)	(.001)	(.002)	(.002)
Linked Fate	.009**	.005	.014**	.002	−.001	.005
	(.003)	(.004)	(.005)	(.003)	(.004)	(.004)
Age	.004	.006	.001	.001	−.001	.003
	(.003)	(.004)	(.004)	(.002)	(.003)	(.003)
Gender (Male)	.004**	.005*	.003	.003*	.002	.003*
	(.001)	(.002)	(.002)	(.001)	(.002)	(.002)
Education	−.002	.001	−.004	−.004	−.009†	.000
	(.004)	(.005)	(.005)	(.003)	(.005)	(.004)
Pol Ideology (Lib)	−.001	−.001	−.001	−.001	−.001	.000
	(.001)	(.002)	(.002)	(.001)	(.002)	(.002)
Constant	.012**	.011**	.013**	.023**	.029**	.017**
	(.004)	(.006)	(.006)	(.004)	(.006)	(.004)
N	733	367	366	735	367	366
R^2	.065	.062	.078	.080	.082	.088

Note: Linear regression, ** indicates statistical significance at the 1 percent level, * significant at the 5 percent level, † significant at the 10 percent level.

they were willing to pay from their own pot of virtual tokens to their counterpart to compensate for an in-group member's deed.

These results hold when controlling for demographics as well. See table 28 for these results. Age and education were also scaled to range from 0 to 1 to for convenience of comparison.

The findings from the simple model held in general when the demographic controls were included as well. Perceptions of linked fate significantly predicted in-group revealed guilt in the overall sample, as well as in the subgroup of Japanese whose guilt toward Chinese was measured. The exception in this model was the sample compared with a South Korean counterpart. In this case linked fate was not significant for in-group revealed guilt, which appears to be related to the fact that it was only mildly significant (p=.066) in the simple model.

As noted, however, when measuring personal revealed guilt, linked fate had no effect across all samples.

To summarize the findings on guilt, NIA led to prosocial attitudes, which then increased guilt admission for both personal and in-group member's actions. This held in the overall sample as well as in each of the country conditions (where the opponent was Chinese and South Korean). This suggests that affirmation of national identity indeed allows people to become more open to concern for others, helping them recognize guilt in a more objective way without becoming defensive, or without hurting the in-group's self-esteem. Besides NIA, the rank order of the effects of self-affirmation and Asia affirmation were mixed and their effects were not statistically significant.

Linked fate did also have a role in guilt recognition, but as hypothesized this only held for guilt they felt for an act of harm someone else from their country committed. In other words, the effect of linked fate on guilt was limited in scope compared to NIA, as it did not apply to direct guilt perceptions regarding something subjects themselves did shortly ago.

Prosocial attitudes induced by NIA was a strong predictor for personal guilt, in-group guilt, and historical guilt. The effect of NIA on guilt can rage widely across context, including personal action in a game setting, a fellow Japanese member's deeds, and questions regarding the actual histories between Japan and its neighbors. Considering questions on the historical context are much more sensitive and difficult compared to those in game settings, the fact that NIA can have an effect here is striking and holds important policy implications. More on historical guilt follows below.

5.3.3 Historical Guilt

To measure actual guilt Japanese respondents felt toward China or South Korea regarding their own history, I combined six items measuring personal perceived guilt, regret, responsibility, compensation will, and the need for apology using a confirmatory factor analysis to create a new, latent guilt variable. Table 29 shows the items that were combined to construct the latent variable. Each of the statements were carefully tailored to connect participants' individual responsibility with their country's past deeds regarding its neighbor countries.

NIA boosts prosocial tendencies, which increases historical guilt recognition.

Importantly and surprisingly, the effect of NIA on guilt was extensive enough to reach beyond contexts of the behavioral game in the experiment. Mediation analyses found prosocial tendencies were positively correlated with reported historical guilt (B = .342, t(918) = 5.014, p < .01). Prosociality mediated NIA and how much guilt Japanese felt for their country's history

TABLE 29. Historical guilt factor analysis

6 items, order randomized. α = 0.83	Factor Loadings
Q1 When I think about things Japanese have done during the war, I sometimes feel guilty.	0.737
Q2 Japanese are not responsible for the bad outcomes received by Chinese/Koreans at the time of WWII (reverse coded).	0.572
Q3 I feel regrettable for the negative things that Japan has done to Chinese/Koreans in the past.	0.717
Q4 I believe I should help repair the damage caused to Chinese/Koreans by my country.	0.784
Q5 Japan has already done enough to compensate for its past (reverse coded).	0.601
Q6 There is no reason for Japan to apologize to countries like China/South Korea now (reverse coded).	0.751

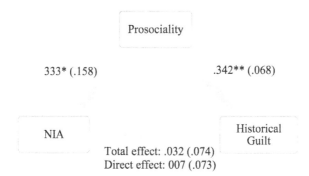

Figure 25. Prosocial attitudes mediate NIA and declared in-group guilt in game
Mediation with indirect effect. Numbers represent unstandardized beta coefficients, with standard errors in parentheses. **Indicates statistical significance at the 1 percent level, *significant at the 5 percent level, †significant at the 10 percent level. Source: Eunbin Chung.

(B = .007, t(918) = .091, p = .927). This finding has the most direct policy implications of NIA for guilt recognition in East Asia. Figure 25 displays the results.

NIA had a significant positive effect on increasing prosociality. In the measure of historical guilt, much like our previous analyses on guilt in the game, the effect of prosociality was strong. The positive boosting effect for prosociality on historical guilt held consistently in each of the subsamples paired with South Korean and Chinese counterparts as well. Figure 26 graphs how much historical guilt was reported by prosocial and proself

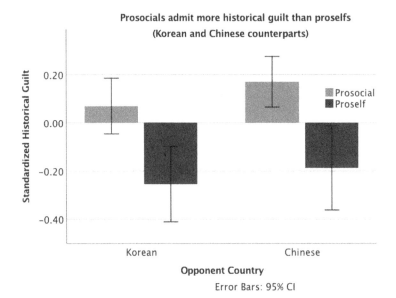

Figure 26. Prosocial attitudes and historical guilt, by opponent nationality. Source: Eunbin Chung.

players. The reason there are negative values of historical guilt on the y-axis is because the dependent variable of historical guilt was standardized, so that its mean was 0 and standard deviation equaled 1.

It is clear from figure 26 that when Japanese were asked about their historical guilt toward Korea and China, people who exhibited prosocial attitudes in the game also reported more historical guilt. Those who played the game to maximize self-interested gain reported less guilt regarding Japan's history with Korea or China.

As reported in table 30, participants who played the game in prosocial ways responded that they held more guilt toward South Korea or China regarding Japan's interaction with those countries. As might be expected, another significant variable was political ideology, as Japanese who self-identified as liberal also reported more historical guilt. An interesting contrast is found here between the tests on historical guilt and guilt in the game, as political ideology did not have a significant effect on declared or revealed guilt in the game.

TABLE 30. Prosocial people report more historical guilt in overall sample as well as South Korean/Chinese counterpart conditions

Historical Guilt	Overall sample	South Korean counterpart	Chinese counterpart
		Coef (SE)	
Prosocial	.346**	.284*	.261*
	(.081)	(.113)	(.109)
Political Ideology (Liberal)	.346**	.311**	.382**
	(.081)	(.118)	(.112)
Age	.006	.004	.007
	(.003)	(.004)	(.004)
Gender (Male)	−.067	−.151	.016
	(.075)	(.109)	(.104)
Education	−.003	−.020	.024
	(.041)	(.061)	(.057)
Constant	−.402	−.298	−.561*
	(.189)	(.277)	(.261)
N	731	367	364
R^2	.056	.051	.068

Note: Linear regression, ** indicates statistical significance at the 1 percent level, * significant at the 5 percent level, † significant at the 10 percent level.

In-group guilt in the game was a predictor for historical guilt.

Table 31 shows the results of a several linear regression tests that identify the relationship between guilt declared by participants regarding an in-group member's deed in the game and historical guilt (motivated by their ancestors' deeds). The dependent variable in the test is historical guilt.

Here Japanese who felt guilty even for another Japanese person's deed (as measured by answers to survey questions) were also the people who felt guilty for their past. These were the people who felt guilty for something their ancestors or contemporary in-group members had done, even if they themselves had not committed or been involved in the deed themselves.

In other words, participants who reported more in-group declared guilt also reported more historical guilt. It should be noted here that both in-group guilt and historical guilt are collective forms of guilt based on the social identity of the country. This is because the measure of in-group guilt in the game followed a statement to participants that a fellow Japanese, or an in-group member that shared the same *national* identity, had committed an act of harm toward the foreign out-group. Similarly, the statements used to measure historical guilt are aimed at gauging whether individual

TABLE 31. People who felt guilty for a fellow in-group member's action in the game also tended to report more historical guilt

Historical Guilt	Overall sample	South Korean counterpart	Chinese counterpart
		Coef (SE)	
In-group Declared Guilt in Game	.788** (.088)	.945** (.120)	.585** (.132)
Political Ideology (Liberal)	.363** (.078)	.315** (.109)	.432** (.112)
Age	.005 (.003)	.003 (.004)	.007 (.004)
Gender (Male)	−.016† (.072)	−.051 (.103)	.016 (.104)
Education	−.024 (.040)	−.003 (.057)	.024 (.057)
Constant	.001 (.177)	−.975** (.310)	−.561* (.261)
N	731	367	364
R²	.131	.177	.104

Note: Linear regression, ** indicates statistical significance at the 1 percent level, * significant at the 5 percent level, † significant at the 10 percent level.

Japanese respondents acknowledge some guilt for actions their country members took in the past.

Judging from the strong positive relationship between in-group guilt in the game and historical guilt, it appears that these people are of the type that perceives of a robust link between the self and membership in their country—or, in other words, a strong national identity. This directly supports this book's central argument that salient national identities are not an impediment to resolving conflict between people from different countries. In addition, it argues against the conventional wisdom that stresses the necessity of creating supranational identities in exchange for national identities. In terms of guilt recognition, affirming national identities increases international guilt by evoking prosocial attitudes. This finding sheds light on the feasibility and potential effectiveness of affirming national identities as a means to narrow the gap of disagreement on the degree of guilt recognition necessary between past inflictor and received states.

In the next section, as a final note to the results section, I end by reemphasizing an important part of the results that has significant policy implications for peace and conflict resolution in Asia.

NIA worked in the hardest case: boosting Japanese' prosociality and guilt recognition toward China.

The most noteworthy finding with meaningful policy relevance comes to focus when zooming in on the sample of Japanese subjects who were paired with a Chinese opponent. Why? Recall that Sino-Japanese relations are arguably the most difficult case among the six dyads of concern in this book. This section gives attention to results on the Japanese sample paired with Chinese counterparts to highlight how effective NIA can be in this "tough case" as well.

Scholars across a wide-range of international relations theories have argued that a rapidly rising China can be destabilizing from Japan's perspective. From the perspective of both offensive *and* defensive realists, China's rise is an uncomfortable one for Japan. Power transition and hegemonic stability theorists note that the challenge from a growing revisionist power would threaten the status-quo to take position as a new hegemon (Gilpin 1981, 1987; Gowa 1989; Keohane 1984; Kindleberger 1981, 1986; Krasner 1976; Organski 1958).

On a regional scale, the most powerful country and economic powerhouse in Northeast Asia was Japan for decades. Even when taking into consideration Japan's defeat in World War II and limits in military power written in the country's constitution, the security alliance with the United States and American forces in Okinawa had enabled an American-led order in Northeast Asia in cooperation with Japan. From a constructivist standpoint, Japan and the United States established a stable culture under the American security umbrella, forming a security community based on decades of cooperative societal interaction. China's political emergence, economic growth, and military expansion pose a challenge to this status-quo.

Perhaps reflecting this reality, Japanese subjects in my tests reported profound negative affect, i.e., strong dislike, against Chinese. Notice from the histograms in figure 27 how strongly hated China was in my surveys. Japanese respondents reported the strongest dislike against the Chinese, which was even worse than their dislike of Koreans. The median affect score is –24 out of a scale from –50 to +50 for Chinese, which is –18 for Koreans in contrast.

However, what is remarkable is that NIA still encouraged Japanese to behave in more prosocial ways toward their Chinese counterparts. This indicates that it is not necessary to change people to emotionally *like* oth-

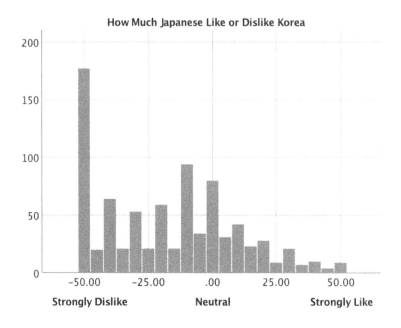

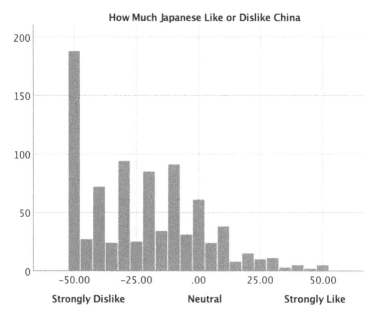

Figure 27. Japanese' reported affect levels toward South Korea and China. Source: Eunbin Chung.

National Identity and Guilt Recognition 153

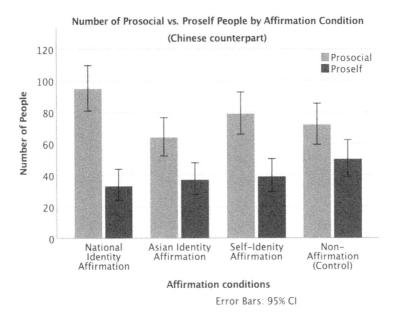

Figure 28. The NIA condition had the largest number of people exhibiting prosocial attitudes when paired with a Chinese counterpart. Source: Eunbin Chung.

ers first, but we can still achieve a sense of prosociality through affirmation. NIA corrects in-group-serving judgments and demolishes defensive reactions publics would otherwise easily exhibit toward citizens of other countries. In this way NIA leads to an increased fairness and concern for people in other countries.

This is visualized in figure 28. People in the national identity affirmation condition were most likely to distribute resources in a prosocial way to their Chinese opponent in the game.

Table 32 shows that Japanese who were affirmed of their national identity exhibited significantly more prosocial attitudes toward their Chinese counterparts in the game. According to the table, subjects who were affirmed of their national identity were most likely to engage in prosociality.

The same effects appeared in a model that controlled for demographic factors. Most remarkably, of all the different modes of identity affirmation, only national identity affirmation had a positive and significant effect on increasing prosociality toward Chinese people. Table 33 presents these results.

TABLE 32. Predictors of prosocial attitudes among Japanese with Chinese counterparts, simple model

Prosocial Attitudes	B	SE	Wald	Exp(B)
Affirmation				
National Identity Affirmation	.693	.273	6.422	1.999*
Asia-Affirmation	.183	.277	.439	1.201
Self-Affirmation	.183	.269	1.613	1.407
Constant	.365	.184	3.924	1.440
χ^2	45.442	p = .000		
Nagelkerke R^2	.191			

Note: Logistic regression, ** indicates statistical significance at the 1 percent level, * significant at the 5 percent level, † significant at the 10 percent level.

TABLE 33. Predictors of prosocial attitudes among Japanese with Chinese counterparts, with controls

Prosocial Attitudes	B	SE	Wald	Exp(B)
Affirmation				
National Identity Affirmation	1.029	.326	9.388	2.799**
Asia-Affirmation	.278	.313	.498	1.320
Self-Affirmation	.388	.309	1.078	1.474
Gender (Male)	−.777	.232	10.603	.460**
Education	−.002	.127	.087	.998
Age	.013	.008	2.417	1.013
Political Ideology (Liberal)	.083	.254	.111	1.086
Constant	.268	.597	.103	1.307
χ^2	45.442	p = .000		
Nagelkerke R^2	.191			

Note: Logistic regression, ** indicates statistical significance at the 1 percent level, * significant at the 5 percent level, † significant at the 10 percent level.

5.4 Conclusion

From examples of discrimination to genocide, very few countries have never at some point devalued, exploited, or persecuted another group, although the nature and severity may vary (Gunn and Wilson 2011). Scholars have noted that denials of past aggression or atrocities elevate fear and create tension between past adversaries (Čehajić-Clancy et al. 2011). In postconflict situations, citizens of countries that consider themselves victims of war or colonization often demand some acknowledgment of their suffering—either through monetary compensation, official apologies by leaders of the country that victims consider to be the past perpetrator, memorials, or mention in history books (Čehajić and Brown 2010; Cohen 2013; Gilbert 2001; Lederach 1997; Minow 1998; Tutu 1999).

However, facing up to actions inflicted by one's group is psychologically challenging. Just as with threats to personal identities, people defend against threats to their social identities. In the context of international conflict, such defensiveness undercuts collective guilt and its prosocial consequences (Gunn and Wilson 2011). Especially in a context where current generations are temporally distant from past acts of war and colonialism, reminders of injustices committed by one's past country members can prompt defensiveness or resentment about being unfairly accused (Branscombe and Miron 2004; Peetz, Gunn, and Wilson 2010; Sahdra and Ross 2007).

This study investigates the potential of national identity affirmation as a way of disarming the defensiveness that is prompted from recognizing guilt of one's country, allowing more prosocial responses to emerge. Affirming the national identities of all countries could be a more viable and appealing approach for national leaders who wish to obtain the benefit of international cooperation with a past adversary but are hesitant to take actions objectionable to their own citizens.

This has critical implications for the Asian case. For decades, China and South Korea have accused Japan's unapologetic remembrance, citing statements made by Japanese leaders or omissions from Japanese history textbooks (Akio 2017; Lawson and Tannaka 2010; Ye 2013). There has been pressure from the United States on countries like Japan and South Korea to put the past in the past. The United States is the most powerful country in the world and, almost completely unarguably, the country with the most strategic leverage and power over both Japan and South Korea. Still this external pressure has not led to successful reconciliation in Asia. National sentiments remain vigorous in China, Japan, and South Korea so leaders must take them into account as they build new international ties. This is especially true for leaders who must win elections in democracies.

For states like Japan, identity affirmation may be more politically feasible than alternative approaches to reconciliation. National leaders may fear the consequences of losing face in front of their own domestic populations. Consequently, when elites find economic, strategic, or geopolitical reasons to build new forms of cooperation among nations with turbulent histories, affirmation of national identities offers a better route to public recognition of guilt, which works through increased prosocial tendencies (i.e., concern for fairness to others).

In the next chapter, I extend these implications of NIA to study its effects on perception and images the public holds of other countries. Using a large survey sample of 7,200 South Korean adults over five years from 2007 to 2012, I find that individuals affirmed of their national identity hold consistently more positive perceptions of South Korea's neighbor countries.

SIX

National Identity and the Ally Image

Surveys in South Korea

In the fourth chapter, we found that national identity affirmation was associated with greater trust toward other countries. Chapter 5 focused on past inflictor states, arguing that affirming national identities releases defensiveness in admitting group-based guilt and willingness to repent. This chapter examines affirmation effects on the images weaker countries hold of stronger states surrounding their own. Namely, can NIA make the general image the public holds of another country more positive? If affirming national identities can nudge general popular images in a positive direction, the repercussions of NIA for foreign policy and international cooperation could be immense.

Thus, to further develop my experimental findings, I conducted a test of NIA and images of other countries. I utilize four categories of "perception of other countries" in existing survey data. These four categories are perceptions of other countries as a candidate for cooperation, competition, caution, or hostility. These four categories allow me to examine more detailed and nuanced distinctions of perceptions of other countries than merely positive or negative.

The study also extends the scope of previous chapters with regard to the target ("opponent" in chapter 4) countries. This allows me to draw predictions that the ramifications of NIA may not just be limited to the three Northeast Asian states. NIA could reach even further beyond the initial scope and theoretical motivation of this study. In particular, I focus on South Koreans' contemporary perceptions (from 2007 to 2012) of four of South Korea's surrounding states who arguably share the most turbulent interactions in the history of Korea's international relations. The four states that, throughout Korea's history, were most eventful in their exchange with Korea are China, Japan, the United States, and Russia. Although not a part of East Asia, the United States and Russia have heavily influenced Korean foreign policy and are significant players in international politics in Asia in general, and are thus included in this analysis.

This chapter adds to the robustness of the empirical analyses in this book. The experiment results in chapters 4 and 5 offer considerable insight into the effects of NIA on trust and guilt at the individual level. Because of random assignment, the manipulation of the independent variable, and the control of extraneous variables, the experiments offer *internal validity* for NIA, or strong support for causal conclusions. In addition, in as much as what the questions in the surveys as well as the economics-style games measure correspond to trust and guilt, the experiments offer *construct validity* as well (Shadish, Cook, and Campbell 2002).

However, there are at least two methodological reasons why it would be worth supplementing these findings. The first reason concerns *external validity*. Experiments, especially those done in labs, are often conducted under conditions that seem artificial (Bauman et al. 2014). This can raise questions to how generalizable the results are beyond the people and situations actually studied. The second reason concerns replication. It has been noted that the conclusions drawn in survey research are often influenced by the types of instrumentation employed (Schuman and Presser 1981). If we find similar results despite utilizing slightly different operationalizations of the key concepts in the study, it offers greater faith in our findings and further confidence in our understanding of the effects of NIA.

Thus I conducted some additional tests of my theory using larger survey data, seeking the generalizability of my experimental findings to the public writ large. I focus on NIA and perception of other countries by South Koreans. I use survey data collected from 7,200 South Korean people over the period of 2007 to 2012. Results of my analysis indicate that people who reported to be prouder to be Korean held more positive images of other countries, considering the countries to be potential allies for cooperation.

6.1 We Like You Better When We Feel Good about Ourselves

Having expanded the cases in focus beyond just China and Japan to include four countries surrounding South Korea, it is worth examining the cur-

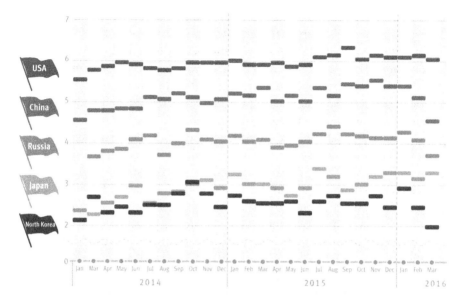

Figure 29. Country favorability by South Koreans (Scale: 0–10. Least favorable = 0; Most favorable = 10). The Asan Poll 2016.

rent state of South Koreans' general perceptions of those countries first. Figure 29 reports results from a public opinion poll performed by the Asan Institute for Policy Studies. In this poll, South Korean respondents were asked to rate the favorability of each country on a scale of 0 to 10, with 0 representing "least favorable."

On the favorability scale, the United States consistently ranked as South Koreans' most favored nation. The countries that followed in order of favorability were China, Russia, and Japan. North Korea is not included in our analysis.

It is noteworthy that China's favorability rose to a peak of 5.54 in favorability in November 2016. Observing significant events around those dates, it can be inferred that the positive perception of China had risen shortly after South Korea, Japan, and China held their first trilateral summit. However, even with this summit that included Japan, the low favorability ratings for Japan remained virtually unchanged.

South Koreans perceive of China and Japan in a profoundly negative image. In the same survey as mentioned above, respondents were asked to identify the nature of South Korea's relationship with the United States, China, and Japan. These responses are reported below in figure 30. An overwhelming 86.1 percent described South Korea's relationship with

National Identity and the Ally Image 159

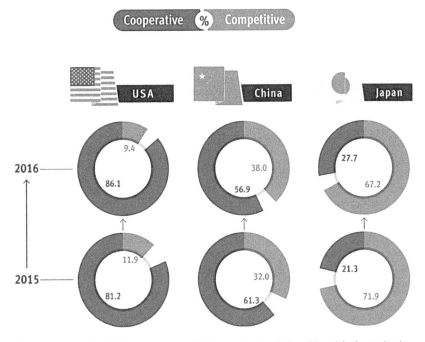

Figure 30. How South Koreans assess their country's relationship with the United States, China, and Japan. The Asan Poll 2016.

the United States as cooperative, while 56.9 percent said the same about its relationship with China. Consistent with the low country favorability ratings, 67.2 percent identified South Korea's relationship with Japan as competitive.

In this chapter, I argue that NIA improves perception of other countries, moving interstate images to a more positive light. In the context of image theory, this means that affirming national identities can help shift negative images toward a positive ally image. In other words, countries will come to perceive of the other as a candidate for cooperation, where both parties can mutually gain from the fruits of cooperation, rather than as a candidate for competition, caution, or hostility.

Recall from the discussion of image theory in chapter 3 that when the public of a country views another country to be a candidate for competition, caution, or hostility, this implies (and/or leads to) a negative perception of the other country. Images reify behavior; they are revelations of the cognitive perception of others that explain and underlie behavior, and at the same time reproduce behavioral tendencies as well. Negative images include enemy, imperialist, colony, or barbarian images (Herrmann and Fischerkeller 1996).

I propose that NIA can move people's perceptions of others toward a more positive direction. To test this hypothesis, this chapter examines whether individuals affirmed of their national identity tend to hold more positive perceptions of other countries. If this argument holds in an empirical finding, based on the results we can expand our theoretical expectations to predict behavioral orientations. The policy implications of image theory apply here, as we can expect the perceptions individuals hold of other countries to generate public support for associated policy. In the case that countries hold ally images of the other, cooperative foreign policy would thus become more popular, making it easier for state leaders to initiate and implement such policies.

On the other hand, negative images such as enemy, imperialist, barbarian, or colony point to a higher probability of competitive, cautious, or hostile foreign policy. The enemy, imperialist, or barbarian image of another country can initiate a security dilemma or spiral model situation, where countries build military strength for defense but by doing so tragically and paradoxically contribute to lessened security (Glaser 1997; Jervis 1976, 1978). A colony image may motivate the in-group to seek to patronize the target country in the colony image through invasion or colonization.

However, an ally image opens doors to the realization of mutual gain between countries. Liberal institutionalists in international relations theory have long emphasized how international cooperation can evolve and solidify in an institutional setting (Keohane 1984; Keohane and Martin 1995; Koremenos, Lipson, and Snidal 2001; Simmons and Martin 2002). A positive image of the other country as a candidate for cooperation with one's country allows for countries to engage in the first step of cooperation, which can lead to reciprocated and continued interaction in the future (Boulding 1978).

6.2 Method

As previously introduced, in this chapter I borrow from an existing dataset, collected through a previously conducted survey. Such a process belongs to a methodological category called secondary data analysis. Secondary data analysis, simply defined, refers to "analysis of data collected by someone else" (Boslaugh 2007), or the method of using any existing datasets (Vartanian 2010).

Borrowing from existing data, my utilization of the national survey data from the Seoul National University holds a number of advantages of secondary data analysis. Most notably, secondary data analysis can make use of existing survey datasets that provide the benefits of representative samples (Smith 2008). Analysis of these datasets offers the opportunities to test or generate theories based on a large representative sample and provide more reliable national estimates. This allows for greater external validity. In the survey data I use, the survey participants look more like the South Korean public as a whole, and compared to the South Korean subjects in the lab experiment, they are older (on average, survey participants were 40.9 years old, compared to 20.8 in the experiment) and less educated (51.6 percent received a high school education or less), and feature lower proportions of males (50.9 percent of respondents identified as male in the survey experiment, compared to 62.6 percent in the lab experiment).

While the fact that the study design and data collection are already completed can be a strength when it comes to saving research time and costs, for the same reason the data may not facilitate the exact research question of the researcher. Because researchers using existing survey datasets were not involved in the study or sampling design, data collection, or the data entry process, working with an existing dataset requires the researcher to work within that dataset under these conditions (Atkinson and Brandolini 2001). Therefore it is necessary to achieve the most appropriate fit between the research question proposed and the datasets available.

To achieve an appropriate fit, existing datasets may require researchers to refine or modify research questions or the scope of the study. Through this modification or refinement, researchers balance the feasibility and limitations of secondary data analysis (Trzesniewski, Donnellan, and Lucas 2011). Similarly, since I am using existing survey data, I need to borrow questions that most closely approximate the concepts in my theory. And since my key motivation of this chapter is to challenge the scope of NIA to examine whether it can cover the general perception of other countries, my variables of interest were slightly modified to support this motivation. At the same time, the four divided categories of images of other countries allow for a finer distinction of what positive or negative perception of other countries may mean. These categories also roughly correspond to the positive and negative images mentioned in image theory.

Modifications were also made for my independent variable. Using an existing dataset, I am not able to include the exact NIA task I used as a manipulation in my experiments, but as an approximate measure to how affirmed individuals already are about their national identity, I use responses to one of the survey items, "How proud are you to be a Korean?" While this may not be the perfect measure to capture how affirmed one is of their national identity, scholars of affirmation theory have used pride measures for affirmation, arguing that the bolstering effect of self-affirmation is accomplished by reflecting on an important value or source of pride irrelevant to the threat at hand (McQueen and Klein 2006). Extending the assumption that when one is group-affirmed one becomes more content in one's sense of self and group identity, we can expect that group-affirmation entails a sense of feeling good about one's self in terms of group membership. Therefore South Korean individuals, for example, who are affirmed on a national level (that have been group-affirmed of their Korean national identity) should feel better about their being Korean.

In sum, benefits of using a larger, representative dataset include expedience, cost effectiveness, and breadth of variables, which allows researchers to choose from the many questions those that most closely resemble their theoretical interest. Data from Seoul National University specifically asks of perception toward a number of countries, with specific distinction as to what these perceptions may mean. The inclusion of South Koreans' perceptions toward the United States, Japan, China, and Russia allow an examination of South Korean's images of the four countries that Korea arguably holds the most turbulent past with, in the history of Korea's international relations. This allows us to expand our scope beyond Northeast Asia, simultaneously challenging and testing the potential of NIA's application in foreign policy. Finally, the dataset asks the same questions over the period of five years (2007 to 2012) to as many as 7,200 South Koreans altogether. Use of this data thus provides good comparison of perception of different countries as well as by generation and changes over time. Using this data, I expect that group members who reported to be prouder to be Korean also hold more positive perceptions of other countries as a candidate for cooperation (i.e., a potential ally). This leads me to the following hypothesis:

> Hypothesis 3 = Individuals affirmed of their national identity exhibit more positive images of other countries.

6.3 Data and Variables

To empirically examine the hypothesis, I use Seoul National University's "National Survey on Korean Perception on Unification." The survey asks

South Korean participants to express their thoughts on various questions regarding unification and foreign policy (Park and Song 2013). Since 2007, the university has been conducting this as an annual survey with face-to-face interviews. I use the data from 2007 to 2012. The typical sample size every year surpasses 1,200.

The primary outcomes of interest here, or main dependent variables, are perceptions toward other countries. To study this I look at responses to the survey question: "How do you perceive of the image of U.S./Japan/China/Russia?" This question offers four response options: "a candidate for (a) cooperation, (b) competition, (c) caution, or (d) hostility" (Park and Song 2013). While the English translation might not perfectly capture the ordinal nature of the choices, these response options are considered to be on an ordinal scale, ranging from positive to negative images. I say this for two reasons. First, the original report of the survey discusses the options as ordered. Second, the options are presented in the stated order and the original report of the survey also discusses them as ordered choices.

Image theorists in international relations have long categorized perception of other states in an ally, imperialist, barbarian, or enemy image, which closely matches the idea of the other as a candidate for cooperation (ally), competition or caution (imperialist or barbarian), or subject of caution or hostility (enemy). As South Korea is undeniably the weakest in power among the states mentioned here, considerations of South Koreans viewing a target state in a colony image is not included. The bigger the number, the stronger the hostility to another country.

Table 34 presents a description and trends of South Koreans' images of surrounding states. Aside from some variations across the years, the overall trends are stable over time. South Koreans tend to perceive the United States most favorably. The average for "Image of U.S." for every year between 2007 and 2012 is the lowest among all dependent variables, suggesting that South Koreans are more likely to recognize the United States as a candidate for cooperation rather than for competition, cau-

TABLE 34. Summary statistics: South Koreans' images of United States, Japan, China, and Russia, 2007–2012

Variable	2007	2008	2009	2010	2011	2012	Total
Image of U.S.	1.75	1.48	1.40	1.33	1.37	1.35	1.45
Image of Japan	2.33	2.48	2.16	2.27	2.42	2.24	2.32
Image of China	2.18	2.19	2.19	2.19	2.23	2.43	2.24
Image of Russia	2.19	2.11	2.06	2.20	2.14	2.24	2.16

Note: Earlier versions of the tests and tables in this chapter have been published in Chung and Woo (2015).

tion, or hostility. In general South Koreans held the most negative images of Japan, with the exception of years 2009 and 2012 only. In those years, South Koreans viewed China in the most negative image. South Korean images of Russia exhibit the least variation over time. This may be due to the notion that relative to the other three states, Russia was the least relevant player to South Korea in the region during the surveyed years.

6.4 Results

6.4.1 NIA and the Ally Image

To capture how affirmed South Koreans are of their national identity, I utilize responses to the question, "How proud are you to be a Korean?" The respondent is provided with the following array of choices "(a) very proud, (b) somewhat proud, (c) a little proud, and (d) not proud at all" (Park and Song 2013). I expect that those who are prouder to be Korean (thus with smaller values of the independent variable) sustain more positive images of states Korea had a rough and complex history of conflict and colonialism with (thus with smaller values of the dependent variables). While this may not be the perfect measure to capture whether one is affirmed of their national identity, I believe it is a reasonable proxy. This extends the theoretical assumption that when one is affirmed of their national identity, one's self-esteem based on membership in that country should be elevated as well. That is precisely how the question is worded.

Methodologically, I use ordered logit models, as the response options in our survey question of interest have an ordered nature to them. Ordered logit models are commonly used when a dependent variable has more than two categories and the values of each category have a sequential order where a value is indeed higher than the previous one, but ordinal scale represents crude measurement of an underlying interval or ratio scale.

I control for a number of sociopolitical variables. Specifically, income and the education levels were controlled for, where higher numbers indicate higher levels of income and education levels, respectively. I also control for political ideology, where a higher number for "Ideology" represents a more conservative political orientation. The variable "Political Knowledge" controls for how much a respondent is interested in politics. In addition, I control for some demographic variables. A dichotomous variable of "Female" was included to control for respondents' gender. Expecting age to influence South Koreans perceptions of the other countries, I include both "Age" and "Age Squared" variables to capture potential nonlinear effects of age.

In the first set of models, I pool the data from all of the years and examine them together with year dummies to parse out potential year effects. Table 35 presents the main results.

The variable "Pride," used here as a proxy for how affirmed a respondent is of their national identity, is statistically significant and consistently positive at the p <0.05 level. The results clearly support my hypothesis. The prouder that a person is to be Korean, the more likely they are to view

TABLE 35. South Koreans' images of four neighbor counties with national pride as main predictor

Variables	Image of U.S.	Image of Japan	Image of China	Image of Russia
	\multicolumn{4}{c}{Coef (SE)}
Pride	.181*	.069*	.078*	.110*
	(.037)	(.032)	(.032)	(.032)
Political Knowledge	−.107*	.053†	.043	.091*
	(.037)	(.031)	(.031)	(.031)
Ideology	−.178*	−.010	.069*	.062*
	(.033)	(.027)	(.028)	(.027)
Female	.084	.071	−.033	.054
	(.054)	(.045)	(.045)	(.045)
Age	.031*	−.033*	−.033*	−.033*
	(.014)	(.012)	(.012)	(.012)
Age Squared	−.0005*	.0004*	.0004*	.0005*
	(.0002)	(.0001)	(.0001)	(.0001)
Education	.047	−.197**	−.199**	−.145*
	(.051)	(.042)	(.042)	(.042)
Income	−.048†	−.021*	.005	−.039†
	(.027)	(.022)	(.022)	(.022)
2007	1.051*	.140*	−.544*	−.151*
	(.089)	(.077)	(.077)	(.077)
2008	.371*	.471*	−.529*	−.316*
	(.094)	(.078)	(.078)	(.077)
2009	.138	−.183*	−.512*	−.392*
	(.095)	(.076)	(.077)	(.076)
2010	−.033	.070	−.488*	−.046
	(.097)	(.075)	(.076)	(.076)
2011	.115	.372*	−.412*	−.220*
	(.096)	(.076)	(.077)	(.076)
Cut1	1.081*	−2.305*	−2.460*	−1.521*
Cut2	2.019	−.284*	−.596*	.144*
Cut3	4.528*	1.679*	1.839*	2.847*
Prob>chi2	.000	.000	.000	.000
N	7138	7134	7133	7132

Note: Ordered logit, standard errors in parentheses. ** Indicates statistical significance at the 1 percent level, * significant at the 5 percent level, † significant at the 10 percent level.

other countries such as the United States, Japan, China, and Russia in a positive image.

There were some interesting differences between the countries respondents were asked about. The relationship between NIA and positive perception seems strongest in the U.S. model, followed by the Russian model. However, without calculating predicted probability changes it is difficult to compare substantive effects across models. It is also difficult to say why effects differ for each model, as this may involve ad hoc reasoning. Instead I emphasize here that the direction and statistical significance from model to model are remarkably consistent, although there is some difference in the coefficient's sizes.

There is also intriguing cross-country variation in the control variables. First, those interested in politics tend to view America less favorably but perceive Japan and Russia in a more favorable image. This result is statistically significant after controlling for annual variation. Second, South Koreans who self-report as political progressives tend to observe China and Russia in a more positive image, but the United States more negatively. In contrast, conservative respondents hold positive views of the United States but less favorable views of China and Russia. These results are predictable considering how a political conservative or liberal may perceive of these countries' ideologies. The results are statistically significant at the $p<0.05$ level.

Among the demographic variables, gender appears to have little effect on the image of other countries. By comparison, the Age and Age Squared variables have a statistically significant effect. However, there is an interesting difference in the respondents' images of the United States and of other countries. Regarding the United States, initially, the older a person is, the lower the favorability of that person's perception of the United States, but as the age of a respondent increases further, the trend is reversed, and the person is more favorable vis-à-vis the United States. This could be due to the fact that many older South Koreans who lived through the Korean War would hold a fairly favorable image of the United States as a close ally. This creates an "inversed-U"-shaped relationship in the overall effect of age. This trend is reversed for Japan, China, and Russia. In other words, the older a person is, the more favorable their position for these countries—up to a certain point. Then after that point, the trend reverses: the older a person is, the less favorable they are vis-à-vis these countries. In such cases, the relationship resembles a "U" shape.

Also, the more educated a respondent is, the more favorable they are toward Japan, China, and Russia, but not the United States. The richer the respondent, the more favorable they are toward the United States, Japan, and Russia, but not toward China.

There are also some time trends. Since 2012 is the excluded year, coefficients for the other years should be understood in comparison to 2012 as the baseline. First, while imagery toward the United States was relatively worse in 2007 and 2008, it improved significantly since 2008. Second, images of China deteriorate over time. Similarly, images toward Russia also decline in our timeframe, although not as consistently as in China's case.

Overall, the results presented in table 35 provide clear empirical support for my hypothesis. *My main independent variable capturing NIA is consistently positive and statistically significant*, although other control variables exhibit cross-national variations. This is especially striking and notable when taking into account that other political and demographic variables often exert almost exact opposite effects on images of the other states.

Other Measures of NIA and Positive Images

While I believe that the measure of how "proud one is of being a Korean" approximates how affirmed survey respondents are of their national identity, nevertheless I try alternative measures to capture how affirmed a person is of their national identity. I use alternative measures of subjective assessments of economic and political development in South Korea over time. This is based on the theoretical assumption that when a person is more affirmed of their Korean-ness, their assessment of the economic or political advancement in South Korea would also be more positive.

The "Economic Satisfaction" variable captures respondents' subjective evaluation of South Korea's economic development. Likewise, the "Democracy" measure represents participants' subjective assessment of political progress in South Korea. Those who judge South Korea to be democratic are coded as "1" and those who evaluate South Korea as undemocratic are coded as "10," with in-between assessments. For ease in interpretation, I recoded the responses so that they were consistent with the "Proud" variable. Along with these measures, other variables such as economic well-being, political ideology, and political knowledge are also included.

The overall results in table 36 are remarkably similar to the results presented in table 35, in which the "Proud" variable was the main predictor. Respondents who evaluate South Korea's economic and political progress more positively tend to hold friendlier images of the other countries. The coefficients for "Economic Satisfaction" are consistently positive and statistically significant at the 5 percent level. Controlling for respondents'

TABLE 36. South Koreans' images of four neighbor counties with economic satisfaction and democracy as main predictors

Variables	Image of U.S.	Image of Japan	Image of China	Image of Russia
		Coef (SE)		
Economic Satisfaction	.143*	.199*	.183*	.127*
	(.039)	(.033)	(.033)	(.033)
Democracy	.165*	.046*	.025†	.023†
	(.016)	(.014)	(.014)	(.014)
Political Knowledge	−.085*	.045	.039	.094*
	(.037)	(.031)	(.031)	(.031)
Ideology	−.159*	−.008	.069*	.063*
	(.033)	(.027)	(.028)	(.027)
Female	.068	.056	−.058	.044
	(.054)	(.045)	(.045)	(.045)
Age	.029*	−.037*	−.035*	−.034*
	(.014)	(.012)	(.012)	(.012)
Age Squared	−.0005*	.0005*	.0004*	.0005*
	(.0002)	(.0001)	(.0001)	(.0001)
Education	.045	−.192*	−.193*	−.139*
	(.051)	(.042)	(.042)	(.042)
Income	−.037	−.014	.010	−.034
	(.027)	(.022)	(.022)	(.022)
2007	1.139*	.142†	−.552*	−.154*
	(.091)	(.077)	(.078)	(.077)
2008	.441*	.455*	−.557*	−.334*
	(.096)	(.079)	(.079)	(.078)
2009	.029	−.232*	−.547*	−.416*
	(.097)	(.077)	(.078)	(.077)
2010	.002	.107	−.460*	−.028
	(.098)	(.076)	(.077)	(.076)
2011	.118	.383*	−.404*	−.218*
	(.097)	(.076)	(.077)	(.076)
Cut1	2.038*	−1.700*	−1.993*	−1.240*
Cut2	2.987	.350*	−.124*	.425*
Cut3	5.510*	2.301*	2.217*	3.130*
Prob>chi2	.000	.000	.000	.000
N	7130	7126	7125	7124

Note: Ordered logit, standard errors in parentheses. ** Indicates statistical significance at the 1 percent level, * significant at the 5 percent level, † significant at the 10 percent level.

own economic status, those who subjectively evaluate the South Korean economy as more developed tend to perceive the other countries in a positive image. Correspondingly, those who subjectively evaluate South Korea as more democratic as opposed to undemocratic view the other countries in a friendlier image. The results are statistically significant at the 5 percent level except the "Democracy" variable for China and Russia, which are significant at the 10 percent level.

Again, these results collectively support the main hypothesis for this chapter on NIA and positive perception/images. The empirical results are consistent and provide strong support for the hypothesis regardless of whether I measure how affirmed a person is of their national identity with feelings of pride in being a Korean, or with their perceived economic and political progress of South Korea.

The control variables in the two tables behave quite similarly. People who are interested in politics tend to view the United States less and Russia more positively. Ideologically, those who self-reported as political progressives tend to see China and Russia more favorably, but perceive the United States in a more negative light. Other demographic variables also remain quite consistent with previous models reported in table 35.

6.5 Conclusion

In this chapter, I significantly broadened my application of NIA to a more general setting. The extension of my study of affirmation effects was mainly made in two areas in this chapter. The first is the larger scope of countries in focus beyond Northeast Asian states. My findings on South Korean public images of as many as four countries Korea had eventful histories with highlights the general applicability of affirmation for countries beyond a particular region. Second, the dependent variables in this chapter looked at general images that a weaker state's public held of powerful and influential states. Images of other countries in public opinion paint a general picture of behavioral inclinations, suggesting support for cooperative or competitive foreign policy.

One of the most striking findings in this chapter is that, in contrast to common belief, pride of people's national identity was *not* associated with disdain or contempt toward other countries. To the contrary, individuals who were proud to be a member of their country (also measured by degrees of satisfaction regarding economic and political progress of the country) viewed other countries in a more positive image. In brief, South Koreans who were most content in their national belongingness also tended to see other countries as a potential candidate for cooperation with South Korea. Keep in mind that this response regarded four powerful countries that Korea had the most dynamic and turbulent interactions with, throughout all of Korea's history. The fact that a psychological difference in how citizens view themselves in terms of country membership actually affects whether they perceive in other countries opportunity for gain via cooperation rather than a threat to be cautious of calls attention to the possible policy implications of NIA. Leaders who perceive mutual benefit from cooperating with another state but are hesitant due to sticky negative images in the populace might find it useful to arouse support for cooperative foreign policy by affirming national identity in the public. More on how this might be done is discussed in the following chapters.

Future research that builds on this chapter's study can supplement it in various ways. First, further tests could establish a tighter connection between image theory and the empirical analysis. This study's analysis was based on existing survey data, so there was less control over the exact variables that would preferably be measured as a test of the theory. For example, data that specify in more detail the three dimensions of image formation—goal compatibility, relative power, and relative status—could investigate exactly what among these NIA impacts and how. The wording of the current question used in the survey delicately refers to how subjects perceive of the goal compatibility between their country and another, but there were no measurements of perceived relative power or status. Here we are able to complement this with guesses regarding how South Koreans would perceive of the relative power of status of the four other states. With power, South Korea is certainly an easier case because it is clearly lower in power on the international stage compared to the four other states. However, further scrutiny is needed to determine perceived relative status, or the effect of NIA on images between states where power gaps are smaller.

While future iterations and extensions of this study will provide finer ideas on how to employ NIA to a policy setting in international relations, my findings that individuals affirmed of their national identity hold consistently positive images of other countries serve as the beginning of a guide for reducing animosity between countries.

SEVEN

Application to Policy 1

Security Cooperation

In an attempt to see whether national identity affirmation can affect foreign policy attitudes, I added questions to the survey in South Korea that had a natural experiment element in them.[1] At the time I was conducting the surveys, a salient and highly contested issue was the GSOMIA (General Security of Military Information Agreement), as well as the agreement of Japan–South Korea bilateral military cooperation. In June of 2012, then-president Lee Myung Bak of South Korea announced that his country would sign its first military cooperation pact with Japan since World War II. The pact would allow Seoul and Tokyo to exchange classified military intelligence on North Korea's nuclear and missile programs as well as information about China's growing military power (Hess and Warden 2014).

Unsurprisingly, considering the public sentiment against Japan in South Korea, the announcement set off a political firestorm in the country. South Koreans expressed deep suspicion over Japan's growing military role and concern that their country would cooperate with Japan militarily without having properly dealt with the legacies of Japan's colonization. Experts called this situation one where the two countries were "aligned, but still not allied" (Bang 2011) in "a stickiness of Cold War thinking" (Cha 2002). Ultimately, faced with mounting political pressure, on June 29 former president Lee Myung Bak abruptly postponed the signing of the treaty.[2]

Hoping to take advantage of this issue at the time, I added questions on South Korean attitudes toward cooperating with Japan militarily. This chapter reports two main findings from my investigation of responses to these questions. First, although South Koreans reported consistently negative perceptions of Japan (as a candidate for competition with South Korea), those who held higher levels of strategic trust in my trust games reported significantly more support for GSOMIA. Strategic trust emerges when actors believe that others have an interest in cooperating (Uslaner 2002). Based on this recognition of mutual interest, South Koreans can come to acknowledge the strategic need for GSOMIA.

Since NIA was found to be a positive predictor of strategic trust, it can be inferred that NIA can boost strategic trust, which then leads to increased support for actual policy. In sum, this chapter tests the implications of my earlier findings on NIA's effects by applying them to public opinion in the context of an existing policy. I find that the positive effects of NIA can extend beyond abstract settings of the experimental game into support for a real policy that is contested between rival states.

Considering the nature of GSOMIA, which was meant to work in preparation against security threats from North Korea and China, the main objecting force in South Korea came from the political liberals, or progressives (Sheen and Kim 2012). This is because in South Korean public opinion political progressives generally tend to side with China and have more favorable attitudes toward North Korea, while conservatives prefer that South Korea have closer relations with the United States and/or Japan. This ideological divide was also observable from our tests on large-scale survey data in chapter 6.

In my analysis, I also find that South Koreans who were most opposed to GSOMIA were a subgroup of political progressives, namely those with linked fate beliefs, or certainty that the fate of the nation is of crucial importance to the individual. This could be due to the viewpoint that cooperating militarily with Japan is a devastating sellout for the fate of the country, one akin to voluntarily choosing to repeat the past, which therefore should be prevented at all costs. Importantly, however, NIA had an effect of pulling the people who were most opposed to the policy into a more moderate middle zone, moving them to be more open to the idea of institutionalized cooperation with Japan.

7.1 The Japan-South Korea General Security of Military Information Agreement

In June 2012, foreign policy elites in South Korea and Japan sought to enact a general agreement that would share military intelligence. Named

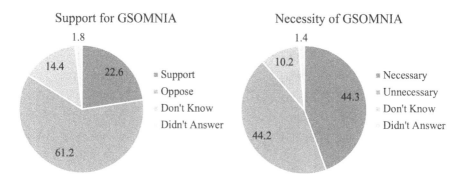

Figure 31. South Koreans' opinions on support for and necessity of GSOMIA (%). Modified and recreated from The Asan Institute of Policy Studies 2012.

GSOMIA (General Security of Military Information Agreement), the treaty was expected to improve cooperation and consensus between the countries. Incentives for the new agreement came from the complex strategic environment that the countries face, namely North Korean nuclear provocations and concerns over China's military growth (Choe 2012b). However, the agreement was abandoned mere hours before the scheduled signing, due to extreme public outrage in South Korea. Members of forty-eight civil society groups gathered to protest the decision outside government offices.

The failure of GSOMIA was broadly interpreted by both foreign and domestic observers as being sparked by anti-Japan sentiment in South Korea (Friedhoff and Kang 2013). It was clear from a survey conducted in the immediate wake of the GSOMIA breakdown that the majority of the public opposed the treaty. Specifically, 61.2 percent opposed the agreement, while only 22.6 percent supported it (Kim, Friedhoff, and Kang 2012). This distribution of opinions is observable from the graph on the left in figure 31.

However, when asked about the *necessity* of GSOMIA, as much as 44.3 percent of respondents answered positively, a huge jump from the mere 22.6 percent who reported support of the treaty. What's going on? In fact, considering the results in the graph on the right in figure 31, the public was split evenly enough to make it difficult to conclude that South Koreans were against GSOMIA in general.

Furthermore, in a poll summarized in figure 32, a striking 63.9 percent of South Korean respondents acknowledge the need for security cooperation with Japan (Kim, Friedhoff, and Kang 2012). Only 26.2 percent said

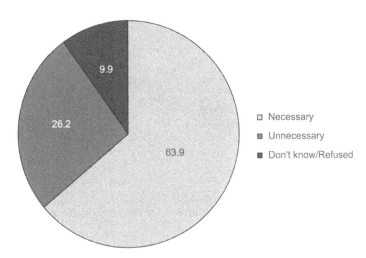

Figure 32. South Koreans' opinions on security cooperation with Japan (%). The Asan Institute of Policy Studies 2013.

it would be unnecessary. This is astonishing considering that the security sector is generally the "hard case" for cooperation. It should be noted that the wording of the question did include mention of cooperation with Japan on security in the event of China's rise, which may have triggered more positive response. However, it is also important to note that this survey was conducted in September 2013, shortly after the Japanese prime minister's visit to the contentious Yasukuni Shrine. Despite this event, the majority of South Koreans expressed that security cooperation with Japan is necessary. This is an especially interesting finding considering that South Koreans consistently reported their perceived country image of China as more favorable compared to their image of Japan, as was noticeable from figure 29 in chapter 6.

In a cross-tab analysis for responses reported in the previous pie charts (see table 37), it was found that among those who supported security cooperation with Japan, 66.0 percent viewed GSOMIA as necessary. However, among those opposed, 75.1 percent viewed GSOMIA as unnecessary.

Judging from the survey responses, it can be inferred that the common assumption that South Koreans do not support engagement with Japan due to anti-Japanese sentiment is inaccurate (Friedhoff and Kang 2013). Of course, it is no secret that the South Korean public holds negative views of Japan, and the public opinion data included throughout the book confirm

TABLE 37. Cross tab analyses with South Korea-Japan security cooperation (%)

		South Korea-Japan Security Cooperation	
		Necessary	Not necessary
GSOMIA	Necessary	66.0	20.3
	Not necessary	25.0	75.1

Source: The Asan Institute of Policy Studies 2013

this. But also according to the survey data, there is a clear desire in the public to take steps to repair the relationship with Japan.

This finding is confirmed by subsequent polling revealing that support for the signing of GSOMIA remains elevated (figure 33). A little more than a year after the initial furor over GSOMIA had passed, opinion polls on GSOMIA reported that support for its passage was still at a relatively high 60.4 percent in September 2013. Over the period of seven months after support for GSOMIA in survey reports peaked in February 2013, support rates only slightly fell by about 4 percent.

The continuation of the support for GSOMIA over time had no relation to a sudden increased favorability of Japan in South Koreans' eyes either. In fact, during this time Japan was consistently viewed in a negative enemy image—a target country for competition rather than cooperation.

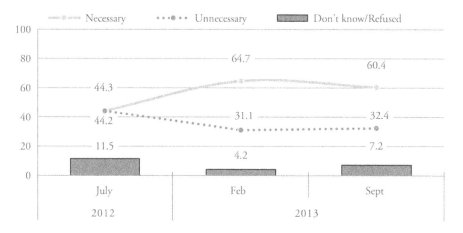

Figure 33. South Koreans' perceived necessity for GSOMIA over time. The Asan Institute of Policy Studies 2013.

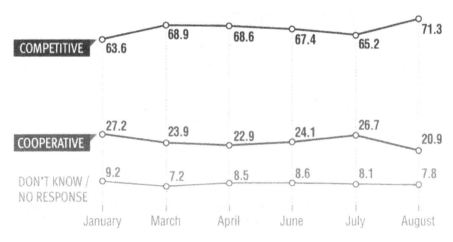

Figure 34. South Koreans' responses to survey question "How do you view the relations between South Korea and Japan?" (%, 2013).

It can be noticed in figure 34 that in August 2013, just before the September 2013 survey represented in the far-right column in figure 33 (in which South Koreans expressed a sustained support for GSOMIA of over 60 percent), the public's unfavorable image of Japan actually topped 70 percent. This implies that South Koreans were able to admit the need for security cooperation with Japan although they did not hold positive images of Japan.

Despite current tensions, the public does not want to see a further deterioration in South Korea-Japan relations. A near majority acknowledge the necessity of GSOMIA. How can these incongruous expressions of opinion be understood?

A closer observation of the polls reveals it is not the case that the public is happy with the status quo of relations or feels no need for improvement or cooperation per se. Japanese and South Korean public opinion in another cross-national survey conducted by Genron NPO in Japan and The East Asia Institute in South Korea (2013–2014) revealed that more than 61 percent of Japanese and 69 percent of South Korean respondents think the current state of Japanese-South Korean relations is undesirable or problematic and needs to be fixed (Genron NPO and East Asia Institute 2014). This suggests support for my theory that the reluctance of countries with a history problem to cooperate is rooted in psychological bias that inhibits updating. The strong negative image of Japan creates a sticky reluctance to cooperate, even when this implies losing potential benefit from cooperation. When South Koreans have the opportunity to engage in systematic processing (Chaiken 1980; Chaiken and Trope 1999; Petty and Cacioppo 1986), however, they acknowledge that cooperation would be beneficial.

In terms of the mechanism through which self-affirmation works, Crocker et al. (2008) identified it as a process in which reminding individuals of larger, self-transcendent values that are also important to the self-concept takes them out of their "angry little selves" to see the larger picture of the self. This enables individuals to realize that reacting in defensive ways toward the issue at hand is no longer necessary. It can be expected that such a route allows people to engage in more objective acceptance of information and moreover logical updating. In other words, people may come to recognize that cooperating with another country can benefit them, rather than to reject working closer with that country due to its negative image.

In addition to potentially reversing the lost opportunities of regional institution-building and the damage of aggravated security concerns discussed in chapters 2 and 3, for South Koreans in particular there is a reason South Korea can benefit from developing and maintaining a cooperative relationship with Japan. Scholars including Ikenberry (2008) and Goldstein (2013) agree that as China rises, other countries will want to balance against it. If this were to be the case, who would South Korea ally with? A clear majority of South Korean respondents stated that if China continues to rise, South Korea must become strategic partners with Japan (Friedhoff and Kang 2013).

When South Korean respondents were questioned on specific events that would ostensibly be seen as a step forward in cooperation with Japan, including the signing of GSOMIA, a majority noted that they were in *support*, not opposition. Relative to South Korea, Japan has been more forward in signaling a willingness to establish a working-level relationship, first proposing to South Korea the idea of the Park-Abe summit (Friedhoff and Kang 2013). Regarding GSOMIA as well, Japan was more willing to sign the agreement, waiting for South Korean signals of a similar readiness.

7.1.1 Strategic Trust and South Koreans' Willingness for Security Cooperation with Japan

In this section, I examine strategic trust as a mechanism through which NIA can influence public opinion on policy. Strategic trust is based on the belief that others will not defect due to their interest in sustaining a mutually beneficial relationship (Hardin 2006).

Figures 33 and 34 imply that the increase in support for GSOMIA did not accompany a positive turn in South Koreans' image of Japan. However, while retaining negative perceptions of Japan, South Koreans were still able to report in surveys that they perceived a need for security cooperation with Japan. This implies that when South Koreans were able to systematically process and carefully calculate and consider the strategic benefits of GSOMIA, they acknowledged its necessity. This was due to the projected gains of working in collaboration with Japan, not because South Koreans necessarily liked Japan.

This idea that willingness to cooperate is possible despite unfavorable affect is the foundation of strategic trust. One might not like the out-group or even believe the character of out-group members is trustworthy, but one can still cooperate with the out-group because mutual benefit is perceived from working together. Of course, this is only possible if the minimum necessary amount of strategic trust exists. That is, if one believes the out-group can be trusted to reciprocate and repeat the mutually beneficial transactions, then interactions can begin. If one does not have the required strategic trust to initiate transactions, this means one believes the out-group will return a sucker payoff, instead of a fruitful outcome for both. In this case, no exchange will occur at all. This is equivalent to the Nash equilibrium in the trust game, where the proposer sends zero tokens to the receiver, and the game ends with no exchange of tokens ever happening between the players at all.

With this understanding of the concept of strategic trust, we can hypothesize that strategic trust South Koreans hold toward Japanese predicts their support for GSOMIA. GSOMIA is employed here as a real-world example for security cooperation with Japan. The questions on Japanese-South Korean security cooperation were asked at the end of the survey used in the trust study (chapter 4) when I was fielding it in South Korea. Thus we are able to analyze the correlation between strategic trust, as represented by the number of tokens South Koreans sent to their Japanese counterparts in the trust game, and South Koreans' reported support of GSOMIA. Since the survey was fielded in June 2012, literally days after Lee Myung Bak announced he would sign GSOMIA with Japan, the issue was of high salience in South Korea. It was also at the period where the majority of South Koreans were vehemently against the treaty, as was illustrated in the far-left column in figure 33. Therefore a significant and positive finding of a predictor that boosted South Koreans' support for GSOMIA would be remarkable, considering the resistance widespread in South Korean public opinion at the time.

This indicates that even at the height of group-based passion and emotional resistance, NIA can remove heuristical judgment and defensive reaction based on superficial processing. It was found in chapter 4 that NIA was positively associated with strategic trust. That is, subjects that were affirmed of their national identities sent more tokens to their foreign opponents in the trust game. Finding a positive relationship between strategic trust and support for GSOMIA, then, suggests that NIA can have desirable outcomes in actual policy settings that require a minimum threshold of strategic trust between rival countries to initiate institutionalized cooperation, even if they perceive of each other in a negative image.

Ideally, countries would come to hold positive images of each other; as discussed in theory in chapters 3 and 6, countries' images are important for foreign policy. However, a positive image might take longer to achieve compared to strategic trust.

Strategic trust is based on a tacit agreement that groups have enough trust to use each other for their own good. When this agreement is established, successful (as in rewarding for both) interaction can occur and continue. Of course, in terms of peaceful and productive interaction between countries, exchange based on moralistic trust (the belief that the outgroup is moral in character) would be preferable and would make for a sturdier interaction than one based on strategic trust. However, moralistic trust is harder to achieve between enduring rival states. We should also be reminded (from figure 6 in chapter 3), however, that with mutually fruitful iterated interactions based on strategic trust, moralistic trust can emerge.

The implications of relationships discussed between strategic trust and institutional cooperation thus far lead to the following hypothesis.

> Hypothesis 4 = NIA nudges South Koreans most extremely against GSOMIA into a more moderate middle zone, leading them to become more supportive of it.
>
> H4a = Strategic trust (increased by NIA) is positively associated with South Koreans' support for GSOMIA.

7.1.2 Ideology and Attitudes toward South Korean Military Cooperation with Japan

Ideology as Source of Social Conflict in South Korea

Ideological cleavages run deep in South Korea. Across a wide range of important political issues including foreign policy, North Korea, the

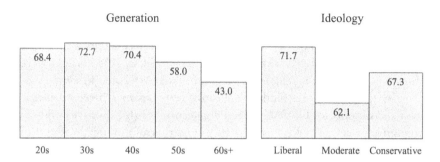

Figure 35. Percentage of respondents (by age groups and ideology) who replied their perceived intensity of the division between liberals and conservatives was "strong" (6–10, on a scale from 0 to 10. 0 was presented as Not Strong; 5: Normal; and 10: Very strong). Modified and recreated from The Asan Institute for Policy Studies 2013.

environment, social welfare, taxation, and minority rights, the country is divided along ideological lines.

The South Korean people are well aware that ideology is a major source of social conflict. Figure 35 reports results from a public opinion poll on how tangible and salient ideological conflict feels for South Koreans. When asked how much South Koreans perceive the intensity of the division between liberals and conservatives in a public opinion poll, roughly 70 percent in each of three age groups of people in their twenties, thirties, and forties all chose the response option that they perceive of ideological conflict as "strong." Younger generations were more likely than older generations in their fifties and up to perceive ideological conflict as "strong" (Kim and Friedhoff 2013).

Perceptions of ideological division also varied along ideological lines: 71.7 percent of self-described liberals and 67.3 percent of self-described conservatives saw ideological conflict as "strong," perhaps because they had more direct experiences or exposure to ideological conflicts (Kim and Friedhoff 2013). In other words, younger and liberal people perceived of ideology as a dividing force in the South Korean public.

Based on this survey data it can be inferred that much of my sample also perceived of ideological differences as a major source of social conflict. With a student sample, most of my participants were younger and more liberal than the average South Korean. It would be interesting and meaningful to see whether NIA can narrow the gap between polarized opinions on a policy that is fiercely contested, especially with a sample that believes in deep ideological cleavages in the country.

As is regularly the case with South Korean foreign policy vis-à-vis Japan, which sharply divides the nation, public opinion on GSOMIA also differed by self-descried ideology and beliefs people held. I describe this in more detail in the next section.

Ideological Divides in Support for GSOMIA

South Korean support for GSOMIA differs across political ideology. As shown in figure 36, conservatives report higher support for GSOMIA than progressives. This is more intuitive than it first appears to be. While one might initially suppose that conservatives would be more against this treaty of military cooperation with Japan, this opposite observation of progressives objecting to the treaty becomes more understandable when we take into consideration that the treaty was designed against security threats from North Korea and China. Traditionally, political progressives in South Korea support forming closer alliances with North Korea and China, and are relatively negative against Japan and the United States.

Although this gap between progressives and conservatives lessens as more time passes after the initial uproar immediately following President Lee Myung Bak's announcement of the plan to sign GSOMIA, progressives consistently oppose GSOMIA relative to conservatives throughout the whole period that responses were recorded. This was until September 2013, or more than a whole year after the first announcement on GSOMIA.

If progressives were initially most against GSOMIA, but gradually reported higher levels of support for GSOMIA with time, then it is possible that the more salient and immediate negative perceptions against Japan are overpowering the concern for the possible benefits of cooperation with Japan. I say this for two reasons. First, it can be understood that military cooperation is a difficult case, especially with a past colonizer who, from a South Korean perspective at least, has not fully atoned for its past. However, GSOMIA concerns merely the sharing of military intelligence, especially with regard to North Korea, which many Japanese and South Koreans may perceive as a common threat, and not joint military action or training. Second, figure 32 reports that close to 63.9 percent of South Korean respondents in the poll believe security cooperation is actually necessary with Japan. As observable in figure 36, over time the progressives actually report increased support for GSOMIA, suggesting that they came to realize possible benefits for South Korea in joining the agreement.

We can assume from figure 32 that the majority of the South Korean public acknowledges the need for security cooperation with Japan. The vis-

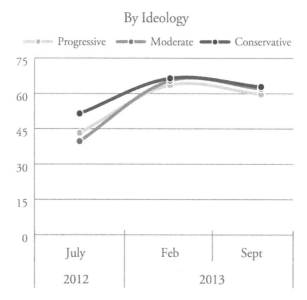

Figure 36. South Korean public support for GSOMIA by ideology. The Asan Institute for Policy Studies 2013.

ible objection to GSOMIA in South Korea, as noticeable in street protests, could be primarily and initially motivated by a strong resistance to working in close cooperation with Japan. It could be the case, then, that if people who most strongly oppose the treaty have a chance to be distanced from this knee-jerk reaction and are able to objectively process the benefits of cooperation with Japan, they will come to support GSOMIA more.

Progressives and Linked Fate

Why were progressives in South Korea against GSOMIA? The public protests that were set off as a result of former president Lee's sudden announcement to sign the agreement reflected strong anxiety about the trajectory of the nation. The Lee administration's proceedings on this issue were considered unilateral and deemed by many as a backroom deal. However, the severest opposition came from progressives who seemed to have the gravest concerns for the destiny of South Korea if it were to sign GSOMIA with Japan.

Idiosyncratically, a defining feature among South Korea's most vocal and patriotic liberals is their emphasis on how deals with adversaries can be self-defeating and harmful to the "fate of the nation." Many of the slogans and rallying cries in protests revealed a heightened apprehension to the extent of comparing the treaty signing to a traitorous act of "selling the nation" or "choosing to be a colony again" (Park and Yun 2016; Yu and Wei 2016).

Similarly, various media outlets in South Korea on the left side of the ideological spectrum that vehemently opposed GSOMIA also expressed "the fate of the nation" as a main cause of objection. Generally, the idea was that the notion of signing a military agreement with Japan was a horrible mistake for the well-being of South Korea as a country, and as its citizens, South Koreans should be personally concerned and seriously worried about the possibility of the nation's destiny heading down that route. Numerous sources, including articles from some of the best-known progressive news and liberal nongovernmental organizations in South Korea, such as The Hankyoreh or People's Solidarity for Participatory Democracy (PPSD), mentioned the country's fate (*oonmyung* in Korean) as an important keyword and reason to fight against GSOMIA (C. Kim 2017; J. Kim 2012; M. Kim 2016; Lee 2016; PPSD 2016a, 2016b). From such reasons stated by objectors to GSOMIA, it can be assumed the progressives that were most concerned about the trajectory of the nation are most against the treaty.

This concern originates from the idea that the fate of the nation is inextricably intertwined with one's own fate as an individual, which is analogous to the concept of linked fate. On a domestic level, the idea that one's belongingness in a country and one's destiny or well-being are inseparably linked has commonly been referred to by scholars as linked fate (Dawson 1994). It is possible that progressives who have a strong sense of linked fate are more sensitive to unsettled postconflict injustice vis-à-vis relations with Japan, leading them to reject the treaty. If it is the case that among political progressives in South Korea, those with strong linked fate beliefs are most against GSOMIA, then what can be done to move these extreme opinions closer to the middle? I propose that the affirmation of national identity can boost support for GSOMIA among the progressives who strongly believe in linked fate, thus mitigating the gap between polarized South Korean public opinion on the treaty.

Why would affirmation of national identity nudge those most against GSOMIA into the direction of supporting it? Members might be worried for the fate of their group in cooperating with a past rival, with concern that the in-group is headed in a detrimental direction. But by reinforcing positive values of the group, identity affirmation can replenish confidence in the group's overall integrity, which can override concern and lead to objective realization that cooperation can benefit the group.

Also, group-affirmation works through a clarification of the concept of group identity and what it means to be a member of the group. Since the mechanism of national identity affirmation involves a process of making national identities salient, it can be assumed that affirmation works best among people who are strongly affected by their conception of national identity. It can be the case that the effect of affirmation will then be most profound for those who believe that the fate of the nation is tied to one's own life and destiny. To those, concern that the nation's fate is headed down the wrong path or repeating history should be most troublesome, as they believe national trajectories directly impact individual well-being. This leads me to the following hypotheses:

> H4b = Progressives report less support for GSOMIA than conservatives.
>
> H4c = Among progressives, those who most believe in linked fate most strongly object to GSOMIA.
>
> H4d = Progressives who strongly believe in linked fate report higher support for GSOMIA when affirmed of their national identity.

7.2 Materials

In the experiments I described in detail in chapter 4, I added a few more questions just for the South Korean sample. (In Japan these questions were not asked due to inappropriate time period of the experiments in Japan. By the time I had traveled to Japan in October 2012 for the experiments, the signing of GSOMIA had already been cancelled due to public opposition in South Korea.) Therefore the sample and set-up of the experiments I discuss here are identical to what I presented in the chapter 4. For this reason, I do not repeat information on the experiments already given.

The time I traveled to South Korea for experiments was June 2012. This was exactly when debates and polemics in the country regarding the signing of GSOMIA were at their peak. Former president Lee had announced the decision to sign the agreement with Japan, and many experts and media outlets supported or expressed concern about the idea of signing a military agreement with Japan.

Taking advantage of this timing, I incorporated the salient issue of GSOMIA into my experiment in South Korea. At the end of all my surveys

---

Box 4

How closely have you been following the recent debate about the treaty on military intelligence sharing between South Korea and Japan?

A lot / Some / Not much / Don't know

Do you favor or oppose South Korea signing this Treaty?

Favor / Oppose / Don't know

How strongly do you feel about that?

Very weakly / Somewhat weakly / Somewhat strongly / Very strongly

---

given in the country, I added a few questions asking respondents to report their views on GSOMIA, which was then at the center of heated debate.

The first question was presented as an introduction to the topic of GSOMIA for the subjects and was not used in my analysis. Of greater interest were responses to the second and third questions. As I had done with some other questions measuring attitudes, as was mentioned in chapter 4, the second and third questions were intended as a two-step response question. These question types have been known to reduce response time and effectively measure politically sensitive attitudes (Sniderman et al. 2004). As I had done when coding other two-step response questions, I again combined responses to these to create a variable that reports each subject's attitude on a continuous scale.

Since these questions about attitudes on GSOMIA were asked of all South Korean participants, I was able to examine whether the responses toward GSOMIA were different in the group of participants that were affirmed of their national identity and the group of participants who were nonaffirmed.

7.3 Results

Strategic Trust and Support for GSOMIA

An OLS regression of South Koreans' support for GSOMIA on strategic trust reported a positive and statistically significant effect. The results are presented in table 38. Responses to the questions on agreement to South Korea's signing GSOMIA with Japan were combined and scaled to range from 0 to 1. This make for easy comparison across different measures. The new variable on South Koreans' reported support for GSOMIA serves as the dependent variable. The predictor variable of strategic trust was a continuous variable that initially ranged from 0 to 100, and was then scaled to range from 0 to 1 as well. This included the whole sample of South Koreans, including all participants who gave 0 to 100 tokens to their counterparts in the trust game.

The effects of NIA on trust found in chapter 4 may appear to be relatively theoretical compared to the application of those findings in this chapter. Here we find reason to be optimistic for the workings of NIA in the context of policy. Based on the model summarized in table 38, we can predict that strategic trust, induced by NIA, can have actual policy implications. For example, if NIA works through boosted strategic trust to influence public support on foreign policy, then a wide-scale affirmation of national identity in the masses could nudge public opinion toward cooperative outcomes with other countries (more on how NIA can be actualized in international politics is discussed in chapter 9, with examples of actual cases from history). To what degree then can we rely on strategic trust for successful initiation and maintenance of international institutions? Would we have to keep affirming national identities throughout the whole operation of international agreements like GSOMIA?

TABLE 38. Strategic trust in experimental game as predictor of support for GSOMIA (South Korean sample)

Support for GSOMIA	Coef (SE)
Strategic Trust	.188*
	(.048)
Constant	.262**
	(.048)
N	206
R^2	.029

Note: Linear regression, robust standard errors in parentheses. ** Indicates statistical significance at the 1 percent level, * significant at the 5 percent level, † significant at the 10 percent level.

An individual's level of strategic trust above zero regarding a specific out-group implies that they believe people in that group also have a self-interest in reciprocating cooperation rather than violating their commitments (Rathbun 2009). Between rival groups, the initial emergence of strategic trust is tricky. But once established, trust can be sustained through an ongoing and consistent exchange of benefits (Uslaner 2002). A lengthened shadow of the future transcends short-term incentives for defection (Axelrod 1984). In this way, cooperation evolves.

At first, the uncertainty about the other's intentions and fears that they will defect from a cooperative agreement can be overcome by strategic conceptions of trust (Kydd 2005). Over time, with accumulation of strategic trust and lessons from repeated positive interactions, the trust between actors transitions into moralistic trust, or a perceived trustworthiness in the other's nature.

International institutions have the role of keeping such actors in check. While not completely binding, international agreements like NPT or organizations like the UN perform the role of monitoring behavior, rewarding compliance and punishing violation or abandonment of the terms of agreement by the agents (Abbott and Snidal 1998; Koremenos, Lipson, and Snidal 2001; cf. Woo and Chung 2018). Once institutional arrangements such as GSMOIA are put in place, therefore, repeated interaction through the institutions can contribute to sustained cooperation.

Figure 37 graphs this model in a simple scatterplot and a fitted line that summarizes the positive relationship between strategic trust and South Korean's support for GSOMIA.

Of course, as chapter 6 revealed, NIA can have positive effects on how people perceive a number of countries, rather than just one target country. However, since the questions assessed how much South Koreans agreed specifically to a security cooperation agreement with Japan, it would be sensible to estimate the same test with just the South Koreans who were specifically assigned in the Japan conditions. This refers to the South Koreans who were asked how much they trusted the Japanese people or government in the moralistic trust questions, and also were told they were paired with a Japanese counterpart in the trust game.

Table 39 and figure 38 illustrate the results. With just the sample of South Koreans who were randomly assigned to the "other country: Japan" conditions, we find here again that strategic trust had a positive and mildly significant (p=.055) effect on South Koreans' support for GSOMIA.

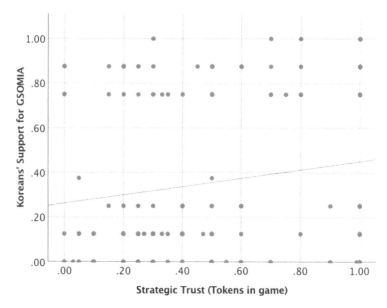

Figure 37. Strategic trust is positively correlated with support for GSOMIA (South Korean sample). Source: Eunbin Chung.

TABLE 39. Strategic trust in experimental game as predictor of support for GSOMIA (South Korean sample paired with Japanese counterpart)

Support for GSOMIA	Coef (SE)
Strategic Trust	.213†
	(.110)
Constant	.301**
	(.073)
N	104
R^2	.036

Note: Linear regression, robust standard errors in parentheses. ** Indicates statistical significance at the 1 percent level, * significant at the 5 percent level, † significant at the 10 percent level.

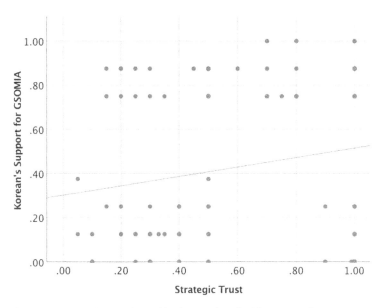

Figure 38. Strategic trust is positively correlated with support for GSOMIA (South Korean sample with Japanese counterpart). Source: Eunbin Chung.

NIA increases support for GSOMIA among progressives with linked fate beliefs.

A first look at the data reveals that progressives were indeed more opposed to GSOMIA than conservatives, confirming my first hypothesis. Again, the dependent variable represents support for GSOMIA, which was scaled to range from 0 to 1. Results from an independent t-test with pooled variance (i.e., equal variances t-test) reveal that progressives expressed lower support for GSOMIA (.269 ± .314) compared to conservatives. (.434 ± .378), $t(168) = -3.106$, $p = .002$. Table 40 shows results of the t-test, which are plotted in figure 39.

Figure 39 graphs the differences in progressives' and conservatives' support for GSOMIA. At a glance, the divide by political ideology is noticeable.

Figure 40 takes a closer look at the subgroups within progressives and conservatives. The distribution of support for GSOMIA by political ideology and linked fate illustrated here reveals that even within progressives, the group members most against GSOMIA were those who had strong

TABLE 40. Results of t-test and descriptive statistics for GSOMIA support by political ideology

	Political Ideology						95% CI for Mean Difference	t	df
	Progressive			Conservative					
	M	SD	N	M	SD	N			
Support for GSOMIA	.269	.314	90	.434	.378	80	−.270, −.060	−3.106**	168

** p < .01.

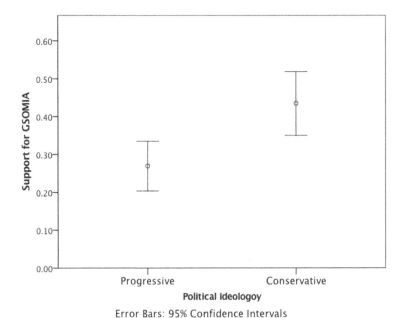

Figure 39. Support for GSOMIA by political ideology. Source: Eunbin Chung.

beliefs of linked fate. In other words, these could likely be the people in the subgroup of the overall South Korean public who most strongly resisted GSOMIA.

What can move public opinion in the group of people most opposed to a policy? To answer this question, I estimated some tests on the effects of NIA on support for GSOMIA that takes into consideration both political ideology and linked fate beliefs.

In order to closely examine what effect NIA has for people most against

Application to Policy 1 191

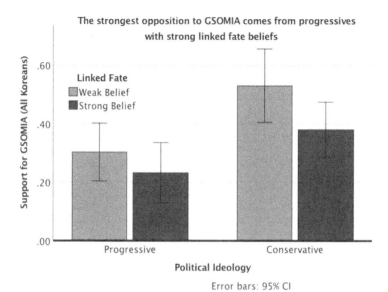

Figure 40. Support for GSOMIA by political ideology and linked fate. Source: Eunbin Chung.

GSOMIA in particular, I tested whether South Koreans who self-identified as political progressives responded to GSOMIA differently when they were affirmed of their national identity. Specifically, I find that those who agreed the fate of South Korea is of crucial importance for them—or in other words reported that their group membership as a South Korean matters immensely for their individual well-being in their daily lives—came to support GSOMIA more when they were affirmed of their national identity. Table 41 and figure 41 summarize the results of tests on people who identified as progressives.

Figure 41 graphs the interaction between affirmation and linked fate among progressives. Affirmation had the effect of increasing support for GSOMIA from those who were strong believers of linked fate and most against GSOMIA. It also decreased the gap in polarized opinion toward a more moderate middle ground. This is because NIA had a large positive effect among progressives who strongly believed in linked fate, and a weak negative effect among progressives who did not have a strong belief in linked fate.

The total number of South Korean respondents who self-reported

TABLE 41. NIA and linked fate on South Korean progressives' support for GSOMIA

Progressives' Support for GSOMIA		Coef (SE)
NIA X Linked Fate	(NIA X Weak Belief in Linked Fate)	−.257†[1] (.130)
NIA		.224* (.094)
Linked Fate	(Weak Belief)	.209* (.096)
Constant		.113 (.069)
N		90
R^2		.076

Note: Linear regression, robust standard errors in parentheses. ** Indicates statistical significance at the 1 percent level, * significant at the 5 percent level, † significant at the 10 percent level.

[1] The interaction variable is midly significant, with a p-value of .051.

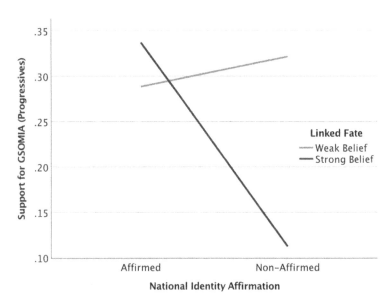

Figure 41. Progressives who believed in linked fate came to support GSOMIA more affirmed of their national identity. Source: Eunbin Chung.

themselves as progressives was 222. The N of this study significantly shrinks, however, leaving just 90. This could be because the questions on GSOMIA were presented to the subjects as the very last questions in the experiment. Since reply to these questions was optional (i.e., subjects were not required to answer them to complete the survey and receive compensation for participation), it is assumed that many chose to opt out. Taking into consideration the sensitivity of the topic at the time of the experiment, I chose not to make response to these questions mandatory.

I also estimated another model that controlled for basic demographics. However, because my sample consisted of university students, variables of age and education were quite narrowly distributed. Therefore including such demographics would not be very meaningful. For this reason, I controlled just for gender. The results are found below in table 42.

Controlling for gender in my model, very similar results held for NIA's effect on linked fate within progressives. The p-value for the interaction variable of NIA and linked fate actually decreased to .037, improving its statistical significance to a 5 percent level.

Several existing studies argue females have different inclinations when it comes to security policy and military alliances (Eichenberg 2016; Fite and Wilcox 1990; Shapiro and Mahajan 1986; Togeby 1994). It is difficult to clearly define the implications of previous research for this model, however, as many earlier studies argue that (from a binary gender perspective) females prefer cooperative foreign policy compared to males, but males tend to express more support for military and security policies. Since the current model estimates support for "security cooperation," I wanted to test whether gender makes a difference in support for GSOMIA, and if so, in what direction.

In my model, males generally reported stronger support for GSOMIA compared to females. Gender had a mildly significant effect on the relationship between NIA and attitudes toward GSOMIA at a 10 percent level. In analysis of my data I found that for my South Korean participants, affirmed and nonaffirmed groups were fairly evenly distributed across genders.

7.4 Conclusion

The primary difficulty the history problem poses for past receivers of atrocities is intransigence in cooperating with the past inflictor. In this chapter I find that NIA can remove such inflexibility on the receivers' side, increasing openness to working closer with the inflictor state. This can be

TABLE 42. NIA and linked fate on South Korean progressives' support for GSOMIA, controlling for gender

Progressives' Support for GSOMIA		Coef (SE)
NIA X Linked Fate	(NIA X Weak Belief in Linked Fate)	−.273* (.129)
NIA		.223* (.093)
Linked Fate	(Weak Belief)	.228* (.095)
Gender	(Male)	.113† (.065)
Constant		.045 (.078)
N		90
R^2		.108

Note: Linear regression, robust standard errors in parentheses. ** Indicates statistical significance at the 1 percent level, * significant at the 5 percent level, † significant at the 10 percent level.

especially helpful in cases of policies that the public at first finds objectionable due to deep-seated and profound negative images of the other, but finds more desirable when systematically processing that information. Such divergent views were observable between South Korean public protests against GSOMIA and public opinion polls that reflected a greater inclination for security cooperation with Japan.

Based on the findings I discussed in chapter 4 on trust, I estimated some additional tests that speak more directly to the policy relevance of NIA. Compared to the more abstract and theoretical dependent variable of trust as in chapter 4, this chapter had a narrower focus on a specific, contested case that exists between Japan and South Korea. These further analyses provide a nice gateway into the feasibility and potential of NIA in practice.

While GSOMIA was canceled just hours before its scheduled signing due to public outrage in Seoul, it was strikingly noticeable from public opinion polls that the majority of South Koreans actually *agreed to* the necessity of the treaty. This supports my theoretical reasoning behind the workings of NIA that I described in chapter 3. That is, fierce opposition against cooperation with a past adversary could be rooted in negative imagery rather than prudent calculations of self-benefit. When people had the chance to "see the larger picture" of how they could benefit through a policy, they were able to objectively acknowledge the necessity of it. I suggest that NIA can be a way for people to step out of their defensive selves that strive to protect their group integrity above all and see the larger picture. In my experiments, when asked about attitudes in a setting of a real policy of heated debate, strategic trust induced by NIA significantly improved public opinion on the policy. In addition, it was found that those who opposed the policy most—progressives in South Korea whose fate was linked to their country—recognized greater need for the policy when they were affirmed of their national identity.

The experimental findings suggest important implications for policymakers. The conventional image of the South Korean public is of an audience highly sensitive to nationalism and, in particular, anti-Japanese sentiment (Cha 2000). If a South Korean government in the Blue House is interested in drumming up support for cooperative foreign policy with Japan it believes to be in the national interest, it may thus consider easier possibilities of garnering support for the policy utilizing measures that affirm South Korean national identity. In this sense, this study could be the beginning of what can become an appealing guidebook for elites: NIA can help push those most extremely opposed to a policy to a more moderate zone and narrow the gap between polarized opinions on the policy.

In Northeast Asia it is simply unrealistic for state leaders to abandon nationalism. South Korea is a democratic country, and leaders will need to engage with nationalism for public support. When leaders find economic, strategic, or geopolitical reasons to cooperate with Japan then, how do they pursue this while still advocating nationalisms? I argue that NIA can move the masses. When leaders perceive of some benefit of cooperation but face domestic opposition, NIA can be a way to nudge the extremely opposed opinions in the public in a moderate direction. It is possible for there to be conditions in which, for example, all three countries have state leaders or strong entrepreneurs with interests in actively promoting xenophobic hatred. In such cases there may be limits to the affirmation effects. More on the possible limits to affirmation is discussed in the concluding chapter.

Among the discourses on the problems of history between South Korea, China, and Japan, the most prevalent ones from South Korea and China are statements that Japan has not adequately compensated for its wartime behavior, and that is most responsible for ongoing tension in the region. In the next chapter, we move to the Japanese side of contested policies for another examination of NIA's effect on actual policy. Specifically, the chapter studies the effect of NIA on Japanese receptiveness to reparatory measures.

EIGHT

Application to Policy 2

Reparation Endorsement

In chapter 4, we found that affirmation of national identities increases trust in the moral character of citizens in a rival country. What does this mean for policy? I theorized in earlier chapters that building moralistic trust can eventually lead to the formation of a security community in Asia. Trust that emerges in the public can accumulate, and with repetition and reciprocation become habitualized and institutionalized to the extent that a security community is born. But this is not an instant process. Although we can theorize the process and probability of a new security community in the context of Asia, it is challenging to test such steady developments in this book.

Instead, in this chapter I examine the more immediate and policy-relevant effects of moralistic trust increased by NIA, namely the motivation in the public to support governmental policy and undertake autonomous action that resolves international conflict. Borrowing from existing work on civil society in international relations, this chapter assumes a change of values in the public can motivate citizens' action, which can progressively and ultimately influence state behavior. I perform quantitative tests that demonstrate how moralistic trust boosted by NIA can lead to a willingness in the Japanese public to take independent and collective action for reparation to China and South Korea.

This is a more direct application of national affirmation theory to policy compared to the experimental trust and guilt chapters (chapters 4 and 5, respectively). In this chapter I ask Japanese respondents directly whether they feel that their government should engage in reparative policy, and if so, what types of measures they should take and to what extent. Whereas the survey items in chapter 4 measured Japanese participants' trust toward Chinese and South Korean people, this was in an abstract game setting, and any mention of practical applications or historical context was absent. And although chapter 5 did study Japanese' declared historical guilt, this was a pure measure of how much guilt Japanese *feel* for their country's past actions, which did not, in connection with the guilt, measure motivation to take actions about this in the real world.

8.1 Psychological Change and Action in the Public Can Impact International Relations

Although the premise of this book and many tests in it argue against constructivist ideas that support a homogenous, common in-group identity as necessary for institutions of lasting peace such as security communities, I do not dismiss the various and wide-ranging schools of constructivist thought as inaccurate. In fact, constructivists have established seminal research foundations on the effects of individual-level agents in international society—an assumption that this book shares. For example, constructivists have provided invaluable insights to the roles of the public and civil society and how grassroots level networks in the populace can affect macro-level change in international relations.

Neorealists and scholars that assign exclusive importance to systemic and structural factors in the international realm remain dubious about the possibility of psychological change in the populace having any substantive influence in the world. What power can a feature like trust in the public have in the sphere of international relations, where the sovereign state reigns supreme?

Chapter 1 included a discussion of why publics matter in world politics. Intuitively, the preferences of voters can affect leaders in countries with democratic elections (Park and Chung 2021). However, the public can also impact policy directly via individual action, rather than merely pressuring for change through political delegates. Experts have noted that public opinion can have a profound impact on public and foreign policy thorough autonomous and collective action (Chanley 1999; Page and Shapiro 1992; Jacobs and Shapiro 2000).

Citizens, often when morally motivated, can create groups or organizations that work to pursue their ethical inclinations (du Gay, Salaman, and

Rees 1996; Lang 2013). These groups are known as civil society. Nongovernmental organizations (NGOs) are an example of civil society. NGOs have impacted intergovernmental organizations (IGOs) and countries' governments on decisions concerning diverse normative issues such as transitional justice, biodiversity, banning landmines, climate change, trade and intellectual property, and sanctions and embargoes (Chung and Yi 2021; Hein 2008).

Civil society can change state behavior in international relations, even in a political order predicated on state sovereignty. Equipped with expertise in specific issue areas, civil society has increasingly grown as active players in policymaking, rather than simply spectators (Barnett and Finnemore 2004). Forming transnational advocacy networks (sometimes abbreviated as TANs), civil society promotes the emergence and socialization of norms (Schneiker 2017). These networks of norm entrepreneurs act as agents of socialization, pressuring IGOs and state leaders to adopt new policies and by monitoring compliance with international standards. As norms promoted by TANs are gradually taken up by other actors and spill over to other policy fields, a tipping point occurs where enough states endorse the new norm to redefine a "logic of appropriateness" (Finnemore and Sikkink 1998). In this sense, states are not the only agents of socialization in the context of international politics. Ideas and values in the citizenry can affect strategic concerns and macro-level change between states in international relations.

The moral motivation of NGOs does not necessarily contrast with state interests either. Hein (2008) argued that NGOs tend to be "aloof from politics and based on compassion," but their action and norm socialization initiated first by compassion can work hand in hand with strategic concerns. As we saw in chapter 4's experimental setting, for example, a moralistic trust of the other would work in accordance with investment in the trust game for strategic trust, rather than offsetting strategic exchange for mutual gain. Finnemore and Sikkink (1998) also agree that the processes of social construction by civil society and strategic bargaining in international relations can be deeply intertwined.

Today citizen groups play the role of moral arbiters, setting standards for human welfare and propelling others—including state leaders—to act. Scholars observe that civil society has particularly emerged on the international scene today as new advocates of victims impacted by war, poverty, and other injustices (Hoffman 2009). For example, many NGOs have successfully articulated new meaningful political topographies of victims and perpetrators in conflict and colonization. Experts have emphasized that communication dynamics are the linchpin to citizen groups in fabricating norms (Hein 2008). In an age of technological advance, unprecedented interconnectedness, and rapid and open access to information, the individual is as efficacious as they have ever been in influencing politics.

8.1.1 How Trust Induced by NIA Can Bring Peace in International Relations

Following the emergence of a norm in civil society, it can "cascade" as it becomes a universalized and consolidated norm through iterated behavior and habit (Finnemore and Sikkink 1998). Extending the discussion from chapter 4, NIA can aid initiation of trust between unlikely publics. Eventually, with iteration the trust can become habitualized and institutionalized to the extent that it makes a difference in state behavior.

I noted in my earlier theoretical model on NIA and trust that repeated positive interactions empowered by NIA can build and reinforce habits of trust. I assume that these can eventually cascade into the creation of a security community. Security communities were mentioned earlier as an example of a preferred ideal of stable peace between sovereign states. What would the first steps of this longer process look like though?

I find that NIA boosts trust between people from different countries, which then increases motivation for personal action to initiate change. In particular, I find that NIA makes Japanese people more receptive to reparatory measures, and this is done through increased trust as a mediator. In particular, not only did Japanese affirmed of their national identity express more need for governmental reparative policies but they also demonstrated a willingness to personally partake in grassroots action for reparation. Iterated beneficial interaction after the initial positive exchange nudged by NIA can build up to create habitual behavior, eventually becoming institutionalized and solidified to the extent that it creates a security community. The repeated positive interaction in the middle steps will include procedures such as confidence-building measures, track-2 diplomacy, and other iterated diplomatic tools that can affect state behavior.

The core argument of European integration put forward by neofunctionalists is that frequent collaboration among people from different countries involving joint endeavors on technical tasks will ultimately create habits of trust (Finnemore and Sikkink 1998). Constructivists emphasize here that identities converge with this habitualized trust, which, with internalization, leads to a security community (Adler and Barnett 1998). The spillover described by both neofunctionalists and constructivists starts from technocratic cooperation in nonpolitical areas but automatically and evolutionarily works toward political convergence, becoming an inadvertent engine of stable peace. In particular, constructivists stress that in the process of this spillover effect people's identification with others shifts to cover previously "othered" parties (Finnemore and Sikkink 1998).

The difference in my theory of affirmation is that it doesn't require convergence of national identities. This book's argument is distinct from the traditional constructivist accounts that point to common, intersubjective understanding as a prerequisite for security communities and view separate identities as a phenomenon that deepens and aligns cleavages across societies, making conflict more likely.

Essentially, I advocate the same outcome of trust leading to relations between states where conflict is unthinkable like a security community. I also agree that trust can become a habit, institutionalized and internalized through peaceful interaction to lead to this favorable outcome. However, I identify a different cause that precedes these desirable effects in international politics. I argue that distinctive, not convergent, national identities can in fact boost a sense of pride and confidence in the self that lowers defensive reaction to other countries. This contentment in group membership enables the mental space for peaceful, evenhanded interaction with other groups. This is the psychological mechanism through which NIA can initiate the first step toward mutually beneficial interaction. With repeated interaction, secure peace between even rival states becomes imaginable.

We examined how NIA can affect behavioral payback through perceived guilt in chapter 5. The amount of payback in the dictator game is considered revealed guilt, as it represents the participant's will to make up for guilt even if that means subtracting from one's own resources. However, that was measured in an abstract game setting. During the game, no mention of historical context or Japan's international relations was given. The abstract nature of the game can be quite theoretical. Also, although participants were asked of their levels of historical guilt later in the survey, this was aimed more at gauging declarations of perceived historical guilt rather than any direct personal willingness to actively do anything about it. Initial experimental results can benefit from and be significantly strengthened by their application to more substantive and practical policy settings.

For added policy relevance, in this chapter we focus on the personal willingness of Japanese people to become involved in grassroots movements. While this grassroots action and civil society may appear as baby steps in international relations, they are things regular citizens can actually do, and in relatively prompt and easy ways if they wish. A huge enterprise of international relations scholars studying this area has been to specify the mechanics of when and how civil society makes a difference in world politics. An analogy to this has been to identify whether mice can roar. Indeed, they have roared, notwithstanding realist doubt, as in the groundbreaking case of landmine bans (Price 1998). This chapter adds to this initiative by theorizing how such noise can contribute to conflict resolution between countries that just can't seem to get along.

What is, then, the connection between NIA and grassroots action? The work of civil society is often based on moral grounds, as citizens act to reify individual commitments and "personal moral enthusiasms" (du Gay, Salaman, and Rees 1996). If NIA increases moralistic trust in other countries, then newfound trust in the out-group's moral goodness can produce a sense of prosocial empathy and justice concerns from the out-group's perspective—even when atrocities were committed by in-group members. This is a radical finding that departs from common psychological tendencies to protect the in-group with defensive, group-serving judgments. What is more, the beauty and surprise of NIA is that it does not even require a weakening of those exact boundaries of identification for this preferred effect to occur. Counterintuitively, by making those national identities salient, people come to afford a mental calmness to put themselves in another's shoes. This becomes the moral foundation that prompts people to take action to make a difference, for example, through civil society.

My tests in chapter 4 discussed how the difficult first step—the initiation of trust between adversarial states with a negative history—can be born. In this chapter, I examine how that trust can influence policy, namely by motivating citizens to initiate and participate in grassroots movements to change their present toxic landscape of international relations. But before discussing the tests, I first provide background information on the reality of some of the unresolved issues at hand between China, Japan, and South Korea that consistently trigger the harshest disputes between the countries' publics. I choose these cases because they are among the areas in which I believe NIA's effect of nudging public opinion to change actual policy can first have an effect. In particular, I hypothesize that NIA can increase the personal willingness of Japanese people to engage in reparative policy.

8.2 Citizens' Actions in Unresolved Issues

Since 1992, every Wednesday there have been *Sooyo Jipwes*, or "Wednesday Assemblies," in front of the Japanese Embassy in Seoul, South Korea (BBC

2014). These "assemblies" are demonstrations consisting of nongovernmental organizations, comfort women, and other South Korean citizens demanding Japanese compensation for Japanese war crimes in Korea during World War II. There have been more than one hundred assemblies since 1992, and they are still taking place in the same spot every Wednesday (BBC 2011).

These assemblies demand justice to Koreans who were sacrificed during wartime. An estimated 200,000 women, mostly Korean but also including Chinese and Dutch, worked as sex slaves by the Japanese army (Adelstein 2014; Kotler 2014). Many of these women claim they were either deceived into a "work opportunity" or even simply snatched out of their villages by Japanese military vehicles (Brooks 2013). A large number of them were teenagers or younger. Demands of the assemblies include an official apology from Abe for Japan's past wrongdoings and compensation to those who suffered (Fackler 2015).

On Japan's side, there is fatigue over such persistent demands from South Korea and China regarding the past. Many taking the Japanese' viewpoint argue that these demands of history have already been settled. In 1995, Japan's then prime minister, Tomichi Murayama, made a statement in which he apologized for wartime actions in Asia (BBC 2014). In addition, many Japanese elites argue that the matter was already settled in bilateral agreements with South Korea in the 1960s, when South Korean dictator Park Chung Hee signed a "Treaty on Basic Relations" with Japan. In it, Park agreed to receive a large amount of developmental aid in exchange for a promise to not bring up historical issues again (Yoon 2008). Japanese experts argue that at the time Japan offered lump-sum compensation to wartime victims.

More than seventy years after the war ended, many South Koreans say these actions are inadequate, accusing the Japanese government of ignoring the demands of the victims with silence and failing to acknowledge the state's responsibility (BBC 2014). Numerous comparisons are drawn in South Korea between Japan's and Germany's attitudes following wartime doings. These analogies are often used to criticize Japan for denying responsibility, which remains the key impediment for cooperative international relations in the region. In addition, with only 56 of the 237 registered South Korean victims surviving, the issue of comfort women and forced wartime laborers is becoming an issue of intense debate as South Koreans demand that Japanese authorities satisfactorily address the issue before the numbers dwindle even lower (BBC 2014).

More recently in June 2015, Japanese prime minister Shinzo Abe and former South Korean president Park Geun Hye were preparing a Park-Abe summit (Halpin 2015). In preparing for the summit, one Japanese request was the removal of the "Little Girl Statue" in front of the Japanese Embassy in South Korea, which was erected by civil societies to mark the 1000th rally in support for their cause (BBC 2011). The statue symbolizes the girls that were used as comfort women for the Japanese army. South Korea rejected Japan's request to tear down the statue (Halpin 2015).

This is just one issue, out of many, that continue to plague international relations in Northeast Asia. If NIA can increase trust, guilt recognition, and positive perception between publics in different countries, how can they have an actual effect in the real world?

8.3 Grassroots Action for Reparation

> NIA motivates individuals to dedicate their own resources to compensate—through a perceived trustworthiness in the out-group's moral character

Numerous unresolved issues exist between Japan and its neighbors, still causing recurrent diplomatic friction today. I offer NIA as an easier way to willingness for reparative policy in the inflictor state's public. In chapter 4, we learned that NIA is associated with higher levels of trust. How could this actually impact reparatory practices in Asia? This chapter incorporates insights from our findings on NIA's effects on trust and applies them to a lingering issue between the countries.

Namely, I conduct multiple mediation analyses to observe the mechanism of how NIA increases moral assessments in the character of the other country's people, which then leads to personal willingness in the inflictor state's public to make up for their country's past doings. Recall from chapter 4 that moralistic trust is a subjective summary of one's assessment of the ethical goodness in the other's disposition. As NIA removes defensive and in-group-serving judgments that would otherwise prevail, it encourages moralistic trust of an out-group. So the in-group comes to perceive the other as a more trustworthy, ethical entity. Because of this enhanced positivity in the subjective evaluation of the out-group's virtuous nature, in-group members become more open to repairing past injustice. If this intention is sincere, then it should be expressed all the same in situations that involve people's dedication of some of their own personal resources (time, money, or energy) to exhibit responsibility. Hence, NIA can lead to personal action aimed at instigating larger change.

To examine how increased trust of the other could actually lead to an improvement in relations, I conducted further analysis studying the effect of affirmation in a more concrete policy setting—namely reparatory measures from Japan. By evaluating the extent of Japanese' willingness to personally partake in actual reparatory measures toward South Korea or China, this chapter takes one step forward from the relatively abstract experimental settings in our previous study of guilt in chapter 5 into the realm of public action, where citizens are willing to take initiative to make a difference, with a sense of agency and free from political interference. I hypothesize that NIA increases trust Japanese have of the other countries, which makes them more receptive to reparatory measures regarding the past.

8.3.1 Moralistic Trust as a Mediator of Affirmation and Reparatory Attitudes

Chapter 4 presented results of tests that showed a positive relationship between NIA and increased trust. How could this affect actual policy? In this part of the analysis, I further explore whether the relationship between affirmation and trust has policy implications that may promote direct public contributions to resolving complications and bettering relations with other countries.

In public opinion polls in 2013 and 2014, Japanese and South Korean people were asked to list the foremost reasons they held negative perceptions of the other. As for the reason why the South Korean public had unfavorable impressions of Japan, more than 70 percent of the respondents answered, "Inadequate repentance over the history of invasion." In comparison, the Japanese raised the concern with "criticism of Japan over historical issues" at 73.9 percent (Genron NPO and East Asia Institute 2014). This view on the Japanese side reflects frustration over South Koreans and Chinese constantly bringing up historical issues from more than seventy years ago. Many Japanese express doubt and distrust regarding the sincerity of such South Korean and Chinese claims. Nationalist movements in the Japanese public express fatigue of being criticized for the past, as well as the wish to put the issues of war crimes and compensation behind them. They believe South Korea and China are strategically using the "history card" to secure further compensation from Japan (Reilly 2011). For example, some experts note that South Korean and Chinese elites started persistently raising the issues of history during the 1980s—and not immediately after the war—as a way of exploiting their "victim" status to advance elites' interests and gain united domestic support (Peattie 2007; Pilling 2009; Wirth 2009).

Moralistic trust increases willingness to compensate

Japanese refusal to believe the sincerity of claims for compensation by South Korea and China reflects a lack of Japan's trust in the character of those making such demands. A belief of the other's trustworthy character is moralistic trust (Uslaner 2002). As a reminder, among the two measures of trust, moralistic trust involves a moralistic assessment of the other's nature (Hardin 2006). Moralistic trust is what allows confident attribution of the capacity for benign motives to another actor, based on the image and moral schemata of that actor (Rathbun 2007). Since strategic trust, on the other hand, is a calculated evolution in the trustworthiness of the other to uphold mutually beneficial institutional arrangements for their self-interest, strategic trust is less relevant here.

In 2015, the Obama administration urged Japan and South Korea to reach an agreement that would put the past behind the two countries. Experts have noted that the United States has various reasons to prefer a strong alliance between Japan and South Korea (Kim 2016). Both are long-standing allies of the United States, liberal democratic states, and middle-to-high-range powers on the global stage with considerable influence (Eilperin 2016). With a Japan-South Korea alliance, America could not only benefit from leverage in balancing behavior against China's rapid rise but also share the burden and costs of American leadership in the region, namely regarding North Korean nuclear provocations (Landler 2014).

Noticing that time and again unresolved historical enmity between Japan and South Korea was the recurrent cause of failed attempts for a closer alliance, however, the Obama administration pressured the two countries to finally sign an agreement to settle some of the main historical issues. As a consequence, on December 28, 2015, Japanese Foreign Minister Fumio Kishida and South Korean Foreign Minister Yun Byung-se announced that both sides had reached a "final and irreversible" deal on the issue of Korean comfort women, or wartime sex-slaves for the imperial Japanese army. However, this sudden announcement caused public outrage in South Korea, with the public problematizing the lack of public consensus behind the agreement and the secret and dogmatic decision-making process of the government (CBS 2015).

The 2015 agreement on comfort women, officially signed between the

Japanese and South Korean governments, is still causing unrest in South Korea. Even today, the majority of South Koreans demand that this treaty should be abolished (Calderwood 2015). From the Japanese perspective, this has been baffling to many. If South Koreans so vehemently reject an agreement concluded by their own government, to the extent that the country cannot effectively and successfully implement the agreed-upon conditions in the treaty, then how much will it take for South Koreans to be satisfied? Will there ever be an agreement that countries can agree on, putting the past in the past? Japanese are growing increasingly skeptical.

This frustration in Japan is rooted in, and further breeds, the idea that the Chinese and South Korean public are dispositionally hostile vis-à-vis Japan (Friedhoff and Kang 2013). The notion is that due to this unchanging character, Chinese and South Koreans will be aggravated and discontented about Japan's past actions regardless of the course of action and amount of effort Japan takes and pays.

Such skepticism has led to a lack of hope and enthusiasm about Japan resolving tension with its neighbors. This sentiment has broadened and hardened in the Japanese public to the extent that there is an idea in Japan that Chinese and South Koreans have "anti-Japanese DNA" that will cause Chinese and South Koreans to dislike and distrust Japan regardless of what efforts the Japanese make to mend relations (Friedhoff and Kang 2013). Observing overwhelming demand from China and South Korea for Japan to reflect on its history and claims of territorial sovereignty (such as Takeshima/Dokdo and Diaoyu/Senkaku islands), the Japanese are increasingly concluding that there is an unchangeable, hostile disposition in Chinese and South Koreans, even if Japan apologizes (Suzuki 2015b; Rich 2018). In other words, in Japan there is little belief in the capacity of Chinese and South Koreans to hold sincere, benign motivations regarding their demands for compensation. Put differently, Japanese lack of moralistic trust vis-à-vis Chinese and South Koreans is a cause of Japanese unwillingness to pay for the past.

On the other hand, from China and South Korea's perspective, the very fact that the majority of Japanese people pinpoint China and South Korea's excessive anti-Japanese sentiment stirs question in China and South Korea as to whether Japan has any sincere intentions to confront their past at all. In other words, the public opinion of both countries is leading to an escalation effect that stimulates and further worsens the opinion of each other.

At the core of this vicious cycle is an absence of trust in the other group's nature, i.e., moralistic trust (Halperin et al. 2012). Japan has frequently been cited as an "impenitent model," or a unique case where, unlike Germany and Austria, the public has been unwilling to more actively and explicitly provide compensation for history (Benedict 2005; Berger 2012; Maruyama 1969). The deficiency of moralistic trust perpetuates a unique psychological deadlock that has been hampering further action in Japan.

I thus hypothesize that moralistic trust is what matters toward inflictor countries' willingness to compensate for their past deeds. In my experiments, moralistic trust was measured by a set of questions that asked subjects to report their trust toward either the other country's people or government.

> Hypothesis 5 = Japanese affirmed of their national identity are more willing to endorse reparatory policy.
>
>> H5a = Moralistic trust mediates NIA and Japanese receptiveness to reparatory policy.
>
>> H5b = NIA increases Japanese citizens' willingness to directly engage in reparatory policy through personal action.

8.4 Materials

In the same survey as discussed in the trust study, following the affirmation manipulation only Japanese subjects were asked to indicate how much they would agree to personally take part in compensation toward either China or South Korea, depending on what condition they were placed in. This was measured by the item below (borrowed from Gunn and Wilson 2011), where subjects were asked to select as many as they would like. They also had the option of choosing nothing at all if they did not agree to any of the options. Of the questions measuring Japanese compensation endorsement below, the third and fourth items ask whether participants are personally willing to take reparative "grassroots action."

Do you think that [Chinese / South Koreans] should be compensated by Japan for the acts of Japan during World War II and imperialism?

Should not be compensated / Should be compensated

Which of the following methods do you want the Japanese government to do as compensation for [China / South Korea]? Please select all that apply.

Formal apology / Community support / Memorial event / History education in Japanese schools about the damage Korea suffered / Monetary compensation / All of the above / Other / Don't Know

Are you personally willing to take any action as compensation for what Japan has done to [China / South Korea] during World War II and imperialism?

Yes, a lot To some extent / Not really Not at all

What do you think can be done personally as part of compensation for [China / South Korea]? Please select all that apply.

Discuss with other people / Sign a petition / Write a letter / Participate in protests or marches / Volunteer in a citizen group for the purpose of restoring the status of Korean elderly people who were forced to work or worked as comfort women / Donate money / All of the above / Other / Don't Know

Each of the four questions above represent various measures of reparation endorsement, respectively: 1) the general perceived need for Japan to compensate, 2) the type of policy actions the Japanese government should specifically take, 3) personal willingness to partake in reparative acts, and 4) the type and number of actions participants would specifically take. Each of these were used as variables of Japanese' openness to reparation. The first and second variable are introductory measures, to gauge the sample's general openness and agreement to the controversial issues of compensation for wartime acts. In comparison, the third and fourth items specifically involved autonomous action that citizens can initiate on their own. The third question measures perceived motivation to personally participate in reparation, whereas the fourth question took this one step further, asking which and how many grassroots movements citizens would be interest in initiating, based on the motivation. Using these variables, I analyze whether enhanced trust in the moral character of the other induced by NIA can spillover to real action in the populace.

Recall that in my survey experiments on trust, moralistic trust was measured by a set of questions that asked subjects to report their trust toward either the other country's people or government. In chapter 4 I had combined the responses to these questions with a Confirmatory Factor Analysis to create a latent variable of moralistic trust. Here, however, in order to closely examine which measure of trust had an effect on each of the reparation variables, instead of using the latent variable right away, I worked with each these items separately or by combining just a few items together if they appeared to be closely relevant.

For example, item QA was combined with the product of QB and B-1 to create a variable of trust in the other country's government. QC is used by itself to gauge the level of trustworthiness Japanese people imagine South Koreans and Chinese have, based on their subjective summary of

Box 5

QA. How much trust do you have about the [Chinese / South Korean] government?

No trust / Little trust / Some trust / A lot of trust

QB. If the [Chinese / South Korean] government could unilaterally use the Japanese government for its own benefit, do you think the [Chinese / South Korean] government will use Japan? Or do you think that, in general, you will treat Japan fairly?

Use unilaterally for benefit / Treat fairly overall

> QB-1. How strongly do you feel about the answer you chose in the question above?
>
> *Very strongly / Somewhat strongly / Somewhat weakly / Very weakly*

QC. How much trust do you have about the [Chinese / South Korean] people?

No trust / Little trust / Some trust / A lot of trust

QD. If the [Chinese / South Korean] come to the point where they can use Japanese unilaterally for their own benefit, do you think the [Chinese / South Korean] will use Japan? Or do you think it will treat Japanese fairly equally?

Use unilaterally for benefit / Treat fairly overall

> QD-1. How strongly do you feel about the answer you chose in the question above?
>
> *Very strongly / Somewhat strongly / Somewhat weakly / Very weakly*

QE. Do you think that the [Chinese / South Korean] are generally good at helping others and are kind, or do they put their interests first?

Good at helping others and are kind / Put self-interest first

> QE-1. How strongly do you feel about the answer you chose in the question above?
>
> *Very strongly / Somewhat strongly / Somewhat weakly / Very weakly*

the people. Finally, responses to QD and D-1 were multiplied, to which the product of QE and E-1 was combined. This new variable measures how fair and other-regarding, or in other words, prosocial, Japanese considered Chinese and South Korean people to be in general.

8.5 Results

In this section, I report strong support for various measures of trust playing a mediating role between Japanese NIA and support for reparative policy. These findings held across four measures of reparation endorsement, in the overall sample (Chinese and South Korean counterpart combined) as well as the sample asked about just reparation toward South Korea. In China, NIA increased the kinds of personal action Japanese participants were willing to take—the fourth dependent variable above—through an increased perceived trust in the Chinese government.

In contrast to the guilt study in chapter 5, which offered robust findings across all tests in the Japanese sample paired with a Chinese opponent, in this chapter's study of individuals' autonomous action for reparation policy, China proved to be a harder case. This could be in part due to the fact that this study was performed on university students, while the guilt project employed a sample representative of gender and age group. The relatively scarce findings on the Chinese conditions here compared to the South Korean conditions may reflect the reality of younger Japanese' enhanced anxiety and antagonism against the threat of a rising China today.

In addition, it could also represent the temporal distance with past atrocities perceived by the younger generation of Japanese. Recall that in chapter 5 older Japanese generally reported more guilt toward Chinese or South Koreans, which can be attributed to the comparative salience of the turbulent history to them. It has been reported that stronger hesitance of younger Japanese to pay reparation can be attributed to frustration and fatigue for being pressured to pay for the past due to a simple "guilt by association" fallacy, and when asked whether they would personally take action for their country's past deeds, this might have triggered more fatigue regarding the issue. In addition, as China happens to a much more palpable threat compared to South Korea today, that salience could have added to the difficulty of younger Japanese in agreeing to the need of compensation and perceiving personal motivation for actively partaking in grassroots movements for it.

Now for a visual presentation of the results. In figure 42, I summarize eight routes of mediation with the first two dependent variables of reparation endorsement, both in the overall sample (in bold) as well as just the subgroup in the sample that were asked about reparation toward South Korea. Mediation analyses were tested using the bootstrapping method with bias-corrected confidence estimates (MacKinnon, Lockwood, and Williams 2004; Preacher and Hayes 2004). In the present study, the 95 percent confidence interval of the indirect effects was obtained with 5,000 bootstrap resamples (Preacher and Hayes 2008).

The first survey question on compensation assessed whether Japanese participants generally perceived of a need for reparative policy regarding Japan's past, without particular regard to whether that agent providing compensation should be the government, autonomous citizens' action, or something else. When combining Japanese participants across all conditions, trust in the other country's (China's or South Korea's) people, as well as a belief in the prosocial and fair nature of those people, mediated NIA's effect on increasing participants' receptiveness to compensation.

The same relationships applied with the second dependent variable of reparation, or in other words, perceived need and degree of compensation by the Japanese government. Participants were asked about which and how many policies in the response options given the Japanese government should implement for reparation. Here, again, trust in the other country's people, as well as a belief in the prosociality of those people, each mediated NIA's boosting effect on compensation. This held both in the overall sample (where Japanese were asked about reparation toward either China or South Korea) as well as when looking at only the group paired with South Korea separately.

Trust in another country's people and their prosocial tendencies mediate Japanese NIA and personal willingness to partake in compensation.

The third survey question on compensation assessed the degree of participants' declared motivation to personally do something for reparation to the opponent countries. The fourth question put this question into context by providing detailed response options participants could choose from. This question measured citizens' willingness to engage in autonomous action. This list of options in the question consisted of actions regular people often take when morally urged of the need to take matters into their own hands to create change. These endeavors are those that commonly grow into movements in civil society and can even prompt changes in public or foreign policy. Autonomous public movement can eventually

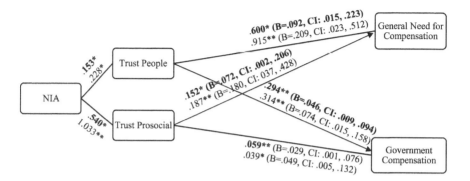

Figure 42. Trust in the other country's people as well as trust in their tendencies to act in fair, prosocial ways mediate Japanese NIA and general perceived need for compensation. Results from overall sample and South Korean conditions, with overall sample in bold.
Multiple mediation models with indirect effects. Numbers outside parentheses represent unstandardized beta coefficients. **Indicates statistical significance at the 1 percent level, *significant at the 5 percent level, †significant at the 10 percent level. B and bias corrected 95 percent CI in parentheses are bootstrap results for indirect effects of predictor on outcome variable through the mediator. Source: Eunbin Chung.

aggregate into larger-scale influence in governmental policy on international reparation.

Across seven mediation models depicted in figure 43, trust in the other country's people in general, and trust in their prosocial tendencies, mediated NIA and personal willingness to compensate as well as to take specific action to participate in and initiate reparation. In the sample of Japanese assigned to the South Korean conditions, trust of South Korean people mediated both outcomes of personal declared agreement for reparation as well as specific options participants chose as actions they would participate in. Trust in South Koreans' prosocial attitudes also mediated personal motivation for compensation, although this did not significantly lead to more choices of action (bottom route in figure 43).

Trust in other governments mediates NIA and personal reparative action in the Chinese and South Korean conditions.

The discussion in section 8.3.1 introduced the current state of Japanese distrust toward the sincerity of Chinese and South Korean governmental demands for reparation. If this is an accurate appraisal of the psychologi-

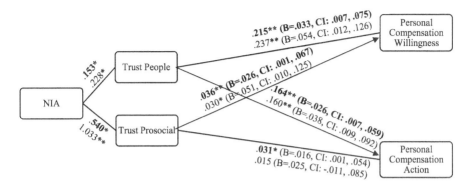

Figure 43. Trust in the other country's people as well as trust in their tendencies to act in prosocial ways mediate Japanese NIA and personal willingness to partake in compensation. Results from overall sample and South Korean conditions, with overall sample in bold. Source: Eunbin Chung.

cal reality across many Japanese, then increasing trust in the foreign governments could encourage personal endorsement of Japanese reparation policy.

The measures of moralistic trust include questions assessing Japanese perceptions of how trustworthy Chinese and South Korean governments are, and whether the governments would use Japan for their interests. I combine responses to these items to create a variable of Japanese trust toward the other governments.

Dividing the overall sample into one that was asked about reparation toward China and the rest that was asked about South Korea, two mediation analyses revealed that trust in the other country's government fully mediated the relationship between NIA and Japanese willingness to personally take action for compensation, in each of the Chinese and South Korean conditions.

When Japanese were asked about their reparative attitudes regarding South Korea, trust regarding the other country's government *and* trust of the other country's people mediated NIA and willingness to compensate. The mediation analysis for trust of people in general in the South Korean condition is included in figure 43.

When examining the Chinese and South Korean conditions, trust of the other country's government mediated the relationship between NIA and Japanese personal willingness to take action in compensation in *both* the South Korean and Chinese conditions.

In figure 44, we see that the relationship is completely mediated by an

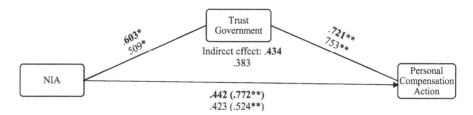

Figure 44. Trust in the Chinese and South Korean governments mediate NIA and Japanese motivation for personal reparative action. Findings from Chinese condition are in bold.
Full mediation. Numbers represent unstandardized beta coefficients. Total effects in parentheses. **Indicates statistical significance at the 1 percent level, *significant at the 5 percent level. Source: Eunbin Chung.

increase of trust of Chinese and South Korean governments. The number .442 in the Chinese condition is the coefficient of NIA on Japanese willingness to personally compensate controlling for trust, or direct effect, which is not significant. But .772 is the total effect, meaning it is the effect of NIA on compensation taking into consideration trust.[1] We see that this coefficient becomes significant. In other words, NIA improves willingness to take reparatory action *through* increased trust of the foreign governments.

When Japanese were asked about their reparative attitudes regarding South Korea, trust of the South Korean government mediated how NIA affected motivation for personal reparatory action. Here again, .423 represents the direct effect between NIA and willingness to compensate, which is not significant when controlling for trust in the South Korean government.

The fact that significant mediation models were found in the Chinese and South Korean conditions with Japanese' perceived trust of the countries' governments speaks directly to the idea that many Japanese presume the other governments use the so-called history card. That is, if it is believed that past conflict is recurrently invoked as a political and strategic tool rather than with sincere motivations, than such beliefs could inhibit Japanese citizens' initiative to establish postconflict justice in their own hands. On the other hand, if some increase of trust is possible by measures like NIA, then the public's readiness to participate in reparation could begin.

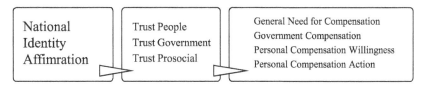

Figure 45. NIA boosted various types of moralistic trust, which enhanced Japanese openness to several reparation measures. Source: Eunbin Chung.

NIA and Reparation in the South Korean Condition

In the South Korean condition, significant mediation effects were found across all the possible connections below (see figure 45), with the exception of trust in South Koreans' prosociality leading to personal action for compensation. That is eleven (calculated by three possible mediators times three outcome variables, minus one nonsignificant relationship) valid routes of mediating relationships, in which NIA works through moralistic trust to increase motivation for compensation.

Another point worth noting is that in chapter 4, I created a latent variable of moralistic trust that combines all of my trust questions. Since I assume that is a summary of one's cognitive image of how trustworthy the people of another country generally are, it is worth checking whether the latent variables of moralistic trust that combines all of the questions also had a mediating effect.

Indeed, in the South Korean condition, moralistic trust mediated all the four compensation variables in our study. These findings are presented in figure 46. These relationships were not significant in the Chinese condition, however. It could be that more mediating effects were overall easily found in the South Korean condition compared to when Japanese faced Chinese opponents because China was the "harder case" for Japan. A possible presumption is that Japanese feel more threatened about China, leading to different dynamics of affirmation effects.

8.6 Conclusion

Though theoretical traditions of international relations are state-centric, key contributors in the study of civil society in global politics have highlighted their role as early promoters of new norms and agenda setters (Finnemore and Sikkink 1998; for a divergent view, see Drezner 2007).

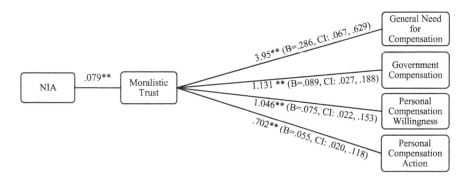

Figure 46. Trust in South Korean people, their tendencies to act prosaically, and the South Korean government mediate NIA and Japanese perceived general need for compensation toward South Korea. Source: Eunbin Chung.

Citizens' movements are especially active in moral arenas, for example, concerning postconflict justice. As providers of analysis and expertise, civil society channels the views of the grassroots upwards to state elites and policy decision makers (Hannah and Scott 2017).

Civil society can drive normative change from the bottom up, as is commonly assumed. However, recent studies discover that civil society increasingly operates as fundamental operators of global governance, rather than peripheral or secondary agents (Hannah and Scott 2017). Citizen groups function as pressure groups and lobbyists for policy and normative change, forming an interconnected and interdependent, almost symbiotic relationship with IGOs and other actors.

Previously I mentioned how leaders can utilize NIA as a policy frame to move sticky antagonism in public opinion toward cooperative foreign policy. But NIA can promote reconciliation and cooperation between enemy states in the other direction too: grassroots movements that start from a morally motivated public can scale up to mass movements that affect foreign policy and governmental decision-making.

This chapter on Japanese reparation policy strengthens our findings on NIA's effect of guilt in reconciliation, by complementing our previous chapter on guilt in various ways. Chapter 5, which focused on guilt recognition in inflictors, found that NIA is associated with an increased willingness in Japanese citizens to admit guilt regarding their country's history. But will these responses to survey questions actually hold implications for Japan's reparative policy toward China and South Korea?

The experimental design in chapter 5 included a dictator game where

Japanese participants were asked to imagine they were paying virtual tokens to their Chinese or South Korean counterpart to make up for any harm their counterpart suffered. This was done in both scenarios where subjects were told the inflictor of harm was the self, or another Japanese participant. We found that the amount subjects offer to give away can be a reliable measure of perceived guilt.

In these cases, since subjects were virtually taking money out of their personal pot of money to give to their counterpart, this can be seen as a measure of a willingness to invest one's own personal resources to compensate for guilt. But this was in an experimental setting, with the "guilty deed" happening in an abstract game context.

How about willingness to devote personal time, energy, and resources to the citizens in other countries regarding Japan's history? This is certainly a harder case, considering the sensitive political connotations of admitting guilt toward another country. The question of whether people in a country are willing to efficaciously take action themselves for their country's deeds many decades ago is also a hard case that connects perceived moral motivation springing from a sense of linked fate to the nation with the resources one personally possesses in her/his hands today.

Linked fate beliefs can reduce some Japanese' frustration of being charged "guilty by association," since continuity of the nation implies present-day Japanese should also share some responsibility for their ancestors' deeds. If linked fate is what encourages people from past inflictor states to admit guilt *and* personally pay resources for reparation, in the interest of achieving peace between enemies quarreling about the appropriate degree of reparation, it might appear as a preferable policy to promote beliefs of linked fate in the public. However, recall that in chapter 7 linked fate was also associated with South Koreans' strong rejection of a joint policy with Japan. Linked fate itself can have mixed effects in international relations, sometimes causing people to passionately push policy in directions that they might have otherwise not agreed to when they systematically processed the costs and benefits of the policy in a coolheaded manner.

At the end of the experiment in chapter 5, participants were asked to report their level of historical guilt concerning Japan's relations with its neighbors. But the willingness to personally make up for historical guilt was not measured. Why does this matter? Many citizens may consider reparation policy to be a matter that falls purely under governmental jurisdiction. This might induce survey participants to more easily respond that they are receptive to admitting historical guilt. However, as discussed in chapter 1, the public has some agency when it comes to foreign policy. In addition, considering the budget that will be needed for reparatory policy, through taxes the public would be, in some part, paying through their own resources for reparation all the same.

In sum, evidence from this chapter suggests that NIA may diminish inflictors' defensive reactions against compensation. When individuals reflect on group values, they become more certain about their priorities and qualities (Wakslak and Trope 2009). This creates a sense of security and contentment in the in-group's overall integrity, allowing members to grow receptive to unfavorable information. Knowing that their perception of their group is not as vulnerable to unfavorable information, members feel less need to act defensively. They embrace the information and thus experience concomitant guilt and shame. To override this guilt and shame, they become receptive to reparation. Importantly, increased trust, expected to be brought about by the NIA manipulation, boosted moralistic trust of the other countries China and South Korea. Since moralistic trust represents trust in the disposition of the other as a moral being, it can be expected that the increased trust led Japanese subjects to take Chinese and Japanese claims as more genuine. Trust in the normative character of the government and people of the other country thus mediated Japanese willingness to endorse compensation.

NINE

Conclusion

How can states with a history of conflict or colonialism reconcile with one another? This book was motivated by seeking answers to this question. Now that my research has been presented, how should we consider the findings as relevant for international politics and policy? What would it take to make NIA an adopted and effectual strategy for international relations? And how could we differently understand the implications of nationalism and historical grievances?

This final chapter reflects on the larger lessons learned from this book. Having first explored how NIA can promote peace and cooperation in earlier chapters, we now turn to some real world examples to visualize how the theoretical insights provided by NIA can be actualized in politics. I present historical examples of NIA, namely in the forms of policy and rhetoric.

I then review the policy implications of NIA and how it can offer insight into finding mutually face-saving resolutions in Asia. I discuss the grave circumstances of current international relations in the region and the urgency and significance of these issues for the United States and world politics, both in the security and economic sectors. The chapter ends with the book's potential limitations, implications for scholarship, and future avenues to pursue in the study of national identity affirmation.

9.1 How Would National Identity Affirmation Look in the Real World?

Robust national identities need not be diverted in the direction of conflict. This book's evidence opens a promising policy space for countries with strong national identities in a counterintuitive yet constructive way. Elites emphasize national pride and greatness for various reasons, and my findings suggest that such acts do not preclude public support for cooperation with a longtime rival. When leaders wish to pursue a reconciliatory policy, this does not require downplaying national identities. Indeed, my test results imply that a tradeoff between the two policies is not inevitable, as long as the policy does not specifically focus on highlighting out-group hatred. National identity and positive engagement with a country previously locked in a negative image do not have to be a zero-sum game. Rather leaders may frame policy with NIA to mobilize public support for cooperative policies with rival states that may otherwise be at the expense of domestic popularity and legitimacy.

9.1.1 Policy and Rhetoric

Political leaders can enact policies of affirmation toward others to help achieve foreign and domestic policy objectives. Applied in the real world, NIA can offer a way of enjoying contentment from an elevated sense of self without a desire for putting down the other. It is a psychologically inward-facing reorientation and refocusing of the self-concept, not an outward projection against the other. This is the strength of NIA and what distinguishes it from chauvinism, potentially making it an attractive tool in foreign policy. In fact, NIA could be put to use via policy, education, media, or leaders' rhetoric, shifting those most opposed to a policy out of their extremes and toward a more moderate center, overall moving the entirety of public opinion (and thus the median voter) closer to supporting the desired policy. While this book takes a more theoretical approach rather than aiming to prescribe specific policy design on best practices for utilizing NIA, I provide a few examples here as precursory evidence to suggest ways in which NIA applied in the real world could be effective.

During Barack Obama's presidency, his foreign policy took the approach of the "Obama Doctrine," which emphasizes collaboration and negotiation and questions why historic U.S. enemies must remain enemies (Goldberg 2016). However, sudden reconciliation with a longtime adversary is bound to be difficult and face fierce opposition from those who cling to a more familiar enemy image of that nation. Facing this challenging situation, Obama managed to successfully pursue the "Cuban Thaw," warming Cuba-U.S. relations (Fullerton, Kendrick, and Broyles 2017). This led to a series of cooperative initiatives that displayed a boost in trust, including the reopening of respective embassies, the loosening of travel and commerce restrictions, the commencement of direct commercial flights, the release of prisoners in both countries who had been accused of spying (DeYoung 2014; Federal Register 2015), and the first historic visit by a sitting U.S. president in almost a century (Davis 2016).

Obama's announcement of this drastic policy change embodied a communication strategy that made use of NIA's effects in nudging policy preference in public opinion to align closer with his own. In his 2015 State of the Union speech, Obama first presented a list of recent accomplishments, bringing up a more politically contentious issue only after that. While most Americans would feel a sense of self-pride about the achievements of their country, not all of them might agree on instantly changing relations with a longtime adversary. A *New York Times* poll conducted before Obama's announcement in October 2014 found opinions on Cuba differed little from a poll conducted in January 1977, with just 54 percent of Americans supporting reestablishing relations with Cuba (Dutton et al. 2014). This indicates that roughly half of Americans were still unprepared to engage in a détente with the longtime Cold War enemy.

In addition, Americans' perceptions of Cuba were sharply polarized along partisan lines. Republicans overwhelmingly disapproved (67 percent) of Obama's handling of the matter, while 72 percent of Democrats approved (Dutton et al. 2014). In this situation, it can be assumed that it was most important for Obama to move the opinions of the Republicans most ardently against him. With our knowledge of the psychological effects of NIA, we can assume that Obama's speech was designed to get the public (and, most considerably, conservatives that were against Obama's policy) on board.

Obama started his State of the Union speech by noting numerous reasons Americans should be proud of themselves:

> Tonight, after a breakthrough year for America, our economy is growing and creating jobs at the fastest pace since 1999. Our unemployment rate is now lower than it was before the financial crisis. More of our kids are graduating than ever before. More of our people are insured than ever before. And we are as free from the grip of foreign oil as we've been in almost 30 years. . . . America, for all that

we have endured; for all the grit and hard work required to come back; for all the tasks that lie ahead, know this: The shadow of crisis has passed, and the State of the Union is strong.[1]

As is evident in this excerpt, Obama's affirmation of America was an inward-looking clarification of what America was about in present times. None of his points were directed outward in a comparison with an outgroup. Rather than defining pride in what it means to be American because it was superior in certain aspects to another nation and by contrasting the current state of success to "the shadow of crisis" that had passed, Obama "othered" the country's own past, saying America is now better than that and has put it behind. In this way he invoked satisfaction and fulfillment in Americans of their national identity.

Following that, he moved on to the more politically contentious issue, presenting it as an important new point of achievement for America:

In Cuba, we are ending a policy that was long past its expiration date. When what you're doing doesn't work for 50 years, it's time to try something new. And our shift in Cuba policy has the potential to end a legacy of mistrust in our hemisphere. It removes a phony excuse for restrictions in Cuba. It stands up for democratic values, and extends the hand of friendship to the Cuban people. And this year, Congress should begin the work of ending the embargo. (Obama 2015)

If Obama's goal when making this point on Cuba was to enable his audience to objectively acknowledge the fruitlessness and thus the need to terminate the old policy of embargo, then the preceding affirmation could be considered effective. As discussed in previous chapters, when accepting incoming information, NIA has been found to enhance the capability for updating.

Did the use of NIA work? Following Obama's attempts to bolster national pride to achieve foreign policy objectives, the percentage of American respondents in a Pew Research Center survey (2015) that approved reestablishing diplomatic relations with Cuba rose from 63 percent in January 2015 to 73 percent in July that year. Importantly, when breaking down such numbers by self-declared political ideology, the greatest increase in approval of reestablishing diplomatic relations came from the most fervent opposers—conservative Republicans. While the lowest support of the policy came from conservative Republicans, the greatest increase during the period also came from that group: a 19 percent increase from 33 percent to

52 percent (Democrats during the same period recorded a 74 to 83 percent increase; the entirety of Republicans, which includes both conservative and moderate/liberal Republicans showed an increase from 40 to 56 percentage points). This means that Obama managed to get more than half of the most conservative Republicans to support his new, dramatic policy of completely shifting U.S. relations with a Cold War enemy around. Of course, political and practical interests were presumably involved in this shift, and I do not claim either NIA or Obama's speech to have been the only cause that enabled this effect; they were most likely one of many efforts to garner public support. However, we can assume from various observations of rhetoric and public opinion at the time that NIA may have had a positive effect in helping the public realize the practical interests in breaking away from an age-old enemy. Public support for U.S. ties with Cuba continued to grow, as 72 percent of Americans favored the United States ending its trade embargo with Cuba, which included 59 percent of Republicans. Based on the results, the report concluded that "support for restoring diplomatic ties with Cuba, and ending the embargo, now spans virtually all groups in the U.S. population" (Pew Research Center 2015).

This trend in public opinion held even after Castro's death and U.S. elections—a *New York Times* survey of U.S. citizens in March 2016 found that 62 percent favored abolishing the ban on trade (Sussman 2016). The Pew Research Center announced in December 2016 that 75 percent of Americans approved of the 2015 decision to resume relations with Cuba, while 73 percent favored ending the U.S. embargo against Cuba (Tyson 2016).

This example suggests that NIA as a policy tool can work in other areas in the world beyond Asia. The next section returns to this book's primary regional focus, to discuss how NIA can be important and beneficial in Northeast Asia. I suggest how we can connect the results from previous chapters to the grim situation of international relations in the region, notably with regard to U.S. interests.

9.2 The U.S.-Japan-South Korea Alliance Triangle

At the time of writing, Japan and South Korea are embroiled in a fierce new trade war that is intertwined with bitter emotion and disagreement on historic grievances. Again, the discord stems from unhealed colonial wounds of forced labor and sexual slavery during Japan's occupation of the Korean Peninsula from 1910 to 1945. South Koreans insist that Japan has not sufficiently apologized for atrocities, while Japanese argue they have done enough, legally and politically (Rich, Wong, and Choe 2019). In 2018, a South Korean court ordered Japanese firms to compensate South Koreans who were forced into labor during the colonial period (Ock 2019). Tokyo claimed they had already paid for damages through a treaty with South Korea in 1965 that normalized bilateral ties. This sequence of events symbolized a downturn in a relationship that is already tainted by a painful history of conflict and colonization (C. Kim 2019).

The long-simmering conflict erupted into full diplomatic crisis when Japan announced in July 2019 that it would tighten its control over trade to South Korea and remove South Korea from its index of reliable trading partners, known as the "white list." This infuriated South Koreans, who responded by actively boycotting Japanese products. In the same month, two South Korean men in their seventies set themselves afire and died in protest against Japan, and multiple candlelight vigils were held in front of the Japanese Embassy with participants calling Japan's move an "economic invasion" and demanding an apology for Japan's wartime atrocities (Ock 2019). Japanese-South Korean relations have hit an all-time low, with public opinion polls in each country showing the highest level of public distrust in each other in decades (Rich, Wong, and Choe 2019).

The consequences of the bilateral conflict will be harmful for the global economy, which is already experiencing another trade war between the United States and China. Furthermore, the toll of the dispute extends beyond economic damage of the trade standoff, with serious implications for American, regional, and international security.

9.2.1 The Alliance Triangle Roots and Implications

The turmoil between Northeast Asian states is most frustrating for the United States. The quagmire for America's position regarding Asia's deep divide is that playing the part of peacemaker is tough, tricky, and with prospects that seem bleak, but ignoring the divide may create threats to practical American security and economic interests. The United States has long relied on its trilateral alliance with Japan and South Korea to help counter China's influence and deter North Korean security threats.

The U.S.-Japan-South Korea security triangle has its roots from several decades ago. From the American perspective, South Korea was at the forefront of the Cold War (Chang 2019). In order to build a reliable fortress of anticommunism in Asia, the United States aided South Korea to emerge from its war ruins into a strong ally. From Japan's point of view, the potential gain of entering this relationship as a mutual ally of the United States and South Korea was also apparent. The security umbrella held together by the American and South Korean militaries in cooperation with Japanese Self-Defense Forces would safeguard an army-less Japan. Economically, Japan was also in a good position to invest in South Korea, with knowledge of the country and a revived postwar economy.

Although the world has changed since then, the United States still needs the trilateral alliance to protect and pursue critical interests. The power dynamics in the international landscapes are shifting, but in such a way that the United States must keep its allies closer than ever in its competition with China and deterrence against North Korean provocations.

Security Concerns

Washington relies on the strategic relationships with both Japan and South Korea to stand alongside it to help counter China's rise and North Korea's nuclear arms (Goodman, cited in C. Kim 2019). In 2019, the U.S. Department of Defense released the first-ever Indo-Pacific Strategy Report (IPSR), a strategic document prepared by outlining Washington's priorities in the region (Panda 2019; U.S. Department of Defense 2019). The term Indo-Pacific Strategy has been used to refer to a partnership between India, Japan, Australia, and other major Asian democracies that will join in curbing the influence of China in what many commentators call the framework of a "new Cold War" (Sim 2019; Walt 2019). The Indo-Pacific Strategy was promoted several times during U.S. President Donald Trump's visit to Japan, reflecting the U.S.-Japan interest in it. For successful implementation of this strategy a strong U.S.-ROK alliance is also crucial, in order to avoid South Korea's siding closer with China, considering the split attitudes regarding North Korea within the South Korean citizenry.

The bitter battle between Japan and South Korea, which stretches back one hundred years, also unsettles American military planners that depend on cooperation between the allies to contain North Korea and secure the region today. In July 2019, North Korea paraded its growing ability to strike its neighbors with devastating firepower through three barrages of short-range missiles (Rich, Wong, and Choe 2019). However, Japan and South Korea, both American allies in the path of those missiles, were locked in a deteriorating combat with each other instead of banding together to deter North Korean threats. In Seoul, thousands of protesters marched the streets, threatening the GSOMIA agreement, which the United States considered crucial to monitoring North Korea's nuclear buildup in cooperation with Japan and South Korea (Rich, Wong, and Choe 2019). Trump administration officials noted that they are particularly concerned about this possibility, as the agreement can be a key element of military cooperation that helps the United States in the region (Glaser, cited in Rich, Wong, and Choe 2019).

Economic Concerns

A close U.S.-Japan-South Korea alliance triangle is vital for the United States concerning China's influence, not just security-wise but in the economic sector too. In 2015, Chinese Premier Li Keqiang and his cabinet issued a strategic plan called "Made in China 2025," with aims to upgrade the manufacturing capabilities of Chinese industries and produce higher-quality products and services (PRC State Council 2015a). Following the announcement of the strategic plan, the premier emphasized the importance of integrating of China's and Russia's development strategies (PRC State Council 2015b). Experts argue that in response to "Made in China 2025," the United States set new regulations to control strategic materials from entering China in 2018, inviting other allied countries to participate (Fukagawa, cited in Y. Kim 2019). In addition, the United States has limited Huawei's sphere of market influence and China's semiconductor production (Klein 2019; Lohr 2019; Sevastopulo 2019).

Success of such policies requires the United States to maintain a close, cooperative relationship with Japan and South Korea. But the two neighbor countries are preoccupied with weaponizing trade in a standoff against each other. This trade dispute poses significant threats to both countries' and the global economies. Simply put, it is a losing battle for everyone involved, including the United States.

Japan and South Korea are among each other's most active trade partners, and both countries' economies will be hurt by the instability and deeply rooted emotions in their relationship. In July 2019, Japan decided to slow down exports of materials essential to South Korean industries, which angered South Koreans. Eventually, however, the export restrictions imposed by the Japanese government could jeopardize markets for Japanese companies too (Rich, Wong, and Choe 2019). While the current trade dispute may look like a bilateral tit-for-tat between Japan and South Korea, given the connected world and deep supply chain the impact is likely to quickly spill over into the region and the rest of the world (Cutler, cited in Rich, Wong, and Choe 2019).

How the United States deals with Asian states impacts their images of the country

The United States is a close and important security ally to both Japan and South Korea. Whenever South Koreans perceived of America's support for Japan, this harms South Korean perceptions of the United States. This kind of backlash in South Korea can weaken the trilateral alliance and U.S. presence in Asia. This is thus a moment for a sensible diplomatic gesture from the United States (Kim et al. 2014).

It is true that the South Korean public's favorable view of the United States has been largely consistent, and the alliance between the countries remains strong. Nevertheless, public opinion is a volatile variable that can fluctuate. In October 2013, then U.S. Secretary of State John Kerry announced that the United States supported Japan's right to expand some aspects of its self-defense. Affected by memories of the past, South Korea and China were very wary of the possibility of Japan pushing for a more aggressive military posture (Rich and Yamamitsu 2019). In public opinion polls conducted by the Asan Institute, 66.8 percent of the South Korean public viewed Japan's perceived military expansion as revisionist, and 64.7 percent stated that Japan would pose a military threat to South Korea in the future (Kim et al. 2014).

As a result, South Koreans' perceived favorability of the U.S. image declined from November to December in 2013. In addition, the percentage of people who viewed the nature of U.S.-Korean relations as competitive rather than cooperative increased from 10 percent to 14.9 percent in December. Although the low numbers did not last for long, they suggest that the South Korean public will react negatively to similar U.S. positions in the future (Kim et al. 2014).

This case hints at how U.S. handling of sensitive issues between the three Asian countries can impact U.S. relations in the region in complex ways. The Trump administration's position on Asia's historical animosity was to largely ignore it, leaving the countries involved to take care of the matters among themselves. However, these issues will not easily disappear, and failure to address them can undermine America's interests in the region. Negligence of the incessant quarrels might be a politically convenient choice, but not a pragmatic one.

Furthermore, China has approached South Korea to work together in addressing shared historical grievances with Japan. This is a prudent move for China, because many South Koreans support the idea of cooperating with China on this issue. In 2013, 74.5 percent of South Koreans in the polls stated that they would support South Korea's cooperation with China to resolve historical disputes with Japan. Shared dissatisfaction with Japan's perceived whitewashing of history and territorial disputes have expanded common ground between China and South Korea. However, this can be damaging for the United States if China is perceived by Koreans as a fellow victim that shares its historical scars while the United States is seen as insensitive to those issues, thus siding with Japan (Kim et al. 2014). In short, America needs to tread carefully between the countries as it helps repair the rift.

In fact, when South Koreans were forced to choose between forging a new cooperative relationship with China and maintaining the alliance with the United States at the risk of damaging relations with China, a clear majority (61 percent) responded that it is more important to forge a new cooperative relationship with China (see fig. 47). This implies that if China's influence does rise as many expect, and U.S. influence relatively declines in South Korea, South Koreans might reexamine the balance between its economic interests (China) and its security interests (United States). From the American perspective, due to these implications China's growth in the region requires adequate and careful planning (The Asan Institute 2013).

With the toxicity of distrust, disagreement on the necessary degree of guilt recognition and reparation, and negative perception of each other, it is easy to assume that the Chinese, Japanese, and South Korean publics do not support attempts at mutual rapprochement. Even institutional measures like summits and GSOMIA have been tough to establish. Understandably, it should not be expected that the people immediately let go of their long-held grudges against each other. However, the public opinion surveys observed in this book indicate that broad swaths of the respective national publics do support a move to improve relations with their neighbors (Friedhoff and Kang 2013). My experimental analyses open a possibility for that. The publics might be prepared for a pragmatic, forward-moving relationship but just have a hard time knowing where to start, or how to get from here to there. I suggest NIA as a way to initiate the first step.

9.3 Implications for Scholarly Debates

Given that many scholars of international relations have already discussed ways to create trust and reassurance in many contexts, what is new about

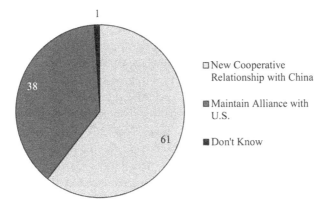

Figure 47. South Koreans prefer forging a new cooperative relationship with China over maintaining alliance with the United States at the risk of damaging relations with China. The Asan Institute of Policy Studies 2013.

my approach? One way in which my study contributes to the scholarship is that I examine underlying micro-foundations of psychological change in public opinion and how this can impact macro-level phenomena in world politics. Many international relations studies that explore interstate enmity focus on the final products of interaction: the external aspects of state behavior. An example is the influential research on enduring rivalries, which defines enduring rivalries as state dyads that have experienced at least five Militarized Interstate Disputes (MID) in the last twenty years (Gochman and Maoz 1984; Goertz and Diehl 1993). Key findings in this literature identify the main causes of termination of rivalries as external shocks or leadership change (Bennett 1996; Goertz and Diehl 1995).

While these seminal findings have contributed to the growth of a rich body of literature, they do not look at the change that actually happens on an individual psychological level when there is a turning point in state relations. The psychological approach of affirmation theory can attempt to fill this gap by focusing on the underpinnings of perception that have a causal effect on international relations. Attention to the actual cognitive foundations of lasting tension can contribute to more effectively identifying the causes, thus eventually relieving the "memory obstacle" that perpetuates a lack of trust and reconciliation.

In addition, while not discussed directly in this book, this study has potential to also contribute to the bargaining literature in international relations in that it suggests a way to lower opposition to cooperation with another country in public opinion, thus enlarging win-sets in negotiation. Why would NIA have effects on bargaining success in particular? In negotiation there exists a barrier to compromise, a barrier that often leads disputing factions to reject even mutually beneficial settlements and instead persist in mutually destructive conflict (Ross and Ward 1995; Sherman, Nelson, and Ross 2003). This barrier concerns, in part, a motivation to defend one's political, national, or regional identity—a motivation that can result in intransigence and stalemate (De Dreu and Carnevale 2003).

However, if protecting one's identity does not have to bring about defensiveness and bias against the out-group, then the cost of initiating a policy that involves closer and cooperative interaction with the out-group can be lessened. From a leader's perspective, if there is less opposition from citizens in cases where benefit from intergroup cooperation is observed, this can connect to more effective implementation of the policy.

In this context, affirmation could lead to higher probability of reaching an agreement in diplomatic negotiation. If NIA can correct for defensive biases, an affirmed domestic audience will be less likely to object to cooperation with the out-group just based on negative imagery alone when the potential of mutual benefit is clear. Additionally, when thinking of interstate negotiation as a two-level game, one could imagine that domestic factions will be more accepting of the outcome of bargaining at the international stage when they are affirmed. In this sense, I suggest that NIA leads to more common ground in negotiation by lowering audience costs that are an impediment to negotiation (Fearon 1994, 1997) and expanding win-sets (Putnam 1988). This especially has policy implications for cases where statesmen conceive potential benefit in international cooperation but fear backlash from the public who have negative sentiments toward each other.

I make several contributions from a perspective of purely progressing academic research as well. First, this study contributes to international relations in that I make an innovative attempt to introduce the social-psychological concept of identity affirmation to the field. This is a first endeavor of applying the theory into a context of international relations.

Second, my findings contribute to social psychology in that I extend the scale of studies on self- and group-affirmation to an international level. To date, I have not been able to find other projects on group-affirmation conducted on national identities across several countries. Furthermore, I construct a novel theory that specifies the conditions under which NIA works. In doing so I integrate several existing psychological studies on self- and group-affirmation into a coherent model that studies the underlying mechanisms. While most studies merely focus on defining more positive effects of self-affirmation, I identify in finer detail which moderators and mediators exist in the process as well.

Third, in terms of theory and scientific methodology, I both horizontally expand the scope of conflict resolution analyses in Asia by including three crucial variables in international reconciliation and vertically deepen the analysis with additional tests using mixed methods. The book focuses on three main dependent variables that are lacking between Northeast Asian countries, causing major impediments to peace: trust, guilt recognition, and positive perception. The breadth of focus allows for an interdisciplinary incorporation of theoretical frameworks popular in international relations, conflict resolution, behavioral economics, and history.

The book takes an eclectic, multimethod approach. I include original experiments in three countries, mediation analyses, and historical cases. The empirical research combines lab, field, natural experiments, and larger-scale surveys, with the experiments merging elements from social psychology and games from behavioral economics. Experiments are an appropriate way to check the internal validity of my theory, as I am first moving to the micro-level to test my basic propositions as a first step that will then be embedded in larger sociological and political factors.

In chapters 5 and 6, samples representative by at least age and gender were used in experiments and observational data. Chapter 6 employed a sample that covers a larger N and longer time period than is generally used in experimental research, with 7,200 South Koreans' perceptions of other countries over the period of six years. This adds an element of external validity that some regard as a potential shortcoming of experimental data.

Finally, I provide a systematic analysis of public opinion in a cross-national setting in Northeast Asia. Unfortunately, and surprisingly, considering the region's importance for peace in the world and significance for the United States, there is a paucity of in-depth analyses that systematically study Asian states' populace and their perceptions. The application of fieldwork or use of primary sources in public opinion studies in the field of international relations is even rarer. Lab experiments in other areas of the world could provide insight into the psychological workings of identity affirmation in general. But national identities are idiosyncratic, and studies on the topic should include consideration for cultural particularities as well by researching in the field. With assumptions on public opinion's ability to influence foreign policy, this book studies ordinary citizens in Asian states that hold deeply engrained national identities they have been socialized into for a long time.

9.4 Scope and Limits of National Identity Affirmation

My findings imply that NIA will increase trust, positive perception, and agreement on the extent of guilt recognition between countries with a history of conflict. A word of caution is needed here, however: I do not propose NIA as a panacea for resolving intergroup animosity, but rather as a catalyst for easing tension when certain conditions are met. By correcting for psychological biases and sticky images, NIA could generate the first move toward affable relations, even if it is not the force that leads toward that as a final state. Initial trust or positive perception generated by affirmation could become the first nudge necessary for initiating positive interaction that benefits both sides. It could be the case that once that minimum necessary level of trust and positive imagery are established, willingness to cooperate with each other opens up, more easily giving rise to reciprocated games of cooperation.

In addition, in places of active military combat, NIA could lose its strength. In cases where lives are lost on a daily basis, for example, intractable conflict could be intuitively understood and chronic suspicion might be unavoidable and justified. NIA could be expected to be more effective in areas where there is persistent tension and negativity between countries but where there is not much rational gain from hostility.

Another possible limit to NIA relates to entrepreneurs with interests in exploiting and manipulating nationalism in a way that perpetuates outgroup hatred. Spinner-Halev and Theiss-Morse (2003) note the difference between "moderate" nationalism, which liberal nationalists argue has the positive effect of reinforcing people's self-esteem, and the nastier, chauvinistic variants of nationalism. When nationalistic leaders with strong interests in promoting and maintaining domestic support based on chauvinism are in power, the positive effects of NIA can be overwhelmed. However, opposite cases also exist, where leaders believe in the benefits of establishing diplomatic relations and hope to cooperate with other states, but they remain unable to make the move due to a potential public backlash. In such cases, NIA could offer an attractive alternative where public opinion can be moved in a more moderate direction. In sum, the scope of this study is most applicable to cases where there is no extreme determining force such as xenophobic elites who have overwhelming power over the country.

9.5 Unanswered Questions

There are several other related avenues to investigate in the future that will add to and strengthen this research. One is to see how long the effects of NIA last. Studies have found the long-term benefits of self-affirmation on students may last for at least two years (Cohen et al. 2009). How long affirmation effects last and in what capacity has direct implications for how attractive and meaningful the application of NIA can be in politics.

Second, and relatedly, how resilient can NIA effects be in response to external and environmental influences? Against what types of countervailing forces may NIA hold or collapse? For example, one could examine whether external or structural changes undo or assist the positive impacts of NIA, depending on their unique situations.

Third, future extensions of this study could replicate it to test its general applicability to other regions and cases of hostility. I chose the three states in Northeast Asia as an example of a region struggling from the history problem, but I also gave examples of other areas where I expect NIA to have a nudging effect toward reconciliation as well. Replications of my experiment in these other areas would greatly reinforce the applicability and feasibility of my theory.

Fourth, examining the effect of matching affirmed with nonaffirmed participants in follow-up experiments would allow for a more refined analysis of exactly how affirmation increases trust and guilt recognition. In each of the economics-style games used in this book, learning patterns may evolve differently in each case, which would be useful to investigate in separate examinations.

Finally, as noted in my scope conditions, the potential risk of applying affirmation of national identities to real world policy would be the danger that it could push people in the undesired direction of xenophobia and self-glorification, especially in the case that chauvinistic entrepreneurs have an interest in promoting such outcomes. By carefully studying how the self-concept clarity enhanced by affirmation is related (or not) to self-esteem, one would be able to broaden the applicability of NIA to policy. It would be interesting to see how enhanced in-group love shows different effects from self-esteem based on a comparison of in-groups and out-groups, which would normally be a source of stronger out-group bias.

All of these additional topics are promising areas for future research. By all means, this project is intended not as the last word but an introduction, to start a conversation on national identity affirmation in international politics.

9.6 Synthesis: Identities in Reconciliation

National identity is among the most salient of social identities today. Cosmopolitans, contact theorists, and common in-group identity theorists alike have argued for a larger, superordinate identity that includes both in-group and out-group and an erosion of existing social identities as a prescription for intergroup peace (Allport 1954; Gaertner and Dovidio 2014; Held 2003). Neofunctionalists studying the European Union look to regional integration that spills over into political arenas (Hoffman 1966). From these perspectives, existing national identities are the foundations that divide one's in-group from an "other," acting as the basis for obstacles to international reconciliation. But is diminishment of robust national identities a prerequisite to move beyond the history problem?

We have witnessed cases of past rivals and enemies achieve reconciliation with each of their respective national identities strong and coexisting. The United States and Mexico have overcome a history of conflict and achieved a pluralistic security community while retaining attachment to strong national identities (Gonzalez and Haggard 1998). As witnessed in this case, an amalgamated entity with a common government or supranational organization is not necessary for reconciliation.

In addition, how willing are people to psychologically and ontologically abandon an existing group identity that they hold close and integrate into a common identity with a past adversary? Forcing people into a larger group together with a distinctive other can actually make people more uncomfortable.

In a larger context, this book speaks to the usefulness of plurality and respect for enduring group identities that many people hold dearly. The idea that an overarching, umbrella identity that subsumes various existing identities should be prioritized might sound idealistic and romantic on the one hand (e.g., projections of the global future as a "world state" [Wendt 2003], or Fukuyama's [1993] "end of history"). On the other hand, however, this can quickly turn into an argument for assimilation into a homogenous bloc. The danger of this argument is the potentially violent approach to enduring identities under the larger bloc, which may be closely knitted with values that are central to a sense of existence and integrity—culture, religion, or even civic values such as a democratic system of governance or rule of law. Multiculturalists have repeatedly argued against strategies of assimilation into a homogenous entity for peace between diverse groups (with different allegiances, religions, and cultures). Diverse identities can not only peacefully coexist but, as I have shown throughout this book, can have positive effects for intergroup relations.

The perceived romanticism of a larger, overarching identity is also related to the question of feasibility. Even political scientist Karl Deutsch (1957), who coined the term security communities, acknowledged that pluralistic security communities are more feasible and easier to maintain than amalgamation under a common government, which is more likely to be unsuccessful and can be overturned—of which he gives the example of the failed union between Sweden and Norway. States in a security community can shelve concerns of future military confrontations while remaining independent in their identities.

Nationalisms have a bad reputation as harmful forces in international peace, but this view neglects the understanding of attachment to *anything* as a double-edged sword. The separation of inward-looking love and pride for one's nation from a sense of superiority over or antagonism toward other nations is indeed a plausible separation, which may become more easily conceived when one considers the example of love for one's own family. Such a purely inward-looking sense of attachment in no way necessitates dislike for others' families. In a similar way, an affirmation of national identity that does not involve comparison to or denigration of other countries is completely possible.

In this sense, strong national identities are not necessarily impediments to peace. Respect for national identities represents a respect for plurality, cultural distinctiveness, and the value of independent groups with diverse cultural and civic markers. Rather than obstacles, these may be tools to help solve the history problem.

Appendixes

Appendix A

Survey Materials

1. Survey Materials for Chapter 4[1]

[NIA (treatment)]

There are many positive aspects about being Korean. Please choose only one of the following items that you think is the most important value for Koreans.

(order of response options randomized)

self-discipline (time management)	family	democracy
loyalty	creativity	originality
appearance / fashion	honesty	concern for others
patience	religion / spirituality	
working hard	self-respect	friendships
personal liberty	health / fitness	achieving your dream
social skills	Courtesy / manners	

> Why did you choose the value you chose above as the most important to Koreans? Why do you think that value is important to Koreans? Please write in 1–2 short paragraphs in the space below. How is the value you chose above expressed among Koreans? Please write in 1–2 short paragraphs in the space below.

[Non-Affirmation (control)]

'Jellybeans' are a chewy candy made in the shape of beans. The following is a list of names of jellybeans. Select just one of the following that you think will be tastiest.

(order of response options randomized)

Sizzling Cinnamon	Tutti-Frutti	Exotic Jalapeno	Wild Island Punch
Apple Jack	Root Beer Rocket	Blueberry Balloon	Tangerine Trampoline
Punch Hole	Maracanã Nuts	Crushed Pear Parachute	Apricot Anvil
Eucalyptus Leaves	Bubble Gum Bouncy Ball	Cosmo Pomegranate	Licorice Ladder
English Cream Cannon	Muscat Mojito	Butter Popcorn	

> In the box provided below, write 1–2 paragraphs about why you think the jellybean you chose will be tastiest.

> When you imagine the taste of the jellybean you chose, what do you think it would taste like compared to the others you did not choose? Write your answer in 1–2 paragraphs.

[Underlined questions included in Japanese surveys only]

> Do you think that Korea [China] should be compensated by Japan for the acts of Japan during World War II and imperialism?
>> *Should not be compensated / Should be compensated*

> Are you personally willing to take any action as compensation for what Japan has done to Korea during World War II and imperialism?
>> *Yes, a lot / To some extent / Not really / Not at all*

> Which of the following methods do you want the Japanese government to do as compensation for Korea? Please select all that apply.
>> *Formal apology / Community support / Memorial event / History education in Japanese schools about the damage Korea suffered / Monetary compensation / All of the above / Other / Don't know*

What do you think can be done personally as part of compensation for Korea? Please select all that apply.

Discuss with other people / Sign a petition / Write a letter / Participate in protests or marches / Volunteer in a citizen group for the purpose of restoring the status of Korean elderly people who were forced to work or worked as comfort women / Donate money / All of the above / Other / Don't know

[Italicized questions not included in Chinese surveys]

*How much trust do you have about the **Japanese government**?*

No trust / Little trust / Some trust / A lot of trust

If the Japanese government could unilaterally use the Korean government for its own benefit, do you think the Japanese government will use Korea? Or do you think that, in general, you will treat South Korea fairly?

Use unilaterally for benefit / Treat fairly overall

How strongly do you feel about the answer you chose in the question above?

Very strongly / Somewhat strongly / Somewhat weakly / Very weakly

*How much trust do you have about the **Japanese people**?*

No trust / Little trust / Some trust / A lot of trust

If the Japanese come to the point where they can use Koreans unilaterally for their own benefit, do you think the Japanese will use Korea? Or do you think it will treat Koreans fairly equally?

Use unilaterally for benefit / Treat fairly overall

How strongly do you feel about the answer you chose in the question above?

Very strongly / Somewhat strongly / Somewhat weakly / Very weakly

Do you think that the Japanese are generally good at helping others and are kind, or do they put their interests first?

Good at helping others and are kind / Put self-interest first

How strongly do you feel about the answer you chose in the question above?

Very strongly / Somewhat strongly / Somewhat weakly / Very weakly

[Trust game instructions]

We will first give 100 tokens to Player A. Player A then has the opportunity to give a portion of his or her 100 tokens to Player B. Player A could give some, all, or none of the 100 tokens. Whatever amount Player A decides to give to Player B will be tripled before it is passed on to Player B. Player B then has the option of returning any portion of this tripled amount to Player A.

Then, the game is over.

Player A receives whatever he or she kept from their original 100 tokens, plus anything returned to him or her by Player B. Player B receives whatever was given to him or her by Player A and then tripled minus whatever they returned to Player A.

We will now run through 3 examples to show you how the game might be played.

(1) Imagine that Player A gives 20 tokens to Player B. We triple this amount, so Player B gets 60 tokens (3 times 20 tokens equals 60 tokens). At this point, Player A has 80 tokens and Player B has 60 tokens. Then Player B has to decide whether to give anything back to Player A, and if so, how much. Suppose Player B decides to return 20 tokens to Player A. At the end of the game Player A will have 100 tokens and Player B will have 40 tokens.

(2) Imagine that Player A gives 50 tokens to Player B. We triple this amount, so Player B gets 150 tokens (3 times 50 tokens equals 150 tokens). At this point, Player A has 50 tokens and Player B has 150 tokens. Then Player B has to decide whether to give anything back to Player A, and if so, how much. Suppose Player B decides to return 0 tokens to Player A. At the end of the game Player A will have 50 tokens and Player B will have 150 tokens.

(3) Imagine that Player A gives 100 tokens to Player B. We triple this amount, so Player B gets 300 tokens (3 times 100 tokens equals 300 tokens). At this point, Player A has 0 tokens and Player B has 300 tokens. Then Player B has to decide whether

to give anything back to Player A, and if so, how much. Suppose Player B decides to return 20 tokens to Player A. At the end of the game Player A will have 20 and Player B will have 280 tokens.

Player B: If you are Player B, the tripled number of tokens Player A decided to give to you will show up on your computer screen. You must decide the amount that you want returned to Player A. Player A could have offered any amount from 0 to 100 tokens, which means you may receive any amount between 0 and 300 total possible tokens. Remember, you can choose to give something back or not. Do what you wish. Type the number of tokens you want to be passed on to Player A.

[Security cooperation questions included in Korean survey only]

Recently, the issue of the military intelligence agreement between Korea and Japan has become a hot topic. Let me ask you a few questions about your thoughts on this.

How interested are you in the subject of the Korea-Japan military intelligence agreement?

A lot of interest / A little interest / No interest / I do not know

Do you think it is good for Korea to conclude this agreement with Japan?

Yes / No / I do not know

How strongly do you feel about the answer you chose in the question above?

Very strongly / Somewhat strongly / Somewhat weakly / Very weakly

Why do you think so? Please write below.

2. Survey Materials for Chapter 5

[Groups 1 and 5: Japanese National Identity Affirmation]

Choose which one among the following values you think is most important to Japanese generally. (order of response options randomized)

self-discipline (time management)	family	democracy
loyalty	creativity	originality
appearance / fashion	honesty	concern for others
patience	religion / spirituality	
working hard	self-respect	friendships
personal liberty	health / fitness	achieving your dream
social skills	courtesy / manners	

> In the box provided below, write 1–2 paragraphs about why you think this value tends to be important to Japanese.
>
> In the box provided below, write 1–2 paragraphs about what you think Japanese have done to demonstrate this value.

[Groups 2 and 6: Asian Identity Affirmation]

Choose which one among the following values you think is most important to Asians generally. (order of response options randomized)

self-discipline (time management)	family	democracy
loyalty	creativity	originality
appearance / fashion	honesty	concern for others
patience	religion / spirituality	
working hard	self-respect	friendships
personal liberty	health / fitness	achieving your dream
social skills	courtesy / manners	

> In the box provided below, write 1–2 paragraphs about why you think this value tends to be important to Asians.
>
> In the box provided below, write 1–2 paragraphs about what you think Asians have done to demonstrate this value.

[Groups 3 and 7: Self-Affirmation]

Choose which one among the following values you think is most important to you. (order of response options randomized)

self-discipline (time management)	family	democracy
loyalty	creativity	originality
appearance / fashion	honesty	concern for others
patience	religion / spirituality	
working hard	self-respect	friendships
personal liberty	health / fitness	achieving your dream
social skills	courtesy / manners	

> In the box provided below, write 1–2 paragraphs about why you think this value tends to be important to you.

> In the box provided below, write 1–2 paragraphs about what you think you have done to demonstrate this value.

[Groups 4 and 8: Nonaffirmation, Control]

'Jellybeans' are a chewy candy made in the shape of beans. The following is a list of names of jellybeans. Select just one of the following that you think will be tastiest. (order of response options randomized)

Sizzling Cinnamon	Tutti-Frutti	Exotic Jalapeno	Wild Island Punch
Apple Jack	Root Beer Rocket	Blueberry Balloon	Tangerine Trampoline
Punch Hole	Maracanã Nuts	Crushed Pear Parachute	Apricot Anvil
Eucalyptus Leaves	Bubble Gum Bouncy Ball	Cosmo Pomegranate	Licorice Ladder
English Cream Cannon	Muscat Mojito	Butter Popcorn	

> In the box provided below, write 1–2 paragraphs about why you think the jellybean you chose will be tastiest.

> When you imagine the taste of the jellybean you chose, what do you think it would taste like compared to the others you did not choose? Write your answer in 1–2 paragraphs.

[All groups receive the questions below]

In this part of the survey, suppose you have been randomly paired with another person, who is of [Groups 1–4: Chinese / Groups 5–8: Korean] nationality. This other person is someone you do not know and that you will not knowingly meet in the future. Both you and your Chinese/Korean counterpart will be making choices by circling either the letter A, B, or C. Each letter represents a different scenario of how you can distribute among yourselves a common pool of resources. The overall size of the pool of resources is unknown.

Your own choices will produce points for both yourself and the Chinese/Korean person. Likewise, your Chinese/Korean opponent's choice will produce points for them and for you. Every point has value: the more points you receive, the better for you, and the more points your opponent receives, the better for them.

Here's an example of how this task works:

	A	B	C
You get	500	500	550
Your Chinese/Korean counterpart gets	100	500	300

In this example, if you chose A you would receive 500 and the other would receive 100 from the common pool of resources. If you chose B, you would receive 500 and the other 500; and if you chose C, you would receive 550 points and the other 300. So, you see that your choice influences both the amount of resources you receive and the amount of resources the other receives from the common pool.

Before you begin making choices, please keep in mind that there are no right or wrong answers—choose the option that you, for whatever reason, prefer most. Also, remember that the points have value; the more of them you accumulate, the better for you. Likewise, from the "other's" point of view, the more points s/he accumulates, the better for him/her. Your answers here won't affect any other part of the survey.

For each of the 5 choice situations, choose A, B, or C, depending on which column you prefer most:

1.	A	B	C
You get	480	540	480
Your Chinese/Korean counterpart gets	80	280	480
2.	A	B	C
You get	560	500	500
Your Chinese/Korean counterpart gets	300	500	100
3.	A	B	C
You get	520	520	580
Your Chinese/Korean counterpart gets	520	120	320

4.	A	B	C
You get	500	560	490
Your Chinese/Korean counterpart gets	100	300	490
5.	A	B	C
You get	560	500	490
Your Chinese/Korean counterpart gets	300	500	90

Imagine that according to your answers, you have taken too much and depleted the pool, harming your opponent by overdrawing. Do you feel any guilt toward your opponent?

Not at all / I feel some guilt / I feel a lot of guilt

You now have the chance of paying back a certain amount of your resources back to your opponent. Let's say you have 500 resources, among which whatever amount you can choose to give to your opponent. From 0 to 500, please write below in the number of resources you would like to give back to the opponent.

Why did you decide on the amount you gave for the last question?

Now imagine that another Japanese player has taken too much and depleted the pool, harming your opponent's group (the Chinese/Korean players) by overdrawing.

Do you feel any guilt toward your opponent's group?

Not at all / I feel some guilt / I feel a lot of guilt

You now have the chance of paying back a certain amount of your resources back to your opponent's group. Let's say you have 500 resources, among which whatever amount you can choose to give to your opponent. From 0 to 500, please write below in the number of resources you would like to give back to the opponent.

Why did you decide on the amount you gave for the last question?

Thank you. You have now reached the second part of the study. Please answer the following questions.

How much do you agree/disagree with the following opinions? (order randomized)

Strongly disagree / Somewhat disagree / Somewhat agree / Strongly agree

When I think about things Japanese have done during the war, I sometimes feel guilty. Japanese at the time of WWII were not responsible for the bad outcomes received by China/Korea.

I feel regrettable for the negative things that Japan has done to Chinese/Koreans in the past.

I believe I should help repair the damage caused to Chinese/Koreans by my country.

Japan has done enough to compensate for its past.

There is no reason for Japan to apologize to countries like China/Korea.

This is the last part of the survey. The following are statements quoted from some historians' opinions.

To what extent does your opinion match the gist of each quotation below? (order randomized)

Strongly disagree / Somewhat disagree / Somewhat agree / Strongly agree

The horrors Asians suffered during World War II were unavoidable.

The happenings during WWII were due to the circumstances (such as militarism and power politics of the time) that could not be avoided.

Japan, China, and Korea all suffered from the disorder and chaos caused at the time of WWII.

Asian states should agree on common ground that it is essential to prevent tragedies such as those happened during WWII from ever occurring again.

Asian states should reach a mutual understanding to cooperate and work together to overcome conflict.

Appendix B

Supplementary Empirical Materials

1. Confirmatory Factor Analysis for Moralistic Trust

From the set of questions I have that measure moralistic trust, I have five trust variables, which I combine to create an overall trust index. To check the correlation between the variables, I used a Confirmatory Factor Analysis to combine them. Treating "overall moralistic trust" as a latent factor, factor analysis helps determine the contribution of each of the five trust variables toward measuring that latent factor.

For questions 2, 4, and 5, which were divided into two steps, the responses to the second questions were combined into the responses from the preceding question. See the box below for the specific wording of these questions.

Q1. How much trust do you have in the [Korean / Japanese / Chinese] (opponent country, given depending on condition subject was in) government?

No trust at all / Little trust / Quite a bit of trust / A lot of trust

Q2. Do you feel the [Korean / Japanese / Chinese] government would try to take advantage of [your country's] government if they got a chance, or do you feel it would be fair?

Take advantage / Try to be fair

Q2-a. How strongly do you feel about this?

Very strongly / Strongly / Weakly / Very weakly

Q3. How much trust do you have in [Korean / Japanese / Chinese] people?

no trust at all / little trust / Quite a bit of trust / A lot of trust

250   *Appendix B*

Q4. Do you feel the [Korean / Japanese / Chinese] people would try to take advantage of [your country's] people if they got a chance, or do you feel it would be fair?

Take advantage / Try to be fair

Q4-a. How strongly do you feel about this?

Very strongly / Strongly / Weakly / Very weakly

Q5. Would you say that most of the time [Korean / Japanese / Chinese] people try to be helpful, or that they are mostly just looking out for themselves?

Try to be helpful / Just looking out for themselves

Q5-a. How strongly do you feel about this?

Very strongly / Strongly / Weakly / Very weakly

I provide an explanation of how these two-step responses were coded, using Question 2 in the box as an example. The response "*take advantage*" was coded as −1, where the response "*try to be fair*" was coded as +1. Then these responses were multiplied by either 4, 3, 2, or 1, where each corresponded to the subsequent responses *very strongly, strongly, weakly, or very weakly*, respectively.

Table 43 shows the results of the Factor Analysis for the combined Japanese and South Korean sample. Each loading can be interpreted as the estimated correlation between the variable and the latent factor. In other words, I estimate that, for Japanese and South Korean participants, their response to Q31 has a correlation of 0.099 to their underlying level of trust. I weight each variable by the factor loading so that variables that were found to be more highly correlated with the latent factor (Q30) carry more weight, and variables that are a little less correlated (like Q31) carry less weight in determining the final trust variable.

I then estimated a Factor Analysis for just South Koreans and just Japanese subjects separately, in order to check that a similar relationship was going on within each country too. As listed in tables 44 and 45, the correlations for each of the trust variables to the latent overall trust were generally similar in South Korea and Japan. Unsurprisingly, in both countries, the two questions that directly asked how much people trusted the govern-

TABLE 43. Factor score weights (all countries—default model)

	Q1	Q2	Q3	Q4	Q5
Moralistic Trust	0.337	0.104	0.563	0.099	0.101

TABLE 44. Factor score weights—South Korea

	Q1	Q2	Q3	Q4	Q5
Moralistic Trust	0.212	0.133	0.459	0.163	0.104

TABLE 45. Factor score weights—Japan

	Q1	Q2	Q3	Q4	Q5
Moralistic Trust	0.467	0.118	0.571	0.107	0.090

ments and people of the other country (Q1 and Q3) were most highly correlated with the latent, overall trust subjects held of the other country. Among these two questions, Q3, or how much subjects trusted the people of the other country, had the highest loading in subjects' latent trust. The less direct, supplementary questions emulating the WVS questions on trust carried less weight in determining overall trust. These results were uniform across both countries as well as in the overall model that combines the two, adding reliability to the factor analysis and the trust index created by the Factor Analysis.

2. Two Groups: 0-99 and 100 Tokens

In observing the data I collected from the trust game, I noticed that there was a peak in the 100 tokens proposers gave to the responders in the game. Noticing this peak, I estimated a mixture model using package flexmix. A mixture model allows my response variable of tokens to be the mixture of two normal distributions with different means and standard deviations (Leisch 2004). The regression assumes there is some underlying density function that is generating my data, and shows what the probability of belonging in each "cluster" is. In this sense the mixture model is different from just cutting data into subsets and running tests on them separately, because the overall density of belonging in each group adds up to 1 (Leisch 2004).

The mixture model gives each observation a probability of belonging to cluster 1 or cluster 2. The two distributions are mixed together with a certain probability. In order to do this, flexmix assigns observations to group 1 or 2 based on all variables provided, and estimates parameters separately. That is, the package doesn't just look at the dependent variable but all the variables to split apart those two clusters, and shows these people were very

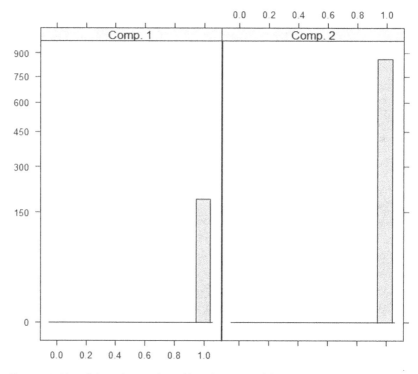

Figure 48. Plot of data clusters found by mixture model. Source: Eunbin Chung.

different on all independent variables as well. It first classifies observations into each cluster and then fits models into them simultaneously, accounting to the fact that they are from the same data or same probability space. Since it assumes the two clusters are related by some probability, it generates two separate functions instead of one (Gruen et al. 2013).

In my data, the model identified people who answered 0–99 and 100 tokens as two distinct groups with a 100 percent probability. In other words, based on all variables in the data, the two groups are very different. Figure 48 shows the probability of individual observations being in each group.

Since the bars are all the way at 1, it means that all the observations are classified into the group with probability 1. That is, the observations can be split into 2 distinct clusters that are 100 percent different: the probability that an observation fits into one cluster is 100 percent. One group happens to be the less than 100 token people, and the other group is the people who gave 100 tokens. There is thus no possibility someone is, for instance,

TABLE 46. Summary statistics for groups 1 and 2 identified in mixture model

	N	Minimum	Maximum	Mean	Std. Deviation
Group 1 (100 tokens)	189	100	100	100.00	.00
Group 2 (0–99 tokens)	857	0	99	39.05	18.96

in group 1 (100 tokens) with a 60 percent probability and group 2 (0–99 tokens) with a 40 percent probability. The y-axis is the number of observations in each group: N = 189 in the 100 tokens group, and N = 857 in the 0–99 tokens group. Table 46 shows the summary statistics for each group.

The mixture model thus identified people answering 0–99 and 100 tokens as two distinct groups in my data. This makes sense, as there is a huge peak at 100 tokens. However, there is no variation in the dependent variable in the second group. In addition, the R function flexmix used for the mixture model does not automatically produce standard errors and is not very user-friendly. So rather than settling on the mixture model as the final method of analysis, I used the Heckman selection model to analyze the distinct groups.

3. Summary Statistics

I summarize in table 47 the number of subjects in each condition, as well as their means and standard deviations of the two dependent variables: the number of tokens given out of 100 (strategic trust) and the latent trust variable (moralistic trust), naturally coded. The numbers in the "Mean" and "SD" columns of moralistic trust represent the means and standard deviations of the latent trust variable in each condition. Since I did not rescale the variables to range from 0 to 1 here, the range of strategic trust is 0 to 100, and the range of the moralistic trust is from 0.85 to 5.46.

Since I found that subjects who gave 100 tokens were different in character from the 0–99 tokens group and removed them subsequently, in table 48 I am reporting the number of subjects here in each condition (nationality, country of opponent, and whether they were affirmed or not) among just the group that gave 0–99 tokens.

TABLE 47. Summary statistics for strategic and moralistic trust, by nationality, opponent, and affirmation conditions

			Strategic trust			Moralistic trust		
Nationality	Opponent	Affirmation	Mean	SD	N	Mean	SD	N
South Korea	Japanese	Affirmed	55.13	32.31	89	3.02	0.77	89
		Nonaffirmed	54.78	31.98	91	2.95	0.74	91
		Total	54.96	32.05	180	2.98	0.76	180
	Chinese	Affirmed	47.27	31.02	98	2.43	0.90	100
		Nonaffirmed	42.7	28.83	170	2.40	0.81	179
		Total	44.37	29.67	268	2.41	0.84	279
	Total	Affirmed	51.01	31.80	187	2.71	0.89	189
		Nonaffirmed	46.91	30.46	261	2.58	0.82	270
		Total	48.62	31.05	448	2.63	0.85	459
Japan	South Korean	Affirmed	52.36	24.93	95	2.46	0.91	96
		Nonaffirmed	57.23	31.89	84	2.13	0.90	85
		Total	54.64	28.43	179	2.30	0.92	181
	Chinese	Affirmed	46.7	28.02	108	2.02	0.71	109
		Nonaffirmed	46.51	27.72	76	2.06	0.72	77
		Total	46.63	27.82	184	2.04	0.71	186
	Total	Affirmed	49.35	26.70	203	2.23	0.84	205
		Nonaffirmed	52.14	30.36	160	2.10	0.82	162
		Total	50.58	28.37	363	2.17	0.83	367
China	South Korean	Affirmed	56.02	28.31	53			
		Nonaffirmed	50.02	25.79	59			
		Total	52.86	27.06	112			
	Japanese	Affirmed	52.63	25.04	62			
		Nonaffirmed	49.77	25.49	61			
		Total	51.21	25.20	123			
	Total	Affirmed	54.19	26.53	115			
		Nonaffirmed	49.89	25.53	120			
		Total	52	26.06	235			
Total	South Korean	Affirmed	53.67	26.16	148	2.46	0.91	96
		Nonaffirmed	54.25	29.64	143	2.13	0.90	85
		Total	53.96	27.88	291	2.30	0.92	181
	Japanese	Affirmed	54.11	29.48	151	3.02	0.77	89
		Nonaffirmed	52.77	29.56	152	2.95	0.74	91
		Total	53.44	29.48	303	2.98	0.76	180
	Chinese	Affirmed	46.97	29.41	206	2.22	0.83	209
		Nonaffirmed	43.88	28.49	246	2.30	0.80	256
		Total	45.29	28.92	452	2.26	0.81	465
	Total	Affirmed	51.07	28.66	505	2.46	0.90	394
		Nonaffirmed	49.12	29.44	541	2.40	0.85	432
		Total	50.06	29.07	1046	2.43	0.87	826

TABLE 48. Number of subjects by condition, excluding the people who gave 100 tokens

Nationality	Opponent			Total
	South Korean	Japanese	Chinese	
South Korea	0	Affirmed 67	Affirmed 79	359
		Nonaffirmed 67	Nonaffirmed 146	
		Total 134	Total 225	
Japan	Affirmed 80	0	Affirmed 92	295
	Nonaffirmed 59		Nonaffirmed 64	
	Total 139		Total 156	
China	Affirmed 44	Affirmed 54	0	203
	Nonaffirmed 51	Nonaffirmed 54		
	Total 95	Total 108		
Total	234	242	381	857

Notes

Chapter 1

1. The very creation of the term "history problem" as an independent concept underscores the significance of the historical debates and the extent to which they complicate relations between concerned parties (Kim and Schwartz 2010).
2. The shrine commemorates the Japanese war dead, which includes some individuals that Chinese and South Koreans regard as war criminals. Chinese protestors boycotted Japanese products, initiated signatory campaigns, and, as the movements grew violent, damaged Japanese-brand cars, department stores, and signs of Japanese enterprises. Incidents of reprisal then followed in Japan, with windows of Chinese banks and schools smashed, threats received by Chinese diplomats, and a petrol bomb thrown at a Bank of China branch in Yokohama by a self-described right-wing Japanese citizen (Chan and Bridges 2006).
3. Psychological studies have shown that group members can respond to threats to their group by affirming alternative sources of the group's integrity, resulting in greater openness to group-threatening information (Sherman et al. 2007).
4. National identity involves an individual's knowledge of their membership in a nation together with the value and emotional significance attached to the membership (Tajfel 1981). This latter element, when involving positive emotions, is analogous to national pride, which is defined as a positive evaluation of the nation. In this sense, national pride can be interpreted as an element, namely the emotional component, of national identity—in other words, it is unlikely one would feel national pride without having any sense of national identity. With this definition, national pride should have similar consequences to national identity (Huddy and Del Ponte 2020). For purposes of investigation and consistency I focus on the concept of national identity in my tests.
5. The definition of the term "nationalism" is described as the attitude members have of a nation when they care about their national identity (Miscevic 2014).

6. For international relations research on the conflictual potential of nationalism, see Mansfield and Snyder 2002; Mearsheimer 2014; Mercer 1995; Van Evera 1994.

7. I use the terms reconciliation and rapprochement synonymously, to describe a relationship characterized by shared expectations of peaceful coexistence in which direct security competition has been suspended. Once countries reach rapprochement, parties involved have decided that armed violence is no longer an appropriate method of competition or dispute resolution (Rock 1989). The terms can be understood as both a state of relations and a process that aims to move toward that state (Jackson 2016).

8. Signaling some implicit symbolic parallels, this term was also taken up by the Japanese media (*South China Morning Post*, April 4, 2005, cited in Chan and Bridges 2006).

9. The discovery of the most precise and effective methods of utilizing NIA as a policy frame would benefit from future extensions of this research.

10. One might argue that North Korea should be included here. However, the inter-Korean relationship is incomparably unique in its characteristics. Excluding North Korea in this analysis also helps ensure analogous level of analysis regarding the target countries South Koreans were asked about in the survey, with those targets limited to entities all Koreans would universally and strictly consider "other countries" that are independent and sovereign.

Chapter 2

1. According to recent media sources, there have been increasingly frequent incursions into both the South Korean and Japanese Air Defense Identification Zones by Russian long-range intelligence, surveillance, and reconnaissance aircraft, and into confined maritime areas by their submarines (Yoon 2019).

2. This analysis pertains to peace between democracies, which would be applicable in the case of relations between Japan and South Korea.

3. When counted as a separate entity, Hong Kong ranks as China's second-largest trading partner, just above Japan.

4. See symbolic politics theory (Kaufman 2015; Sears 1993).

5. Title borrowed and edited from Choe and Gladstone (2018), *New York Times*.

6. Japan-U.S. Feminist Network for Decolonization (2012). Robert Dujarric, director of the Institute of Contemporary Asian Studies at Temple University Tokyo, highlights that Japanese Prime Minister Shinzo Abe is listed as an assenter for this ad (Evans 2015).

7. A more detailed account of each of the images in image theory and its application follows in chapter 3.

8. This was originally an editorial published in the Japanese newspaper *Jiji Shimpo* on March 16, 1885. I cite Datsu-A Ron here to highlight the ideas elaborated in it.

9. This was the first American military action in Korea, in which American land and naval forces supported an American diplomatic delegation sent to establish trade and political relations with Korea and a treaty assuring aid for shipwrecked sailors. This followed the General Sherman incident just years prior in 1866, when

Koreans destroyed an American armed merchant marine side-wheel steamer named General Sherman that landed in Ganghwa Island without permission (Ch'oe et al. 2000; Grimmett 2011).

10. In 1853, American Commodore Matthew C. Perry arrived in Japan in large warships, requesting a treaty that would open up Japanese ports to trade (U.S. Department of State).

Chapter 3

1. Donga Ilbo News, April 11, 2001; Joongang Ilbo News, July 10, 2001 cited in Cho and Park. 2011.

2. Lind (2009a) notes the European example in which, contrary to Asia, states were able to reconcile due to a recovery of trust of Germany. At the 1990 Chequers Conference, advisers told British Prime Minister Margaret Thatcher that since West Germany could now be trusted, the reunification of West and East Germany should be encouraged, in part because of its good record of confronting its past.

3. Seminar on "History, Identity and Collective Memory: In Search of Modern China" (International Institute for Asian Studies 2012).

4. This is a behavioral decision-making game frequently used in economics-style experiments to measure trust between participants (Berg, Dickhaut, and McCabe 1995; Duffy, Xie, and Lee 2013).

5. Rationality assumes that people will respond to the external environment to maximize the payoffs available given an objective situation (Herrmann 2013).

6. Moralistic trust can be divided into generalized trust and particularized trust. Generalized trust does not target a specific person or group of people but is a general sense of trust toward the world as a whole. Resting on a belief in human benevolence and the honesty of others, it is the belief that most others can be trusted (Cook and Cooper 2003). Particularized trust is trust regarding a certain group of people, where one trusts that specific group to be inherently moral (Rathbun 2007). In contrast to generalized trust, particularized trust is relational in nature. Distrust between states with the history problem is particularized distrust.

7. As an example, drafters of the interim constitution in South Africa recognized the primacy of reconciliation and reconstruction to the pursuit of national unity, and they accepted the principle of amnesty as a necessary tool for this purpose (Sarkin 1996).

8. Lind 2008a; Lyall 1997; Nobles 2008; Ward 2007 provide historical examples of domestic opposition following apologies in France, Britain, the United States, Australia, and New Zealand.

9. The study of perception was driven by the failure of theories that relied on purely material factors to explain international relations (Herrmann 2013). This led to what is called the cognitive revolution, a movement that started in the field of psychology in the 1950s and impacted several social sciences for decades. The central argument of the cognitive revolution is that any simple prediction about the ideational world from the material world is problematic (Howard 1985).

10. Perceived superiority in cultural status backed caste and racial systems in many societies and was typical in European empires toward their African and Asian colonies (Herrmann 2013; Herrmann and Fischerkeller 1995).

11. Rather than listing every single hypothesis for each chapter here, I break this down into more detail in the chapters. See chapter 7 for specific subhypotheses under H4.

12. Again, I break this down into finer hypotheses in chapter 8. I do not list all of the hypotheses in detail here.

Chapter 4

1. Survey items (translated to English) can be found in the appendix. The experiments took place at Chung-Ang University, South Korea; Wuhan University, China; and Waseda University, Japan, during the periods of July 9–13, 2012, July 25–27, 2012, and October 1–9, 2012, respectively.

2. The World Values Survey (WVS, www.worldvaluessurvey.org) is a global research project in which social scientists have been exploring people's values and beliefs, their stability or change over time, and their impact on social and political development of the societies in different countries of the world (WVS 2014). The social scientists conduct representative national surveys in almost one hundred countries, and the WVS is the only source of empirical data on attitudes covering nearly 90 percent of the world's population (WVS 2014). Although no measure of an attitudinal source such as trust may be judged to be perfect, the World Values Survey is a well-known and widely cited source, having been downloaded by more than 100,000 researchers, journalists, policymakers, and workers in media (WVS 2014). I thus borrow from the trust questions in the World Values Survey based on the assessment that it is considerably reliable enough to emulate.

3. Naef and Schupp (2009) conclude there are strong indications that the trust game is a valid measure of trust, finding that trust measured in the trust game is surprisingly robust, not subject to social desirability bias, and not dependent on the exact stake size or on the size of the strategy space.

4. I ran a pilot study at Ohio State University as a preliminary test before I went into the field to conduct experiments. During this pilot study the trust game was interactive, having subjects come in to a computer lab where they were matched in pairs to play a trust game on z-Tree (Fischbacher 2007). The results from this pilot study were congruent with my findings in this book (Chung 2015b). Preliminary results of the field experiments are also reported in Chung (2015c).

5. The main difference between trust and of trustworthiness in the trust game is that the former must incorporate expectations about responders' trustworthiness, while the latter can draw on observed actions by proposers (Brülhart and Usunier 2008, 2012). For work on trustworthiness in the trust game, see Ben-Ner et al. 2004; Cox, Friedman, and Gjerstad 2007; McCabe, Rigdon, and Smith 2003; Minozzi et al. 2015.

6. The "communication" here refers to how it was perceived from the participants' perspective, whereas in fact the interaction itself is stimulated.

7. Brülhart and Usunier (2008) find evidence that trust is the dominant motivation in trust games, rather than other motives like altruism. Some scholars have also made intercultural comparisons in how different nationals play the trust game. Buchan, Croson, and Johnson (2006) observe that there are only small differences in how American, Chinese, South Korean, and Japanese subjects play the game.

8. Faculty and staff members at the three universities generously gave approval and support for the study to be fielded at their schools, helped as liaisons in the field research, and oversaw conduct of the study. Although the value of tokens roughly corresponded in each country, I did also give attention and respect to the exact range of monetary awards for students as recommended by the respective faculty and staff members.

9. A total of 6.4 percent of the sample was omitted as the respondents indicated they did not believe the trust game was truly interactive, or that they had some previous knowledge of game theory or the trust game. This resulted in my N dropping from my total sample of 1,118 to 1,046.

10. See Chung and Pechenkina (2020) for a field experimental design that examines the effects of NIA and an overarching common identity on trust.

Chapter 5

1. The absolute versus relative gain frames had mixed effects for guilt recognition. For reasons of clarity, I only distinguish between proselfness and prosociality in this chapter's analysis of guilt recognition.

2. My initial survey draft included a third "other" response option; however, this was removed in the process of review of my survey for approval to field overseas.

3. Because the analysis includes a dichotomous mediator (prosociality), I use MacKinnon and Dwyer's (1993) statistical procedure for mediation via logistic regression.

Chapter 7

1. Technically, for this to be a natural experiment I would have to have asked the questions before the event and after the event to randomly assigned groups. To be exact, rather than a complete natural experiment, mine was closer to a survey taking place at a convenient time. These questions were removed from the Japanese survey because the issue lost salience by the time I traveled to Japan.

2. After the completion of the research in this chapter, the Japanese and South Korean governments signed to GSOMIA in 2016 but only briefly until South Korea withdrew from the agreement in August 2019. The cancelation was in part due to another emotional combat between the countries' citizens concerning historical grievances and followed a series of public protests in Seoul rejecting cooperation with Japan and demanding withdrawal from the agreement. With the currency of the issue, no public opinion polls on this new whirlwind of events are yet available. However, my findings in this chapter, which are based on the first instance that the governments agreed to sign GSOMIA but eventually decided against it due to public outrage in 2012, can offer guidelines and lessons for the resurgent dispute on GSOMIA.

Chapter 8

1. The relationship between the total effect, direct effect, and indirect effect in a complete mediation can be presented as: total effect = direct effect + indirect effect.

Or, using symbols, $c = c' + ab$. The reason my coefficients do not add up perfectly in the manner of $c = c' + ab$ is because of the different scales of the variables. Since the variables are not continuous, they are rescaled in the test. The numbers are just slightly off but the mechanism is the same.

Chapter 9

1. Barack Obama 2015. State of the Union Address. January 20. https://obamawhitehouse.archives.gov/the-press-office/2015/01/20/remarks-president-state-union-address-january-20-2015

Appendix

1. For convenience, I am showing here the questions South Korean participants in the affirmation condition against Japanese saw in the survey. Variations across conditions are explained within the survey.

References

Abbott, Kenneth W., and Duncan Snidal. 1998. "Why states act through formal international organizations." *Journal of Conflict Resolution* 42(1): 3–32.

Adams, Glenn, Teceta Thomas Tormala, and Laurie T. O'Brien. 2006. "The effect of self-affirmation on perception of racism." *Journal of Experimental Social Psychology* 42(5): 616–26.

Adelstein, Jake. 2014. "The uncomfortable truth about 'comfort women.'" *Japan Times*, November 1. http://www.japantimes.co.jp/news/2014/11/01/national/media-national/uncomfortable-truth-comfort-women/#.VZYYDfl_Okp

Adler, Emanuel, and Michael Barnett. eds. 1998. *Security Communities*. Cambridge, UK: Cambridge University Press.

Akio, Takahara. 2017. "Forty-four years of Sino–Japanese diplomatic relations since normalization," in Lam Pang Er, ed., *China-Japan relations in the 21st century: Antagonism despite interdependency*, 291–317. Singapore: Palgrave Macmillan.

Aldrich, John H., John L. Sullivan, and Eugene Borgida. 1989. "Foreign affairs and issue voting: Do presidential candidates 'waltz before a blind audience?'" *American Political Science Review* 83(1): 123–41.

Alexander, Michele G., Marilynn B. Brewer, and Richard K. Herrmann. 1999. "Images and affect: A functional analysis of out-group stereotypes." *Journal of Personality and Social Psychology* 77(1): 78–93.

Alexander, Michele G., Marilynn B. Brewer, and Robert W. Livingston. 2005. "Putting stereotype content in context: Image theory and interethnic stereotypes." *Personality and Social Psychology Bulletin* 31(6): 781–94.

Allport, Gordon. 1954. *The nature of prejudice*. New York: Addison-Wesley.

Ariely, Gal. 2012. "Globalization, immigration and national identity: How the level of globalization affects the relations between nationalism, constructive patriotism and attitudes toward immigrants." *Group Processes & Intergroup Relations* 15(4): 539–57.

Aronson, Elliott, Phoebe C. Ellsworth, J. Merrill Carlsmith, and Marti Hope Gonzales. 1990. *Methods of Research in Social Psychology*, 2nd ed. New York: McGraw-Hill.

Aronson, Joshua, Carrie B. Fried, and Catherine Good. 2002. "Reducing the effects of stereotype threat on African American college students by shaping theories of intelligence." *Journal of Experimental Social Psychology* 38(2): 113–25.

Asan Institute for Policy Studies. 2012. "South Korea in a changing world: Foreign affairs. Results of the Asan Institute's 2012 Annual Survey of South Korean Public Opinion."

Asan Institute for Policy Studies. 2013. "Special Survey: South Koreans and their neighbors." https://en.asaninst.org/contents/south-koreans-and-their-neigbors/

Asan Institute for Policy Studies. 2013. "2012 Asan Annual Survey." https://en.asaninst.org/contents/2012-asan-annual-survey-2/

Atkinson, Anthony B., and Andrea Brandolini. 2001. "Promise and pitfalls in the use of 'secondary' data-sets: Income inequality in OECD countries as a case study." *Journal of Economic Literature* 39(3): 771–99.

Axelrod, Robert M. 1984. *The evolution of cooperation*. New York: Basic Books.

Axelrod, Robert M., and William D. Hamilton. 1981. "The evolution of cooperation." *Science* 211(4489): 1390–96.

Bandow, Doug. 2013. "Japan as a normal country." *Japan Times*. February 13. http://www.japantimes.co.jp/opinion/2013/02/13/commentary/japan-commentary/japan-as-a-normal-country/#.VByrB5R5NmA

Bang, Jiun. 2011. "Aligned but not allied: ROK—Japan bilateral military cooperation," Joint U.S.-Korea Academic Studies. Emerging Voices Vol. 22, Special Edition. Korea Economic Institute.

Barbieri, Katherine. 1996. "Economic interdependence: A path to peace or a source of interstate conflict?" *Journal of Peace Research* 33(1): 29–49.

Barbieri, Katherine. 2002. *The liberal illusion: Does trade promote peace?* Ann Arbor: University of Michigan Press.

Barboza, David, 2010. "China passes Japan as second-largest economy." *New York Times*, August 15. https://www.nytimes.com/2010/08/16/business/global/16yuan.html

Barkan, Elazar. 2001. *The guilt of nations: Restitution and negotiating historical injustices*. Baltimore: Johns Hopkins University Press.

Barnett, Michael, and Martha Finnemore. 2004. *Rules for the world: International organizations in global politics*. Ithaca: Cornell University Press.

Barry, Brian. 2002. *Culture and equality: An egalitarian critique of multiculturalism*. Cambridge, MA: Harvard University Press.

Barucco, Armando. 2007. "National identity in the age of globalization—Changing patterns of national identity in India." Harvard University. http://programs.wcfia.harvard.edu/files/fellows/files/barucco.pdf

Bauman, Christopher W., A. Peter McGraw, Daniel M. Bartels, and Caleb Warren. 2014. "Revisiting external validity: Concerns about trolley problems and

other sacrificial dilemmas in moral psychology." *Social and Personality Psychology Compass* 8(9): 536–54.
Baumeister, Roy F., Arlene M. Stillwell, and Todd F. Heatherton. 1994. "Guilt: An interpersonal approach." *Psychological Bulletin* 115(2): 243–67.
Baumeister, Roy F., and Stephen Hastings. 1997. "Distortions of collective memory: How groups flatter and deceive themselves." In James W. Pennebaker, Bernard Rim, and Dario Paez, eds., *Collective memory of political events: Social psychological perspectives*, 277–293. Mahwah, NJ: Lawrence Erlbaum.
BBC. 2011. "South Korea 'comfort women' in diplomatic tussle over statue." December 14. http://www.bbc.com/news/world-16176575
BBC. 2014. "India cancels talks with Pakistan over Kashmir row." August 19. https://www.bbc.com/news/world-asia-28832477
BBC. 2014. "S Korean 'comfort women' still waiting for apology after 22 years." January 8. http://www.bbc.com/news/world-asia-25654865
BBC World Service Poll. 2014. "Media release on the country rating poll." June 3. https://downloads.bbc.co.uk/mediacentre/country-rating-poll.pdf
Bechhofer, Frank, and David McCrone. 2009. *National identity, nationalism and constitutional change*. Basingstoke: Palgrave Macmillan.
Benedict, Ruth. 2005. *The chrysanthemum and the sword: Patterns of Japanese culture*. Boston: Houghton Mifflin.
Ben-Ner, Avner, Louis Putterman, Fanmin Kong, and Dan Magan. 2004. "Reciprocity in a two-part dictator game." *Journal of Economic Behavior and Organization* 53(3): 333–52.
Bennett, D. Scott. 1996. "Security, bargaining, and the end of interstate rivalry." *International Studies Quarterly* 40(2): 157–83.
Berg, Joyce, John Dickhaut, and Kevin McCabe. 1995. "Trust, reciprocity, and social history." *Games and Economic Behavior* 10(1): 122–42.
Berg, Linda, and Mikael Hjerm. 2010. "National identity and political trust." *Perspectives on European Politics and Society* 11(4): 390–407.
Berger, Thomas U. 2003. "The construction of antagonism: The history problem in Japan's foreign relations." In G. John Ikenberry and Takashi Inoguchi, eds., *Reinventing the alliance: U.S.-Japan security partnership in an era of change*, 63–90. New York: Palgrave.
Berger, Thomas U. 2008. "Overcoming a difficult past: The history problem and institution building in Northeast Asia." In Martina Timmermann and Jitsuo Tsuchiyama, eds., *Institutionalizing Northeast Asia: Regional steps toward global governance*, 98–117. Tokyo: United Nations University Press.
Berger, Thomas U. 2012. *War, guilt, and world politics after World War II*. Cambridge: Cambridge University Press.
Bernstein, Richard, and Ross Munro. 1998. *The coming conflict with China*. New York: Alfred A. Knopf.
Betts, Richard. 1993. "Wealth, power, and instability." *International Security* 18(3): 34–77.

Beugelsdijk, Sjoerd, Henri de Groot, and Anton van Schaik. 2004. "Trust and economic growth: A robustness analysis." *Oxford Economic Papers* 56(1): 118–34.

Biletzki, Anat. 2013. "Peace-less reconciliation." In Alice MacLachlan and Allen Speight, eds., *Justice, responsibility and reconciliation in the wake of conflict*. Boston Studies in Philosophy, Religion and Public Life. Vol 1. Dordrecht: Springer.

Bollen, Kenneth A. 2002. Latent variables in psychology and the social sciences. *Annual Review of Psychology* 53(1): 605–34.

Booth, Ken, and Nicholas Wheeler. 2008. *The security dilemma: Fear, cooperation, and trust in world politics*. Basingstoke: Palgrave Macmillan.

Borsboom, Denny, Gideon J. Mellenbergh, and Jaap Van Heerden. 2003. "The theoretical status of latent variables." *Psychological Review* 110(2): 203–19.

Boslaugh, Sarah. 2007. *Secondary data sources for public health: A practical guide*. Cambridge: Cambridge University Press.

Boulding, Kenneth E. 1978. *Stable peace*. Austin: University of Texas Press.

Bowles, Paul. 2002. "Asia's post-crisis regionalism: bringing the state back in, keeping the (United) States out." *Review of International Political Economy* 9(2): 244–70.

Bracken, Paul. 1999. *Fire in the East*. New York: HarperCollins.

Branigan, Tania. 2012. "China and Japan relations tense after standoff over disputed islands in Beijing." *The Guardian*. September 14. https://www.theguardian.com/world/2012/sep/14/china-japan-senkaku-diaoyu-islands

Branscombe, Nyla R., and Anca M. Miron. 2004. "Interpreting the ingroup's negative actions toward another group: Emotional reactions to appraised harm." In Larissa Z. Tiedens and Colin Wayne Leach, eds., *The social life of emotions*. Cambridge: Cambridge University Press.

Branscombe, Nyla R., and Daniel L. Wann. 1994. "Collective self-esteem consequences of outgroup derogation when a valued social identity is on trial." *European Journal of Social Psychology* 24(6): 641–57.

Branscombe, Nyla R., Bertjan Doosje, and Craig McGarty. 2002. "Antecedents and consequences of collective guilt." In Diane M. Mackie and Eliot R. Smith, eds., *From prejudice to intergroup emotions: Differentiated reactions to social groups*, 49–66. Philadelphia: Psychology Press.

Brewer, Marilynn B. 1999. "The psychology of prejudice: Ingroup love or outgroup hate?" *Journal of Social Issues* 55(3): 429–44.

Brewer, Marilynn B. 2003. "Optimal distinctiveness, social identity, and the self." In Mark Leary and June Tangney, eds., *Handbook of Self and Identity*, 480–91. New York: Guilford Press.

Brewer, Paul R., Kimberly Gross, Sean Aday, and Lars Willnat. 2004. "International trust and public opinion about world affairs." *American Journal of Political Science* 48(1): 93–109.

Brody, Richard. 1991. *Assessing the president: The media, elite opinion, and public support*. Stanford: Stanford University Press.

Brofenbrenner, Urie. 1961. "The mirror image in Soviet-American relations. A social psychologist's report." *Journal of Social Issues* 17(3): 45–56.

Brooks, Katherine. 2013. "The History Of 'Comfort Women': A WWII Tragedy We Can't Forget." *Huffington Post*. November 25. http://www.huffingtonpost.com/2013/11/25/comfort-women-wanted_n_4325584.html

Brülhart, Marius, and Jean-Claude Usunier. 2008. "Verified Trust: Reciprocity, Altruism, and Randomness in Trust Games." IRM Working Paper #0809, Institute of Research in Management, University of Lausanne.

Brülhart, Marius, and Jean-Claude Usunier. 2012. "Does the trust game measure trust?" *Economics Letters* 115(1): 20–23.

Buchan, Nancy R., Eric J. Johnson, and Rachel T. A. Croson. 2006. "Let's get personal: An international examination of the influence of communication, culture and social distance on other regarding preferences." *Journal of Economic Behavior and Organization* 60(3): 373–98.

Buzan, Barry, and Gerald Segal. 1995. "Asia: Skepticism about optimism." *National Interest* 39: 82–84.

Byrne, Barbara M. 2013. *Structural equation modeling with LISREL, PRELIS, and SIMPLIS: Basic concepts, applications, and programming*. Mahwah, NJ: Lawrence Erlbaum.

Calderwood, Imogen. 2015. "South Korean 'comfort women' blast Japan apology for keeping them as sex slaves during World War Two amid anger British POWs have still not been offered one." *Daily Mail*. December 28. https://www.dailymail.co.uk/news/article-3376360/South-Korean-Comfort-women-blast-Japan-apology-keeping-sex-slaves-World-War-Two-amid-anger-British-POWs-not-offered-one.html

Calhoun, Craig. 2007. *Nations matter: Culture, history and the cosmopolitan dream*. London: Routledge.

Camerer, Colin. 2003. *Behavioral game theory: Experiments in strategic interaction*. Princeton: Princeton University Press.

Camerer, Colin, and Ernst Fehr. 2004. "Measuring social norms and preferences using experimental games: A guide for social scientists." In Joseph Henrich, Robert Boyd, Samuel Bowles, Colin Camerer, Ernst Fehr, and Herbert Gintis, eds., *Foundations of human sociality: Economic experiments and ethnographic evidence from fifteen small-scale societies*, 55–95. Oxford: Oxford University Press.

Castano, Emanuele, and Roger Giner-Sorolla. 2006. "Not quite human: Infrahumanization as a response to collective responsibility for intergroup killing." *Journal of Personality and Social Psychology* 90(5): 804–18.

CBS. 2015. "South Korea, Japan reach agreement over 'comfort women.'" *CBS*. December 28. https://www.cbsnews.com/news/south-korea-japan-reach-deal-over-world-war-2-comfort-women/

Čehajić, Sabina, and Rupert Brown. 2010. "Silencing the past effects of intergroup contact on acknowledgment of in-group responsibility." *Social Psychological and Personality Science* 1(2): 190–96.

Čehajić-Clancy, Sabina, Daniel A. Effron, Eran Halperin, Varda Liberman, and Lee D. Ross. 2011. "Affirmation, acknowledgment of in-group responsibility, group-based guilt, and support for reparative measures." *Journal of Personality and Social Psychology* 101(2): 256–70.

Cha, Victor D. 2000. "Hate, power, and identity in Japan-Korea security: Towards a synthetic material-ideational analytical framework." *Australian Journal of International Affairs* 54(3): 309–23.

Cha, Victor D. 2002. "Hawk engagement and preventive defense on the Korean Peninsula." *International Security* 27(1): 40–78.

Cha, Victor D. 2003. "Hypotheses on history and hate in Asia: Japan and the Korean Peninsula." In Yoichi Funabashi, ed., *Reconciliation in the Asia-Pacific*. Washington, DC: United States Institute of Peace.

Chaiken, Shelly. 1980. "Heuristic versus systematic information processing and the use of source versus message cues in persuasion." *Journal of Personality and Social Psychology* 39(5): 752–66.

Chaiken, Shelly, and Yaacov Trope, eds. 1999. *Dual-process theories in social psychology*. New York: Guilford Press.

Chan, Che-po, and Brian Bridges. 2006. "China, Japan, and the clash of nationalisms." *Asian Perspective* 30(1): 127–56.

Chang, Booseung. 2019. "Japan is trying to repel Korea from the Korea-US-Japan framework" (translated). *JoongAng Daily*. August 8. https://mnews.joins.com/article/23546594?sfns=xmwa#home

Chanley, Virginia A. 1999. "U.S. public views of international involvement from 1964 to 1993: Time-series analyses of general and militant internationalism." *Journal of Conflict Resolution* 43(1): 23–44.

Charnysh, Volha, Christopher Lucas, and Prerna Singh. 2015. "The ties that bind: National identity salience and pro-social behavior toward the ethnic other." *Comparative Political Studies* 48(3): 267–300.

Chen, Jidong, Jennifer Pan, and Yiqing Xu. 2016. "Sources of authoritarian responsiveness: A field experiment in China." *American Journal of Political Science* 60(2): 383–400.

Cho, Il Hyun, and Seo-Hyun Park. 2011. "Anti-Chinese and anti-Japanese sentiments in East Asia: The politics of opinion, distrust, and prejudice." *Chinese Journal of International Politics* 4(3): 265–90.

Choe, Sang-Hun. 2012. "South Korea postpones military pact with Japan." *New York Times*. June 29. http://www.nytimes.com/2012/06/30/world/asia/south-korea-postpones-military-data-pact-with-japan.html?_r=0

Choe, Sang-Hun, and Rick Gladstone. 2018. "How a World War II-era reparations case is roiling Asia." *New York Times*. October 30. https://www.nytimes.com/2018/10/30/world/asia/south-korea-japan-compensation-world-war-two.html?module=inline

Ch'oe, Yŏng-ho, William Theodore De Bary, Martina Deuchler, and Peter Hacksoo Lee. 2000. *Sources of Korean tradition: From the sixteenth to the twentieth centuries*. New York: Columbia University Press.

Chopparapu, Ramasaranya. 2005. "The European Union. A model for East Asia?" *Asia Europe Journal* 3(2): 133–36.

Christensen, Thomas J. 1999. "China, the US-Japan alliance, and the security dilemma in East Asia." *International Security* 23(4): 49–80.

Chung, Eunbin. 2015a. "Explaining the coexistence of globalization and nationalism in East Asia: An analytical framework on the case of Hallyu (The Korean Wave)." *Peace Studies* 23(1): 329–81.

Chung, Eunbin. 2015b. "Can affirming national identity increase international trust? Experimental evidence from South Korean, Chinese, and Japanese nationals." *International Studies Review* 16(1): 75–97.

Chung, Eunbin. 2015c. "Overcoming the history problem: Group-affirmation and trust in international relations." PhD diss., Ohio State University.

Chung, Eunbin, and Anna O. Pechenkina. 2020. "Group-affirmation and trust in international relations: Evidence from Ukraine." *PLoS ONE* 15(12): e0239944.

Chung, Eunbin, and Byungwon Woo. 2015. "We like you better when we feel good about ourselves: Group-affirmation in an international context." *Korea Observer* 46(2): 387–417.

Chung Eunbin, and Jaehee Yi. 2021. "Pandemic priorities: The impact of South Korea's COVID-19 policies on vulnerable populations. *International Journal of Public Administration* 44(11–12): 1–11.

Cohen, Geoffrey L., Joshua Aronson, and Claude M. Steele. 2000. "When beliefs yield to evidence: Reducing biased evaluation by affirming the self." *Personality and Social Psychology Bulletin* 26(9): 1151–64.

Cohen, Geoffrey L., and Julio Garcia. 2005. "'I am us': Negative stereotypes as collective threats." *Journal of Personality and Social Psychology* 89(4): 566–82.

Cohen, Geoffrey L., Julio Garcia, Valerie Purdie-Vaughns, Nancy Apfel, and Patricia Brzustoski. 2009. "Recursive processes in self-affirmation: Intervening to close the minority achievement gap." *Science* 324(5925): 400–3.

Cohen, Stanley. 2013. *States of denial: Knowing about atrocities and suffering*. Malden, MA: Polity Press.

Collingwood, Loren, Nazita Lajevardi, and Kassra A. R. Oskooii. 2018. "A change of heart? Why individual-level public opinion shifted against Trump's 'Muslim Ban.'" *Political Behavior* 40(4): 1035–72.

Cook, Karen S., and Robin M. Cooper. 2003. "Experimental studies of cooperation, trust, and social exchange." In Elinor Ostrom and James Walker, eds., *Trust and Reciprocity: Interdisciplinary Lessons from Experimental Research*, Vol. 6, 209–44. New York: Russell Sage Foundation.

Copeland, Dale. 2000. *The origins of major war*. Ithaca: Cornell University Press.

Corning, Gregory P. 2011. "Trade regionalism in a realist East Asia: Rival visions and competitive bilateralism." *Asian Perspective* 35(2): 259–86.

Cottam, Richard W. 1977. *Foreign policy motivation: A general theory and a case study*. Pittsburgh: University of Pittsburgh Press.

Cox, James C., Daniel Friedman, and Steven Gjerstad. 2007. "A tractable model of reciprocity and fairness." *Games and Economic Behavior* 59(1): 17–45.

Crawcour, Sydney. 1980. "Alternative models of Japanese society: An overview." *Social Analysis* 5: 184.

Crick, Nicki R., and Jennifer K. Grotpeter. 1995. "Relational aggression, gender, and social-psychological adjustment." *Child Development* 66(3): 710–22.

Critcher, Clayton R., David Dunning, and David A. Armor. 2010. "When self-affirmations reduce defensiveness: Timing is key." *Personality and Social Psychology Bulletin* 36(7): 947–59.

Crocker, Jennifer, and Riia Luhtanen. 1990. "Collective self-esteem and ingroup bias." *Journal of Personality and Social Psychology* 58(1): 60–67.

Crocker, Jennifer, Yu Niiya, and Dominik Mischkowski. 2008. "Why does writing about important values reduce defensiveness? Self-affirmation and the role of positive, other-directed feelings." *Psychological Science* 19(7): 740–47.

Davis, Julie Hirschfeld. 2016. "Obama plans visit to Cuba, as talks on expanding trade begin." *New York Times*. February 17. http://www.nytimes.com/2016/02/18/us/politics/new-talks-begin-with-cuba-on-expanding-business-ties.html?_r=0

Dawson, Michael. 1994. *Behind the mule: Race and class in African-American politics*. Princeton: Princeton University Press.

De Dreu, Carsten K. W., and Peter J. Carnevale. 2003. "Motivational bases of information processing and strategy in conflict and negotiation." *Advances in Experimental Social Psychology* 35: 235–291.

Dent, Christopher M., and David W. F. Huang, eds. 2002. *Northeast Asian regionalism: Learning from the European experience*. London: Routledge.

Denyer, Simon. 2018. "Japan's Abe stakes out new identity in region: Stronger leadership and wider military reach." *Washington Post*. October 20. https://www.washingtonpost.com/world/asia_pacific/japans-abe-stakes-out-new-identity-in-region-stronger-leadership-and-wider-military-reach/2018/10/19/c0e4ee8e-d12b-11e8-a275-81c671a50422_story.html?noredirect=on&utm_term=.64bf5c550a81

Deutsch, Karl W., et al. 1957. *Political community and the North Atlantic area: International organization in the light of historical experience*. Princeton: Princeton University Press.

Devine, Patricia G., Margo J. Monteith, Julia R. Zuwerink, and Andrew J. Elliot. 1991. "Prejudice with and without compunction." *Journal of Personality and Social Psychology* 60(6): 817–30.

DeYoung, Karen. 2014. "Obama moves to normalize relations with Cuba as American is released by Havana." *Washington Post*. December 17. http://www.washingtonpost.com/world/-security/report-cuba-frees-american-alan-gross-after-5-years-detention-on-spy-charges/2014/12/17/a2840518-85f5-11e4-a702-fa31ff4ae98e_story.html

Doosje, Bertjan, Nyla R. Branscombe, Russell Spears, and Antony S. R. Manstead. 1998. "Guilty by association: When one's group has a negative history." *Journal of Personality and Social Psychology* 75(4): 872–86.

Drezner, Daniel W. 2008. *All politics is global: Explaining international regulatory regimes*. Princeton: Princeton University Press.

Dudden, Alexis. 2014. *Troubled apologies among Japan, Korea and the United States*. New York: Columbia University Press.

Duffy, John, Huan Xie, and Yong-Ju Lee. 2013. "Social norms, information, and trust among strangers: Theory and evidence." *Economic Theory* 52(2): 669–708.

Du Gay, Paul, Graeme Salaman, and Bronwen Rees. 1996. "The conduct of management and the management of conduct: Contemporary managerial discourse and the constitution of the 'competent' manager." *Journal of Management Studies* 33(3): 263–82.

Dujarric, Robert. 2013. "Japan's history problem." *The Diplomat*. October 14. http://thediplomat.com/2013/10/japans-history-problem/

Dunn, John. 1999. "Nationalism." In Ronald Beiner, ed., *Theorizing nationalism*, 27–50. Albany: State University of New York Press.

Dutton, Sarah, Jennifer De Pinto, Anthony Salvanto, and Fred Backus. 2014. "How do Americans feel about reestablishing relations with Cuba?" *CBS News*. December 22. https://www.cbsnews.com/news/what-americans-think-of-normalizing-relations-with-cuba/

Economist. 2012. "Could Asia really go to war over these? The bickering over islands is a serious threat to the region's peace and prosperity." September 22. https://www.economist.com/leaders/2012/09/22/could-asia-really-go-to-war-over-these

Economist. 2013. "The Senkaku/Diaoyu islands: Dangerous shoals." January 19. https://www.economist.com/leaders/2013/01/19/dangerous-shoals

Economist. 2015. "Still fighting: In Asia memories of the Second World War still bring more recrimination than reconciliation." February 5. https://www.economist.com/asia/2015/02/05/still-fighting

Edwards, Jeffrey R., and Richard P. Bagozzi. 2000. "On the nature and direction of relationships between constructs and measures." *Psychological Methods* 5(2): 155–74.

Eichenberg, Richard C. 2016. "Gender difference in American public opinion on the use of military force, 1982–2013." *International Studies Quarterly* 60(1): 138–48.

Eilperin, Juliet. 2016. "Agreement on 'comfort women' offers strategic benefit to U.S. in Asia-Pacific." *Washington Post*. January 9. https://www.washingtonpost.com/politics/agreement-on-comfort-women-offers-ancillary-benefit-to-us-in-asia-pacific/2016/01/09/41a03d84-b54c-11e5-a842-0feb51d1d124_story.html?noredirect=on&utm_term=.50d5b94b5e86

Elster, Jon. 1998. "Emotions and economic theory." *Journal of Economic Literature* 36(1): 47–74.

Evans, Stephen. 2015. "Bad blood between Japan and Korea persists." *BBC*. April 28. https://www.bbc.com/news/world-asia-32477794

Everard, John. 2014. "Are China, Japan and South Korea fanning the flames of war?" *The Telegraph*. January 6. https://www.telegraph.co.uk/news/worldnews/

asia/china/10553628/Are-China-Japan-and-South-Korea-fanning-the-flames-of-war.html

Fackler, Martin. 2015. "Ahead of World War II anniversary, questions linger over stance of Japan's premier." *New York Times*. April 9.http://www.nytimes.com/2015/04/10/world/asia/ahead-of-world-war-ii-anniversary-questions-linger-over-stance-of-japans-premier.html?_r=2

Feagin, Joe R., and Vera Hernan. 2000. *White racism: The basics*. New York: Routledge.

Fearon, James D. 1994. "Domestic political audiences and the escalation of international disputes." *American Political Science Review* 88(3): 577–92.

Fearon, James D. 1997. "Signaling foreign policy interests: Tying hands versus sinking costs." *Journal of Conflict Resolution* 41(1): 68–90.

Federal Register. 2015. "Cuban assets control regulations." Washington, DC. January 16. https://www.federalregister.gov/articles/2015/01/16/2015-00632/cuban-assets-control-regulations

Fehr, Ernst, Urs Fischbacher, Bernhard Von Rosenbladt, Jürgen Schupp, and Gert G. Wagner. 2003. "A nation-wide laboratory: Examining trust and trustworthiness by integrating behavioral experiments into representative survey." *Schmollers Jahrbuch* 122: 519–42.

Fein, Steven, and Steven J. Spencer. 1997. "Prejudice as self-image maintenance: Affirming the self through derogating others." *Journal of Personality and Social Psychology* 73(1): 31–44.

Festinger, Leon. 1957. *A theory of cognitive dissonance*, Vol. 2. Stanford: Stanford University Press.

Fifield, Anna. 2014. "Japan's Abe avoids Yasukuni Shrine in hopes of meeting with China's Xi Jinping." *Washington Post*. August 15. http://www.washingtonpost.com/world/japans-abe-stays-away-from-yasukuni-in-hopes-of-meeting-with-chinas-xi/2014/08/15/f55bdcc8-ba8c-4c94-9ba2-032124c84a9a_story.html

Finnemore, Martha, and Kathryn Sikkink. 1998. "International norm dynamics and political change." *International Organization* 52(4): 887–917.

Fischbacher, Urs. 2007. "z-Tree: Zurich toolbox for ready-made economic experiments." *Experimental Economics* 10(2): 171–78.

Fisher, Max. 2013. "Japan and South Korea can't even cooperate over peacekeeping in South Sudan." *Washington Post*. December 26. https://www.washingtonpost.com/news/worldviews/wp/2013/12/26/japan-and-south-korea-cant-even-cooperate-over-peacekeeping-in-south-sudan/?noredirect=on&utm_term=.3321ae3e260b

Fitch, Asa, Joshua Mitnick, and Mohammed Najib. 2014. "Eyes turn to Cairo talks as cease-fire holds in Gaza." *Wall Street Journal*. August 14. https://www.wsj.com/articles/gaza-cease-fire-holds-after-truce-extension-1408005383

Fite, David, Marc Genest, and Clyde Wilcox. 1990. "Gender differences in foreign policy attitudes: A longitudinal analysis." *American Politics Quarterly* 18(4): 492–513.

Fitzsimons, Gráinne M., and James Y. Shah. 2008. "How goal instrumentality shapes relationship evaluations." *Journal of Personality and Social Psychology* 95(2): 319–37.
Foddy, Margaret, Michael J. Platow, and Toshio Yamagishi. 2009. "Group-based trust in strangers: The role of stereotypes and expectations." *Psychological Science* 20(4): 419–22.
Friedberg, Aaron L. 1993. "Ripe for rivalry: Prospects for peace in a multipolar Asia." *International Security* 18(3): 5–33.
Friedhoff, Karl, and Kang Chungku. 2013. "Rethinking public opinion on Korea-Japan relations." *Asan Institute for Policy Studies*, no. 73 (October 15).
Fukuyama, Francis. 2006. *The end of history and the last man*. New York: Free Press.
Fullerton, Jami, Alice Kendrick, and Sheri Broyles. 2017. "Attitude change among US adults after the Castro-Obama announcement: The role of soft power in agenda setting." *Palgrave Communications* 3(1): 1–9.
Gächter, Simon, Benedikt Herrmann, and Christian Thöni. 2004. "Trust, voluntary cooperation, and socio-economic background: Survey and experimental evidence." *Journal of Economic Behavior & Organization* 55(4): 505–31.
Gaertner, Samuel L., and John F. Dovidio. 2014. *Reducing intergroup bias: The common ingroup identity model*. Philadelphia: Psychology Press.
Gaertner, Samuel L., John F. Dovidio, Phyllis A. Anastasio, Betty A. Bachman, and Mary C. Rust. 1993. "The common ingroup identity model: Recategorization and the reduction of intergroup bias." *European Review of Social Psychology* 4(1): 1–26.
Gardner, Howard. 1987. *The mind's new science: A history of the cognitive revolution*. New York: Basic Books.
Genron NPO and China Daily. 2014. "The 10th Japan-China public opinion poll analysis report on the comparative data." September 9. http://www.genron-npo.net/en/pp/docs/10th_Japan-China_poll.pdf
Genron NPO and East Asia Institute. 2014. "The 2nd joint Japan-South Korea public opinion poll (2014) analysis report on comparative data." http://www.genron-npo.net/pdf/forum_1407_en.pdf
Gernet, Jacques. 1996. *A history of Chinese civilization*. Cambridge: Cambridge University Press.
Gibbons, Frederick X., Tami J. Eggleston, and Alida C. Benthin. 1997. "Cognitive reactions to smoking relapse: The reciprocal relation between dissonance and self-esteem." *Journal of Personality and Social Psychology* 72(1): 184–95.
Gibney, Mark, Rhoda E. Howard-Hassmann, Jean-Marc Coicaud, and Niklaus Steiner, eds. 2008. *The age of apology: Facing up to the past*. Philadelphia: University of Pennsylvania Press.
Gilbert, Margaret P. 2001. "Collective remorse." In Aleksandar Jokic, ed., *War crimes and collective wrongdoing*, 216–35. Oxford: Blackwell.
Gilpin, Robert. 1981. *War and change in world politics*. Cambridge: Cambridge University Press.

Gilpin, Robert. 1987. *The political economy of international relations.* Princeton: Princeton University Press.

Glaeser, Edward L., David I. Laibson, Jose A. Scheinkman, and Christine L. Soutter. 2000. "Measuring trust." *Quarterly Journal of Economics* 115(3): 811–46.

Glaser, Charles L. 1997. "The Security dilemma revisited." *World Politics* 50(1): 171–201.

Glosserman, Brad, and Scott A. Snyder. 2015. *The Japan–South Korea identity clash: East Asian security and the United States.* New York: Columbia University Press.

Glover, Jonathan. 1997. "Nations, identity and conflict." In Rober McKim Içinde and Jeff McMahan, eds., *The morality of nationalism*, 11–29. New York: Oxford University Press.

Gochman, Charles S., and Zeev Maoz. 1984. "Militarized interstate disputes, 1816–1976: Procedures, patterns, and insights." *Journal of Conflict Resolution* 28(4): 585–616.

Goertz, Gary, and Paul F. Diehl. 1993. "Enduring rivalries: Theoretical constructs and empirical patterns." *International Studies Quarterly* 37(2): 147–71.

Goertz, Gary, and Paul F. Diehl. 1995. "The initiation and termination of enduring rivalries: The impact of political shocks." *American Journal of Political Science* 39(1): 30–53.

Goh, Evelyn. 2011. "How Japan matters in the evolving East Asian security order." *International Affairs* 87(4): 887–902.

Goldberg, Jeffrey. 2016. The road to Havana. *The Atlantic.* March 20. https://www.theatlantic.com/international/archive/2016/03/united-states-cuba-obama-visit/474510/

Goldstein, Avery. 2013. "First things first. The pressing danger of crisis instability in US-China relations." *International Security* 37(4): 48–89.

Gonzalez, Guadalupe, and Stephan Haggard. 1998. "The United States and Mexico: A pluralistic security community." In Emanuel Adler and Michael Barnett, eds., *Security Communities.* Cambridge: Cambridge University Press.

Gordon, Andrew. 2003. *A modern history of Japan: From Tokugawa times to the present.* Oxford: Oxford University Press.

Gowa, Joanne. 1989. "Rational hegemons, excludable goods, and small groups: An epitaph for hegemonic stability theory?" *World Politics* 41(3): 307–24.

Grieco, Joseph M. 1988. "Anarchy and the limits of cooperation: A realist critique of the newest liberal institutionalism." *International Organization* 42(3): 485–507.

Gries, Peter Hays. 2005. "The Koguryo controversy, national identity, and Sino-Korean relations today." *East Asia* 22(4): 3–17.

Grimmett, Richard F. 2011. "Instances of use of United States armed forces abroad 1798–2010." *Congressional Research Service.* March 10. https://fas.org/sgp/crs/natsec/R41677.pdf

Gronau, Reuben. 1974. "Wage comparisons—A selectivity bias." *Journal of Political Economy* 82(6): 1119–43.

Gruen, Bettina, Friedrich Leisch, Deepayan Sarkar, Frederic Mortier, and Nicolas Picard. 2013. "flexmix: Flexible mixture modeling." http://CRAN. R-project.org/package= flexmix. R package version, 2–3.

Gruenfeld, Deborah H., M. Ena Inesi, Joe C. Magee, and Adam D. Galinsky. 2008. "Power and the objectification of social targets." *Journal of Personality and Social Psychology* 95(1): 111–27.

Guibernau, Montserrat. 2001. "Globalisation and the nation-state." In Montserrat Guibernau and John Hutchinson, eds., *Understanding nationalism*, 242–68. Cambridge: Polity Press.

Gunn, Gregory R., and Anne E. Wilson. 2011. "Acknowledging the skeletons in our closet: The effect of group affirmation on collective guilt, collective shame, and reparatory attitudes." *Personality and Social Psychology Bulletin* 37(11): 1474–87.

Gustafsson, Karl. 2014. "Memory politics and ontological security in Sino-Japanese relations." *Asian Studies Review* 38(1): 71–86.

Gustavsson, Gina, and David Miller, eds. 2020. *Liberal nationalism and its critics: Normative and empirical questions*. Oxford: Oxford University Press.

Gustavsson, Gina, and Ludvig Stendahl. 2020. "National identity, a blessing or a curse? The divergent links from national attachment, pride, and chauvinism to social and political trust." *European Political Science Review* 12(4): 449–68.

Haas, Ernst B. 1958. *The uniting of Europe*. Stanford: Stanford University Press.

Hagström, Linus, and Karl Gustafsson. 2015. "Japan and identity change: Why it matters in International Relations." *Pacific Review* 28(1): 1–22.

Hajari, Nisid. 2015. "The legacy of India-Pakistan partition." *Economic Times*. June 30. http://blogs.economictimes.indiatimes.com/et-citings/the-legacy-of-india-pakistan-partition/

Halperin, Eran, Daniel Bar-Tal, Keren Sharvit, Nimrod Rosler, and Amiram Raviv. 2010. "Socio-psychological implications for an occupying society: The case of Israel." *Journal of Peace Research* 47(1): 59–70.

Halperin, Eran, Richard J. Crisp, Shenel Husnu, Kali H. Trzesniewski, Carol S. Dweck, and James J. Gross. 2012. "Promoting intergroup contact by changing beliefs: Group malleability, intergroup anxiety, and contact motivation." *Emotion* 12(6): 1192–95.

Halpin, Dennis P. 2015. "Japan Pushes South Korea Into China's Arms." *Weekly Standard*. June 29. http://www.weeklystandard.com/blogs/japan-pushes-south-korea-china-s-arms_979076.html

Hamilton, Valerie. 2014. "California statue stirs passions in South Korea and ire in Japan." *PRI*. January 29. https://www.pri.org/stories/2014-01-29/california-statue-stirs-pride-south-korea-and-protest-japan

Hannah, Erin, and James Scott. 2017. "Rethinking NGOs in global economic governance." International Studies Association Global South Caucus Workshop.

Hardin, Russel. 2006. *Trust*. London: Polity Press.

Hardy-Chartrand, Benoit. 2014. "The dangers of nationalism in China and Japan."

Centre for International Governance Innovation. September 26. https://www.cigionline.org/articles/dangers-nationalism-china-and-japan

Harlan, Chico. 2012. "At last minute, S. Korea postpones signing first military pact with Japan since World War II." *Washington Post*. June 29. http://www.washingtonpost.com/world/at-last-minute-s-korea-postpones-signing-first-military-pact-with-japan-since-world-war-ii/2012/06/29/gJQABZ35AW_story.html

Harris, Bryan, and Robin Harding. 2018a. "South Korea-Japan relations sour over wartime slavery decision." *Financial Times*. October 30. https://www.ft.com/content/26237866-dc07-11e8-9f04-38d397e6661c

Harris, Bryan, and Robin Harding. 2018b. "Japan-South Korea 'comfort women' deal under threat." *Financial Times*. November 20. https://www.ft.com/content/2b50b1f2-ed3a-11e8-89c8-d36339d835c0

Harvey, Richard D., and Debra L. Oswald. 2000. "Collective guilt and shame as motivation for white support of black programs." *Journal of Applied Social Psychology* 30(9): 1790–1811.

Harvie, Charles, Fukunari Kimura, Hyun-Hoon Lee, eds. 2005. *New East Asian regionalism: Causes, progress and country perspectives*. Northampton, MA: Edward Elgar.

Hayashi, Hirofumi. 2008. "Disputes in Japan over the Japanese military "comfort women" system and its perception in history." *The Annals of the American Academy of Political and Social Science* 617(1): 123–32.

Hayashi, Yuka. 2013. "Anti-Korean voices grow in Japan small but venomous rallies become more frequent, prompt soul-searching over hate speech." *Wall Street Journal*. May 16. http://online.wsj.com/news/articles/SB10001424127887324031404578482570250163826

He, Yinan. 2006. "National mythmaking and the problem of history in Sino-Japanese relations." In Lam Peng Er, ed., *Japan's foreign relations with China: Facing a rising power*, 68–91. London/New York: Routledge.

He, Yinan. 2008. "Ripe for cooperation or rivalry? Commerce, realpolitik, and war memory in contemporary Sino-Japanese relations." *Asian Security* 4(2): 162–97.

He, Yinan. 2009. *The search for reconciliation: Sino-Japanese and German-Polish relations since World War II*. Cambridge: Cambridge University Press.

He, Yinan. 2011. "Comparing postwar (West) German-Polish and Sino-Japanese reconciliation: A bridge too far?" *Europe-Asia Studies* 63(7): 1157–94.

He, Yinan. 2013. "Forty years in paradox: Post-normalisation Sino-Japanese relations." *China Perspectives* 2013/4 (December 1): 7–16.

Heckman, James J. 1976. "The common structure of statistical models of truncation, sample selection and limited dependent variables and a simple estimator for such models." *Annals of Economic and Social Measurement* 5(4): 475–92.

Heckman, James J. 1979. "Sample selection bias as a specification error." *Econometrica: Journal of the Econometric Society* 47(1): 153–61.

Heider, Fritz. 1946. "Attitudes and cognitive organization." *Journal of Psychology* 21(1): 107–12.

Hein, Laura Elizabeth, and Mark Selden. 2000. *Censoring history: Citizenship and memory in Japan, Germany, and the United States.* Armonk, NY: M. E. Sharpe..

Heins, Volker. 2008. *Nongovernmental organizations in international society: Struggles over recognition.* Basingstoke, UK: Palgrave Macmillan.

Held, David. 2003. "Cosmopolitanism: Globalisation tamed?" *Review of International Studies* 29(4): 465–80.

Herrmann, Richard K. 2013. "Perceptions and image theory in international relations." In Leonie Huddy, David O. Sears, and Jack S. Levy, eds., *The Oxford handbook of political psychology*, 334–63. New York: Oxford University Press.

Herrmann, Richard K., and Michael P. Fischerkeller. 1995. "Beyond the enemy image and spiral model: Cognitive-strategic research after the Cold War." *International Organization* 49(3): 415–50.

Herrmann, Richard K., Philip E. Tetlock, and Penny S. Visser. 1999. "Mass public decisions to go to war: A cognitive-interactionist framework." *American Political Science Review* 93(3): 553–73.

Herrmann, Richard K., Pierangelo Isernia, and Paolo Segatti. 2009. "Attachment to the nation and international relations: Dimensions of identity and their relationship to war and peace." *Political Psychology* 30(5): 721–54.

Herz, John. 1950. "Idealist internationalism and the security dilemma." *World Politics* 2(2): 171–201.

Hess, Ashley A. C., and John K. Warden. 2014. "Japan and Korea: Opportunities for cooperation." *National Interest.* March 19. http://nationalinterest.org/commentary/japan-korea-opportunities-cooperation-10076

Heydarian, Richard Javad. 2018. "Shinzo Abe strikes back." *National Interest.* December 14. https://nationalinterest.org/feature/shinzo-abe-strikes-back-39447

Hjerm, Mikael. 1998. "National identities, national pride and xenophobia: A comparison of four Western countries." *Acta Sociologica* 41(4): 335–47.

Hoffman, Peter J. 2009. "Making sense of NGOs: The mice that roar?" *International Studies Review* 11(1): 192–94.

Hoffmann, Stanley. 1966. "Obstinate or obsolete? The fate of the nation-state and the case of Western Europe." *Daedalus* 95(3): 862–915.

Holsti, Oli R. 1967. "Cognitive dynamics and images of the enemy." *Journal of International Affairs* 21(1): 16–39.

Hook, Glenn D., Julie Gilson, Christopher W. Hughes, and Hugo Dobson. 2003. *Japan's international relations: politics, economics and security.* London: Routledge.

Hopf, Ted. 2010. The logic of habit in international relations. *European Journal of International Relations* 16(4): 539–61.

Hopkins, Nick. 2001. "Commentary. National identity: pride and prejudice?" *British Journal of Social Psychology* 40(2): 183–86.

Horowitz, Donald L. 2000. *Ethnic groups in conflict.* Berkeley: University of California Press.

Huddy, Leonie. 2013. "From group identity to political cohesion and commitment." In Leonie Huddy, David O. Sears, and Jack S. Levy, eds., *Oxford Handbook of Political Psychology*, 737–73. New York: Oxford University Press.

Huddy, Leonie, and Alessandro Del Ponte. 2020. "National identity, pride, and chauvinism—Their origins and consequences for globalization attitudes." In Gina Gustavsson and David Miller, eds., *Liberal nationalism and its critics: Normative and empirical questions*. Oxford: Oxford University Press.

Hughes, Christopher. 2013. "Overview." In "Viewpoints: How serious are China-Japan tensions?" BBC. February 8. https://www.bbc.com/news/world-asia-21290349

Hund, Markus. 2003. "ASEAN Plus Three: Towards a new age of pan-East Asian regionalism? A skeptic's appraisal." *Pacific Review* 16(3): 383–417.

Hurwitz, Jon, and Mark Peffley. 1987. "How are foreign policy attitudes structured? A hierarchical model." *American Political Science Review* 81(4): 1099–1120.

Hurwitz, Jon, and Mark Peffley. 1990. "Public images of the Soviet Union: The impact on foreign policy attitudes." *Journal of Politics* 52(1): 3–28.

Ienaga, Saburo. 1993. "The glorification of war in Japanese education." *International Security* 18(3): 113–33.

Ijiri, Hidenori. 1996. "Sino-Japanese controversy since the 1972 Diplomatic Normalization." In Christopher Howe, ed., *China and Japan: History, trends, and prospects*, 60–82. Oxford: Clarendon Press.

Ikenberry, G. John. 2008. "The rise of China and the future of the West. Can the liberal system survive?" *Foreign Affairs* 87(1): 23.

International Institute for Asian Studies. 2012. Seminar on "History, identity and collective memory: In search of modern China." https://www.iias.asia/event/history-identity-collective-memory-search-modern-china

Jackson, Jay W., and Eliot R. Smith. 1999. "Conceptualizing social identity: A new framework and evidence for the impact of different dimensions." *Personality and Social Psychology Bulletin* 25(1): 120–35.

Jackson, Van. 2016. "Threat consensus and rapprochement failure: Revisiting the collapse of US-North Korea relations, 1994–2002." *Foreign Policy Analysis* 14(2): 235–53.

Jacobs, Lawrence R., and Robert Y. Shapiro. 2000. *Politicians don't pander: Political manipulation and the loss of democratic responsiveness*. Chicago: University of Chicago Press.

Jansen, Marius B. 2002. *The making of modern Japan*. Cambridge, MA: Harvard University Press.

Japan Times. 2007. "Severed pinkie sent to LDP to protest Abe's Yasukuni no-show." August 24. http://www.japantimes.co.jp/news/2007/08/24/news/severed-pinkie-sent-to-ldp-to-protest-abes-yasukuni-no-show/#.VBysw5R5NmB

Japan-U.S. Feminist Network for Decolonization (FeND). 2012. "Yes, we remember the facts (2012)." http://fendnow.org/encyclopedia/yes-we-remember-the-facts-2012/

Jervis, Robert. 1976. *Perception and misperception in international politics.* Princeton: Princeton University Press.
Jervis, Robert. 1978. "Cooperation under the security dilemma." *World Politics* 30(2): 167–214.
Jervis, Robert. 2010. *Why intelligence fails: lessons from the Iranian Revolution and the Iraq War.* Ithaca: Cornell University Press.
Jervis, Robert, and Jack Snyder, eds. 1991. *Dominoes and bandwagons: Strategic beliefs and great power competition in the Eurasian rimland.* New York: Oxford University Press.
Jiang, Junyan. 2018. "Making bureaucracy work: Patronage networks, performance incentives, and economic development in China." *American Journal of Political Science* 62(4): 982–99.
Johnson, Jesse. 2016. "80% of Japanese fear military clash around Senkakus, poll finds." *Japan Times.* https://www.japantimes.co.jp/news/2016/09/14/national/pew-poll-finds-80-japanese-fear-possible-clash-china-senkakus/#.XK_VP5hKhyx
Johnston, Alastair Iain. 2013. "How new and assertive is China's new assertiveness?" *International Security* 37(4): 7–48.
Johnston, Richard, Keith Banting, Will Kymlicka, and Stuart Soroka. 2010. "National identity and support for the welfare state." *Canadian Journal of Political Science* 43(2): 349–77.
Kaldor, Mary. 2004. "Nationalism and globalisation." *Nations and Nationalism* 10(1–2): 161–77.
Katzenstein, Peter J. 2003. "Same war—different views: Germany, Japan, and counterterrorism." *International Organization* 57(4): 731–60.
Katzenstein, Peter J. 2005. *A World of Regions: Asia and Europe in the American Imperium.* Ithaca: Cornell University Press.
Kaufman, Stuart J. 2009. "Narratives and symbols in violent mobilization: The Palestinian-Israeli case." *Security Studies* 18(3): 400–34.
Kaufman, Stuart J. 2015. *Nationalist passions.* Ithaca: Cornell University Press.
Kawasaki, Akira, and Céline Nahory. 2013. "Revision of Japan's peace constitution—A matter of global concern." *Common Dreams.* July 21. https://www.commondreams.org/view/2013/07/21-2
Kelman, Herbert C. 1997. "Social-psychological dimensions of international conflict." In I. William Zartman and J. Lewis Rasmussen, eds., *Peacemaking in international conflict: Methods & techniques,* 191–237. Washington, DC: U.S. Institute of Peace.
Keohane, Robert O. 1984. *After hegemony: Cooperation and discord in the world political economy.* Princeton: Princeton University Press.
Keohane, Robert O., and Joseph S. Nye. 1977. *Power and Interdependence.* Boston: Little, Brown.
Kertzer, Joshua D. 2016. *Resolve in international politics.* Princeton: Princeton University Press.

Kertzer, Joshua D., and Brian C. Rathbun. 2015. "Fair is fair: Social preferences and reciprocity in international politics." *World Politics* 67(4): 613–55.

Kim, Catherine. 2019. "The escalating trade war between South Korea and Japan, explained: This dispute is all about colonialism and historical grievances." *Vox*. August 9. www.vox.com/world/2019/8/9/20758025/trade-war-south-korea-japan?sfns=xmwa

Kim, Chung-hwan. 2017. "[Candlelight Diary by Kim Chung-hwan] With persistent struggle, the enemy begins to collapse" (translated). *News Min*. October 20. http://www.newsmin.co.kr/news/24326/

Kim, Jiyoon, and Karl Friedhoff. 2013a. "Source of social conflict: Ideology. public opinion on social division." Asan poll—The Asan public opinion brief. The Asan Institute for Policy Studies. https://en.asaninst.org/contents/source-of-social-conflict/

Kim, Jiyoon, and Karl Friedhoff. 2013b. "Korea-Japan relations: Public opinion on Korea-Japan relations." Asan poll—The Asan public opinion brief. The Asan Institute for Policy Studies. https://en.asaninst.org/contents/test2-test2-test2-test2-test2-test2-test2-test2-test2-test2/

Kim, Jiyoon, and Karl Friedhoff. 2013c. "December brief." Asan poll—The Asan public opinion brief. The Asan Institute for Policy Studies. https://en.asaninst.org/contents/asan-public-opinion-brief-december-2013/

Kim, Jiyoon, Karl Friedhoff, and Chungku Kang. 2012. "The Asan Monthly Opinion Survey." July. The Asan Institute for Policy Studies. http://mansfieldfdn.org/mfdn2011/wp-content/uploads/2012/08/July-2012-Asan-Monthly-Public-Opinion-Report.pdf

Kim, Jiyoon, Karl Friedhoff, Chungku Kang, and Euicheol Lee. 2014. "Asan Report: Challenges and opportunities for Korea-Japan relations in 2014." The Asan Institute for Policy Studies. http://en.asaninst.org/wp-content/uploads/2014/02/Challenges-and-Opportunities-for-Korea-Japan-Relations-in-2014.pdf

Kim, Jongdae. 2012. "[Interview] Moon Jeong-in, Professor, Department of Political Science and Diplomacy, Yonsei University" (translated). *Hankyoreh*. January 12. http://plug.hani.co.kr/dndfocus/105467

Kim, Mikyoung. 2008. "Myths, milieu, and facts: History textbook controversies in Northeast Asia." In Tsuyoshi Hasegawa and Kazuhiko Togo, eds., *East Asia's haunted present: Historical memories and the resurgence of nationalism*, 103–13. Westport: Praeger Security International.

Kim, Mikyoung. 2016. "The US the big winner in 'comfort women' agreement." January 7. East Asia Forum. http://www.eastasiaforum.org/2016/01/07/the-us-is-the-big-winner-in-comfort-women-agreement/

Kim, Mikyoung, and Barry Schwartz, eds. 2010. *Northeast Asia's Difficult Past: Essays in Collective Memory*. London/New York: Palgrave Macmillan.

Kim, Yookyung. 2019. "Who is Korea friends with, the US or China? Japan fired a warning shot: Conflict between Korea and Japan—Professor Yukiko Fukagawa" (translated). *Joongang Sunday*. July 27. mnews.joins.com/article/23537246?sfns=xmwa#home

Kimura, Kan. 2019. "Japan-South Korea rupture shakes political balance in Northeast Asia." *Diplomat*. February 19. https://thediplomat.com/2019/02/japan-south-korea-rupture-shakes-political-balance-in-northeast-asia/

Kinder, Donald R., and Cindy D. Kam. 2009. *Us against them: Ethnocentric foundations of American opinion*. Chicago: University of Chicago Press.

Kindig, Jessie. n.d. "Nightmares must be told." *Jacobin* (accessed April 24, 2019). https://www.jacobinmag.com/2017/08/south-korea-japan-comfort-stations

Kindleberger, Charles P. 1981. "Dominance and leadership in the international economy: Exploitation, public goods, and free rides." *International Studies Quarterly* 25(2): 242–54.

Kindleberger, Charles P. 1986. *The world in depression, 1929–1939*. Vol. 4. Berkeley: University of California Press.

Kirk, Don. 2001. "South Korea asks U.S. for help in peace talks with the North." *New York Times*. August 16. http://www.nytimes.com/2001/08/16/world/south-korea-asks-us-for-help-in-peace-talks-with-the-north.html

Kissinger, Henry A. 2011. *On China*. New York: Penguin Press.

Kitaoka, Shinichi. 2010. "A look back on the work of the joint Japanese-Chinese history research committee." *Asia-Pacific Review* 17(1): 6–20.

Klare, Michael. 1993. "The next great arms race." *Foreign Affairs* 72(3): 136–52.

Klein, Jodi Xu. 2019. "US agencies banned from doing business with Huawei and other Chinese tech companies, as Trump administration cites security concerns." *South China Morning Post*. August 8. www.scmp.com/news/china/politics/article/3021888/trump-administration-bans-us-agencies-doing-business-huawei-and?sfns=xmwa

Knack, Stephen, and Philip Keefer. 1997. "Does social capital have a payoff? A cross-country investigation." *Quarterly Journal of Economics* 112(4): 1251–88.

Koremenos, Barbara, Charles Lipson, and Duncan Snidal. 2001. "The rational design of international institutions." *International Organization* 55(4): 761–99.

Korhonen, Pekka. 2013. "Leaving Asia? The meaning of Datsu-A and Japan's modern history." *Asia-Pacific Journal: Japan Focus* 11(50): 1–19.

Kotler, Mindy. 2014. "The comfort women and Japan's war on truth." *New York Times*. November 14. http://www.nytimes.com/2014/11/15/opinion/comfort-women-and-japans-war-on-truth.html

Krasner, Stephen D. 1976. "State power and the structure of international trade." *World Politics* 28(3): 317–47.

Kraus, Charles, Sergey Radchenko, and Yutaka Kanda. 2014. "More friends than foes: Sino-Japanese relations in 1984." Cold War international history project, e-Dossier No. 48, Woodrow Wilson International Center for Scholars. https://www.wilsoncenter.org/publication/more-friends-foes-sino-japanese-relations-1984

Kray, Laura J., Linda G. George, Katie A. Liljenquist, Adam D. Galinsky, Philip E.

Tetlock, and Neal J. Roese. 2010. "From what might have been to what must have been: Counterfactual thinking creates meaning." *Journal of Personality and Social Psychology* 98(1): 106–18.
Kristof, Nicholas D. 1998. "The problem of memory." *Foreign Affairs* 77(6): 37–49.
Kupchan, Charles A. 2010. *How enemies become friends: The sources of stable peace*. Princeton: Princeton University Press.
Kuran, Timur. 1998. "Social mechanisms of dissonance reduction." In Peter Hedstrom and Richard Swedberg, eds., *Social mechanisms. An analytical approach to social theory*, 147–71. Cambridge: Cambridge University Press.
Kwok, Tat Wai Dwight. 2009. "A translation of Datsu-a ron: Decoding a prewar Japanese nationalistic theory." PhD diss., University of Toronto.
Kydd, Andrew. 1997. "Sheep in sheep's clothing: Why security seekers do not fight each other." *Security Studies* 7(1): 114–55.
Kydd, Andrew. 2007. *Trust and mistrust in international relations*. Princeton: Princeton University Press.
Kymlicka, Will. 1995. *Multicultural citizenship: A liberal theory of minority rights*. Oxford: Clarendon Press.
Kymlicka, Will. 1998. *Finding our way: Rethinking ethnocultural relations in Canada*. Vol. 19. Toronto, Ontario, Canada: Oxford University Press.
Kymlicka, Will. 2003. "Conclusion: The future of nationalism." In Umut Özkırımlı, ed., *Nationalism and its futures*. New York: Palgrave.
Lai, Yew Meng. 2013. *Nationalism and power politics in Japan's relations with China: A neoclassical realist interpretation*. New York: Routledge.
Landler, Mark. 2014. "Obama offers support to South Korea at a moment of trauma and tension." *New York Times*. April 25. https://www.nytimes.com/2014/04/26/world/asia/obama-asia.html
Landman, Janet. 1993. *Regret: The persistence of the possible*. New York: Oxford University Press.
Landry, Pierre F., Xiaobo Lü, and Haiyan Duan. 2018. "Does performance matter? Evaluating political selection along the Chinese administrative ladder." *Comparative Political Studies* 51(8): 1074–1105.
Lang, Andrew T. F. 2013. "The legal construction of economic rationalities?" *Journal of Law and Society* 40(1): 155–71.
Larson, Deborah W. 1997. *Anatomy of mistrust: US-Soviet relations during the Cold War*. Ithaca: Cornell University Press.
Lawson, Stephanie, and Seiko Tannaka. 2011. "War memories and Japan's 'normalization' as an international actor: A critical analysis." *European Journal of International Relations* 17(33): 405–28.
Lazare, Aaron. 2004. *On apology*. New York: Oxford University Press.
Lebow, Richard Ned. 1984. *Between peace and war: The nature of international crisis*. Baltimore: Johns Hopkins University Press.
Lebow, Richard Ned. 2004. "The politics of memory in postwar Europe." In Rich-

ard Ned Lebow, Kansteiner Wulf, and Fogu Claudio, eds., *The politics of memory in postwar Europe*, 1–39. Durham: Duke University Press.

Lederach, John Paul. 1997. *Building peace: Sustainable reconciliation in divided societies*. Washington, DC: United States Institute of Peace Press.

Lee, Amanda. 2019. "China should boost ties with Japan, South Korea to counter increasingly hostile US, analysts say." *South China Morning Post*. February 22. https://www.scmp.com/economy/china-economy/article/2187321/china-should-boost-ties-japan-south-korea-counter-increasingly

Lee, Gwangkil. 2016. "Opposition to the THAAD deployment and Korea-Japan military information agreement" (translated). *Tongil News*. April 19. http://www.tongilnews.com/news/articleView.html?idxno=116297

Lee, Shin-wha. 2008. "Northeast Asian security community: From concepts to practices." In Martina Timmermann and Jitsuo Tsuchiyama, eds., *Institutionalizing Northeast Asia: Regional steps toward global governance*. Tokyo: United Nations University Press.

Lee, Suk-jong. 2005. "The Achievement of president Kim Dae-jung's visit to Japan and future prospects" (translated). *Joongang Ilbo News*. October 9.

Leisch, Friedrich. 2004. "Flexmix: A general framework for finite mixture models and latent glass regression in R." *Journal of Statistical Software* 11(8): 1–18.

Leland, Jonathan, Daniel Houser, and Jason Shachat. 2005. "Measuring trust and trustworthiness." In Hans-Hermann Höhmann and Friederike Welter, eds., *Trust and entrepreneurship: A West-East perspective*, 87–96. Cheltenham, UK: Edward Elgar.

Levendusky, Matthew S. 2018. "Americans, not partisans: Can priming American national identity reduce affective polarization?" *Journal of Politics* 80(1): 59–70.

Lewis, H. Gregg. 1974. "Comments on selectivity biases in wage comparisons." *Journal of Political Economy* 82(6): 1145–55.

Lieberthal, Kenneth, and Wang Jisi. 2012. *Addressing U.S.-China strategic distrust*. Vol. 4. Washington, DC: John L. Thornton China Center at Brookings.

Lind, Jennifer. 2008. *Sorry states: Apologies in international politics*. Ithaca: Cornell University Press.

Lind, Jennifer. 2009. "The perils of apology: What Japan shouldn't learn from Germany." *Foreign Affairs* 88(3): 132–46.

Lind, Jennifer. 2012. "Japan, the never normal." Council on Foreign Relations. November 30. https://www.cfr.org/blog/jennifer-lind-japan-never-normal

Lohr, Steve. 2019. "U.S. moves to ban Huawei from government contracts." *New York Times*. August 7. www.nytimes.com/2019/08/07/business/huawei-us-ban.html

Longman, Timothy, and Theoneste Rutagengwa. 2004. "Memory, identity, and community in Rwanda." In Eric Stover and Harvey M. Weinstein, eds., *My neighbor, my enemy: Justice and community in the aftermath of mass atrocity*, 162–82. Cambridge: Cambridge University Press.

Lyall, Sarah. 1997. "Past as prologue: Blair faults Britain in Irish potato blight." *New York Times*. June 3. https://www.nytimes.com/1997/06/03/world/past-as-prologue-blair-faults-britain-in-irish-potato-blight.html

Mackie, Diane M., Thierry Devos, and Eliot R. Smith. 2000. "Intergroup emotions: Explaining offensive action tendencies in an intergroup context." *Journal of Personality and Social Psychology* 79(4): 602.

MacKinnon, David P., and James H. Dwyer. 1993. "Estimating mediated effects in prevention studies." *Evaluation Review* 17(2): 144–58.

MacKinnon, David P., Chondra M. Lockwood, and Jason Williams. 2004. "Confidence limits for the indirect effect: Distribution of the product and resampling methods." *Multivariate Behavioral Research* 39(1): 99–128.

Major, Patrick. 2010. *Behind the Berlin Wall: East Germany and the frontiers of power*. Oxford: Oxford University Press.

Mansfield, Edward. D., and Diana C. Mutz. 2009. "Support for free trade: Self-interest, sociotropic politics, and out-group anxiety." *International Organization* 63(3): 425–57.

Mansfield, Edward D., and Jack Snyder. 2002. "Democratic transitions, institutional strength, and war." *International Organization* 56(2): 297–337.

March, James G., and Johan P. Olsen. 2004. "The logic of appropriateness." *The Oxford handbook of political science*. Oxford: Oxford University Press.

Martin, Alexander, and Eleanor Warnock Connect. 2014. "Japan Prime Minister Shinzo Abe avoids shrine on war anniversary." *Wall Street Journal*. August 15. http://online.wsj.com/articles/japan-prime-minister-shinzo-abe-avoids-shrine-on-war-anniversary-1408079636

Maruyama, Masao. 1969. *Thought and behavior in modern Japanese politics*. Ivan Morris, ed. New York: Oxford University Press.

Mazzini, Giuseppe. 2009. *A cosmopolitanism of nations: Giuseppe Mazzini's writings on democracy, nation building, and international relations*. Nadia Urbinati and Stefano Recchia, eds. Princeton: Princeton University Press.

McCabe, Kevin A., Mary L. Rigdon, and Vernon L. Smith. 2003. "Positive reciprocity and intentions in trust games." *Journal of Economic Behavior and Organization* 52(2): 267–75.

McClain, Paula D., Jessica D. Johnson Carew, Eugene Walton Jr., and Candis S. Watts. 2009. "Group membership, group identity, and group consciousness: Measures of racial identity in American politics?" *Annual Review of Political Science* 12: 471–85.

McCormack, Gavan. 2000. "Nationalism and identity in post-Cold War Japan." *Pacifica Review* 12(3): 247–63.

McQueen, Amy, and William M. P. Klein. 2006. "Experimental manipulations of self-affirmation: A systematic review." *Self and Identity* 5(4): 289–354.

Mearsheimer, John J. 1994. "The false promise of international institutions." *International Security* 19(3): 5–49.

Mearsheimer, John J. 2014. *The tragedy of great power politics*. Updated ed. New York: Norton.

Mercer, Jonathan. 1995. "Anarchy and identity." *International Organization* 49(2): 229–52.
Miguel, Edward. 2004. "Tribe or nation: Nation building and public goods in Kenya versus Tanzania." *World Politics* 56(3): 327–62.
Miller, David. 1995. *On nationality*. Oxford: Clarendon Press.
Miller, David, and Sundas Ali. 2014. "Testing the national identity argument." *European Political Science Review* 6(2): 237–59.
Ministry of Foreign Affairs of Japan. 1993. "Statement by the Chief Cabinet Secretary Yohei Kono on the result of the study on the issue of comfort women." August 4. https://www.mofa.go.jp/policy/women/fund/state9308.html
Ministry of Foreign Affairs of Japan. 1995. "Statement by Prime Minister Tomiichi Murayama, 'On the occasion of the 50th anniversary of the war's end.'" August 15. https://www.mofa.go.jp/announce/press/pm/murayama/9508.html
Ministry of Foreign Affairs of Japan. 2001. "Letter from Prime Minister Junichiro Koizumi to the former comfort women." https://www.mofa.go.jp/announce/press/pm/murayama/9508.html
Minow, Martha. 1998. *Between vengeance and forgiveness: Facing history after genocide and mass violence*. Boston: Beacon Press.
Minozzi, William, Eunbin Chung, Matthew P. Hitt, and Andrew Rosenberg. 2015. "Anarchy in the lab." Working paper.
Miscevic, Nenad. 2014. *Stanford Encyclopedia of Philosophy*. https://plato.stanford.edu/entries/nationalism/
Mitzen, Jennifer. 2006. "Ontological security in world politics: State identity and the security dilemma." *European Journal of International Relations* 12(3): 341–70.
Morgenthau, Hans J. 1973. *Politics among nations: The struggle for power and peace*. New York: Alfred A. Knopf.
Mounk, Yascha. 2018. *The people vs. democracy: Why our freedom is in danger and how to save it*. Cambridge, MA: Harvard University Press.
Mummendey, Amelie, Andreas Klink, and Rupert Brown. 2001. "Nationalism and patriotism: National identification and out-group rejection." *British Journal of Social Psychology* 40(2): 159–72.
Mutua, Makau W. 1997. "Never again: Questioning the Yugoslav and Rwanda tribunals." *Temple International & Comparative Law Journal* 11(167): 167–87.
Naef, Michael, and Jürgen Schupp. 2009. "Measuring trust: Experiments and surveys in contrast and combination." March 23. SOEPpaper No. 167.
New York Times. 2012. "A lost deal for South Korea and Japan." July 7. https://www.nytimes.com/2012/07/08/opinion/sunday/a-lost-deal-for-south-korea-and-japan.html
New York Times. 2015. "Japan's apologies for World War II." August 14. https://www.nytimes.com/interactive/2015/08/13/world/asia/japan-ww2-shinzo-abe.html
Neyer, Jürgen. 2012. *The justification of Europe: A political theory of supranational integration*. Oxford: Oxford University Press.
Nicolas, Françoise. 2014. "Economic regionalism in East Asia, the end of an excep-

tion?" In Zhiqun Zhu, Benny Cheng Guan Teh, Sarah Y. Tong, Jie Li, Chi-Jen Yang, and Jieli Li, eds., *Globalization, development and security in Asia*, 105–30. Singapore: World Scientific Publishing.

Nincic, Miroslav. 2011. *The logic of positive engagement*. Ithaca: Cornell University Press.

Nisbett, Richard E., and Lee Ross. 1980. *Human inference: Strategies and shortcomings of social judgment*. Englewood Cliffs, NJ: Prentice-Hall.

Nobles, Melissa. 2008. *The politics of official apologies*. Cambridge: Cambridge University Press.

Norton, Michael I., Benoit Monin, Joel Cooper, and Michael A. Hogg. 2003. "Vicarious dissonance: Attitude change from the inconsistency of others." *Journal of Personality and Social Psychology* 85(1): 47–62.

Nussbaum, Martha C. 1994. "Patriotism and cosmopolitanism." *Boston Review* 19(5): 3–6.

Nussbaum, Martha C. 2008. "Toward a globally sensitive patriotism." *Daedalus* 137(3): 78–93.

Nussbaum, Martha C., et al. 1996. *For love of country: Debating the limits of patriotism*, edited by Joshua Cohen. Boston: Beacon Press.

Nye, Joseph S. Jr. 2004. *Soft power: The means to success in world politics*. New York: Public Affairs.

Obama, Barack. 2015. State of the Union Address. Washington, DC. January 20. https://obamawhitehouse.archives.gov/the-press-office/2015/01/20/remarks-president-state-union-address-january-20-2015

Ock, Hyun-ju. 2019. "[Feature] Koreans reject 'No Japan' campaign, focus on criticizing Abe." *Korea Herald*. August 12. http://www.koreaherald.com/view.php?ud=20190812000777

Ohmae, Kenichi. 1995. *The end of the nation-state: The rise of regional economies*. New York: Simon and Schuster.

Oneal, John R., and Bruce M. Russett. 1997. "The classical liberals were right: Democracy, interdependence, and conflict, 1950–1985." *International Studies Quarterly* 41(2): 267–94.

O'Neill, Barry. 1999. *Honor, symbols, and war*. Ann Arbor: University of Michigan Press.

Onishi, Norimitsu. 2007. "Denial reopens wounds of Japan's ex-sex slaves." *New York Times*. March 8. https://www.nytimes.com/2007/03/08/world/asia/08japan.html

Orentlicher, Diane F. 1991. "Settling accounts: The duty to prosecute human rights violations of a prior regime." *Yale Law Journal* 100(8): 2537–2615.

Organski, A. F. K. 1958. *World politics*. New York: Alfred A. Knopf.

Osgood, Charles E. 1962. *An alternative to war or surrender*. Champagne: University of Illinois Press.

Oye, Kenneth A. 1985. "Explaining cooperation under anarchy: Hypotheses and strategies." *World Politics* 38(1): 1–24.

Paez, Dario, and James H. Liu. 2011. "Collective memory of conflicts." In Daniel Bar-Tal, ed., *Intergroup conflicts and their resolution: A social psychological perspective.* New York: Psychology Press.

Page, Benjamin I., and Marshall M. Bouton. 2008. *The foreign policy disconnect: What Americans want from our leaders but don't get.* Chicago: University of Chicago Press.

Page, Benjamin I., and Robert I. Shapiro. 1992. *The rational public: Fifty years of trends in Americans' policy preferences.* Chicago: University of Chicago Press.

Panda, Ankit. 2019. "The 2019 US Indo-Pacific Strategy Report: Who's it for?" *The Diplomat.* June 11. https://thediplomat.com/2019/06/the-2019-us-indo-pacific-strategy-report-whos-it-for/Park, Hahn-Kyu. 2017. "The China-Japan-South Korea Trilateral Summit: Realpolitik or liberal peace?" In Lam Pang Er, ed., *China-Japan relations in the 21st century: Antagonism despite interdependency,* 291–317. Singapore: Palgrave Macmillan.

Park, June, and Eunbin Chung. 2021. "Learning from past pandemic governance: Early response and Public-Private Partnerships in testing of COVID-19 in South Korea. *World Development* 137: 105198-105198.

Park, Jaehan, and Sangyoung Yun. 2016. "Korea and Japan's military information agreement: A final touch for the pivot?" November 24. *The Diplomat.* https://thediplomat.com/2016/11/korea-and-japans-military-information-agreement-a-final-touch-for-the-pivot/

Park, Madison. 2013. "Yasukuni shrine visits: Japan honoring the dead or insulting the neighbors?" *CNN.* December 26. http://www.cnn.com/2013/10/21/world/asia/yasukuni-japan/

Park, Myung-Kyu, and Young-Hoon Song. 2013. "Perceptions on reunification 2013" (translated). Seoul National University Research Center on Reunification and Peace.

Patten, Christopher. 2015. "Don't lose track of the conflict between Palestinians and Israelis." *Daily Star.* June 30. https://www.dailystar.com.lb/Opinion/Commentary/2015/Jun-30/304378-dont-lose-track-of-the-conflict-between-palestinians-and-israelis.ashx

Pavlović, Srđa. 2016. "Montenegro's 'stabilitocracy': The West's support of Đukanović is damaging the prospects of democratic change." LSE European Politics and Policy (EUROPP) Blog. December 23. https://blogs.lse.ac.uk/europpblog/2016/12/23/montenegros-stabilitocracy-how-the-wests-support-of-dukanovic-is-damaging-the-prospects-of-democratic-change/

Peattie, Mark R. 2007. "The poisoned well: Fifty years of Sino-Japanese animosity." In Gi-Wook Shin and Daniel C. Sneider, eds., *Cross currents: Regionalism and nationalism in Northeast Asia.* Stanford, CA: Walter H. Shorenstein Asia-Pacific Research Center.

Peetz, Johanna, Gregory R. Gunn, and Anne E. Wilson. 2010. "Crimes of the past: Defensive temporal distancing in the face of past in-group wrongdoing." *Personality and Social Psychology Bulletin* 36(5): 598–611.

Peffley, Mark and Jon Hurwitz. 1992. "International events and foreign policy beliefs: Public response to changing Soviet-US relations." *American Journal of Political Science* 36(2): 431–61.

Pei, Minxin. 2010. "Rights and Resistance: The changing contexts of the dissident movement." In Elizabeth J. Perry and Mark Selden, eds., *Chinese society: Change, conflict and resistance*. New York: Routledge.

Petty, Richard E., and John T. Cacioppo. 1986. *The elaboration likelihood model of persuasion*. New York: Springer.

Pew Research Center. 2014. "Chapter 4: How Asians view each other." July 14. https://www.pewresearch.org/global/2014/07/14/chapter-4-how-asians-view-each-other/

Pew Research Center. 2015. "Growing public support for U.S. ties With Cuba—And an end to the trade embargo." July 21. https://www.pewresearch.org/politics/2015/07/21/growing-public-support-for-u-s-ties-with-cuba-and-an-end-to-the-trade-embargo/

Pilling, David. 2009. "Beijing finds fine words for its old enemy." *Financial Times*. December 16. https://www.ft.com/content/0b636690-ea7a-11de-a9f5-00144feab49a

Pilling, David. 2012. "Japan, China and their 'history problem.'" *Financial Times*. August 22. http://www.ft.com/intl/cms/s/0/497f8d14-ec43-11e1-a91c-00144feab49a.html#axzz3CxC68Wl4

Platow, Michael J., Margaret Foddy, Toshio Yamagishi, Li Lim, and Aurore Chow. 2012. "Two experimental tests of trust in in-group strangers: The moderating role of common knowledge of group membership." *European Journal of Social Psychology* 42(1): 30–35.

Polyakova, Alina, and Neil Fligstein. 2016. "Is European integration causing Europe to become more nationalist? Evidence from the 2007–9 financial crisis." *Journal of European Public Policy* 23(1): 60–83.

PPSD (People's Solidarity for Participatory Democracy). 2016a. "[Comment] Immediately Stop the Provisional Signing of the Korea-Japan Military Information Protection Agreement" (translated). November 14. http://www.peoplepower21.org/Peace/1461629

PPSD (People's Solidarity for Participatory Democracy). 2016b. "[Press Conference] Opposition to the Korea-Japan Military Information Protection Agreement Passing the Cabinet" (translated). November 22. http://www.peoplepower21.org/Peace/1463970

PRC State Council. 2015a. "Highlights of government work report." March 5. http://english.www.gov.cn/premier/news/2015/03/05/content_281475066011469.htm

PRC State Council. 2015b. "Premier emphasizes China-Russia development strategy integration." December 17. http://english.www.gov.cn/premier/news/2015/12/17/content_281475255751161.htm

Preacher, Kristopher J., and Andrew F. Hayes. 2004. "SPSS and SAS procedures

for estimating indirect effects in simple mediation models." *Behavior research methods, instruments, & computers* 36(4): 717–31.
Preacher, Kristopher J., and Andrew F. Hayes. 2008. "Asymptotic and resampling strategies for assessing and comparing indirect effects in multiple mediator models." *Behavior research methods* 40(3): 879–91.
Price, Richard. 1998. "Reversing the gun sights: Transnational civil society targets land mines." *International Organization* 52(3): 613–44.
Putnam, Robert D. 1988. "Diplomacy and domestic politics: The logic of two-level games." *International Organization* 42(3): 427–60.
Putnam, Robert D. 2007. "E pluribus unum: Diversity and community in the twenty-First century." The 2006 Johan Skytte Prize Lecture. Nordic Political Science Association.
Rajagopalan, Rajeswari Pilla. 2018. "Where Is Japan in Its military push under Abe?" *The Diplomat*. March 29. https://thediplomat.com/2018/03/where-is-japan-in-its-military-push-under-abe/
Rathbun, Brian C. 2007. "Uncertain about uncertainty: Understanding the multiple meanings of a crucial concept in international relations theory." *International Studies Quarterly* 51(3): 533–57.
Rathbun, Brian C. 2009. "It takes all types: Social psychology, trust and the international relations paradigm in our minds." *International Theory* 1(3): 345–80.
Rathbun, Brian C. 2011. "Before hegemony: Generalized trust, international cooperation and the design of international organizations." *International Organization* 45(2): 243–73.
Ravenhill, John. 2001. *APEC and the construction of Pacific Rim regionalism*. Cambridge: Cambridge University Press.
Reilly, James. 2011. "Remember history, not hatred: Collective remembrance of China's war of resistance to Japan." *Modern Asian Studies* 45(2): 463–90.
Reilly, James. 2012. *Strong society, smart state: The Rise of public opinion in China's Japan policy*. New York: Columbia University Press.
Reséndez, Andrés. 2005. *Changing national identities at the frontier: Texas and New Mexico, 1800–1850*. Cambridge: Cambridge University Press.
Reynolds, Isabel, and Youkyung Lee. 2019. "Why can't Japan and South Korea be friends?" *Bloomberg*. April 17. https://www.bloomberg.com/news/articles/2019-04-17/trump-needs-them-to-be-friends-but-japan-and-south-korea-feud
Rich, Motoko. 2017a. "Shinzo Abe announces plan to revise Japan's pacifist constitution." *New York Times*. May 3. https://www.nytimes.com/2017/05/03/world/asia/japan-constitution-shinzo-abe-military.html
Rich, Motoko. 2017b. "A pacifist Japan starts to embrace the military." *New York Times*. August 29. https://www.nytimes.com/2017/08/29/world/asia/korea-missile-japan-pacifism.html
Rich, Motoko. 2018. "Japan balks at calls for new apology to South Korea over 'comfort women.'" *New York Times*. January 12. https://www.nytimes.com/2018/01/12/world/asia/japan-south-korea-comfort-women.html

Rich, Motoko, and Eimi Yamamitsu. 2019. "Good news for Shinzo Abe: Japan's young voters lean right, if they vote at all." *New York Times*. July 18. www.nytimes.com/2019/07/18/world/asia/japan-shinzo-abe-election.html?module-inline

Rich, Motoko, Edward Wong, and Choe Sang-Hun. 2019. "As Japan and South Korea feud intensifies, U.S. seems unwilling, or unable, to help." *New York Times*. August 4. www.nytimes.com/2019/08/04/world/asia/japan-south-korea-feud.html

Riek, Blake M., Eric W. Mania, and Samuel L. Gaertner. 2006. "Intergroup threat and outgroup attitudes: A meta-analytic review." *Personality and Social Psychology Review* 10(4): 336–53.

Riek, Blake M., Eric W. Mania, Samuel L. Gaertner, Stacy A. McDonald, and Marika J. Lamoreaux. 2010. "Does a common ingroup identity reduce intergroup threat?" *Group Processes & Intergroup Relations* 13(4): 403–23.

Robinson, Amanda Lea. 2014. "National versus ethnic identification in Africa: Modernization, colonial legacy, and the origins of territorial nationalism." *World Politics* 66(4): 709–46.

Roccas, Sonia, Yechiel Klar, and Ido Liviatan. 2006. "The paradox of group-based guilt: Modes of national identification, conflict vehemence, and reactions to the in-group's moral violations." *Journal of Personality and Social Psychology* 91(4): 698–711.

Rock, Stephen R. 1989. *Why peace breaks out: Great power rapprochement in historical perspective*. Chapel Hill: University of North Carolina Press.

Rosamond, Ben. 2000. *Theories of European integration*. Hampshire: Palgrave Macmillan.

Ross, Lee, and Andrew Ward. 1995. "Psychological barriers to dispute resolution." *Advances in Experimental Social Psychology* 27: 255–304.

Ross, Robert S. 2009. "China's naval nationalism: Sources, prospects, and the US response." *International Security* 34(2): 46–81.

Rotella, Katie N., and Jennifer A. Richeson. 2013. "Motivated to 'forget' the effects of in-group wrongdoing on memory and collective guilt." *Social Psychological and Personality Science* 4(6): 730–37.

Rousseau, David L., and Rocio Garcia-Retamero. 2007. "Identity, power and threat perception: A cross-national experimental study." *Journal of Conflict Resolution* 51(5): 744–71.

Roy, Denny. 1994. "Hegemon on the horizon? China's threat to East Asian security." *International Security* 19(1): 149–68.

Rozman, Gilbert. 2004. *Northeast Asia's stunted regionalism: Bilateral distrust in the shadow of globalization*. Cambridge: Cambridge University Press.

Rutayisire, John, John Kabano, and Jolly Rubagiza. 2004. "Redefining Rwanda's future: The role of curriculum in social reconstruction." In Sobhi Tawil and Alexandra Harley, eds., *Education, conflict and social cohesion*. Geneva, Switzerland: UNESCO, International Bureau of Education.

Saeki, Toshiro. 2001. "Amendment is just a grand illusion." *Japan Quarterly* 48(4): 72–79.

Sahdra, Baljinder, and Michael Ross. 2007. "Group identification and historical memory." *Personality and Social Psychology Bulletin* 33(3): 384–95.

Sarkin, Jeremy. 1996. "The trials and tribulations of the truth and reconciliation commission in South Africa." *South African Journal on Human Rights* 12(4): 617–40.

Sarkin, Jeremy. 1999. "The necessity and challenges of establishing a truth and reconciliation commission in Rwanda." *Human Rights Quarterly* 21(3): 767–823.

Sarkin, Jeremy. 2001. "The tension between justice and reconciliation in Rwanda: Politics, human rights, due process and the role of the Gacaca courts in dealing with the genocide." *Journal of African Law* 45(2): 143–72.

Sartori, Anne E. 2003. "An estimator for some binary-outcome selection models without exclusion restrictions." *Political Analysis* 11(2): 111–38.

Sasaki, Takeshi. 2001. "A new era of nationalism?" *Journal of Japanese Trade and Industry* 20/1: 8–11.

Scanlon, Charles. 2005. "S Korean fury over island dispute." BBC. March 14. http://news.bbc.co.uk/2/hi/asia-pacific/4347851.stm

Schlenker, Andrea. 2013. "Cosmopolitan Europeans or partisans of fortress Europe? Supranational identity patterns in the EU." *Global Society* 27(1): 25–51.

Schneiker, Andrea. 2017. "NGOs as norm takers: Insider–outsider networks as translators of norms." *International Studies Review* 19(3): 381–406.

Schuman, Howard, and Stanley Presser. 1981. *Questions and answers in attitude surveys: Experiments on question form, wording, and context*. New York: Academic Press.

Schuman, Robert. 1950. "La déclaration du 9 mai 1950," Paris; online: "Declaration of 9th May 1950." 2011. *European Issue* (204): 1–3. https://www.robert-schuman.eu/en/doc/questions-d-europe/qe-204-en.pdf

Sears, David O. 1993. "Symbolic politics: A socio-psychological theory." In Shanto Iyengar and William J. McGuire, eds., *Explorations in political psychology*, 113–49. Durham: Duke University Press.

Sevastopulo, Demetri. 2019. "US agencies barred from buying Huawei equipment." *Financial Times*. August 7. www.ft.com/content/fc23eebe-b951-11e9-8a88-aa6628ac896c

Shadish, William R., Thomas D. Cook, and Donald Thomas Campbell. 2002. *Experimental and quasi-experimental designs for generalized causal inference*. Boston, MA: Houghton Mifflin.

Shapiro, Robert Y., and Harpreet Mahajan. 1986. "Gender differences in policy preferences: A summary of trends from the 1960s to the 1980s." *Public Opinion Quarterly* 50(1): 42–61.

Sheen, Seongho, and Jina Kim. 2012. "What went wrong with the ROK-Japan Military Pact?" *Asia Pacific Bulletin*, East-West Center. July 31. http://www.eastwestcenter.org/sites/default/files/private/apb176.pdf

Sherman, David K., and Geoffrey L. Cohen. 2006. "The psychology of self-defense: Self-affirmation theory." *Advances in Experimental Social Psychology* 38: 183–242.

Sherman, David K., and Heejung S. Kim. 2005. "Is there an "I" in "team"? The role of the self in groupserving judgments." *Journal of Personality and Social Psychology* 88(1): 108–20.

Sherman, David K., Leif D. Nelson, and Lee D. Ross. 2003. "Naï realism and affirmative action: Adversaries are more similar than they think." *Basic and Applied Social Psychology* 25(4): 275–89.

Sherman, David K., Zoe Kinias, Brenda Major, Heejung S. Kim, and Mary Prenovost. 2007. "The group as a resource: Reducing biased attributions for group success and failure via group affirmation." *Personality and Social Psychology Bulletin* 33(8): 1100–12.

Shimko, K. L. 1991. *Images and arms control: Perceptions of the Soviet Union in the Reagan administration*. Ann Arbor: University of Michigan Press.

Silverstein, Brett. 1989. "Enemy images: The psychology of US attitudes and cognitions regarding the Soviet Union." *American Psychologist* 44(6): 903–13.

Sim, Dewey. 2019. "Asia fears 'second cold war' as Donald Trump pushes Iran into Chinese arms." *South China Morning Post*. August 13. www.scmp.com/week-asia/geopolitics/article/3022654/trump-pushes-iran-chinese-arms-asia-fears-second-cold-war

Simoes, Alexander James Gaspar, and César A. Hidalgo. 2011. "The economic complexity observatory: An analytical tool for understanding the dynamics of economic development." Workshops at the Twenty-Fifth AAAI Conference on Artificial Intelligence, MIT. https://atlas.media.mit.edu/en/profile/country/jpn/, https://atlas.media.mit.edu/en/profile/country/chn/

Simon, Bernd, Claudia Kulla, and Martin Zobel. 1995. "On being more than just a part of the whole: Regional identity and social distinctiveness." *European Journal of Social Psychology* 25(3): 325–40.

Sivanathan, Niro, Daniel C. Molden, Adam D. Galinsky, and Gillian Ku. 2008. "The promise and peril of self-affirmation in de-escalating commitment." *Organizational Behavior and Human Decision Processes* 107(1): 1–14.

Smith, Anthony D. 1993. *National identity*. London: Penguin.

Smith, Eliot R. 2014. "Social identity and social emotions: Toward new conceptualizations of prejudice." In Diane M. Mackie and David L. Hamilton, eds., *Affect, cognition and stereotyping: Interactive processes in group perception*. New York: Academic Press.

Smith, Eliot R., and Susan Henry. 1996. "An in-group becomes part of the self: Response time evidence." *Personality and Social Psychology Bulletin* 22(6): 635–42.

Smith, Eliot R., Charles R. Seger, and Diane M. Mackie. 2007. "Can emotions be truly group level? Evidence regarding four conceptual criteria." *Journal of Personality and Social Psychology* 93(3): 431–46.

Smith, Emma. 2008. *Using secondary data in educational and social research*. London: Open University Press.

Sniderman, Paul M., Louk Hagendoorn, and Markus Prior. 2004. "Predisposing factors and situational triggers: Exclusionary reactions to immigrant minorities." *American Political Science Review* 98(1): 35–49.

Sobel, Michael E. 1994. "Causal inference in latent variable models." In Alexander Ed von Eye and Clifford C. Clogg, eds., *Latent variables analysis: Applications for developmental research*, 3–35. Newbury Park, CA: Sage.

Soesastro, Hadi. 2006. "East Asia: many clubs, little progress." *Far Eastern Economic Review* 169(1): 50–53.

Soeya, Yoshihide. 1995. *Nihon gaikou to chugoku 1945–1972 [Japanese diplomacy and China 1945–1972]*. Tokyo: Keio University Publishers.

Soeya, Yoshihide, David A. Welch, and Masayuki Tadokoro, eds. 2011. *Japan as a normal country? A nation in search of its place in the world. Japan and global society*. Toronto: University of Toronto Press.

Solingen, Etel. 2007. *Nuclear logics: Contrasting paths in East Asia and the Middle East*. Princeton: Princeton University Press.

Soroka, Stuart, Matthew Wright, Richard Johnston, Jack Citrin, Keith Banting, and Will Kymlicka. 2017. "Ethnoreligious identity, immigration, and redistribution." *Journal of Experimental Political Science* 4(3): 173–82.

Spencer, Steven J., Steven Fein, and Christine D. Lomore. 2001. "Maintaining one's self-image vis-à-vis others: The role of self-affirmation in the social evaluation of the self." *Motivation and Emotion* 25(1): 41–65.

Spinner-Halev, Jeff, and Elizabeth Theiss-Morse. 2003. "National identity and self-esteem." *Perspectives on Politics* 1(3): 515–32.

Steele, Brent J. 2008. *Ontological security in international relations: Self-identity and the IR state*. London: Routledge.

Steele, Claude. M. 1988. "The psychology of self-affirmation: Sustaining the integrity of the self." In Leonard Berkowitz, ed., *Advances in experimental social psychology* 21: 261–302. New York: Academic Press.

Steele, Shelby. 2006. *White guilt: How blacks and whites together destroyed the promise of the civil rights era*. New York: HarperCollins.

Stein, Arthur A. 1982. "Coordination and collaboration: Regimes in an anarchic world." *International Organization* 36(2): 299–324.

Stephan, Walter G., and Cookie White Stephan. 2000. "An integrated threat theory of prejudice." In Stuart Oskamp, ed., *Reducing prejudice and discrimination*, 23–45. Mahwah, NJ: Lawrence Erlbaum Associates.

Stets, Jan E., and Peter J. Burke. 2000. "Identity theory and social identity theory." *Social Psychology Quarterly* 63(3): 224–37.

Strelan, Peter. 2007. "Who forgives others, themselves, and situations? The roles of narcissism, guilt, self-esteem, and agreeableness." *Personality and Individual Differences* 42(2): 259–69.

Stuart, Douglas, and Harvey Starr. 1981. "The 'inherent bad faith model' reconsidered: Dulles, Kennedy, and Kissinger." *Political Psychology* 3(3/4): 1–33.

Sullivan, Daniel, Mark J. Landau, Nyla R. Branscombe, and Zachary K. Rothschild. 2012. "Competitive victimhood as a response to accusations of ingroup harm doing." *Journal of Personality and Social Psychology* 102(4): 778–95.

Sussman, Dalia. 2016. "Most Americans support ending Cuba embargo, Times poll finds." *New York Times*. March 21. http://www.nytimes.com/interactive/projects/cp/international/obama-in-cuba/type/analysis

Suzuki, Shogo. 2008. "Seeking legitimate great power status in post-Cold War international society: China's and Japan's participation in UNPKO." *International Relations* 22(1): 45–63.

Suzuki, Shogo. 2015a. "The rise of the Chinese 'Other' in Japan's construction of identity: Is China a focal point of Japanese nationalism?" *Pacific Review* 28(1): 95–116.

Suzuki, Shogo. 2015b. "Will Japan's war apologies ever satisfy China?" *East Asia Forum*. November 5. http://www.eastasiaforum.org/2015/11/05/will-japans-war-apologies-ever-satisfy-china/

Swaine, Michael D. 2010. "China's assertive behavior, part one: On 'core interests.'" *China Leadership Monitor* 34: 8-11.

Tajfel, Henri. 1978. *Differentiation between social groups: Studies in the social psychology of intergroup relations*. London: Academic Press.

Tajfel, Henri. 1981. *Human groups and social categories: Studies in social psychology*. Cambridge: Cambridge University Press.

Tajfel, Henri, and John C. Turner. 1979. "An integrative theory of intergroup conflict." In Stephen Worchel and William G. Austin, eds., *The social psychology of intergroup relations*, 33–47. Monterey, CA: Brooks/Cole.

Tamir, Yael. 1995. *Liberal nationalism*. Princeton: Princeton University Press.

Tang, Wenfang, and Benjamin Darr. 2012. "Chinese nationalism and its political and social origins." *Journal of Contemporary China* 21(77): 811–26.

Tate, Katherine. 1994. *From protest to politics: The new black voters in American elections*. Cambridge, MA: Harvard University Press.

Tatsumi, Yuki. 2018. "The Japan-South Korea 'comfort women' agreement survives (barely)." *The Diplomat*. January 11. https://thediplomat.com/2018/01/the-japan-south-korea-comfort-women-agreement-survives-barely/

Taylor, Charles. 1998. "Nationalism and modernity." In John A. Hall, ed., *The state of the nation: Ernest Gellner and the theory of nationalism*, 191–218. Cambridge: Cambridge University Press.

Tetlock, Philip E., and Richard Ned Lebow. 2001. "Poking counterfactual holes in covering laws: Cognitive styles and historical reasoning." *American Political Science Review* 95(4): 829–43.

Theiss-Morse, Elizabeth. 2009. *Who counts as an American? The boundaries of national identity*. Cambridge: Cambridge University Press.

Thies, Cameron. 2009. "Role theory and foreign policy." *Oxford Research Encyclopedia of International Studies*. https://oxfordre.com/internationalstudies/view/10.1093/acrefore/9780190846626.001.0001/acrefore-9780190846626-e-291

Todd, Jennifer, Lorenzo Cañás Bottos, and Nathalie Rougier, eds. 2013. *Political transformation and national identity change: Comparative perspectives*. London: Routledge.

Togeby, Lise. 1994. "The gender gap in foreign policy attitudes." *Journal of Peace Research* 31(4): 375–92.

Torpey, John, ed. 2004. *Politics and the past: On repairing historical injustices*. Lanham, MD: Rowman & Littlefield.

Torres, Ida. 2013. "Anti-Korean demonstrations hurt businesses in Shin-Okubo district." *Japan Daily Press*. August 5. http://japandailypress.com/anti-korean-demonstrations-hurt-businesses-in-shin-okubo-district-0533307/

Transue, John E. 2007. "Identity salience, identity acceptance, and racial policy attitudes: American national identity as a uniting force." *American Journal of Political Science* 51(1): 78–91.

Trzesniewski, Kali H., M. Donnellan, and Richard E. Lucas. 2011. *Secondary data analysis: An introduction for psychologists*. Washington, DC: American Psychological Association.

Tselichtchev, Ivan. 2018. "Why can't Japan and South Korea get past their battle scars?" *South China Morning Post*. April 15. https://www.scmp.com/week-asia/geopolitics/article/2141313/why-cant-japan-and-south-korea-get-past-their-battle-scars

Turner, John C., Michael A. Hogg, Penelope J. Oakes, Stephen D. Reicher, and Margaret S. Wetherell. 1987. *Rediscovering the social group: A self-categorization theory*. Oxford: Basil Blackwell.

Tusicisny, Andrej. 2007. "Security communities and their values: Taking masses seriously." *International Political Science Review* 28(4): 425–49.

Tutu, Desmond. 1999. *No future without forgiveness*. London: Rider.

Twining, Daniel. 2012. "The Chinese military's great leap forward." *Real Clear World*. March 8. http://www.realclearworld.com/articles/2012/03/08/the_chinese_militarys_great_leap_forward_99944.html

Tyler, Tom R., and P. Degoey. 2004. "Trust in organizational authorities: The influence of motive attributions on willingness to accept decisions." In R. M. Kramer and K. S. Cook, eds., *Trust and distrust in organizations: Dilemmas and approaches*, Vol. 7, 331–56. Thousand Oaks, CA: Sage.

Tyson, Alec. 2016. "Americans still favor ties with Cuba after Castro's death, U.S. election." Pew Research Center. December 13. https://www.pewresearch.org/fact-tank/2016/12/13/americans-still-favor-ties-with-cuba-after-castros-death-u-s-election/

U.S. Department of Defense. 2019. "Indo-Pacific Strategy report preparedness, partnerships, and promoting a networked region." June 1. https://media.defense.gov/2019/Jul/01/2002152311/-1/-1/1/DEPARTMENT-OF-DEFENSE-INDO-PACIFIC-STRATEGY-REPORT-2019.PDF

U.S. Department of State. n.d. "The United States and the opening to Japan, 1853." Office of the Historian, Foreign Service Institute. https://history.state.gov/milestones/1830-1860/opening-to-japan#:~:text=On%20July%208%2C%201853%2C%20American,Japan%20and%20the%20western%20world

Uslaner, Eric M. 2002. *The moral foundations of trust*. Cambridge: Cambridge University Press.

Van Evera, Stephen. 1994. "Hypotheses on nationalism and war." *International Security* 18(4): 5–39.

Van Lange, Paul A. M., Ellen De Bruin, Wilma Otten, and Jeffrey A. Joireman. 1997. "Development of prosocial, individualistic, and competitive orientations:

theory and preliminary evidence." *Journal of Personality and Social Psychology* 73(4): 733–46.

Varandani, Suman. 2014. "Shinzo Abe's offering to Yasukuni Shrine angers China, South Korea." *International Business Times*. August 15. https://www.ibtimes.com/shinzo-abes-offering-yasukuni-shrine-angers-china-south-korea-1659368

Vargas, Jose Antonio. 2012. "Spring awakening." *New York Times*. February 17. https://www.nytimes.com/2012/02/19/books/review/how-an-egyptian-revolution-began-on-facebook.html

Vartanian, Thomas P. 2010. *Secondary data analysis*. New York: Oxford University Press.

Vogel, Ezra. 1979. *Japan as number one: Lessons for America*. New York: Harper & Row.

Vogel, Ezra. 2003. "Foreward." In Yoichi Funabashi, ed., *Reconciliation in the Asia-Pacific*. Washington, DC: United States Institute of Peace.

Wakslak, Cheryl J., and Yaacov Trope. 2009. "Cognitive consequences of affirming the self: The relationship between self-affirmation and object construal." *Journal of Experimental Social Psychology* 45(4): 927–32.

Waldron, Jeremy. 2002. "One law for all-The logic of cultural accommodation." *Washington & Lee Law Review* 59: 3.

Walt, Stephen M. 1987. *The origins of alliances*. Ithaca: Cornell University Press.

Walt, Stephen M. 2019. "Yesterday's Cold War shows how to beat China today." *Foreign Policy*. July 29. https://foreignpolicy.com/2019/07/29/yesterdays-cold-war-shows-how-to-beat-china-today/

Waltz, Kenneth N. 1979. *Theory of international politics*. Boston: Addison-Wesley.

Walzer, Michael. 2008. *Spheres of justice: A defense of pluralism and equality*. New York: Basic books.

Ward, David. 2007. "Archbishop of York urges PM to apologise for slavery." *The Guardian*. March 26. https://www.theguardian.com/politics/2007/mar/26/race.past

Wendt, Alex. 1999. *Social theory of international politics*. Cambridge: Cambridge University Press.

Wendt, Alex. 2003. "Why a world state is inevitable." *European Journal of International Relations* 9(4): 491–542.

White, Ralph K. 1965. "Images in the context of international conflict." In Herbert C. Kelman, ed., *International behavior: A social-psychological analysis*, 236–76. New York: Holt, Rinehart & Winston.

White, Ralph K. 1968. *Nobody wanted war: Misperception in Vietnam and other wars*. New York: Doubleday.

White, Ralph K. 1991. "Enemy images in the United Nations-Iraq and East-West conflicts." In Robert W. Rieber, ed., *The psychology of war and peace*, 59–70. New York: Plenum Press.

Whiteley, Paul F. 2000. "Economic growth and social capital." *Political Studies* 48(3): 443–66.

Wimmer, Andreas. 2019. "Why nationalism works and why it isn't going away." *Foreign Affairs*. March/April. https://www.foreignaffairs.com/articles/world/2019-02-12/why-nationalism-works

Wirth, Christian. 2009. "China, Japan and East Asian regional cooperation: The views of 'self' and 'other' from Beijing to Tokyo." *International Relations of the Asia-Pacific* 9(3): 469–96.

Wittkopf, Eugene R. 1990. *Faces of internationalism: Public opinion and American foreign policy*. Durham: Duke University Press.

Wohl, Michael J. A., Nyla R. Branscombe, and Yechiel Klar. 2006. "Collective guilt: Emotional reactions when one's group has done wrong or been wronged." *European Review of Social Psychology* 17(1): 1–37.

Woo, Byungwon, and Eunbin Chung. 2018. Aid for vote? United Nations General Assembly voting and American aid allocation. *Political Studies* 66(4): 1002–26.

World Bank. 2013. "Military expenditure (% of GDP)." http://data.worldbank.org/indicator/MS.MIL.XPND.GD.ZS

World Bank. 2017. World integrated trade solution. https://wits.worldbank.org/CountryProfile/en/Country/CHN/Year/2017/TradeFlow/EXPIMP/Partner/by-country, https://wits.worldbank.org/CountrySnapshot/en/JPN

World Values Survey. n.d. http://www.worldvaluessurvey.org/wvs.jsp

Yahuda, Michael. 2006. "The limits of economic interdependence: Sino-Japanese Relations." In Alastair Iain Johnston and Robert S. Ross, eds., *New directions in the study of China's foreign policy*. Stanford: Stanford University Press.

Yamagishi, Toshio, and Midori Yamagishi. 1994. "Trust and commitment in the United States and Japan." *Motivation and Emotion* 18(2): 129–66.

Yamamoto, Yoshinobu. 2008. "Institutionalization in Northeast Asia: Is outside-in regionalization enough?" In Martina Timmermann and Jitsuo Tsuchiyama, eds., *Institutionalizing Northeast Asia: Regional steps toward global governance*. Tokyo: United Nations University Press.

Yasuaki, Onuma. 2002. "Japanese war guilt and postwar responsibilities of Japan." *Berkeley Journal of International Law* 20(3): 600–620.

Yoon, Sukjoon. 2019. "Rethinking Japan-South Korea defense relations." *The Diplomat*. March 2. https://thediplomat.com/2019/03/rethinking-japan-south-korea-defense-relations/

Yoon, Tae-Ryong. 2008. "Learning to cooperate not to cooperate: Bargaining for the 1965 Korea-Japan Normalization." *Asian Perspective* 32(2): 59–91.

Yu, Tian, and Zeng Wei. 2016. "Who benefits most from GSOMIA?" December 8. Ministry of National Defense, People's Republic of China. http://eng.mod.gov.cn/Opinion/2016-12/08/content_4769057.htm

Zak, Paul J., and Stephen Knack. 2001. "Trust and growth." *Economic Journal* 111(470): 295–321.

Zarakol, Ayşe. 2010. "Ontological (in) security and state denial of historical crimes: Turkey and Japan." *International Relations* 24(1): 3–23.

Index

Abe, Shinzo
   efforts to amend constitution, 58
   and reparations, 29, 67, 113, 203, 258n6
   and Yasukuni Shrine, 11, 58, 174
Aboriginal peoples in Canada and reparations, 7, 68
absolute gains, 121
affirmation. *See* group-affirmation; national identity affirmation; self-affirmation
age
   and generational differences in guilt recognition, 6, 7, 28, 118–19, 129, 141, 155, 210
   in guilt recognition experiment, 122–23, 128, 129, 142, 143, 149, 154
   in image survey, 161, 164, 165, 166, 168
   and perception of political ideology conflicts, 180
ally image
   China as, 34, 51
   and cooperation, 72, 160, 163
   and effect on policy, 160
   and goal compatibility, 75, 78
   in image theory, 31, 74, 75
   Japan as, 79, 80
   and mutual gain, 160
   need for, 37–38
   shifting with national identity affirmation, 72–73, 76, 77, 78, 79–80
   US as, 163, 166
ambassadors, recall of, 55
amnesty, 69
anti-China protests in Japan, 257n2
anti-Japanese protests, 1, 21–22, 224
anti-Korean protests in Japan, 58
apologies
   Abe on, 113
   in guilt recognition experiment, 146, 147
   motivations for, 52
   in Murayama Statement, 28, 202
   negative consequences of, 70
   pressure on Japan for, 10, 27–30, 70
   role in reconciliation, 69–70
   undermining of, 29, 66
appropriateness, logic of, 63, 198
Asian attachment
   in guilt recognition experiment, 119, 126, 128, 153, 154
   in trust experiment, 84–85, 96–97, 99–101, 107–11
Asian commonality
   attempts at promoting, 44–45
   in trust experiment, 84–85, 96–97, 99–101, 107–11
Asian Financial Crisis of 1997, 54

barbarian image
  and caution, 163
  of China, 31, 33, 34, 79
  effect on policy, 160
  in image theory, 31, 74, 75, 78, 163
barriers to compromise, 230
belonging, sense of, 4, 5, 41, 43
Berlin Wall, 23
bias, 45, 47
Bosnia-Serbia relations, 7
Brexit, 23

Canadian reparations, 7, 68
caution in image survey, 156, 163–64
Chaudhry, Aizaz Ahmad, 11
chauvinism
  as barrier to reconciliation, 41
  exploiting, 232, 233
  and leaders, 20, 21
  as outward-looking, 5
China
  ally image, 34, 51
  anti-China protests in Japan, 257n2
  anti-Japanese protests in China, 1, 21–22
  barbarian image, 31, 33, 34, 79
  colony image, 31–33, 79–80
  decline of communism in, 56–57
  development integration with Russia, 226
  Diaoyu/Senkaku islands dispute, 9, 35, 45, 58
  dislike of Chinese, 151–54
  dislike of Japan, 206
  dissatisfaction with Japanese reparations, 7, 10, 27–30, 54–55, 67, 70, 202, 204–5
  distrust of, general, 26–27, 110, 151
  distrust of in reparations endorsement survey, 208–10, 212–14, 215
  distrust of in trust experiment, 97, 99, 106, 110
  distrust of Japan remilitarization, 26–27, 56, 57–58, 227
  economic cooperation with Japan, 19, 50
  economic rise of, 33–34, 145, 226
  enemy image, 32, 33, 34
  example of shift in images, 22
  in image survey, 162–69
  and Indo-Pacific Strategy, 225
  Joint History Research Committee, 44
  Nanjing Massacre, 29, 31
  opposition to Japan UN Security Council membership, 55
  perceptions of in Japan, 30, 31–33
  perceptions of in South Korea, 35–36, 37, 77, 80, 158–59, 163–69
  perceptions of Japan, 30, 31, 33–34, 35, 80–81
  public opinion in, 25
  rise of, 33–34, 145, 151, 205
  as security threat, 19, 24, 38, 55–59, 172, 173, 177, 224, 225
  Sino-Japanese honeymoon period, 3, 49–51
  and South Korea cooperation, 227–28, 229
  trade with Hong Kong, 258n3
  trade with US, 12, 224, 226
  and undermined gain, 54–55
  See also comfort women; forced labor; guilt recognition experiment; Japan reparations and guilt recognition; trust experiment
civil society
  and comfort women issue, 1, 29, 201–3
  effect on policy, 196, 197–99, 211–12, 215–16
  and GSOMIA protests, 173
  and moralistic trust, 196, 198, 201
  and reparations, 34, 196, 200–201
class and self-affirmation, 46
cognitive revolution, 259n9
Cold War, 224
collective action
  effect on policy, 23–24, 197–99
  and institution building, 54
  and moralistic trust, 196
  and reparations, 196
colony image
  of China, 31–33, 79–80
  and colonialism, 259n10
  and dehumanization, 31–32
  effect on policy, 160
  and guilt recognition, 75

in image theory, 31, 74, 75, 78
of South Korea, 31, 32, 33, 79–80
comfort women
   apology by Koizumi, 28
   and damage to security alliance triangle, 223–24
   protests, 1, 201–3
   2015 agreement on, 205–6
   undercutting of apologies for, 29, 67
commonality, Asian. *See* Asian commonality
common pool game in guilt recognition experiment
   and dictator game results, 135, 138–39
   instructions for, 121, 245–47
   and linked fate, 142–43
   measuring guilt in, 116, 117, 119
   methodology, 119, 120–22
   results, 123–37
communism, decline of, 56–57
competition
   and effect on policy, 160
   and enemy image, 72, 160
   in image survey, 156, 163–64
   and imperialist image, 163
   Japan as, 159, 175–76
   US as, 227
compromise, barriers to, 230
confidence
   and institution building, 54
   and moralistic trust, 66, 205
   in Sino-Japanese honeymoon period, 50
   and trust building, 60, 66
conflicts and war
   and enemy image, 31, 35
   and group-affirmation, 48
   and interdependence, 42
   and limits of national identity affirmation, 232
   origins of history problem in, 20–21
   perceptions of other countries as factor in, 73, 74
   potential for military conflict in region, 35, 56, 57
   pride as factor in, 1–2
   spirals of, 30, 56, 73, 78, 160
   as unthinkable in security communities, 59–60

conservative orientation
   and Cuba-US relations, 221, 222–23
   and GSOMIA support, 172, 181–82, 184, 189, 190, 191
   in guilt recognition experiment, 123
   in image survey, 164, 166
   and perception of political ideology conflicts, 180
   in trust experiment, 94
constructivism
   and common historical interpretation, 16, 20, 44
   effects of individuals on policy, 197
   and habit, 73, 199–200
   and history interpretation in trust experiment, 84, 85–86, 97, 99–101
   on public opinion and change, 23, 197
   and security community between Japan and US, 151
   on trust, 59–60
construct validity, 157
cooperation
   and ally image, 72, 160, 163
   between China and South Korea, 227–28, 229
   in image survey, 156, 163–64
   perceptions of in South Korea survey, 159
   perceptions of need for between Japan and South Korea, 175–77, 181
   role of trust in, 59–61, 63, 65, 178
   and sense of belonging, 5, 41
   spillover cooperation, 35, 41, 42, 199–200
   as stunted, 8–9, 10, 12, 18–20, 176, 193
   and subsuming identities strategy, 4
   and undermined gain, 53–55
   and willingness to shift images, 22
   See also economic cooperation; security cooperation; strategic trust
Cuba-US relations, 220–23
cultural products, 20, 50, 55, 58

Datsu-A Ron, 32
declared guilt
   in guilt recognition experiment, 116–17, 123–38, 149–50
   and linked fate, 141–46

personal, 124–26, 130–31, 132, 135–46
  relation to historical guilt, 149–50
  relation to revealed guilt, 135–38
dehumanization, 31–32
Deng, Xiaoping, 49
Diaoyu/Senkaku islands dispute, 9, 35, 45, 58
dictator game, 122, 135–46, 216–17
dignity, 5, 41
distrust
  defined, 26
  See also trust; trust and national identity affirmation; trust experiment; trust games
Dokdo/Takeshima islands dispute, 9

economic cooperation
  between China and Japan, 19, 50
  and Japan, South Korea, US triangle, 226
  between South Korea and Japan, 19–20
  stunting of, 8, 12, 19–20
  See also gain
economic satisfaction in image survey, 167–69
education level
  in guilt recognition experiment, 149, 154
  in image survey, 161, 164, 165, 166, 168
Egypt, collective action in, 24
emotions, group, 48
enduring rivalries, 229
enemy image
  and caution, 163
  China as, 32, 33, 34
  and competition, 72, 160
  and conflict, 31, 35
  and dehumanization, 32
  effect on policy, 160
  and hostility, 163
  in image theory, 31, 74, 75, 78
  of Japan, 34–35
  and perceived power and status, 75, 78
  research focus on, 73–74
Ethiopia, example of shift in images, 22
European Union

  general trust in by South Korea, 26, 27
  model in trust experiment, 96–97, 99–100, 107–9
  national identities *vs.* European identity, 42
  reconciliation in, 69–70
  security community in, 69
experiments
  in methodology overview, 13
  as tool, 231
exploitation
  and colony image, 31, 32, 33, 75, 78
  and imperialist image, 76
  and limits of national identity affirmation, 232
external validity, 157

fairness
  and national identity affirmation, 126–27, 153
  and prosociality, 114, 115–16, 117, 124, 155
  and reparations, 52
  and self-affirmation, 46
first gestures, 63
forced labor, 28, 202, 223–24
Fukuzawa, Yukichi, 32

gain
  absolute *vs.* relative, 121
  and ally image, 160
  and goal compatibility, 78
  and neoliberalism, 74
  undermined, 39, 52, 53–55, 59, 61–62, 64, 65, 66, 92
games. *See* common pool game in guilt recognition experiment; dictator game; trust game in trust experiment; trust games
gender
  and GSOMIA support, 193, 194
  in guilt recognition experiment, 123, 128, 129, 142, 143, 149, 154
  in image survey, 161, 164, 165, 166, 168
  and perception of political ideology conflicts, 180
generalized trust, 259n6

General Security of Military Information Agreement. *See* GSOMIA (General Security of Military Information Agreement)
General Sherman incident, 258n9
generational differences in guilt recognition, 6, 7, 28, 118–19, 129, 141, 155, 210
See also age
Genron NPO, 44
Germany
Berlin Wall, 23
reconciliation in, 69–70, 202, 206–7, 259n2
Global Attitudes Survey, 56
globalization and subsuming of national identities, 10, 42
goal compatibility, 74, 75–76, 78, 80
Graduated and Reciprocated Initiative in Tension-Reduction (GRIT), 63–64
grassroots action
effect on policy, 216
reparation efforts, 199, 200–201, 203, 207, 208, 210
See also civil society; collective action
group-affirmation
and bias, 47
and emotions, 48
and guilt recognition, 68, 117–18, 120, 126
in image survey, 162
and information processing, 48–49, 68, 76
in national identity affirmation theory, 15, 39, 47–51, 76–77, 184
scholarly implications on, 230–31
and self-affirmation, 39, 47–51
in trust experiment, 86, 87
group emotions, 48
GSOMIA (General Security of Military Information Agreement)
background on, 171, 172–73
and distrust between inflictors and receivers, 80–81
failure of and public opinion, 12–13, 67, 171, 173, 175, 194
and gender, 193, 194
and linked fate, 172, 182–84, 189–93, 194

in overview, 12–13, 14
and political orientation, 172, 181–83, 184, 189, 190, 191
reactions to, 171, 172–77
recognition of need for cooperation, 172, 173–77, 181, 194–95
and strategic trust, 171, 177–79, 186–89
in trust survey, 171–72, 178–79, 184–93, 194, 243
and US, 225–26
guilt recognition
in Balkan states, 7
and colony image, 75
and conflict resolution, 114–15
definition of group guilt, 114
definition of guilt, 114
and generational differences, 6, 7, 28, 115, 118–19, 129, 141, 155, 210
in Germany, 69–70
and group-affirmation, 68, 117–18, 120, 126
"guilt by association," 118–19, 129, 141, 210, 217
in Israeli-Palestinian relations, 7
and linked fate, 118–19, 141–46, 217
measuring, 116–17
and national identity affirmation potential, 3, 5, 13–14, 29–30
and national identity affirmation psychological mechanisms, 51–53, 117–19, 124–25, 141
and national identity affirmation theory, 40, 66–72, 81, 117–19
obstacles to, 6–7
overview of, 113–15
and punishment, 68–69
and rationality, 113–14
and self-affirmation, 46–47
as variable in research, 231
See also declared guilt; Japan reparations and guilt recognition; revealed guilt
guilt recognition experiment
about, 114, 115, 116–17
affirmation treatment in, 120
Asian commonality in, 119, 126, 128, 153, 154

guilt recognition experiment (*continued*)
  declared guilt in, 116–17, 123–38, 149–50
  demographics, 122–23, 128–29, 142, 143, 145, 148, 149, 150, 154, 161
  dictator game, 122, 135–46, 216–17
  and dislike of Chinese, 151–54
  and historic guilt, 146–54, 217
  linked fate in, 141–46
  materials, 243–48
  methodology, 116–17, 119–22
  and opponent country variable, 126–29, 134, 139, 140, 143–45, 147–48, 151–54
  payment for, 122
  results, 122–54
  revealed guilt in, 116–17, 124, 135–46
  survey, 116, 117, 119–20, 122, 135, 142–43, 146, 147, 243–48
  theory and hypotheses, 117–19
  See also common pool game in guilt recognition experiment; prosociality in guilt recognition experiment

habit
  and images, 73
  and trust, 199–201
hate, out-group, 5
Hatoyama, Yukio, 55
historic guilt in guilt recognition experiment, 146–54, 217
history
  and common historical interpretation, 16, 20, 44
  interpretation in trust experiment, 84, 85–86, 97, 99–101, 107–9
  pride in, 3
history problem
  and Asian commonality attempts, 44–45
  and common historical interpretation, 20
  examples of, 11
  and general distrust of Japan, 26, 27–30
  and images of other countries, 21, 22–23, 30–36
  leaders' role in, 20–21
  origins and causes of, 20–22

political use of, 20–21, 58, 204
public's role in, 21–26
and stunting of cooperation, 18–20, 176, 193
as term, 1
and trust, 6, 12–13, 26–30, 39–40
undermined gain and security, 53–61
See also Japan reparations and guilt recognition
Hong Kong, China trade with, 258n3
hostility in image survey, 156, 163–64

ideology. *See* political orientation
images of other counties
  effect on policy, 30, 73–74, 159–60
  and history problem, 21, 22–23, 30–36
  importance of, 24, 73–74
  and learning behavior, 30–31
  in national identity affirmation theory, 40, 51–53, 72–81, 159
  in overview, 3, 5, 13, 14
  and public opinion, 24
  shifting images, 22, 72–73, 79, 80
  and status of in-groups, 72–73, 80
  in trust game, 90
  as variable in research, 231
  See also image survey; *specific countries*
image survey
  baseline perceptions, 157–60
  data and variables, 162–64
  demographics, 161, 164–65, 166, 167–69
  economic satisfaction in, 167–69
  measuring affirmation in, 161–62, 164–65, 167–69
  methodology, 160–62, 164
  overview, 156–57
  results, 164–69
  time trends in, 167
image theory
  and effects of images, 74–76, 159–60
  and goal compatibility, 74, 75–76, 78, 80
  and habit, 73
  and history problem, 21, 22–23
  images, defined, 72
  and learning behavior, 30–31, 73
  in overview, 7, 40

and relative power/status, 74–77, 78, 80
shifting images, 72
and stereotypes, 40, 72
and "sticky" images, 21, 22
types of images in, 31, 74
See also ally image; barbarian image; colony image; enemy image; image survey; imperialist image
imperialist image
and competition, 163
effect on policy, 160
in image theory, 31, 74, 76, 78
of Japan, 31, 32, 34, 79, 80
shifting to ally image, 72–73, 79, 80
income in image survey, 164, 165, 166–67, 168
India
national identity, 43
-Pakistan relations, 11, 12
individuals
effects of on policy, 197
interactions and stereotypes, 42
reparation efforts, 81, 199, 200–201, 203, 207, 208, 210, 211–12, 216–17
Indo-Pacific Strategy Report, 225
inflictors
and cooperation, 12, 15, 80–82
and dictator game, 216–17
and generational distance, 115, 154–55
and group-affirmation, 46–47
and GSOMIA support, 80–81
and individual action, 203
and linked fate, 217
and moralistic trust, 207
in national identity affirmation theory, 40, 51–53, 66–72, 115, 150
in overview, 12, 13, 14, 15, 16, 17
and security communities, 60
and self-affirmation, 46
in trust experiment survey, 85–86, 110
See also guilt recognition
information processing
and group-affirmation, 48–49, 68, 76
and psychological mechanisms of national identity affirmation, 51–52
and self-affirmation, 45–46
in-groups

and affirmation mechanisms, 40–41, 76–77, 80, 82, 113, 115–16, 203, 218
aversion to guilt recognition, 67, 68, 201
creation of, 41
and declared guilt, 6, 16, 126–37, 149–50
and historical guilt, 149–50
and image theory, 75–76, 160
and linked fate, 118–19, 141–46
love, 5, 233, 235
and revealed guilt, 135–46
status of, 72–73, 76–77, 80
See also guilt recognition experiment; trust experiment
institution building
and ally image, 160
gains from, 39, 53–54
and game theory, 91
stunting of in region, 6, 26, 53–54, 55
and trials, 69
and trust, 6, 11, 13, 39–40, 60–63, 65, 66, 67, 179, 186–87
and undermined gain, 53–55
See also cooperation; security cooperation
integration theory, 35, 41, 42, 44, 199, 234
internal validity, 157
Israel-Palestine relations, 7, 11, 12, 21

Japan
ally image, 79, 80
anti-China protests in, 257n2
anti-Japanese protests, 1, 21–22, 224
anti-Korean protests in, 58
as competition, 159, 175–76
constitution, 34, 58, 118
defense and remilitarization, 26–27, 34, 56, 57–58, 227
defense and US, 151, 225
defense spending, 58
Diaoyu/Senkaku islands dispute, 9, 35, 45, 58
dislike of, 206
dislike of Chinese, 151–54
dislike of closer ties by South Koreans, 48–49
dislike of Koreans, 151, 152

Japan (*continued*)
  distrust in China and South Korea in reparations endorsement survey, 208–10, 212–14, 215
  distrust of, 26–30, 56, 57–58, 206, 227
  distrust of China, 26–27, 56, 57–58, 97, 99, 106, 110, 151, 206, 228
  economic cooperation with China, 19, 50
  economic cooperation with South Korea, 19–20
  as economic power, 151
  enemy image, 34–35
  example of shift in images, 22
  in image survey, 162–69
  imperialist image, 31, 32, 34, 79, 80
  Joint History Research Committee, 44
  modernization and opening of, 32–33
  perceptions of China, 30, 31–33
  perceptions of in China, 30, 31, 33–34, 35, 80–81
  perceptions of in South Korea, 30, 31, 34–36, 37, 77, 80–81, 158–59, 162–69
  perceptions of South Korea, 30, 31–33
  security alliance triangle with US and South Korea, 9, 223–28
  security community with US, 151
  and Sino-Japanese honeymoon period, 3, 49–51
  Takeshima/Dokdo islands dispute, 9
  trade conflict with South Korea, 223, 224, 226
  trade with China, 8, 19
  trade with South Korea, 8, 19–20
  UN Security Council membership, 55
  See also GSOMIA (General Security of Military Information Agreement); guilt recognition experiment; Japan reparations and guilt recognition; Japan reparations endorsement survey; security cooperation; trust experiment
Japan-East Asia Student and Youth Exchange Network, 44–45
Japan-Korea Treaty of 1876, 33
Japan reparations and guilt recognition
  apologies, 10, 27–30, 67, 70, 113, 202
  coordination between China and South Korea on, 227–28
  endorsement survey, 14, 81, 196–99, 203–17
  fatigue over, 16, 28, 67, 81, 129, 204–5, 206, 224
  and general distrust of Japan, 26, 27–30
  generational differences in, 6, 7, 28, 118–19, 129, 141, 210
  as inadequate, 7, 10, 27–30, 54–55, 67, 69–70, 81, 202, 204–5, 223–24
  and individual efforts, 81, 199, 200–201, 203, 207, 208, 210, 211–12, 216–17
  Kono Statement, 29, 67
  Murayama Statement, 27–28, 67, 202
  political use of by China and Japan, 21, 58, 204, 205, 212–14
  protests on, 201–3
  and Sino-Japanese honeymoon period, 51
  Treaty on Basic Relations (1965), 28–29, 224
  undercutting and denials of, 29, 66–67, 113
  and undermined gain, 54–55
  See also comfort women; forced labor; guilt recognition
Japan reparations endorsement survey
  and impact of public, 197–99
  and linked fate, 217
  materials, 207–10
  and moralistic trust, 203–10
  and need for action, 209
  overview of, 14, 81, 196–97
  questions, 208–10
  results, 210–16
  trustworthiness of South Korea and China, 208–10, 212–14, 215
Joint History Research Committee, 44

Kerry, John, 227
Kim, Dae Jung, 26
Kim, Sam Hoon, 55
Kishida, Fumio, 205
Koizumi, Junichiro, 1, 28, 60
Kono, Yohei, 29
Kono Statement, 29, 67

leaders
  and decline of communism in China, 56–57
  and effect of public opinion on, 8, 10, 24
  and group-affirmation, 49–51
  political use of nationalism, 57
  role in history problem, 20–21
  and self-affirmation, 47
  and Sino-Japanese honeymoon period, 49–51
learning
  cognitive revolution, 259n9
  and image theory, 30–31, 73
  and national identity affirmation mechanisms, 70–71
  and security communities, 63
Lee, Myung Bak, 171, 178, 182–83, 185
Li, Hongzhang, 33
Li, Keqiang, 226
liberal nationalism
  and dignity, 5, 41
  and expectations of reduced conflicts, 19–20
  on institutions and cooperation, 160
  on "moderate" nationalism, 232
  on public opinion, 23
  on trust, 60
liberal orientation
  and Cuba-US relations, 223
  and GSOMIA support, 172, 181–83, 189–93, 194
  in guilt recognition experiment, 123, 128, 142, 143, 148, 149, 150, 154
  in image survey, 166
  and linked fate, 182–84
  and perception of political ideology conflicts, 180
  in trust experiment, 94
liking
  Chinese dislike of Japan, 206
  Japanese dislike of Koreans, 151, 152
  vs. prosociality, 151–53
  South Korean dislike of Japan, 206
  in trust experiment, 101–2
linked fate
  and guilt recognition and reparations, 118–19, 141–46, 217
  and opposition to GSOMIA, 172, 182–84, 189–93, 194
logic of appropriateness, 63, 198
love, in-group, 5, 233, 235

"Made in China 2025," 226
Mexico
  national identity changes, 43
  security community with US, 234
moralistic trust
  building, 63, 64–66, 67, 179, 187
  and civil society, 196, 198, 201
  and confidence, 66, 205
  confirmatory factor analysis of, 249–51
  correlation with national identity affirmation, 65, 203
  defined, 62
  and generalized trust, 259n6
  and institution building, 6
  measuring with surveys, 64, 65
  measuring with surveys in trust experiment, 86–89, 92, 94–102, 110
  in overview, 6, 13
  and particularized trust, 259n6
  and reparations endorsement, 203–7
  and reparations survey, 196–97, 207–15, 216
  and security, 39–40, 61, 62–64, 65, 67
Murayama, Tomiichi, 28, 202
Murayama Statement, 27–28, 67, 202

Nakasone, Yasuhiro, 49, 51
Nanjing Massacre, 29, 31
Nash equilibrium, 62, 89, 178
national identity
  components of, 48
  defined, 2–3
  examples of changes in, 43
  as factor preventing cooperation, 2
  as hard to change, 4, 42–43
  vs. national pride, 257n4
  and need for belonging, 4, 43
  positive effects of, 41
  and prevalence of subidentities, 4
  and regional identities as rising alongside, 10
  subsuming of, 2, 3–5, 10, 40–45, 64, 199–200, 234
  and xenophobia, 2, 3

national identity affirmation
  and bargaining, 230
  defined, 2–3
  examples in real world, 220–23
  flow charts, 53, 65, 71
  future research areas, 233
  policies for, 220
  psychological mechanisms of, 51–53, 117–19, 124–25, 141, 200
  scholarly implications, 228–32
  scope and limits of, 232
  theory overview, 5–13, 39–40, 45–53, 66–72
  uses and potential, 3, 5, 7–9, 13–14, 29–30, 41–42, 186, 220–23, 230
  See also GSOMIA (General Security of Military Information Agreement); guilt recognition; guilt recognition experiment; image survey; image theory; Japan reparations and guilt recognition; Japan reparations endorsement survey; prosociality; trust and national identity affirmation; trust experiment
nationalism
  age of, 42–43
  as barrier to cooperation, 195
  as barrier to reconciliation, 40–41
  and chauvinism, 5
  exploiting, 232
  and foreign policy, 8–9, 10
  increase in China, 57
  political use of, 57
  as term, 257n5
National Survey on Korean Perception on Unification, 161, 162–64
  See also image survey
neofunctionalism and spillover cooperation, 35, 41, 199–200, 234
neoliberalism, 60, 63, 74
Nippon Steel & Sumitomo Metal, 28
nongovernmental organizations (NGOs), 198
North Korea
  and GSOMIA, 172, 173, 181
  as potential security threat, 8, 9, 19, 38, 56, 172, 173, 181, 224, 225–26
  sanctions on, 9
  and security triangle between Japan, South Korea, and US, 224, 225–26
  as subject, 258n10

Oba, Mintaro, 9
Obama Doctrine, 220–23
ontological security, 4, 43, 118, 234
opponent nationality in guilt recognition experiment, 126–29, 134, 139, 140, 143–45, 147–48, 151–54
othering
  and chauvinism, 5
  and colony image, 33
  and image theory, 76, 163
  lack of in national identity affirmation, 5–6, 52, 72, 220
  lack of in Sino-Japanese honeymoon period, 50
  of past, 222
  political use of, 21
  and receiver side of guilt recognition, 68
  and stereotypes, 21, 72
out-groups
  cooperating with, 178, 230
  creation of, 41
  hate, 5
  and image theory, 75–76
  and increasing in-group status, 76–77, 80
  shifting perceptions of, 53, 72, 78
  See also guilt recognition experiment; Japan reparations endorsement survey; prosociality; trust experiment
overseas experience in trust experiment, 104–5, 108, 109, 112

Pakistan-India relations, 11, 12
Palestine-Israel relations, 7, 11, 12, 21
Park, Chung Hee, 202
Park, Geun Hye, 203
particularized trust, 259n6
past, othering of, 222
peace
  and accepting multiple national identities, 4–5, 42–43, 235
  and habit, 199–201
  and image theory, 73, 74
  and Japan's constitution, 34, 58, 118
  obstacles to, 6–7

potential of national identity affirmation, 3, 4–6, 10, 11, 12, 42–43
role of reconciliation in, 69
and subsuming national identities, 2, 3–5, 40–41, 234–35
perceptions. *See* images of other countries; image theory
Perry, Matthew C., 259n10
personal declared guilt in guilt recognition experiment, 124–26, 130–31, 132, 135–46
policy
and civil society, 196, 197–99, 211–12, 215–16
and collective action, 23–24, 197–99
effect of images on, 30, 73–74, 159–60
effect of public opinion on, 8, 10, 23–26, 55, 197–99
on national identity affirmation, 220
and nationalism, 8–9, 10
See also GSOMIA (General Security of Military Information Agreement); security cooperation
political knowledge in image survey, 164, 165, 166, 167–69
political orientation
and GSOMIA support, 172, 181–83, 184, 189–93, 194
in guilt recognition experiment, 123, 128, 129, 142, 143, 148, 149, 150, 154
and historic guilt, 148
in image survey, 164, 165, 166, 167–69
and linked fate, 182–84, 189–93, 194
and Obama Doctrine, 221, 222–23
and perception of conflicts in political ideology, 180
as source of conflict in South Korea, 179–81
in trust experiment, 94
power
relative power in image theory, 74–76, 77, 78, 80
soft power, 19–20
pride, national
defined, 257n4
effect on peace, 5
framing as inward looking, 3, 169–70
role in conflicts, 1–2

and Sino-Japanese honeymoon period, 50–51
prisoners' dilemma, 62
prosociality
association with national identity affirmation, 40, 125–35, 141, 147
and civil society, 201
effects on international relations, 116
vs. liking, 151–53
and linked fate, 141–46
in reparations endorsement survey, 211–12
prosociality in guilt recognition experiment
about, 71, 113, 115–19
and Chinese opponents, 151–54
and declared guilt, 123–35, 149–50
and historic guilt, 146–54
and revealed guilt, 138–45
protests
anti-Chinese protests in Japan, 257n2
anti-Japanese protests, 1, 21–22, 224
anti-Korean protests, 58
on GSOMIA, 173, 225
over comfort women, 1, 201–3
public opinion
and Asian commonality attempts, 44–45
and collective action, 23–24
effect of national identity affirmation on, 8, 24, 25–26
effect on policy, 8, 10, 23–26, 55, 197–99
and failure of GSOMIA, 12–13, 67, 171, 173, 175, 194
as force, 23–26
on Japan–South Korea relations, 48–49, 176
on military conflict in region, 35, 56, 57
poll of South Korea perceptions of other countries, 157–59
poll on South Korea–Japan relations, 204
research on, 25
role in history problem, 21–26
and Sino-Japanese honeymoon period, 49–51
punishment, 68–69

race and racism, 7, 46–47
rapprochement
  as term, 258n7
  See also reconciliation
rationality
  and guilt, 113–14
  rational choice model, 89–90, 111, 134–35
  rational gain in institutions, 53–54
  and strategic trust, 62
realism
  on cooperation in region, 18–19
  and perception of power, 77
  on public opinion, 23
  and relative power, 74
  and rise of China, 151
receivers
  and cooperation, 15, 80–82, 193–94
  and GSOMIA support, 80–81
  in national identity affirmation theory, 40, 51–53, 66–68, 70, 71, 150
  in overview, 14, 15, 17
  and security communities, 60
  in trust experiment, 85–86
reconciliation
  and apologies, 69–70
  and first gestures, 63
  in Germany, 69–70, 202, 206–7, 259n2
  Graduated and Reciprocated Initiative in Tension-Reduction (GRIT), 63–64
  in national identity affirmation theory, 66–72
  in Rwanda, 20
  in South Africa, 259n7
  and subsuming national identities, 3–5, 40–45, 234–35
  as term, 258n7
  US desire for in area, 9, 155, 205
  See also guilt recognition; Japan reparations and guilt recognition; Japan reparations endorsement survey; reparations
relative gains, 121
remilitarization of Japan, 26–27, 34, 56, 57–58, 227
reparations
  and amnesty, 69
  in Germany, 69–70, 202, 206–7, 259n2
  and punishment, 68–69
  and trials, 68–69
  See also guilt recognition; Japan reparations and guilt recognition; Japan reparations endorsement survey; reconciliation
replication, 157
reputation building, 91
revealed guilt
  in guilt recognition experiment, 116–17, 124, 135–46
  and linked fate, 144–45
  and prosociality, 138–45
  relation to declared guilt, 135–38
rivalries, enduring, 229
Russia
  development integration with China, 226
  example of shift in images, 22
  in image survey, 162–69
  as incentive for cooperation in region, 9, 19
  perceptions of in South Korea, 77, 80, 158–59, 163–69
Rwanda, reconciliation in, 20

scapegoating, 20–21
security communities
  and common identity approach, 64
  defined, 59
  EU as, 69
  maintaining separate identities in, 200, 234–35
  and moralistic trust, 63, 64, 65, 67
  and trust, 59–60, 63, 64, 199
  US and Japan as, 151
  US and Mexico as, 234
security cooperation
  aggravated security dilemma and trust, 39–40, 52, 55–59, 61, 62–64, 65
  China as potential security threat, 19, 24, 38, 55–59, 172, 173, 177, 224, 225
  Japan remilitarization as threat to, 26–27, 56, 57–58, 227
  North Korea as potential security threat, 8, 9, 19, 38, 56, 172, 173, 181, 224, 225–26
  perceptions of need for between Japan

and South Korea, 172, 173, 175–77, 181, 194
security alliance triangle with US, Japan, and South Korea, 9, 223–28
as stunted, 8–9, 12, 18–20
See also GSOMIA (General Security of Military Information Agreement)
self-affirmation
and group-affirmation, 39, 47–51
in guilt recognition experiment, 120, 126, 128, 146, 153, 154
in national identity affirmation theory, 39, 45–47
and security cooperation, 177
trust as variable in, 46
use in experiments, 86
Senkaku/Diaoyu islands dispute, 9, 35, 45, 58
Serbia-Bosnia relations, 7
Shimazu, Nariakira, 33
Singh, Sujatha, 11
Sino-Japanese honeymoon period, 3, 49–51
slavery. *See* comfort women; forced labor
smokers and self-affirmation, 45–46
social media, 23–24
soft power, 19–20
Somalia, example of shift in images, 22
South Africa, reconciliation in, 259n7
South Korea
anti-Japanese protests in, 1, 224
anti-Korean protests in Japan, 58
and Cold War, 224
colony image, 31, 32, 33, 79–80
cooperation with China, 227–28, 229
dislike of closer ties to Japan, 48–49
dislike of Japan, 206
dislike of Koreans, Japanese, 151, 152
dissatisfaction with Japanese reparations, 7, 10, 27–30, 54–55, 67, 70, 202, 204–5, 223–24
distrust of China, 26–27, 56, 57–58, 97, 99, 106, 110, 228
distrust of Japan, 26–30, 56, 57–58, 206, 227
economic cooperation with Japan, 19–20
General Sherman incident, 258n9

opposition to Japan UN Security Council membership, 55
perceptions of China, 35–36, 37, 77, 79, 80, 158–59, 163–64
perceptions of in Japan, 30, 31–33
perceptions of Japan, 30, 31, 34–36, 37, 77, 79, 80–81, 158–59
perceptions of Russia, 77, 80, 158–59, 163–69
perceptions of US, 35–36, 37, 77, 80, 158–59, 163–69, 227, 229
political orientation conflicts in, 179–81
recall of ambassador to Japan, 55
security alliance triangle with US and Japan, 9, 223–28
Takeshima/Dokdo islands dispute, 9
trade conflict with Japan, 223, 224, 226
trust in EU, 26, 27
trust in US, 26, 27
trust of in reparations endorsement survey, 208–10, 212–14, 215
See also comfort women; forced labor; GSOMIA (General Security of Military Information Agreement); guilt recognition experiment; image survey; Japan reparations and guilt recognition; security cooperation; trust experiment
spillover cooperation, 35, 41, 42, 199–200
status
and colonialism, 259n10
increasing with national identity affirmation, 72–73, 76–77, 80
relative status in image theory, 74–77, 78
stereotypes, 20–21, 42, 72, 74
strategic trust
building moralistic trust with, 63, 64, 65, 66, 179, 187
building with national identity affirmation, 64–66, 67, 172, 187
and confidence, 66
defined, 61
and GSOMIA support, 171, 177–79, 186–89
incentives for, 61

and institution building, 6, 13, 39–40, 61, 66, 67, 179, 186–87
and mutual gain, 61–62, 64, 66
in overview, 6, 13
and trust games, 62, 64, 65, 89–93, 94, 102–11
student exchange programs, 44–45
sucker payoff, 62, 76, 92–93
surveys
  GSOMIA in trust survey, 171–72, 178–79, 184–93, 194, 243
  guilt recognition experiment, 116, 117, 119–20, 122, 135, 142–43, 146, 147, 243–48
  and linked fate, 142–43
  measuring moralistic trust in trust experiment, 64, 65, 86–89, 92, 94–102, 110
  National Survey on Korean Perception on Unification, 161, 162–64
  poll on perception of South Korea and Japan, 204
  reparations endorsement in trust survey, 196–99, 207–17
  South Korea image survey, 156–57, 160–70
  South Korean ASAN poll on other countries, 157–59

Taiwan Strait, 59
Takeshima/Dokdo islands dispute, 9
Tanaka, Kakuei, 49
TANs (transnational advocacy networks), 198
territorial disputes, 9, 35, 45, 58, 59
Texas, identity changes in, 43
textbooks, 20, 28, 51, 55
Thatcher, Margaret, 259n2
Tokyo-Beijing Forum, 44
trade
  conflict between Japan and South Korea, 223, 224, 226
  between Japan and China, 8, 19
  between Japan and South Korea, 8, 19–20
  and stunted economic cooperation in region, 8, 12, 19–20
  US-China trade, 12, 224, 226

transnational advocacy networks (TANs), 198
Treaty on Basic Relations (1965), 28–29, 202, 224
trials, 68–69
trust
  and chauvinism, 5
  chronic distrust, 6
  chronic distrust in Asia, 26–27, 35, 37
  defined, 24, 26
  general distrust in China, 26–27, 110, 151
  general distrust in Japan, 26–27, 35
  generalized trust, 259n6
  and group-affirmation, 48–49
  and habit, 199–201
  and history problem, 6, 12–13, 26–30, 39–40
  and images of other counties, 24
  and institution building, 6, 11, 13, 39–40, 60–63, 65, 66, 67, 179, 186–87
  measuring with surveys, 64
  measuring with trust games, 64, 65
  particularized, 259n6
  and repetition, 91, 111
  role in cooperation, 59–61, 63, 65, 178
  and security communities, 59–60, 63, 64, 199
  and security dilemma, 39–40, 52, 55–59, 61, 62–64, 65
  and self-affirmation, 46
  and subsuming national identity strategy, 4
  vs. trustworthiness, 260n5
  and undermined gain, 39, 52, 53–55, 59, 61–62, 64, 65
  as variable in research, 231
  See also moralistic trust; strategic trust
trust and national identity affirmation
  building trust, 64–66, 67, 81
  in national identity affirmation theory, 53–66
  in overview, 3, 5, 6–7, 13
  and psychological mechanisms of national identity affirmation, 51–53, 200
  and public opinion, 13
  in theory overview, 39–40

trust experiment
  affect/liking in, 101–2
  affirmation treatment in, 84, 86, 87, 93
  applications of, 112
  Asian commonality in, 84–85, 96–97, 99–101, 107–11
  community integration in, 84–85, 96–97
  demographics, 94
  GSOMIA survey in, 171–72, 178–79, 184–93, 194, 243
  history interpretation in, 84, 85–86, 97, 99–101, 107–9
  methodology, 83–84, 184–85
  and moralistic trust, 86–89, 92, 94–102, 110
  payment, 93
  pilot study, 260n4
  reparations endorsement survey in, 14, 81, 196–99, 207–17
  research design and materials, 84–93, 110–11, 239–43
  results, 94–111
  and strategic trust, 89–93, 94, 102–11
  survey questions, 86–89, 92, 239–42, 243
  trust game, 89–93, 94, 102–11, 186–89, 242–43, 251–55
trust game in trust experiment
  and GSOMIA support, 186–89
  instructions for, 242–43
  measuring trust with, 89–93, 94, 102–11
  results, 102–11
  subsets by numbers of tokens, 104–5, 251–53
  summary statistics, 253–55
trust games
  differences in play style by nationality, 260n7
  and reputation building, 91
  and strategic trust, 62, 64, 65, 91–92
  sucker payoff in, 62, 76, 92–93
  in trust experiment, 89–93, 94, 102–11, 186–89, 242–43, 251–55

United Nations Security Council, 55
United States
  ally image, 163, 166
  Cuba-US relations, 220–23
  desire for cooperation and reconciliation in area, 9, 19, 38, 155, 205, 225
  example of shift in images, 22
  first expedition to Korea, 33
  general trust in by South Korea, 26, 27
  and GSOMIA, 225–26
  guilt recognition in, 7
  in image survey, 162–69
  Indo-Pacific Strategy, 225
  national identity changes in, 43
  and North Korea, 9, 225–26
  perceptions of in South Korea, 35–36, 37, 77, 80, 158–59, 162–69, 227, 229
  security alliance triangle with Japan and South Korea, 9, 223–28
  security community with Japan, 151
  security community with Mexico, 234
  trade with China, 12, 224, 226
universalism
  as strategy, 2, 41–45, 234–35
  in trust experiment, 85

victim role, 48
  See also receivers

war. *See* conflicts and war
white list, 224
World Values Survey, 86
World War II. *See* Japan reparations and guilt recognition

xenophobia, 2, 3, 6, 195, 232, 233
Xi, Jinping, 29

Yasukuni Shrine, 1, 11, 58, 60, 174
Yugoslavia, collective action in, 23
Yun, Byung-se, 205